The Millennium

Loraine Boettner

Author of

Immortality
The Reformed Doctrine of Predestination
Studies in Theology
Roman Catholicism
A Harmony of the Gospels
The Christian Attitude Toward War
The Reformed Faith

Presbyterian and Reformed Publishing Company
Phillipsburg, New Jersey

Anyone is at liberty to use material from this book with or without credit. In preparing this book the writer has received help from may sources, some acknowledged and many unacknowledged. He believes the material herein set forth to be a true statement of Scripture teaching, and his desire is to further, not to restrict, its use.

Library of Congress Catalog Card Number 57-12170

Revised Edition 1984

ISBN 0-87552-113-4

Printed in the United States of America

CONTENTS

III. *Premillennialism*

I.

Postmillennialism

Chapter I

INTRODUCTION

Broadly speaking there are three general systems which profess to set forth the teaching of Scripture regarding the Second Coming of Christ and the future course of the Kingdom. They are: *Postmillennialism, Amillennialism,* and *Premillennialism.*

The essential presuppositions of the three systems are similar. Each holds that the Scriptures are the word of God and authoritative. Each holds to the same general concept of the death of Christ as a sacrifice to satisfy Divine justice and as the only ground for the salvation of souls. Each holds that there will be a future, visible, personal Coming of Christ. Each holds that every individual is to receive a resurrection body, that all are to stand before the judgment seat of Christ, that the righteous are to be rewarded in heaven, and that the wicked are to be punished in hell. Each of the systems is, therefore, consistently evangelical, and each has been held by many able and sincere men. The differences arise, not because of any conscious or intended disloyalty to Scripture, but primarily because of the *distinctive method employed by each system in its interpretation of Scripture,* and they relate primarily to the time and purpose of Christ's coming and to the kind of kingdom that is to be set up at His coming.

It should be helpful at the beginning of this study to define each of the systems as clearly as possible. Exact definitions cannot be given since numerous variations are found within each system. However, we submit the following as essentially correct. The first is our own. The latter three, including that of Dispensationalism, which is a radical form of Premillennialism, are given by Dr. J. G. Vos, a recent writer and son of Dr. Geerhardus Vos who for many years was a professor in Princeton Theological Seminary. These definitions are presented as the most accurate and comprehensive that we have found.

POSTMILLENNIALISM

Postmillennialism is that view of the last things which holds that the Kingdom of God is now being extended in the world through the preaching of the Gospel and the saving work of the Holy Spirit, that the world eventually will be Christianized, and that the return of Christ will occur at the close of a long period of righteousness and peace commonly called the *Millennium*.

This view is, of course, to be distinguished from that optimistic but false view of human betterment and progress held by Modernists and Liberals which teaches that the Kingdom of God on earth will be achieved through a *natural* process by which mankind will be improved and social institutions will be reformed and brought to a higher level of culture and efficiency. This latter view presents a spurious or pseudo Postmillennialism, and regards the Kingdom of God as the product of natural laws in an evolutionary process, whereas orthodox Postmillennialism regards the Kingdom of God as the product of the supernatural working of the Holy Spirit in connection with the preaching of the Gospel.

AMILLENNIALISM

"Amillennialism is that view of the last things which holds that the Bible does not predict a 'Millennium' or period of world-wide peace and righteousness on this earth before the end of the world. (Amillennialism teaches that there will be a parallel and contemporaneous development of good and evil—God's kingdom and Satan's kingdom—in this world, which will continue until the second coming of Christ. At the second coming of Christ the resurrection and judgment will take place, followed by the eternal order of things—the absolute, perfect Kingdom of God, in which there will be no sin, suffering nor death)."

PREMILLENNIALISM

"Premillennialism is that view of the last things which holds that the second coming of Christ will be followed by a period of world-wide peace and righteousness, before the end of the world, called 'the Millennium' or 'the Kingdom of God,' during which

Christ will reign as King in person on this earth. (Premillennialists are divided into various groups by their different views of the order of events associated with the second coming of Christ, but they all agree in holding that there will be a millennium on earth *after* the second coming of Christ but *before* the end of the world)."

DISPENSATIONALISM

"The false system of Bible interpretation represented by the writings of J. N. Darby and the Scofield Reference Bible, which divides the history of mankind into seven distinct periods or 'dispensations,' and affirms that in each period God deals with the human race on the basis of some one specific principle. (Dispensationalism denies the spiritual identity of Israel and the Church, and tends to set 'grace' and 'law' against each other as mutually exclusive principles)."

The word *millennium* is derived from two Latin words, *mille*, meaning thousand, and *annum*, meaning year. Hence the literal meaning is a thousand years. The term is found just six times in Scripture, all in the first seven verses of the twentieth chapter of Revelation, an admittedly difficult and highly symbolical portion of Scripture. The prefixes Post-, A-, and Pre-, as used with the word designate the particular view held regarding the thousand years. Premillennialists take the word literally, holding that Christ will set up a Kingdom on earth which will continue for precisely that length of time. Postmillennialists and Amillennialists take the word figuratively, as meaning an indefinitely long period, held by some to be a part, and by others to be the whole, of the Christian era.

Similarly, the word *Chiliasm,* more commonly used in early Church history than at the present time, comes from the Greek word *chilias,* also meaning thousand. The early Christians who believed that Christ at His coming would set up a one thousand year Kingdom were called *Chiliasts.* In their historical setting the words *Chiliasm* and *Premillennialism* have been used as synonyms, and it is commonly understood that today those who bear the name Premillennialists are logically the same as those who formerly were known as Chiliasts, although their systems differ in several important respects.

It should be said further in regard to Dispensationalism

that while historic Premillennialism has held that the Church will go through the Tribulation, Dispensationalism holds that the Church will be raptured and so taken out of the world before that event, and that following the Rapture there will be a seven year period, during the first half of which the Jews are in covenant relationship with the Antichrist and dwell in Palestine but during the last half they endure terrible presecution under the Antichrist. At the end of the seven year period Christ returns, annihilates the Antichrist, and establishes His Kingdom in Jerusalem. The Jews are to have a position of special favor in the Kingdom, and are to remain a body distinct from the Gentiles throughout eternity. Dispensationalists are thus double "pre-s" —pre-tribulation Pre-millennialists. This distinction is of great importance to the Dispensationalists, for it gives them a seven year period, allegedly the 70th week of Daniel's prophecy (9:24–27), during which time all the events foretold in Revelation chapters 4 through 19 are to be fulfilled. That the Dispensationalists do attach great importance to this distinction is shown by the vigor with which they attack their fellow Premillennialists who are Post-tribulationalists, that is, who hold that the Church does go through the Tribulation.

Another prominent feature of Dispensationalism is its doctrine that when the Jews rejected Christ's alleged offer of the Davidic Kingdom, the Kingdom was withdrawn, and the Church was then set up as a substitute,—this present church age being therefore an interlude or parenthesis period, during which time God deals with man through the Church until the return of Christ, when in turn the Church is to be taken away and the Kingdom established.

Dispensationalism is a comparatively recent development. These distinctive views were first effectively set forth by John N. Darby, a leader in the Plymouth Brethren group in England, about 1830, and later popularized by the *Scofield Reference Bible*. The real origin of the system, however, was considerably earlier, as we shall show when we discuss the history of the movement.

Primarily through the influence of the Scofield Reference Bible, with its explanatory Notes printed on the same page with the text, these views have now become the prevailing tenets of Premillennialism in the United States. They have never found creedal statement in any of the larger Protestant denominations, but are held by individuals throughout the denominations, and they are the standard belief of various Pentecostal and Holiness groups, which as a rule are not noted for scholarship or scientific research. They have been further popularized by the Bible institutes, most of which are dispensational in their teaching. These views have been just as consistently rejected and opposed in most of the theological seminaries, where scholarship and research are given more prominence, and by a large majority of the outstanding theologians.

There can be no doubt but that Premillennialism lends itsself more to an emotional type of preaching and teaching than does Postmillennialism or Amillennialism. It gives something definite to look for in the immediate future and charges the present with portentous possibilities. While many who hold it do not so exploit it, it often has been used in that manner by those who are less restrained.

Premillennialism tends to make the Bible a textbook of ready reference, rather than a source book from which statements are to be collected, compared, placed in their logical relations, and so worked up into a Systematic Theology. It professes to "take God at His word," and to "accept the plain statement of truth as God has revealed it." Such reasoning has its place when directed against the Modernists who reject the doctrine of the full inspiration of the Scriptures. But it is out of place when directed against those who while accepting the doctrine of the full inspiration of Scripture nevertheless acknowledge that much truth is conveyed through figurative expressions. The fact of the matter is that God's revelation as found in the Bible contains many deep mysteries and secrets which always have and probably always will challenge the intellects of even the wisest of men. Superficial statements about taking God at His word and about the plain harmony of God's word are illusory and ought to be their own refutation. Rejecting such easy solutions, we are deeply grateful for the rich heritage that the scholars and theologians of the Church have handed down to us. The deeper understanding of the Scriptures and the correlation of these doctrines is not something that can be completed in a day, or even in a lifetime, but is a task for the Church throughout the centuries. Dr. William H. Rutgers writing on this subject has well said: "If men are engaged in intellectual battle for centuries to settle the Christological problem, and so many other theological questions, it is not to be expected that eschatology, the most difficult problem of theological science, will be solved differently. The positiveness and assurance with which many of these Bible students speak concerning the future of God's program, is but pride and arrogance" (*Premillennialism in America*, p. 42).

Premillennialism thrives best and makes its greatest gains in time of war or of national crisis when people are anxious and worried about the future. Premillennial clergymen from all denominations gather in "prophetic conferences" to discuss impending events such as the establishment of the nation of Israel in Palestine, the future movements of Russia or Germany, signs that the apostasy has about run its course, etc., as these are assumed to be foretold in the "hidden" wisdom of Daniel, Ezekiel, Zechariah, or the Book of Revelation.

The earlier forms of Premillennialism as well as the present dispensational doctrines have been held usually, if not always, by a minority of Christian people. The distinctive dispensational doctrines occupy a much less prominent place in European than in American church life.

There are, then, three principal views concerning the return of Christ: the Postmillennial, which holds that He will return after the Millennium; the Premillennial, which holds that His return precedes the Millennium; and the Amillennial, which holds that there is to be no Millennium at all in the generally accepted sense of the term. Dispensationalism, sometimes looked upon as a fourth view, is in reality only a more extreme form of Premillennialism.

Little pretense can be made to originality in this book. Most of what is said here has been said before by scholars much superior to the present writer. The primary purpose of the present work is to make available in summarized and systematized form the information concerning these eschatological problems that has been wrought out through generations of careful study by the best scholars that the Church has produced, to separate truth from error, and to express that truth as clearly and convincingly as possible. The Scripture quotations are from the American Standard Version of 1901 rather than the King James Version since the former is a more accurate translation.

Chapter II

REPRESENTATIVE THEOLOGIANS IN THE DIFFERENT SYSTEMS

We have said that each of the millennial views has been held by men of unquestioned sincerity and ability. Among Postmillennialists should be mentioned first of all the great Augustine, whose eminently sound interpretation of Scripture set the standard for the Church for nearly a thousand years. In later times there were Rev. David Brown, a Scotch Presbyterian minister, and a considerable number of systematic theologians, the Hodges at Princeton (Drs. Charles, Archibald A., and Caspar Wistar Hodge, Jr., the latter having been the writer's revered teacher), Dr. W. G. T. Shedd, Dr. Robert L. Dabney, Dr. Henry B. Smith, Dr. Augustus H. Strong, and Dr. Benjamin B. Warfield. Probably the most influential books from the postmillennial viewpoint have been *The Second Advent,* by David Brown (1846, revised 1849), which for many years was recognized as the standard work on the subject, and Dr. Charles Hodge's *Systematic Theology* (1871). In more recent times Dr. Warfield (died, 1921) has been recognized as the outstanding postmillennial theologian. His influence was exerted through a period of more than thirty-three years as Professor of Systematic Theology in Princeton Theological Seminary and as Editor of the *Presbyterian and Reformed Review* and later as one of the chief contributors to the *Princeton Theological Review.* A book by Dr. James H. Snowden, *The Coming of the Lord* (1919), has proved to be of special value. This latter book contains a strong refutation of Premillennialism, although Dr. Snowden did not distinguish clearly between Premillennialism and Dispensationalism.

The postmillennial position has been much neglected during the past third of a century, most of the discussion having centered around Premillennialism and Amillennialism. This has led some to conclude that Postmillennialism is no longer worthy of serious consideration. Alexander Reese, for instance, a Premillennialist, in his book *The Approaching Advent of Christ* (1937), expressed his opinion in these words: "Here one can but make the arbitrary statement that the postmillennial interpretation of Origen, Jerome, Augustine, and the majority of the Church theologians ever since, is now as dead as Queen Ann, and just as honorably buried." (p. 306.) Dr. Lewis Sperry Chafer in an Introduction to Dr. Charles Feinberg's book, *Premillennialism or Amillennialism?* (1936), says, "Postmillennialism is dead," a statement which he later qualifies by saying that it is dead in the sense that it offers no living voice in its own defense when the millennial question is under discussion. That, however, is not true today, and it was at least debatable at the time it was made. That such was also Dr. Feinberg's opinion was indicated by the title of his book, and by his almost complete ignoring of Postmillennialism.

But such statements are, to say the least, premature. Since Postmillennialism has been so ably supported by outstanding theologians and ministers whose influences continue at the present time, and since it occupies such a prominent place in a number of standard theological works, it seems rather curious to find Premillennialists attempting to assign it merely an antiquarian interest. One cannot help but feel that in these cases the wish is father to the thought. Dr. Warfield, who in the opinion of the present writer is to be ranked with Augustine, Calvin, and Charles Hodge as one of the four outstanding theologians in the entire history of the Church, was a Postmillennialist, and his collected writings, reprinted in ten large volumes, continue to exert a strong influence in theological circles. Postmillennialism, like Christianity itself, has often suffered reverses. But after each such period of neglect or misunderstanding it has been re-asserted with even more power and conviction. Such no doubt will be the case after the present period of neglect has run its course. We must remember that Premillennialism too was in almost total eclipse for a thousand years, between the time of Augustine and the Reformation, and that during the Reformation period and for a long time afterward it was held by only a few small sects that were considered quite heretical. Furthermore, Amillennialism as a system was not clearly developed nor aggressively set forth until very recent times. Four recent books have been written from the postmillennial viewpoint. They are: *An Eschatology of Victory* (1955), by J. Marcellus Kik; *Israel and the New Covenant* (1954), by Roderick Campbell; *Thy Kingdom Come* (1974), by R. J. Rushdoony; and *The Puritan Hope* (1971), by Iain Murray (England). We believe that the true eschatological system can be set forth only on the basis of Postmillennialism, and that a careful study of Scripture will establish that fact.

Among Amillennialists we find a considerable number of able men, nearly all in recent years: Dr. Louis Berkhof, *Systematic Theology* (Revised Edition, 1941); Dr. Geerhardus Vos, *The Pauline Eschatology* (1930); Dr. Albertus Pieters, *Studies In The Revelation of St. John* (1937), and *The Seed of Abraham* (1950); Professor Floyd E. Hamilton, *The Basis of Millennial Faith* (1942); Dr. George L. Murray, *Millennial Studies* (1948); Dr. William H. Rutgers, *Premillennialism in America* (1930); Dr. Abraham Kuyper, *Chiliasm or the Doctrine of Premillennialism* (pamphlet); Dr. Martin J. Wyngaarden, *The Future of the Kingdom* (1934); Dr. William Hendriksen, *More Than Conquerors* (1939); Dr. William Masselink, *Why Thousand Years?*; Rev. William J. Grier, *The Momentous Event* (1945); and Prof. Everett I. Carver, *When Jesus Comes Again* (1979). Among these the present writer has found the books by Pieters, Hamilton and Carver particularly helpful.

Outstanding writers from the viewpoint of Historic Premillennialism include: Rev. Alexander Reese, *The Approaching Advent of Christ* (1937); Dean Alford, *The Greek Testament* (1874); Dr. Nathaniel West, *The Thousand Years in Both Testaments* (1880); Dr. E. B. Elliott, *Horae Apocalypticae* (4 vols., 5th ed., 1862); Dr. H. Grattan Guinness, *The Approaching End of the Age* (1880); Dr. S. H. Kellogg, *The Jews, or Prediction and Fulfillment* (1883); Dr. Henry W. Frost, *The Second Coming of Christ* (1934); and Dr. George E. Ladd, *Crucial Questions About the Kingdom of God* (1952), and *The Blessed Hope* (1956).

Outstanding dispensational writers include: John N. Darby, *Synopsis of the Books of the Bible* (5 vols.), and other writings; Dr. C. I. Scofield, *The Scofield Reference Bible* (1909, revised 1967); Dr. William E. Blackstone, *Jesus Is Coming* (1878, revised 1908); Dr. Jesse F. Silver, *The Lord's Return* (1914); Rev. James M. Brookes, *Maranatha* (1870); Dr. James M. Gray, *Prophecy and the*

Lord's Return (1917); Dr. Arno C. Gaebelein, *The Return of the Lord* (1925); Dr. Lewis Sperry Chafer, *Systematic Theology* (1948); Dr. Charles L. Feinberg, *Premillennialism or Amillennialism?* (1936, enlarged 1954); Dr. John F. Walvoord, *The Rapture Question* (1957); and Dr. J. Dwight Pentecost, *Things to Come* (1958).

There are also other writers who have dealt with special aspects of the Second Coming, as for instance, Dr. Oswald T. Allis, whose valuable book, *Prophecy and the Church,* deals particularly with the dispensational view. Dr. Allis is an Anti-Chiliast, but is not to be classed as either a Post- or Amillennialist.

Chapter III

STATEMENT OF THE DOCTRINE

We have defined Postmillennialism as that view of the last things which holds that the Kingdom of God is now being extended in the world through the preaching of the Gospel and the saving work of the Holy Spirit in the hearts of individuals, that the world eventually is to be Christianized, and that the return of Christ is to occur at the close of a long period of righteousness and peace commonly called the "Millennium." It should be added that on postmillennial principles the second coming of Christ will be followed immediately by the general resurrection, the general judgment, and the introduction of heaven and hell in their fullness.

The Millennium to which the Postmillennialist looks forward is thus a golden age of spiritual prosperity during this present dispensation, that is, during the Church age, and is to be brought about through forces now active in the world. It is an indefinitely long period of time, perhaps much longer than a literal one thousand years. The changed character of individuals will be reflected in an uplifted social, economic, political and cultural life of mankind. The world at large will then enjoy a state of righteousness such as at the present time has been seen only in relatively small and isolated groups, as for example in some family circles, some local church groups and kindred organizations.

This does not mean that there ever will be a time on this earth when every person will be a Christian, or that all sin will be abolished. But it does mean that evil in all its many forms eventually will be reduced to negligible proportions, that Christian principles will be the rule, not the exception, and that Christ will return to a truly Christianized world.

Postmillennialism further holds that the universal proclamation of the Gospel and the ultimate conversion of the large majority of men in all nations during the present dispensation was the express command and meaning and promise of the Great Commission given by Christ Himself when He said: "All authority hath been given unto me in heaven and on earth. Go ye therefore, and make disciples of all the nations, baptizing them in the name of the Father and of the Son and of the Holy Spirit; teaching them to observe all things whatsoever I commanded you: and lo, I am with you always, even unto the end of the world" (Matt. 28:18–20).

We believe that the Great Commission includes not merely the formal and external announcement of the Gospel preached as a "witness" to the nations, as the Premillennialists and Amillennialists hold, but the true and effectual evangelization of all the nations so that the hearts and lives of the people are transformed by it. That seems quite clear from the fact that *all authority* in heaven and on earth and an endless sweep of conquest has been given to Christ and through Him to His disciples specifically for that purpose. The disciples were commanded not merely to preach, but *to make disciples of all the nations*. It was no doubtful experiment to which they were called, but to a sure triumph. The preaching of the Gospel under the direction of the Holy Spirit and during this dispensation is, therefore, the all-sufficient means for the accomplishment of that purpose.

We must acknowledge that the Church during the past nineteen centuries has been extremely negligent in her duty, and that the crying need of our time is for her to take seriously the task assigned to her. Instead of discussions of social and economic and political problems, book reviews and entertaining platitudes from the pulpit the need is for sermons with real Gospel content, designed to change lives and to save souls. The charge of negligence applies, of course, not only to ministers, but equally to the laity. Every individual Christian is called to give his witness and to show his faith by personal testimony, or through the distribution of the printed word, or through the generous and effective use of his time and money for Christian purposes. Christ commanded the evangelization of the world. That is our task. Surely He will not, and in fact cannot, come back and say to His Church, "Well done, good and faithful servant," until that task has been accomplished. Rev. J. Marcellus Kik has said:

"That there is still a remnant of paganism and papalism in the world is chiefly the fault of the Church. The Word of God is just as powerful in our generation as it was during the early history of the Church. The power of the Gospel is just as strong in this century as in the days of the Reformation. These enemies could be completely vanquished if the Christians of this day and age were as vigorous, as bold, as earnest, as prayerful, and as faithful as Christians were in the first several centuries and in the time of the Reformation"(*An Eschatology of Victory*, p. 250).

In contrast with this, Premillennialism holds that the world is not to be converted during this dispensation, that it is, in fact, vain to hope for its conversion before the return of Christ. It holds rather that the world is growing progressively worse, that the present age is to end in a great apostasy and rebellion climaxed by the reign of the Antichrist and the battle of Armageddon, at which time Christ comes with sudden and overwhelming power to rescue His people, destroy His enemies, and establish a one thousand year earthly kingdom with Jerusalem as its capital. Many seem convinced that we now are in the last stage of the Laodicean apostasy, and that the end is very near. Premillennialism thus despairs of the power of the Gospel to Christianize the world, and asserts rather that it is to be preached only as a witness. Whereas Postmillennialism holds that Christ's coming closes this age and that it is to be followed by the eternal state, Premillennialism holds that His coming is to be followed by another dispensation, the Millennium, or kingdom age, and that the final resurrection and judgment do not take place until one thousand years later. It has also been a standard doctrine of Premillennialism in every age that the coming of Christ is "near" or "imminent," although every generation of Premillennialists from the first century until the present time has been mistaken on that point.

Premillennialism, in its dispensational form, divides the second coming of Christ into two parts: (1) the Rapture, or His coming "for" His saints, at which time the righteous dead of all ages are to be raised in the "first resurrection," the righteous living translated, and both groups caught up to meet the Lord in the air; and (2) the Revelation, which occurs seven years later, at the close of the Great Tribulation, at which time Christ re-

turns to earth "with" His saints, overpowers the Antichrist, defeats and suppresses all His enemies, raises the righteous dead
who have died or who have been killed during the Great Tribulation, and establishes His Kingdom on this earth. At the close of
the Millennium the wicked dead are to be raised in a final resurrection, and this in turn is followed by their judgment and the
introduction of the eternal state. The Millennium in which the
Premillennialist believes is thus a direct and personal rule of
Christ over this earth.

Amillennialism, too, differs from Postmillennialism in that it
holds that the world is not to be Christianized before the end
comes, that the world will in fact continue much as it now is,
with a parallel and continuous development of both good and
evil, of the Kingdom of God and the kingdom of Satan. It agrees
with Postmillennialism, however, in asserting that Christ does not
establish an earthly, political kingdom, and that His return will
be followed by a general resurrection and general judgment.
Post- and Amillennialists thus agree that the Kingdom of Christ
in this world is not political and economic, but spiritual and now
present in the hearts of His people and outwardly manifested
in the Church.

Amillennialism, as the term implies, does not set forth a
Millennium at all. Some Amillennialists apply the term to the
entire Christian era between the first and second advent of Christ.
Some apply it to a relatively Christian and peaceful era, such as
the Church enjoyed after the bitter persecution of the first three
centuries, at which time Emperor Constantine made Christianity
the preferred religion of the Roman Empire. Others apply it to
the intermediate state. The position of the Amillennialist does not
necessarily preclude him from believing that the world may be
Christianized before the end comes, but most Amillennialists have
not so held. Rather they have preferred to say that there probably will not be much relative change. In support of this they
cite the parable of the wheat and the tares, in which both grow
together until the harvest. Historically the main thrust of Amillennialism has been much stronger against Premillennialism than
against Postmillennialism, since it interprets Revelation 20 symbolically and does not believe that Christ will reign personally in
an earthly kingdom.

It should be remembered, however, that while Post-, A-, and Premillennialists differ in regard to the manner and time of Christ's return, that is, in regard to the events that are to precede or follow His return, they agree in regard to the *fact* that He will return personally and visibly and in great glory. Each alike looks for "the blessed hope and appearing of the glory of the great God and our Saviour Jesus Christ" (Titus 2:13). Each acknowledges Paul's statement that, "The Lord himself shall descend from heaven, with a shout, with the voice of the archangel, and with the trump of God" (I Thess. 4:16). Christ's return is taught so clearly and so repeatedly in Scripture that there can be no question in this regard for those who accept the Bible as the word of God. They also agree that at His coming He will raise the dead, execute judgment, and eventually institute the eternal state. No one of these views has an inherent liberalizing tendency. Hence the matters on which they agree are much more important than those on which they differ. This fact should enable them to cooperate as evangelicals and to present a united front against Modernists and Liberals who more or less consistently deny the supernatural throughout the whole range of Bible truth.

Chapter IV

INADEQUATE TERMINOLOGY

One difficulty that we constantly face in this discussion is that of an inadequate terminology. The use of the prefixes "pre-" and "post-", as attached to the word "millennial," is to some extent unfortunate and misleading. For the distinction involves a great deal more than merely "before" or "after." The Millennium expected by the Premillennialist is quite a different thing from that expected by the Postmillennialist, not only in regard to the time and manner in which it will be set up but primarily in regard to the nature of the Kingdom and the manner in which Christ exercises His control.

The Postmillennialist looks for a golden age that will not be essentially different from our own so far as the basic facts of life are concerned. This age gradually merges into the millennial age as an increasingly larger proportion of the world's inhabitants are converted to Christianity. Marriage and the home will continue, and new members will enter the human race through the natural process of birth as at present. Sin will not be eliminated but will be reduced to a minimum as the moral and spiritual environment of the earth becomes predominantly Christian. Social, economic and educational problems will remain, but with their unpleasant features greatly eliminated and their desirable features heightened. Christian principles of belief and conduct will be the accepted standards. Life during the Millennium will compare with life in the world today in much the same way that life in a Christian community compares with that in a pagan or irreligious community. The Church, much more zealous in her testimony to the truth and much more influential in the lives of the people, will continue to be then as now the outward and visible manifestation of the Kingdom of God on earth. And the Millennium will close with the second coming of Christ, the resurrection and final judgment. In short, Postmillennialists set forth a spiritual Kingdom in the hearts of men.

On the other hand the Millennium expected by the Premillennialist involves the personal, visible reign of Christ as King in Jerusalem. The Kingdom is to be established not by the conversion of individual souls over a long period of time, but suddenly and by overwhelming power. The Jews are to be converted not as individuals and along with other groups of the population, but suddenly and *en masse* at the mere sight of Christ, and are to become the chief rulers in the new Kingdom. Nature is to share in the millennial blessings and is to become abundantly productive, and even the ferocious nature of the wild beasts is to be tamed. Evil, however, does not cease to exist, nor is it necessarily decreased in amount, but it is held in check by the rod-of-iron rule of Christ, and at the end of the Millennium it breaks out in a terrible rebellion that all but overwhelms the saints and the holy city. During the Millennium the saints in glorified bodies mingle freely with men who still are in the flesh. This latter element in particular seems to us to present an inconsistency,—a mongrel kingdom, the new earth and glorified sinless humanity mingling with the old earth and sinful humanity, Christ and the saints in immortal resurrection bodies living in a world that still contains much of sin and amid scenes of death and decay. To bring Christ and the saints to live again in the sinful environment of this world would seem to be the equivalent of introducing sin into heaven. As the amillennialist William J. Grier has observed, such a company would indeed be a "mixtum gatherum."

Amillennialists, of course, reject both the post- and the premillennial conception, and are usually content to say that there will be no Millennium at all in either sense of the word.

The terms are, therefore, somewhat inaccurate and misleading. For that reason some theologians hesitate to label themselves either post-, a-, or premillennial. But no more appropriate terms are available. These terms serve at least to distinguish the different schools of thought, and their meaning is generally understood.

But while the three schools differ in regard to the meaning of the word "millennium," that does not mean that the word itself is meaningless, nor that the distinctions between the systems are imaginary or unimportant. Quite the contrary. Actually these systems represent widely divergent views concerning this very important subject, which, as we shall see, have far-reaching consequences.

A broader and perhaps more accurate terminology has been suggested by some—that of Chiliasts and Anti-Chiliasts. Chiliasts would then include both Historic Premillennialists and Dispensationalists, while Anti-Chiliasts would include both Post- and Amillennialists without making it necessary to choose between these.

Furthermore, the fact that some who designate themselves Amillennialists hold that the present Church age constitutes the Millennium and that Christ will come at the close of the Church age might seem to make them Postmillennialists. But since the primary tenet of Postmillennialism as generally understood is that the coming of Christ is to follow a golden age of righteousness and peace, those who look upon the entire Church age as the Millennium are not commonly referred to as Postmillenialists.

Chapter V

A REDEEMED WORLD OR RACE*

On postmillennial principles a strong emphasis is thrown on the universality of Christ's work of redemption, and hope is held out for the salvation of an incredibly large number of the race of mankind. Since it was the world, or the race, which fell in Adam, it was the world, or the race, which was the object of Christ's redemption. This does not mean that every individual will be saved, but that the race as a race will be saved. Jehovah is no mere tribal deity, but is described as "the Lord of the whole earth," "a great King over all the earth" (Ps. 97:5; 47:2). The salvation that He had in view cannot be limited to a little select group or favored few. The good news of redemption was not merely local news for a few villages in Palestine, but was a world message; and the abundant and continuous testimony of Scripture is that the kingdom of God is to *fill* the earth, "from sea to sea, and from the River to the ends of the earth" (Zech. 9:10).

Early in the Old Testament we have the promise that "all the earth shall be filled with the glory of Jehovah" (Nu. 14:21); and Isaiah repeats the promise that all flesh shall see the glory of Jehovah (40:5). Isaiah was set for "a light to the Gentiles," and for "salvation unto the end of the earth" (Is. 49:6; Acts 13:47). Joel made the clear declaration that in the coming days of blessing, the Spirit hitherto given only to Israel would be poured out upon the whole earth. "And it shall come to pass afterward," said the Lord through His prophet, "that I will pour out my Spirit upon all flesh" (2:28); and Peter applied that prophecy to the outpouring that was begun at Pentecost,—"But this is that which hath been spoken through the prophet Joel . . ." (Acts 2:16f).

Nothing could well exceed the plainness, directness and pre-

* Some of the material in pages 22 to 47 is taken from an earlier book by the present writer, *The Reformed Doctrine of Predestination*, pp. 130–143.

22

cision with which the conversion of the nations is announced in the Psalms:

"All nations whom thou hast made shall come and worship before thee, O Lord;
And they shall glorify thy name" (Ps. 86:9).

"All the ends of the earth shall remember and turn unto Jehovah;
And all the kindreds of the nations shall worship before thee" (Ps. 22:27).

"Ask of me, and I will give thee the nations for thine inheritance,
And the uttermost parts of the earth for thy possession" (Ps. 2:8).

The 47th Psalm sings of the sovereignty of God, and of His rulership over the nations:

"For Jehovah Most High is terrible;
He is a great King over all the earth.
He subdueth peoples under us,
And nations under our feet . . .
For God is the King of all the earth;
Sing ye praises with understanding,
God reigneth over the nations:
God sitteth upon his holy throne" (vss. 2–8).

Probably nowhere is the universal reign of Christ stated more strongly than in the Messianic 72nd Psalm:

"In his day shall the righteous flourish,
And abundance of peace, till the moon be no more.
He shall have dominion also from sea to sea,
And from the River unto the ends of the earth.
They that dwell in the wilderness shall bow before him;
And his enemies shall lick the dust.
The kings of Tarshish and of the isles shall render tribute:
The kings of Sheba and Seba shall offer gifts.
Yea, all kings shall fall down before him:
All nations shall serve him . . .
All nations shall call him happy . . .
And let the whole earth be filled with his glory" (vss. 7–11, 17, 19).

"All nations whom thou hast made shall come and worship before thee, O Lord;
And they shall glorify thy name" (Ps. 86:9).

"Jehovah saith unto my Lord, Sit thou at my right hand,
Until I make thine enemies thy footstool" (Ps. 110:1).

We call special attention to the fact that this latter verse from
the 110th Psalm means that Christ is to conquer all. The right-
hand position is the position of power and influence. This conquest is now in process of accomplishment as He advances against
His enemies. His mediatorial reign from the right hand of God
is to continue until all of His enemies have been subdued. In the
New Testament Christ Himself quoted this verse to prove His
Deity (Luke 20:42,43). Peter too quoted this verse (Acts 2:34,35)
to prove that what had happened at Pentecost was the fulfillment
of Psalm 110:1. He thus saw its fulfillment, not as a cataclysmic
act coming at the day of judgment, but in the outpouring of the
Holy Spirit upon the Church during the present age. This process
is to continue until all of Christ's enemies have been placed under
His feet, so that He reigns over all the earth.

There is no mistaking the meaning of these announcements
found in the Psalms. They are as unambiguous as anything that
can be spoken by the most sanguine advocates of foreign missions
in this twentieth century. Yet they come from the time of David,
and most of them are from his pen. By him the Holy Spirit, for
twenty-nine centuries, has been bearing witness that God's visible
Church is destined to embrace all the nations that He has created
on the whole face of the earth. A time is coming when they shall
acknowledge the Lord as their Ruler. They have long forgotten
Him, but one day they shall acknowledge His claims and turn to
Him, even in the uttermost parts of the earth. Says Mr. Kik:

"The Covenant concept of 'all nations blessed' comes to the
fore in the poetry of the Psalter. The composers of the Book of
Praise of the Old Testament looked for the triumph of the Church
upon earth. There are no better missionary hymns than those
contained in the Psalms. One of the contributing factors to present-day pessimism, gloominess, defeatism within the Church is
the omitting of the Psalms from the hymn books" (*An Eschatology
of Victory*, p. 22).

In Isaiah 2:2,3 we read: "And it shall come to pass in the latter days, that the mountain of Jehovah's house shall be established on the top of the mountains, and shall be exalted above the hills; and all nations shall flow unto it. And many peoples shall go and say, Come ye, and let us go up to the mountain of Jehovah, to the house of the God of Jacob; and he will teach us of his ways, and we will walk in his paths: for out of Zion shall go forth the law, and the word of Jehovah from Jerusalem." In the book of Hebrews "Mount Zion," God's holy mountain, is spiritualized to mean the Church (12:22). Hence in this prophecy it must mean that the Church, having attained a position so that it stands out like a mountain on a plain, will be prominent and regulative in all world affairs.

Ezekiel gives us the picture of the increasing flow of the healing waters which issue from under the threshold of the temple; waters which first were only to the ankles, then to the knees, then to the loins, then a great river, waters which could not be passed through (47:1–5). Daniel's interpretation of King Nebuchadnezzar's dream taught the same truth. The king saw a large image, with various parts of gold, silver, brass, iron and clay. Then he saw a stone cut without hands, which stone smote the image so that the gold, silver, brass, iron and clay were carried away like the chaff of the summer threshing floor. These various elements represented great world empires which were to be broken in pieces and completely destroyed, while the stone cut out without hands represented a spiritual kingdom which God Himself would set up and which figuratively would become a great mountain and *fill the whole earth.* "And in the days of those kings shall the God of heaven set up a kingdom which shall never be destroyed, nor shall the sovereignty thereof be left to another people; but it shall break in pieces and consume all these kingdoms, and it shall stand for ever" (Dan. 2:44). The generally accepted interpretation of the dream is that the four parts of the image represented four successive empires, the Babylonian, the Medo-Persian, the Macedonian empire of Alexander the Great, and the Roman empire. In the light of the New Testament we see that the final kingdom, represented by the stone cut out without hands, was the one that Christ set up, which indeed was set up while the Roman empire still was in existence. The Church, an institution not of human but of divine origin and therefore described as "cut out without hands," was destined to outlast and break in pieces all of the anti-Christian kingdoms, that is, convert and transform them, and so, figuratively, to become a great mountain and fill the whole earth, so prominent will it be in every phase of human life.

In the vision which Daniel saw, recorded in chapter 7, the beast made war against the saints and prevailed against them for a time,—but, "the time came that the saints possessed the kingdom" (vs. 22).

Jeremiah gives the promise that the time is coming when it will no longer be necessary for a man to say to his brother or to his neighbor, "Know Jehovah"; "for they shall all know me, from the least of them unto the greatest of them" (31:34). The last book of the Old Testament contains a promise that "from the rising of the sun even unto the going down of the same my name shall be great among the Gentiles, saith Jehovah of hosts" (Mal. 1:11).

In the New Testament we find the same clear teaching. At the Jerusalem Conference James cited the prophecy of Amos 9:11,12, that in the days to come God would pour out spiritual blessings on His people, "that they may possess the remnant of Edom, and all the nations that are called by my name,"—Edom here being taken as typical of Jehovah's enemies; and James, speaking by inspiration and quoting this prophecy, gives it a wider interpretation, saying that "the residue of men," and "all the Gentiles," are to "seek after the Lord" (Acts 15:17). This clearly implies the world-wide conversion of the nations.

The New Testament puts a strong emphasis on the fact that it is the *world* that is the object of Christ's redemption. "Christ is the propitiation for our sins, and not for ours only, but also for the whole world" (I John 2:2). "For God so loved the world, that he gave his only begotten Son, that whosoever believeth on him should not perish, but have eternal life. For God sent not the Son into the world to judge the world; but that the world should be saved through him" (John 3:16, 17). "The Father hath sent the Son to be the Saviour of the world" (I John 4:14). "Behold the Lamb of God, that taketh away the sin of the world!" (John 1:29). "We have heard for ourselves, and know that this is indeed the Saviour of the world" (John 4:42). "I am the light of the world" (John 8:12). "God was in Christ reconciling the world unto himself" (II Cor. 5:19).

The parable of the leaven teaches the universal extension and triumph of the Gospel, and it further teaches that this development is accomplished through the gradual development of the Kingdom, not through a sudden and cataclysmic explosion. There we are told that "The kingdom of heaven is like unto leaven, which a woman took, and hid in three measures of meal, till it was all leavened" (Matt. 13:33). The Kingdom of heaven, like leaven, transforms that with which it comes in contact. All the meal was transformed by its contact with the leaven. Similarly, Christ teaches, society is to be transformed by the Kingdom of heaven, and the result will be a Christianized world. Premillennialists cannot admit this. To do so would contradict their whole system. Hence they seek another meaning, and where Christ says *the Kingdom of heaven is like leaven,* they say that the leaven is not symbolical of the Kingdom of heaven, but of evil. J. S. Silver, one of their representative writers, says: "Literally, it denotes sin, therefore here it means apostasy" (*The Lord's Return,* p 247). And another representative writer, W. E. Blackstone, says: "We believe that the leaven in the parable of Matthew 13 represents . . . the false doctrines which have crept in and so pervaded the professing church that it has, in the main, become merely formal and nominal" (*Jesus Is Coming,* p. 95). We are at a loss to understand how any one professing to take the Bible at face value, particularly those who lay great stress on literal interpretation, can deliberately contradict the words spoken so clearly and unequivocally and make them mean the exact opposite, in this case, false doctrine. These are the very people who protest so strongly against "spiritualizing." Anyone who can so change the meaning of Scripture can make it mean anything that he pleases. According to this interpretation Christ is to be understood as saying in effect that, "The kingdom of heaven is like an evil influence which brings the whole world into a state of apostasy." This is an example of the extremity to which some will go, the forced interpretation to which they will resort, in defending a theory. They would never arrive at such a meaning if they were not attempting to avoid the clear implication of the parable.

Premillennialists seize upon the words of Jesus in Matthew 24:14, "And this gospel of the kingdom shall be preached in all the world for a witness unto all nations; and then shall the end come" (King James Version), as proving their doctrine that the gospel is to be preached only as a "witness," or as a "testimony" (American Standard Version), and therefore that it is not intended to convert the world. This verse in itself may not be decisive as to the purpose and effect of such preaching. But such definitely was not the case when Christ gave the Great Commission to the disciples. There He said: "All authority hath been given unto me in heaven and on earth. Go ye therefore, and make disciples of all the nations, baptizing them in the name of the Father and of the Son and of the Holy Spirit: teaching them to observe all things whatsoever I commanded you: and lo, I am with you always, even unto the end of the world" (Matt. 28:18–20).

Here we are told that "all authority" in heaven and on earth has been given to Christ for the performance of this work. Commenting on this point Dr. Snowden says: "All authority includes all power of every kind that is applicable to this task. Jesus Christ can never have any more power than He has now, for He now has all there is. Premillenarians put their confidence in some 'rod of iron' with which Christ will 'smite down all opposition' when He comes, but Christ now has omnipotence and has pledged it to the present work of preaching the gospel for the conversion of the world." He goes on to say that, "The Greek word translated 'make disciples of' is a strong one, meaning not merely to 'preach' or 'evangelize' but to convert into disciples . . . We have in this commission express and inescapable teaching that the gospel is preached not simply for 'evangelizing' or 'for a witness', but for the deeper work of conversion . . . These nations are to be converted into Christian disciples, and this work is not done but only begun when they are 'evangelized,' or simply had the gospel preached to them. Jesus here speaks in world terms, here is the splendid universality of His gospel . . . Premillenarians say that Christ the King is absent and tell us what great things He will do when He comes again. But Christ Himself assures us He is present and is even now with us in our work . . . To reduce this great commission to the premillenarian program of preaching the gospel as a witness to a world that is to grow worse and worse until it plunges into its doom in destruction, is to emasculate the gospel of Christ and wither it into pitiful impotency. This is to send the gospel out into the world as a futile thing, foreordained to failure from the start. No, the gospel is the power of God unto salvation, and Jesus Christ, marching in the greatness of His strength, sends us on no empty errand of uttering a message that will die away in the air on an unheeding and hostile world, gathering only a few out of its innumerable multitudes and consigning the vast majority to destruction, but He sends us to 'make disciples of all the nations' and thereby win the world itself" (*The Coming of the Lord,* pp. 98–103).

We find that Christ's work of redemption truly has as its object the people of the entire world and that His Kingdom is to become universal. And since nothing is told us as to how long the earth shall continue after that goal has been reached, possibly we can look forward to a great "golden age" of spiritual prosperity continuing for centuries, or even for millenniums, during which time Christianity shall be triumphant over all the earth, and during which time the great proportion even of adults shall be saved. It seems that the number of the redeemed shall then be swelled until it far surpasses that of the lost.

Chapter VI

THE VASTNESS OF THE REDEEMED MULTITUDE

The writer of the Apocalypse says: "I saw, and behold, a great multitude, which no man could number, out of every nation and of all the tribes and peoples and tongues, standing before the throne and before the Lamb, arrayed in white robes, and palms in their hands; and they cried with a great voice, saying, Salvation unto our God who sitteth on the throne, and unto the Lamb" (Rev. 7:9,10). God has chosen to redeem untold millions of the human race. Just what proportion of the race has been included in His purposes of mercy, we have not been informed; but in view of the future days of prosperity which are promised to the Church, it may be inferred that much the greater part eventually will be found among that number. Assuming that those who die in infancy are saved, as most churches have taught and as most theologians have believed, already much the larger proportion of the human race has been saved.

In Revelation 19:11–21 we have a vision setting forth in figurative language the age-long struggle between the forces of good and the forces of evil in the world, with its promise of complete victory. There we read:

"And I saw the heaven opened; and behold, a white horse and he that sat thereon called Faithful and True; and in righteousness he doth judge and make war. And his eyes are a flame of fire, and upon his head are many diadems; and he hath a name written which no one knoweth but himself. And he is arrayed in a garment sprinkled with blood; and his name is called The Word of God. And the armies which are in heaven followed him upon white horses, clothed in fine linen, white and pure. And out of his mouth proceedeth a sharp sword, that with it he should smite the nations: and he shall rule them with a rod of iron: and he treadeth the winepress of the fierceness of the wrath of God, the Almighty. And he hath on his garment and on his thigh a name written, KING OF KINGS, AND LORD OF LORDS.

"And I saw an angel standing in the sun; and he cried with a loud voice, saying to all the birds that fly in mid heaven, Come and be gathered together unto the great supper of God; that ye may eat the flesh of kings, and the flesh of captains, and the flesh of mighty men, and the flesh of horses and of them that sit thereon, and the flesh of all men, both free and bond, and small and great.

"And I saw the beast, and the kings of the earth, and their armies, gathered together to make war against him that sat upon the horse, and against his army. And the beast was taken, and with him the false prophet that wrought the signs in his sight, wherewith he deceived them that had received the mark of the beast and them that worshipped his image: they two were cast alive into the lake of fire that burneth with brimstone: and the rest were killed with the sword of him that sat upon the horse, even the sword which came forth out of his mouth: and all the birds were filled with their flesh."

The best explanation of this passage we believe is that given by Dr. Warfield. He says:

"The section opens with a vision of the victory of the Word of God, the King of Kings and Lord of Lords over all His enemies. We see Him come forth from heaven girt for war, followed by the armies of heaven; the birds of the air are summoned to the feast of corpses that shall be prepared for them; the armies of the enemy—the beasts and the kings of the earth—are gathered against him and are totally destroyed; and 'all the birds are filled with their flesh.' It is a vivid picture of a complete victory, an entire conquest, that we have here; and all the imagery of war and battle is employed to give it life. This is the symbol. The thing symbolized is obviously the complete victory of the Son of God over all the hosts of wickedness. Only a single hint of this signification is afforded by the language of the description, but that is enough. On two occasions we are carefully told that the sword by which the victory is won proceeds *out of the mouth* of the conqueror (verses 15 and 21). We are not to think, as we read, of any literal war or manual fighting, therefore; the conquest is wrought by the spoken word—in short, by the preaching of the Gospel. In fine, we have before us here a picture of the victorious career of the Gospel of Christ in the world. All the imagery of the dread battle and its hideous details are but to give us the impression of the completeness of the victory. Christ's Gospel is to conquer the earth; He is to overcome all His enemies . . .

"What we have here, in effect, is a picture of the whole period between the first and the second advents, seen from the point of view of heaven. It is the period of advancing victory of the Son of God over the world, emphasizing, in harmony with its place at the end of the book, the completeness of the victory. It is the eleventh chapter of Romans and the fifteenth chapter of I Corinthians in symbolical form: and there is nothing in it that was not already in them—except that, perhaps the completeness of the triumph of the Gospel is possibly somewhat more emphasized here . . .

"As emphatically as Paul, John teaches that the earthly history of the Church is not a history merely of conflict with evil, but of conquest over evil: and even more richly than Paul, John teaches that this conquest will be decisive and complete. The whole meaning of the vision of Revelation 19:11–21 is that Christ Jesus comes forth not to war merely but to victory; and every detail of the picture is laid in with a view precisely to emphasizing the thoroughness of this victory. The Gospel of Christ is, John being witness, completely to conquer the world. He says nothing, any more than Paul does, of the period of the endurance of this conquered world. Whether the last judgment and the consummated kingdom are to follow immediately upon its conquest—his visions are as silent as Paul's teaching. But just on that account the possibility of an extended duration for the conquered earth lies open: and in any event a progressively advancing conquest of the earth by Christ's Gospel implies a coming age deserving at least the relative name of 'golden' " (Article, *The Millennium and the Apocalypse*; reprinted in *Biblical Doctrines*, pp. 647, 648, 662).

To us who live between the first and the second coming of Christ it is given to see that conquest taking place. Revelation 19:11–21, we believe, is a description of the spiritual warfare which rages through the centuries, in which as followers of our great Captain it is our privilege to have a part. In verse 14 we are told that those who follow the Rider on the white horse are "clothed in fine linen, white and pure." Surely Christ's elect are His soldiers. Earlier in this same chapter, verse 8, we were told that the Church, as the bride of the Lamb, has arrayed herself "in fine linen, bright and pure: *for the fine linen is the righteous acts of the saints.*" Hence the righteous acts of the saints who through the centuries constitute the Church evidently play an important part in this great conquest. Paul gives an insight into the nature of this battle when he says: "Put on the whole armour of God, that ye may be able to stand against the wiles of the Devil. For our wrestling is not against flesh and blood, but against the principalities, against the powers, against the world rulers of this darkness, against the spiritual hosts of wickedness in the heavenly places" (Eph. 6:11,12). Here we learn who the real enemies of Christ's kingdom are. Our conflict is revealed as not primarily against evil human beings, but rather against spiritual hosts of wickedness. Here, too, we learn that in this holy war Christians are Christ's soldiers, and that it is through their victory that His victory is won.

How long the conquest continues before it is crowned with victory—we purposely use the word "conquest," rather than "conflict," for Christ is not merely striving against evil, but progressively overcoming it—or how long the converted world is to await her coming Lord, we are not told. Today we are living in an era that is relatively golden as compared with the first century of the Christian era. This progress is to go on until on this earth we shall see a practical fulfillment of the prayer, "Thy kingdom come, thy will be done in earth as it is in heaven"—and the mere fact that Christ Himself taught His disciples thus to pray certainly indicates that it is a petition that God desires and wills to answer. As we get the broader view of God's gracious dealings with the sinful world, we see that He has not distributed His saving grace with a miserly hand, but that His purpose has been the restoration to Himself of the whole world.

We have quoted Warfield's view regarding a future golden age. Another of America's most brilliant theologians, Jonathan Edwards, gives the following exposition of the postmillennial position.

"The visible kingdom of Satan shall be overthrown, and the

kingdom of Christ set up on the ruins of it, everywhere throughout the whole inhabitable globe. Now shall the promise made to Abraham be fulfilled, that 'in him and in his seed all the families of the earth shall be blessed'; and Christ now shall become the desire of all nations, agreeable to Hagai 2:7. Now the kingdom of Christ shall in the most strict and literal sense be extended to all nations, and the whole earth. There are many passages of Scripture that can be understood in no other sense. What can be more universal than that in Isaiah 11:9, 'For the earth shall be full of the knowledge of the Lord, as the waters cover the sea.' As much as to say, as there is no part of the channel or cavity of the sea anywhere, but what is covered with water; so there shall be no part of the world of mankind but what shall be covered with the knowledge of God. It is foretold in Isaiah 45:22, that all the ends of the earth shall look to Christ, and be saved. And to show that the words are to be understood in the most universal sense, it is said in the next verse, 'I have sworn by myself, the word is gone out of my mouth in righteousness, and shall not return, that unto me every knee shall bow, every tongue shall swear.' So the most universal expression is used (Dan. 7:27), 'And the kingdom and dominion, and the greatness of the kingdom under the whole heaven, shall be given to the people of the saints of the Most High God.' You see the expression includes *all* under the *whole heaven*."

Early in the Old Testament the promise was given to Abraham that his posterity should be a vast multitute,—"In blessing I will bless thee, and in multiplying I will multiply thy seed as the stars of the heavens, and as the sand which is upon the sea-shore" (Gen. 22:17); "I will make thy seed as the dust of the earth; so that if a man can number the dust of the earth, then may thy seed also be numbered" (Gen. 13:16). And in the New Testament we discover that this promise refers not merely to the Jews as a separate people, but that those who are Christians are in the highest sense the true "sons of Abraham." "Know therefore," says Paul, "that they that are of faith, the same are sons of Abraham"; and again, "If ye are Christ's, then are ye Abraham's seed, heirs according to promise" (Gal. 3:7, 29).

Isaiah declared that the pleasure of Jehovah should prosper in the hand of the Messiah, that He should see of the travail of

His soul and be satisfied (53:10,11). And in view of what He suffered on Calvary we know that He will not be easily satisfied.

The idea that the saved shall far outnumber the lost is also carried out in the contrasts drawn in Scripture. Heaven is uniformly pictured as the next world, as a great kingdom, a country, a city; while on the other hand hell is uniformly represented as a comparatively small place, a prison, a lake (of fire and brimstone), a pit (perhaps deep, but narrow): (Luke 20:35; Rev. 21:1; Matt. 5:3; Heb. 11:16; I Peter 3:19; Rev. 19:20; 21:8–16). When the angels and saints are mentioned in Scripture they are said to be hosts, myriads, an innumerable multitute, ten thousand times ten thousand and many more thousands of thousands; but no such language is ever used in regard to the lost, and by contrast their number appears to be relatively insignificant (Luke 2:13; Is. 6:3; Rev. 5:11). The description of the great white throne judgment as found in Revelation 20:11–15 closes with the statement: "And if any was not found written in the book of life, he was cast into the lake of fire"—language which indicates that in the judgment the *normal* thing will be that the names of the great majority of earth's population *are* written in the book of life. Such language implies that those whose names are not written there are the exceptional—we may even say, rare—cases.

"The circle of God's election," says Dr. W. G. T. Shedd, "is a great circle of the heavens and not that of a treadmill. The kingdom of Satan is insignificant in contrast with the kingdom of Christ. In the immense range of God's dominion, good is the rule, and evil is the exception. Sin is a speck upon the azure of eternity; a spot upon the sun. Hell is only a corner of the universe."

Judging from these considerations it appears, if we may hazard a guess, that the number of those who are saved may eventually bear some such proportion to those who are lost as the number of free citizens in our commonwealth today bears to those who are in the prisons and penitentiaries; or that the company of the saved may be likened to the main stalk of the tree which grows and flourishes, while the lost are but as the small limbs and prunings which are cut off and which are destroyed in the fires. This is the prospect that Postmillennialism is able to offer. Who even among those holding other systems would not wish that it were true?

But, it may be asked, do not the verses, "Narrow is the gate, and straightened the way, that leadeth to life, and few are they that find it," and "Many are called, but few chosen" (Matt. 7:14; 22:14), teach that many more are lost than saved? We believe that these verses are meant to be understood in a temporal sense, as describing the conditions which Jesus and the disciples saw existing in Palestine in their day. The great majority of the people about them were not walking in the way of righteousness, and the words were spoken from the standpoint of the moment rather than from the standpoint of the distant Judgment Day. In these words we have presented to us a picture that was true to life as they saw it about them, and which in general has been true even up to the present time. But we may ask, in view of the future prosperity promised to the Church, are we not entitled to believe that as the years and the centuries and ages flow on the proportion following "the two ways" shall be reversed?

These verses are also designed to teach that the way of salvation is a way of difficulty and sacrifice, and that it is our duty to address ourselves to it with diligence and persistence. No one is to take his salvation for granted. Those who enter into the kingdom of heaven do so through many tribulations; hence the command. "Strive to enter in by the narrow door" (Luke 13:24). The choice in life is represented as a choice between two roads, —one is broad, smooth, and easy to travel, but leads to destruction. The other is narrow and difficult, but leads to life. "There is no more reason," says Dr. Warfield, "to assume that this similitude teaches that the saved shall be fewer than the lost than there is to suppose that the parable of the Ten Virgins (Matt. 25:1ff) teaches that they shall be precisely equal in number; and there is far less reason to suppose that this similitude teaches that the saved shall be few comparatively to the lost than there is to suppose that the parable of the Tares in the Wheat (Matt. 13:24ff) teaches that the lost shall be inconsiderable in number in comparison with the saved—for that, indeed, is an important part of the teaching of that parable" (Article, *Are They Few That Be Saved?*). And we may add that there is no more reason to suppose that this reference to the two ways teaches that the number of the saved shall be fewer than the number of the lost than there is to suppose that the parable of the Lost Sheep teaches that only one out of a hundred goes astray and that even that one eventually will be brought back—which indeed would be absolute restorationism.

Chapter VII

THE WORLD IS GROWING BETTER

The redemption of the world is a long, slow process, extending through the centuries, yet surely approaching an appointed goal. We live in the day of advancing victory, although there are many apparent set-backs. As seen from the human viewpoint it often looks as though the forces of evil are about to gain the upper hand. Periods of spiritual advance and prosperity alternate with periods of spiritual decline and depression. But as one age succeeds another there is progress. Looking back across the nearly two thousand years that have passed since the coming of Christ we can see that there has indeed been marvelous progress. This process ultimately shall be completed, and before Christ comes again we shall see a Christianized world. This does not mean that all sin ever will be eradicated. There always will be some tares among the wheat until the time of harvest—and the harvest, the Lord tells us, is the end of the world. Even the righteous fall, sometimes grievously, into temptation and sin. But it does mean that Christian principles of life and conduct are to become the accepted standards in public and private life.

That a great spiritual advance has been made should be clear to all. Consider, for instance, the awful moral and spiritual conditions that existed on earth before the coming of Christ,— the world at large groping helplessly in pagan darkness, with slavery, polygamy, the oppressed conditions of women and children, the almost complete lack of political freedom, and the ignorance, poverty, and extremely primitive medical care that was the lot of nearly all except those who belonged to the ruling classes. Today the world at large is on a far higher plane. Christian principles are the accepted standards in many nations even though they are not consistently practiced. Slavery and polygamy have practically disappeared. The status of women and children has been improved immeasurably. Social and economic conditions in almost all nations have reached a new high plateau. A spirit of cooperation is much more manifest among the nations than it has ever been before. International incidents which only a few years ago would have resulted in wars are now usually settled by arbitration. As an evidence of international good will witness the fact that the United States this fiscal year (July, 1957 to July, 1958) appropriated more than three billion dollars for the foreign aid and mutual security program, and since the end of World War II has given to other nations more than sixty billion dollars for these purposes. Since our population is approximately 170,000,000, this means an average contribution of $350 for every man, woman and child in the United States. And this does not include the other very considerable sums that have been given by individuals, churches and other organizations. This huge amount of goods and services has been given freely by this enlightened and predominantly Protestant nation to nations of other races and religions, with no expectation that it ever will be paid back, an effective expression of unselfishness and international good will. That record has never been even remotely approached before by this or any other nation in all the history of the world.

Recently the London Times, the leading newspaper in England, after commending the wisdom and generosity with which the United States acted, said: "There are other things so obvious to us that we take them for granted. But because silence can be misunderstood it is worth saying once again that no nation has ever come into possession of such power for good or ill, for freedom or tyranny, for friendship or enmity among the peoples of the world, and that no nation in history has used those powers, by and large, with greater vision, restraint, responsibility and courage" (Issue of March 23, 1954).

Today there is much more wealth consecrated to the service of the Church than ever before; and, in spite of the defection toward Modernism in some places, we believe there is far more really earnest evangelistic and missionary activity than at any time in the past. This is indicated by a number of developments. We cite particularly the following.

Up until the time of the Reformation the Bible had been a book for priests only. It was written in Latin, and the Roman

Church refused to allow it to be translated into the languages of the common people. But when the Reformers came on the scene all that was changed. The Bible was soon translated into all of the vernacular tongues of Europe, and wherever the light of the Reformation went it became the book of the common people. Decrees of popes and church councils gave way to the Word of life. Luther translated the entire Bible into German for the people of his native land, and within 25 years of its appearance one hundred editions of the German Bible came off the press. The same was true in France, Holland, England, and Scotland. Protestant Bible societies now circulate more Bibles each year than were circulated in the fifteen centuries that preceded the Reformation.

Publishers report that more than 8,000,000 copies of the complete Bible were sold in the United States in 1956. Sales were up about 10 per cent from 1955, which was the previous record year. Incidentally, it is interesting to notice that of the above number the King James Version easily held its place as the popular favorite, its total sales being more than 6,000,000 copies. The Revised Standard Version sold nearly 1,000,000 copies; the Douay Version, the standard Bible for American Roman Catholics, about 750,000; Jewish Bibles about 70,000; modern speech translations such as Moffatt, Goodspeed, etc., about 25,000; the American Standard Version of 1901 and others about 150,000. In addition to the above total many millions of copies of the New Testament and of portions of the Bible were sold.

During the last 150 years the Bible has been translated into all of the major languages of the world. According to the report given at the 1957 annual meeting of the American Bible Society the complete Bible, Old and New Testament, is now available in 210 languages and dialects, the complete New Testament is available in 270 more, and at least one book of the Bible, usually one of the gospels, has been translated into 629 more, for a total of 1109 languages and dialects into which the Bible has been translated in whole or in part. (United Press report, Jan. 12, 1957).

Today the Bible is available in whole or in part in the native tongue of 98 per cent of the people of the world. Surely that must be acknowledged as great progress and as a very broad and substantial basis on which to rear the future structure of Christianity. None of the so-called "best seller" books attain more than a small fraction of the number of Bibles sold.

Furthermore, the Christian message is being broadcast by radio and television in all the principal languages of the world. Several evangelical programs, with nation-wide or world-wide coverage have been launched within recent years—e.g., The Lutheran Hour, Missouri Synod (broadcasting in more than 50 languages); Coral Ridge Ministries (Presbyterian); The Back To God Hour (Christian Reformed, broadcasting in 8 languages); and Family Radio (independent), to name only a few. There are literally hundreds of other radio and television programs, many of which are heard daily. The gospel is thus brought into many a home and into many a sick room where it would not otherwise be heard, and to many a distant farm or lonely mining or lumber camp, to people on the highways and to ships at sea. How marvelous that is, compared with the very limited proclamation that prevailed for so many centuries! The over-all result is that for the first time in history the people of the entire world have the evangelical Christian message made available to them.

The number of theological seminaries, Bible institutes and Christian colleges in which the Bible is studied systematically is growing faster than the population, and the enrollment is increasing steadily. Numerous Christian magazines with very wide circulations have been established within recent years. A considerable proportion of the new books that come from the press either deal directly with Christianity or with some phase of religion.

During the past two centuries the Christian Church has made great progress and has established thousands upon thousands of local churches. It has become customary in the United States to think of the Colonial period as an age of deep faith. Yet the fact is that a large number of the people who came to these shores during that time did so to escape religious oppression in European countries, and they were slow in establishing new churches. Many had no church connection to begin with, or dropped the connection they did have, as has so often been the case in frontier or pioneer settlements. The Pilgrims and Puritans were the exception to the rule, but while they were strong in some sections other sections were quite different. Professor Leonard Verduin, of the Department of History in the University of Michigan has this to say regarding church membership in the colonial period:

"The first century and a half of American history was a mere elongation of European establishmentism. Throughout the colonies by and large there was a favored church. And, contrary to a legend which one often hears that those were golden days, America was never so near to being post-Christian as it was at the end of those 150 years. Competent historians find not more than 6 per cent of the adult population church-related. Then came the Revolution, and out of it was born the federal constitution. As by a divine economy it was laid down once and for all in the First Amendment that establishment was to be 'out' in this new commonwealth. And, even as a patient sometimes rallies in an amazing fashion at the injection of sulfa, so did this new commonwealth from that moment on witness the return of religion. Steadily, without fluctuation, the figure of the percentage of church membership rises, until today we stand at an all time high—not far below 60 per cent of the population today holding church membership" (*The Reformed Journal*, Jan. 1953).

We may add that in 1870 church membership in the United States stood at 18 per cent, a percentage increase three times that of the Revolutionary War period. Today it stands at an all time high of 61 per cent, an increase of 4 per cent within the last five years. Of these, 35 per cent are members of Protestant churches, 20 per cent are Roman Catholics (*Yearbook of American Churches*, 1956). So-called Modernism or Liberalism has indeed risen in some quarters to deny a greater or lesser portion of the faith. But Modernism has nothing positive to offer. Its leading advocates set forth conflicting systems, and in effect acknowledge that the system is bankrupt. We are confident that after the present season of criticism and testing of the foundations is over we shall have a grander and stronger edifice of theology than the ages have yet seen.

Statistics indicate that the world over Christianity has grown more in the last one hundred years than in the preceding eighteen hundred, and that it now has a considerably larger number of nominal adherents than the combined total of any other two world religions. These figures show that of a total world population of about two and one-half billion there are approximately 800,000,000 Christians, 350,000,000 Confucianists (including Taoists), 320,000,000 Moslems, 310,000,000 Hindus, 150,000,000 Buddhists, 20,000,000 Shintoists, and 12,000,000 Jews. And while many of those who are counted as Christians are only "nominally" such, the proportion of true Christians probably is as great or greater than is the proportion of true adherents in any of the pagan religions. All of the other religions, with the exception of Mohammedanism, are much older than Christianity. All of the false religions are dying. Christianity alone is able to grow and flourish under modern civilization, while all of the others soon disintegrate when brought under its glaring light.

We feel perfectly confident in asserting that all of the anti-Christian religions and anti-Christian philosophies of our day are demonstrably false. Their histories show what complete failures they have been so far as raising the moral, spiritual and intellectual standards of their adherents is concerned. They await only the *coup de grace* of an aroused and energetic Christianity to send them into oblivion. In this connection Dr. Albertus Pieters has well said: "In the early church Ebionitism, Gnosticism, Montanism, Arianism and Pelagianism endangered the life of the church. They are rememberd now only by church historians. Later it was Romanism and Socinianism. In modern life it is Unitarianism, Modernism, Mormonism, Russellism, Christian Science, Spiritualism, etc.,—a long list of movements of Satanic origin that comes on like a flood, and for a time make timid believers afraid that the church will be overwhelmed and the gospel permanently lost to the world—but it never comes to pass. The present heresies will disappear as did those of the past" (*Studies in the Revelation of St. John*, p. 165).

Only within the last one hundred years have foreign missions really come into their own. As they have recently been developed, with great church organizations behind them and with extensive facilities for translating and publishing Christian literature in many languages, they are in a position to carry on a work of evangelism in foreign lands such as the world has never seen before. It is safe to say that the present generation living in India,

China, Japan, Korea, Indo-China and the Near East have seen greater changes in religion, society and government than occurred in the preceding two thousand years. Not only has the foundation been laid in most of these countries for a further evangelical advance, but under the benign influence of the Church innumerable local churches, schools and hospitals have been founded, ethical culture and social services have advanced greatly, and moral standards are much higher today than when the Church was first established. That we may get a truer view of the progress that has been made we cite the following picture of the early world into which Christianity came, as given by Dr. William Hendriksen:

"Let us transplant ourselves to the world of John the apostle, and imagine that the slow finger of history's clock is pointing to the first century A. D. Now, look around you in every direction. What a picture of spiritual darkness and desolation! Try to count the many idols that disgrace the streets and sanctuaries of imperial Rome. The abominations, the filth and corruption attendant upon the celebration of pagan festivals, the superstitions, vices, etc., are very staggering. Temples and shrines throughout the world are crowded with ignorant, half-despairing worshippers. We see a few scattered churches established by the efforts of Paul and others. For the rest, heathendom is everywhere triumphant. All the nations—with the exception of the Jews—are under the thraldom of Satan!" (*More Than Conquerors*, p. 224).

When we contrast the rapid spread of Christianity in recent years with the rapid disintegration that is taking place in all of the other world religions, it becomes very clear that Christianity is the future world religion. There are, however, some who tell us in all seriousness that the world is getting worse. Surely they are prompted to do so only in defense of a theory that clearly is contradicted by the facts. In response to such reasoning Dr. Snowden says:

"The true way of judging the world is to compare its present with its past condition and note in which direction it is moving. Is it going backward, or forward, is it getting worse or better? It may be wrapped in gloomy twilight, but is it the twilight of the evening, or of the morning? Are the shadows deepening into starless night, or are they fleeing before the rising sun? One glance at the world as it is today compared with what it was ten or twenty centuries ago shows us that it has swept through a wide arc and is moving toward the morning" (*The Coming of the Lord*, p. 250).

But while great progress has been made as the Church has extended her witness to the far corners of the earth, much the greater part of the work yet remains to be accomplished. Adherents of the pagan religions still outnumber those of the Christian faith, and even within the Church there is a crying need for a fuller knowledge of the contents of the Christian faith and for a much more consistent living in accordance with those principles on the part of professing Christian people. The binding of Satan, described in Revelation 20:1–3, we now perceive to be not a sudden event, but a very long, slow process. It has been in process of accomplishment for more than nineteen centuries, and much progress has been made. But no time limit can be set as to how much longer the process may have to be continued before it is crowned with success, nor how long the era of righteousness will prevail over the earth before the Lord returns. The nineteen centuries that have elapsed since the Christian era began may well indicate that several more centuries, perhaps even millenniums, may be required, particularly if devastating wars yet remain to be fought, as is of course perfectly possible.

Skeptics sometimes point to present day evils and tell us that we are living in a post-Christian age. But, no, there has never yet been a truly Christian age, nor has so much as one nation ever been consistently Christian. The age in which we are living is still pre-Christian.

That the progress of the Church through these years has been slow is due to the fact that Christians in general have not taken seriously Christ's command to evangelize the world. The Great Commission is addressed not merely to ministers and missionaries, but *to all Christians everywhere*. No distinction is made in this command between ministers and laymen. The command applies to parents rearing their children, to children in regard to their parents, to individuals in whatever relationship they stand to their neighbors or business or social companions, to those who teach in the schools, to employers and employees in their mutual relationships, to writers, newsmen, statesmen, to Christians in general regardless of occupation or station in life. The Gospel is the "good news" of the salvation that God has provided for sinful men, and it should be given out by all who have it,—given out by word of mouth, through the example of a Christian life, and by the effective and generous use of money or property or time as opportunity affords. Oftentimes a word sincerely spoken by a friend or neighbor to one who is outside the Church is more persuasive than what is said by the minister. It has been said: "No one can perform a higher service than this—to make more accessible the riches that are in Christ Jesus." Let Christians everywhere take seriously the command to evangelize the world and the work will be accomplished in a comparatively short time.

Roderick Campbell has well said:

"Some day the Christian church will learn to profit by the bitter experience of the church and nation of the Old Covenant. Two very pointed and useful lessons may be learned from the records of the past. Israel had been commanded by God to march in and take possession of the Promised Land. About one year after they left Egypt they reached the borders of the land. Then their faith and their courage failed. 'Let us make a captain,' they say, 'and let us return into Egypt.' What is the result?—forty weary years of wandering among the rocks and the sand of the desert, and the death of that entire adult generation with the exception of two men of faith (cf. Nu. 14; 32:10–13).

"The other lesson is equally profitable and clear. A new army under Joshua entered the land. It won its first signal victory at Jericho. It then met bitter and humiliating defeat. Why? Israel had sinned. The guilty party must be punished and every forbidden thing destroyed before victory could be achieved. When this was done Israel found itself on the side of the Almighty (Joshua 7). God fought for Israel with a mighty hand. The fulfillment of prophecy awaits the day when the church will really believe that God will do all that He has promised to do, and when the church will sincerely aim at entire conformity to the revealed will of God. Then, by the agency of imperfect but faithful men, we may expect God to do what He has promised to do" (*Israel and the New Covenant*, p. 162).

Premillennialists sometimes try to refute this general view by citing the question asked in Luke 18:8, "When the Son of man cometh, shall he find faith on the earth?" And they infer that the answer must be "No." But in order to give a negative answer to this question it is necessary to ignore the many statements in Scripture which describe the latter day glory of the Church. Surely an answer which at first might seem to be implied but which is not given in Scripture should not be allowed to overweigh the many references which speak of the triumph of righteousness in the earth. We submit that a question such as that in Luke 18:8 does not necessarily require a negative answer. When in the farewell discourse to the disciples Jesus asked, "Do ye now believe?" (John 16:31), no answer is given, but we do not believe that the implied answer is "No." When Paul asked, "King Agrippa, believest thou the prophets?" (Acts 26:27), the implied answer might seem to be "No," for there was little to indicate that Agrippa did believe. But Paul quickly adds, "I know that thou believest."

In closing this chapter we should point out that some postmillennial writers, as well as others, have fallen into the error of assuming too rapid progress. Dr. Snowden, for instance, after showing so clearly the error of the Premillennialists in date-setting and in assuming the near return of Christ, went on to make the same kind of an error in assuming that the Millennium was just about to dawn. In his book, *The Coming of the Lord*, written while the First World War was in progress, he assumed that the successful conclusion of the war, which he saw as in the near future, would put an end to militarism forever, and that it would be followed by a rapid development toward the millennial era. That the lessons learned from the First World War should have had that effect we readily agree. But whether the time will be long or short we have no way of knowing. This we can say: Postmillennialism does not despair of the power of the Gospel to convert the world, but holds rather that it cannot be defeated, that over the centuries it will win its way, and that eventually the goal will be achieved.

In the light of these facts we face the future confident that the best is yet to be. Let Christians everywhere thank God for the progress that has been made and take courage. Their future is as bright as the promises of God.

Chapter VIII

MATERIAL PROSPERITY
DURING THE MILLENNIUM

The great material prosperity of which the Bible speaks as accompanying the millennial era will be, to a large extent, the natural result of the high moral and spiritual life of that time. These blessings too are from God. In numerous prophecies temporal blessings are expressly represented as following in the train of the new covenant blessings. Surely it need not be doubted that when the other characteristics of the millennial era are realized this material prosperity also shall find its place. Godliness and sober living in a real sense bring their own reward. "Seek ye first his kingdom, and his righteousness; and all these things shall be added unto you," said Jesus (Matt. 6:33). "Godliness is profitable for all things, having promise of the life that now is," as well as "of that which is to come" (I Tim. 4:8). "The wilderness and the dry land shall be glad; and the desert shall rejoice, and blossom as the rose" (Is. 35:1). And how appropriate is the prophetic Messianic 72nd Psalm:

"Give the king thy judgments, O God,
 And thy righteousness unto the king's son.
 He shall judge the people with righteousness,
 And thy poor with justice. . . .
 He shall redeem their soul from oppression and violence;
 And precious will their blood be in his sight:
 And they shall live; and to him shall be given of the gold of
    Sheba:
 And men shall pray for him continually;
 They shall bless him all the day long.
 There shall be abundance of grain in the earth upon the top
    of the mountains;
 The fruit thereof shall shake like Lebanon;

And they of the city shall flourish like grass of the earth.
His name shall endure for ever;
His name shall be continued as long as the sun:
And men shall be blessed in him;
All nations shall call him happy. . . .
And blessed be his glorious name for ever;
And let the whole earth be filled with his glory." (vss. 1, 2, 14–19).

In this connection David Brown quotes a writer of his day as follows:

"We need not have recourse to the miraculous fruitfulness of the earth which Papias feigned, in order to fulfill this prophecy (Ps. 72). Plenty is the natural consequence of the moral change which takes place in the world at the millennium. The universal righteousness of that happy period will prevent despotism in government, anarchy in the people, as well as the devastations of war, by which the earth is left uncultivated, or its produce destroyed. The religion of that period will civilize savages, and destroy among civilized nations the numerous occupations that minister to the lawless passions of men; thus directing a great multitute of the human race to the useful arts of agriculture, who had been formerly idle and a burden upon the labor of others. The love universally felt and practiced in that period will lead those who have abundance to distribute cheerfully and freely to the necessities of those who may be in need" (*The Second Advent*, p. 400).

By way of background we should remember that when man was created and placed in the garden of Eden he was commanded not only to dress and keep the garden, but that he was given the broader command to "subdue" the earth and to "have dominion over the fish of the sea, and over the birds of the heavens, and over every living thing that moveth upon the earth" (Gen. 1:28; 2:15). That meant that he was to search out the laws of nature and learn how to use them, develop new substances, and in general make himself master of the whole creation. Certainly he is a long way behind schedule on that assignment.

In the Genesis account of the origin of sin we read that as a part of the penalty placed on man for his sin the ground was cursed (3:17,18). Thenceforth it would bring forth thorns and thistles, so that he would have a never-ending struggle to maintain his existence. The plants and animals and the forces of nature in general, which formerly were for his use and service, then came into a different relationship to him and became in a degree antagonistic to him. His previously pleasant task of dressing and keeping the garden then became "toil," irksome labor; and he must thenceforth earn his bread by the sweat of his face (3:19). And in reality is not much of the waste land condition of the earth the natural and inevitable result of man's indolence, ignorance and generally perverted nature which has come about as a result of his fall into sin? The barren and unimproved stretches of land witness to his neglect. Proper irrigation and cultivation has made many a desert to blossom like the rose. One who has traveled through our arid southwest, particularly through New Mexico, Arizona and southern California, has had opportunity to see what great changes take place when water, fertilizer, improved plant varieties and cultivation are applied to the soil. The luxurious growths and beautiful landscapes that now are to be found in some limited areas are but a small sample of what can be done more efficiently and on a world-wide scale when man returns to the proper performance of the task that was assigned to him in Eden. A field that this year has a beautiful crop of wheat or corn may next year lie untilled, with the result that weeds and thistles take possession. Man's proper management of the earth, the task assigned to him before the fall, will go far toward restoring a profitable plant and animal life. Remedy the sin condition in man and a marvelous transformation will take place in nature. Luther Burbank and others have done much to bring back toward their original condition many varieties of plants and fruits that in their wild and neglected state had degenerated until they were practically worthless.

A revolution has occurred in transportation, communications, home furnishings, etc., within our own lifetime. Our modes of travel and transportation have changed more within the last 150 years than in the preceding 2,000. George Washington, using the horse-drawn stagecoach which was the best means available in his day, travelled in much the same manner as did the ancient Persians and Egyptians. The automobile, hard-surface highways, electrical power for lighting and other household uses, the airplane, radio, television, etc., are all comparatively new. And now the new sciences of atomic and solar energy with the prospect for extremely cheap power, and the whole new field of electronics, in which we have as yet hardly more than scratched the surface, give great promise for the future. A leading industrialist recently said: "America is about to enter a new golden age of prosperity which will hinge upon the harnessing of the atom, and the advent of the electronic age." One new discovery follows another, and we see more and more clearly the tremendous potentials that are available for good, potentials that through all these many centuries have remained largely unused.

Knowledge has become very widespread. Schools, even for advanced study, have been made available for all classes of people, and books, magazines, newspapers, libraries, scientific laboratories, etc., make available for all of our people vast stores of knowledge that only two or three generations ago was confined almost exclusively to favored, limited groups.

In the administration of justice great progress has been made as Christian principles have gained wider acceptance. British and American justice today is world-renowned for its meticulous consideration for the rights of the accused and of prisoners. But this is a comparatively recent development. Even in England, generally regarded as the most enlightened of the European nations, as late as the nineteenth century prisoners convicted of comparatively minor offenses were often given long prison terms or even death. A recent book, *The Old Bailey And Its Trials,* by Bernard O'Donnell (1951), gives a history of one of the most famous law courts, and tells a shocking story of professional witnesses and bribed juries being used to secure convictions, and of executions before drunken hysterical throngs. Conditions among the prisoners were revolting. Sanitation was almost unknown, disease ran rampant among prison inmates. Tortures such as flogging and pressing were used to extract confessions. Prisoners convicted of slandering royalty might have their hands cut off. The vicious practice of fees charged inmates by jail-keepers whereby prisoners had to pay to be supplied with water, a bed and other necessities, was not stopped until the nineteenth century. There were half-hearted attempts at reform from time to time, but it took parliamentary action during the Victorian period to establish the justice and fairness which prevails today.

Similarly, the progress that already has been made in the fields of health and sanitation have raised the human life span in the United States from 32 years in 1750 until now it is just short of 70 years. Modern surgery and medicine have developed largely within the past 100 years. Medical practice has been changed from a mystic and superstitious procedure to an advanced science. The so-called "miracle drugs," including the sulphas, cortisone and antibiotics, date back only about 20 years, the sulphas having been discovered in 1935. It is not unreasonable to assume that with the continued advance of science, and particularly with the better modes of living that come with moral and spiritual advance, man's life span shall be extended considerably more. Isaiah seems to indicate great longevity for the righteous,—the sinner dying at the age of one hundred years will be accursed, and so unnatural will his death be that it will be looked upon as the death of a child: "There shall no more thence be an infant of days, nor an old man that hath not filled his days: for the child shall die a hundred years old, and the sinner being a hundred years old shall be accursed" (65:20). Only recently Dr. Robert A. Davidson, Department of General Practice at the University of Tennessee medical college, declared to a group of doctors that, "Doctors of the future will spend most of their time maintaining health rather than restoring it. To live to be 115 or 120 will be expected. To live to be 140 will be desired." He added that science estimates the metabolic potential of the human body as it now is at 140 years (*The Kansas City Times*, Oct. 21, 1955).

But no matter how marvelous this material prosperity may become, it will ever remain but the by-product of the moral and spiritual prosperity that already to some extent characterizes the partially Christianized nations. It is abundantly clear that these blessings do not originate under pagan religions. Many nations that are the victims of those religions have lain in their poverty and ignorance and moral degradation for centuries or even for thousands of years while making practically no progress. The progress that has already occurred, originating largely in the Protestant nations of western Europe and in the United States, has been achieved in connection with only a limited amount of progress toward the Millennium. What marvels must lie ahead when nations the world over are Christian—when the Millennium becomes a reality!

Thus Postmillennialism holds that Christianity is to become the controlling and transforming influence not only in the moral and spiritual life of some individuals, but also in the entire social, economic and cultural life of the nations. There is no reason why this change should not take place over the entire earth, with pagan religions and false philosophies giving place to the true, and the earth being restored in considerable measure to that high purpose of righteousness and holiness for which it was created.

Chapter IX

THE MILLENNIUM NOT A PERFECT OR SINLESS STATE

There seems to be a general impression that when we speak of a Millennium we mean a time when the world will be sinless or practically so. We do believe that a time is coming when the people of the world in general will be Christians, a time when Satan will no longer be able to "deceive the nations" (Rev. 20:3). But we do not believe that the Kingdom in this world, even in its millennial fullness and power, will be a perfect or sinless state. Nor do we believe that every person will be a Christian. Yet it is not uncommon to find pre- and amillennial writers inferring or declaring that such are the tenets of Postmillennialism, and using such terms as "ideal perfection," "a perfect world," "convert every individual," and "sinless perfection," to describe the postmillennial position. No representative Postmillennialist teaches those things. Certainly such was not the teachings of Hodge, Dabney, Shedd, Strong, Snowden, or Warfield. Nor is it the teaching of Scripture.

Sinless perfection belongs only to the heavenly life. As long as the person remains in this world, even though he is a truly born again Christian, remnants of the old nature still cling to him, and he falls victim to some extent to such things as selfish desires, envy, jealousy, impatience, etc. All of us still have occasion to say with Paul, "The good which I would I do not; but the evil which I would not, that I practice" (Rom. 7:19). Sanctification is a *process* which is not complete until death. As long as the present world continues all those born into it are born members of a fallen, sinful race. They can be brought to a state of saving knowledge of God and be turned to a righteous life only through the regenerating and sanctifying power of the Holy Spirit. Some experience regeneration in early childhood, others in middle

54

life or old age, and some never experience it at all. There will always remain problems to vex the saints. In a Christian environment temptations do become much more limited in scope and intensity, but they are never completely eliminated. The wheat and the tares continue to grow together until the harvest, which is the end of the world.

What a tremendous difference there would be in this world if the rank and file of the people were Christians, and if Christian standards were the generally accepted rule in our social, economic, educational and political life! Progress would be incredibly more rapid and permanent, poverty and disease would be largely eliminated, economic and political rivalry would be reduced to a minimum, and the accomplishments of a prolonged era of peace would be preserved instead of being destroyed by periodic wars as has so often been the case up to the present time.

The Millennium is, in fact, simply the full development of the Kingdom of grace as it comes to fruition in this world. This Kingdom begins very small, but it grows and eventually it dominates the whole earth.

In some Old Testament prophecies God's future Kingdom is described under the symbolism of a mountain. In these we have set before us the triumph of the now existing Church as it becomes prominent and influential in all phases of human life. No new weapons are needed for the conquest of the world, nor is there any change of dispensations. Says David Brown, "The Church is already all that she needs to be. She is complete in her living and ever-present Head, having 'all power in heaven and in earth' at her command, and getting it too at the destined periods, when 'the time to favor her is come, even the set time'" (*The Second Advent*, p. 342).

Snowden expresses his idea of what the Millennium is in the following words: "The world is yet young. Humanity is in its infancy. The centuries stretch out before it in vast vistas. There is before it a prospect of hope and splendid opportunism. The future is rosy with morning light. . . . Truth shall be taken from the scaffold, and wrong driven from the throne. More and more shall He whose right it is reign and the will of God be done on earth as it is in heaven. This will be the millennium. The visions of the Hebrew prophets of the Messianic kingdom shall be fulfilled in their true spiritual and glorious meaning . . . As we gird ourselves for the work of life we may look forward to the time when in the truest sense the kingdoms of this world shall become the kingdom of Christ, and He shall reign forever and ever, Kings of kings, and Lord of lords' (*The Coming of the Lord*, p. 275).

What then will the Millennium be like? In Acts 9:31 we read that after the bloody persecutor, Saul of Tarsus, had been transformed into a warm-hearted Christian, "The church throughout all Judaea and Galilee and Samaria had peace, being edified; and, walking in the fear of the Lord and in the comfort of the Holy Spirit, was multiplied." Such rest and its blessed consequences will be one of the chief features of the Millennium. Up until the present time we have seen such rest only within limited circles and over short periods of time. But during the Millennium such a state will exist throughout the Church and over the whole world. "What, then, is the difference between the present and the millennial state?" asks David Brown. "Just the difference," he answers, "between plucking more brands out of the fire than now—between a less and a greater number of converted and holy persons. That is all" (p. 393).

There will be no difference in principle between the teaching and preaching of the Gospel then and now. The difference will be in the *extent* to which it will become effective in the lives of the people. As Christianity is triumphant now in some family groups and local communities, so it will be then over the entire world. The Millennium, therefore, does not mean an entirely new and different state of things on this earth, but rather the elimination of the great majority of the evil influences that still are so prominent throughout the world, and a correspondingly higher moral and spiritual tone in the lives of the people. Thus, figuratively, the wolf and the lamb shall lie down together,—things formerly antagonistic and hateful to each other will work together in one harmonious purpose. The desert will blossom as the rose— literally, as economic and scientific conditions lead to the development of natural resources and generally prosperous conditions over the world, and figuratively, as moral and spiritual conditions are improved. Poverty and ignorance will be largely eliminated. Health and education will be the general rule, and wealth will be vastly more abundant and more widely distributed.

In general, then, the Millennium will not involve any change in the nature of Christianity, but only its much wider extension. There will be no elements in it that are not now present on a smaller scale. Then it will be said, "The kingdom of the world is become the kingdom of our Lord, and of his Christ: and he shall reign for ever and ever." In the words of David Brown:

"When the kingdom and the dominion, and the greatness of the kingdom, under the whole heaven, is given to the people of the saints of the Most High; when Christ's dominion is from sea to sea, and from the River to the ends of the earth; when men are blessed in Him, and all nations call Him blessed; when they have beaten their swords into plough-shares, and their spears into pruning-hooks—nation not lifting up sword against nation, and none learning war any more:—then, of course, all the earth will be at rest and be still, save in the unwearied activities of well-doing. But even then, as the flesh will lust against the spirit, and the spirit against the flesh, so salvation in every case will then be as much a triumph of grace over nature as now" (p. 397).

Chapter X

THE MILLENNIAL AGE
APPROACHES BY
IMPERCEPTIBLE DEGREES

The golden age of righteousness is, of course, not to be thought of as beginning suddenly, or on any particular date. It cannot be pinpointed on the calendar, for it comes as the result of a long, slow process. "The kingdom of heaven cometh not with observation" (Luke 17:20). It is "first the blade, then the ear, then the full grain in the ear" (Mark 4:28). Or again, it is "precept upon precept, precept upon precept; line upon line, line upon line; here a little, there a little" (Is. 28:10).

The coming of the Millennium is like the coming of summer, although ever so much more slowly and on a much grander scale. In the struggle between the seasons there are many advances and many apparent setbacks. Time and again the first harbingers of spring appear, only to be overcome by the winter winds. It often seems that the struggle has been lost and that the cold of winter will never be broken. But gradually the moderate spring breezes take over, and after a time we find ourselves in the glorious summer season.

Trying to pinpoint the date on which the Millennium begins is like trying to distinguish the day or year when Medieval history ended and Modern history began. The discovery of America by Columbus usually is taken as the landmark dividing the two. At least for us as Americans that is where medievalism ends and where the story of America begins. But that discovery made no immediate change in the life of the world, and in fact Columbus himself died without ever knowing that he had discovered a new world. In retrospect and for convenience we arbitrarily choose a date as the division point between two eras. But in reality one such age blends into another so slowly and so imperceptibly that no change is recognizable at the time. Only with the perspective of history can we look back and set an approximate date, perhaps within a century or two, as to when one era ceased and another began. So it is with the coming of the Millennium. Undoubtedly it will follow the law of all of the other great periods in the history of the Church, being gradual and uncertain in its approach.

We find that time and again during the Church age there has been progress toward higher moral and spiritual standards, only to suffer tragic setback through a series of wars or retrogressions. Looked at from the standpoint of present day events it may not be possible to say which way the tides are moving. But over the centuries there is progress, great progress if we look back five hundred, or a thousand, or two thousand years. Certainly many of those who tell us that the world is getting worse would change their minds very quickly if they suddenly found themselves back in colonial days, or in the Dark Ages, or in the pre-Christian era.

The following paragraph by Dr. William Hendriksen, Professor in Calvin Seminary, in regard to the "binding" of Satan in Revelation 20:1-3, is much to the point. We differ with Dr. Hendriksen only in that we regard the millennial age as belonging primarily to a future era, while he as an Amillennialist understands it as embracing the entire Church age. But that is beside the point. Says he:

"The Church has become international. The international Church is very powerful; 'like a mighty army moves the Church of God! . . . The particularism of the Old Testament has made place for the universalism of the New. The Bible, just recently, was translated into its thousandth (!) tongue. The influence of the Gospel upon the thought and life of mankind can scarcely be overestimated. In some countries the blessed truth of Christianity affects life in all its phases: political, economic, social, and intellectual. Only the individual who lacks the historical sense and is, therefore, unable to see the present in the light of conditions which prevailed throughout the world before Christ's ascension, can fail to appreciate the glories of the millennial age in which we are now living. Truly, the prophecy found in

Psalm 72 is being fulfilled before our very eyes" (*More than Conquerors,* p. 227).

We have made much progress during the Christian era, but still, on postmillennial grounds, it hardly seems that even in the most advanced nations of the earth we have seen anything that is worthy of being called more than the early dawn of the Millennium. We might say that as yet we still are engaged primarily in laying the foundation rather than building the superstructure. Some Amillennialists, as we have just seen, deny that there is to be a future golden age on either post- or premillennial principles, and hold instead that the term embraces the entire period between the first and second coming of Christ. We believe, however, that while we are making progress we still have a long distance to go, and that the Millennium will be something much more advanced and glorious than anything that has yet been seen.

We hold that Christ is not merely the potential victor, but the actual victor over sin. During the interadventual reign He is steadily putting into effect the victory that He has won, gradually overcoming the forces of evil, until all His enemies shall have been made the footstool of His feet (Acts 2:35). The dispensation in which we now are is a period of advancing conquest, so that when He returns it is to a converted world. Appropriate here are the words of Dr. Samuel G. Craig:

"Certainly on the basis of Scripture we are warranted in looking forward to a period relatively golden as compared with that which we now enjoy. Christ is today the head of a kingdom, a kingdom that is not merely engaged in conflict with evil but that is triumphing over evil. We are today living in the midst of a period that is relatively golden as measured with the period in the midst of which the New Testament was written. Moreover, Christ is to go on conquering and to conquer until the kingdoms of this world shall have become the kingdom of our Lord and His Christ, until in fact the prayer He taught His disciples to pray shall have been realized, 'Thy kingdom come, Thy will be done, as in heaven, so on earth'" (*Jesus As He Was And Is,* p. 278).

A truly Christianized world was the goal set before the disciples by Christ Himself, for he said, "Go ye therefore, and make disciples of all the nations." And that this might be a long, slow process was indicated by the form of the promise that he gave in connection with that command: "Lo, I am with you always, even unto the end of the world" (Matt. 28:20). The leaven is to work until it leavens the whole lump. The kingdom, like the little mustard seed, is to grow until it becomes a tree. Here too is to be found the fulfillment of the promise, "For the earth shall be full of the knowledge of Jehovah, as the waters cover the sea" (Is. 11:9). John gives us the prophecy that the Devil shall be bound for a thousand years, "that he should deceive the nations no more" (Rev. 20:3). And that this latter prophecy relates not to the intermediate state, nor to the eternal order, but to the present world order, should be clear from the fact that John saw the angel "coming down out of heaven" to the earth, and from the fact that the *nations*, entities which relate to this present world order, are specifically mentioned. The nations as such have no place in the heavenly kingdom.

The earth during the present dispensation never can, of course, become paradise regained. But a Christianized world can afford a foretaste of heaven, an earnest of the good things that God has in store for those who love Him. In principle Christians already are partakers of the heavenly life. They have been "born anew" or "born from above" (John 3:3); they have been "made alive," whereas they formerly were "dead" through trespasses and sins (Eph. 2:1): they are "partakers of a heavenly calling" (Heb. 3:1); they have "tasted of the heavenly gift" (Heb. 6:4); their "citizenship is in heaven" (Phil. 3:20); and Paul says that already God has "raised us up with him, and made us to sit with him in the heavenly places in Christ Jesus" (Eph. 2:6). When we are born anew we are born into the Kingdom and partake of the preliminary benefits of the Kingdom even in this world.

Hence we see the world progressing slowly but surely toward an appointed goal. Much progress has been made. Already the beams of the rising Sun of Righteousness are beginning to displace the darkness and confusion and wretchedness and ruin that they are destined to chase away. Says Dr. Warfield, "According to the New Testament, this time in which we live is precisely the time in which our Lord is conquering the world to Himself; and it is the completion of this conquest which, as it marks the completion of His redemptive work, so it sets the time for His return to earth to consummate His kingdom and establish it in its eternal form" (Article, *The Gospel of the Second Coming,* in *The Bible Magazine,* April 1915).

Chapter XI

THE THOUSAND YEARS A SYMBOLICAL FIGURE

As we read the book of Revelation figurative or symbolical expressions are met on every hand. The churches are symbolized by the seven golden candlesticks. Seven spirits before the throne are used to symbolize the fullness of the one Holy Spirit. We read of the Lamb having seven horns. We do not expect to see a literal lamb, nor seven literal horns, but know that this symbolizes the fullness of the power of Christ. Twelve is the number of the Church, and wherever the Church is mentioned we have this number or its mulitple,—twelve apostles, twenty-four elders, or the totality of God's people symbolized by the number 144,000. In the Bible the number ten stands for rounded totals. Hence we have the moral law summarized in the ten commandments. Ten plagues on Egypt, each directed at a god worshipped by the Egyptians, showed the complete superiority of the God of the Hebrews over the gods of Egypt. In the tabernacle the Holy of Holies, the place in which God manifested His presence, was ten cubits long, ten cubits wide, and ten cubits high. The cube, with all sides equal, symbolizes perfection. A thousand is the cube of ten, and symbolizes vastness of number or time. In Psalm 50:10 the expression "the cattle upon a thousand hills" does not mean that only the cattle on a thousand hills are the Lord's but that all of the cattle on all of the hills of the world are His. When the Lord told Peter that he should forgive his brother not seven times, but seventy times seven (Matt. 18:22), He did not mean 490 times, but that he should forgive him as many times as he sincerely asked to be forgiven. The New Jerusalem, of which we read in Revelation 21, is pictured as a city in the form of a cube, 12,000 furlongs (1500 miles) on an edge, a figure which symbolizes prefection, grandeur and vastness. "The length and breadth and the height are equal," says John. The city was surrounded by a wall 144 cubits high (12 squared), or 216 feet, which to the people to whom John wrote would symbolize absolute safety. Neither the shape nor the dimensions of the city can be taken with mathematical exactness, as if it were a gigantic apartment house.

In Revelation 20 we do not understand John to write of a literal dragon or of a literal serpent. Nor do we understand him to say that the angel has a literal key or a literal chain in his hand with which he binds the Devil. The "thousand years" is quite clearly not to be undestood as an exact measure of time but rather as a symbolical number. Strict arithmetic has no place here. The term is a figurative expression, indicating an indefinitely long period of time, a complete, perfect number of years, probably not less than a literal one thousand years, in all probability very much longer. It is, however, a definitely limited period, during which certain events happen, and after which certain other events are to follow.

Concerning this symbolism of numbers Dr. Warfield says:

"It is quite certain that the number 1000 represents in Bible symbolism absolute perfection and completeness; and that the symbolism of the Bible includes also the use of a period of time in order to express the idea of greatness, in connection with thoroughness and completeness. It can scarcely be necessary to insist here afresh on the symbolical use of numbers in the Apocalypse and the necessity consequently laid upon the interpreter to treat them consistently not merely as symbols but as embodying definite ideas. They constitute a language, and like any other language they are misleading unless intended and read as expressions of definite ideas. When the seer says seven or four or three or ten, he does not name these numbers at random but expresses by each a specific notion. The sacred number seven in combination with the equally sacred number three forms the number of holy perfection, ten, and when this ten is cubed into a thousand the seer has said all he could say to convey to our minds the idea of absolute completeness. It is of more importance doubtless, however, to illustrate the use of time-periods to the idea of completeness. Ezekiel 39:9 provides an instance. There the completeness of the conquest of Israel over its enemies is expressed by saying that seven years shall be consumed in the burning up of the debris of battle: they 'shall go forth,' we read, 'and shall make fires of the weapons and burn them, both the shields and the bucklers, the bows and the arrows, and the hand-staves and the spears, and they shall *make fires of them seven years.'* It were absurd to suppose that it is intended that the fires shall actually endure seven years. We have here only a hyperbole to indicate the greatness of the mass to be consumed and the completeness of the consumption. A somewhat similar employment of the time-phrase to express the idea of greatness is found in the twelfth verse of the same chapter, where, after the defeat of Gog 'and all his multitude,' it is said, 'And seven months shall the children of Israel be in burying of them that they may cleanse the land.' That is to say, the multitude of the dead is so great that by way of hyperbole their burial is said to consume seven months. The number seven employed by Ezekiel in these passages is replaced by the number a thousand in our present passage, with the effect of greatly enhancing the idea of greatness and completeness conveyed. When the saints are said to live and reign with Christ a thousand years the idea intended is that of inconceivable exaltation, security and blessedness beyond expression of ordinary language" (Article, *The Millennium and the Apocalypse,* reprinted in *Biblical Doctrines,* p. 654).

Similarly Dr. Abraham Kuyper says:

"The numbers and the indications of persons appearing in this book, are not actual numbers but figurative numbers. There were more than seven churches in Asia Minor. We are not to take the number 144,000 as if that was the number of a man, of those who were saved first. The 1600 furlongs of the stream of blood which reaches unto the bridles of the horses, is not a geographical designation. All these figures are to be understood symbolically" (Article, *Chiliasm or Premillennialism,* p. 28).

That Calvin understood the "thousand years" figuratively is clear beyond doubt. He dismisses the idea with one brief reference:

"Not long after arose the millenarians, who limited the reign of Christ to a thousand years. Their fiction is too puerile to deserve refutation" (Institutes, Book III; Ch. 25; Sec. 5).

We should point out, however, that in Revelation 20 the

"thousand years" of verses 1–3 and the "thousand years" of verses 4–6 do not relate to the same thing. The Millennium of verses 1–3 relates to a period of the future *on earth*, during which time the Devil is bound so that he can no longer deceive *the nations*. The Millennium of verses 4–6, during which time the souls of "them that had been beheaded for the testimony of Jesus and for the word of God" are living and reigning with Christ, relates to *the intermediate state,* and for each individual soul it covers that period between death and the resurrection. That these "souls" who are living and reigning with Christ are in the intermediate state is indicated: (1) by the fact that John saw them as "souls," not as people with bodies; (2) by the fact that they are contrasted with a second group, "the rest of the dead" (verse 5), hence both groups must be identified with the dead—those who have died in the Lord, of which Revelation 14:13 speaks, and those who have died in their sins and who therefore have no part in the intermediate reign with Christ; and (3) by the contrast between the expression, "the first resurrection," and another figurative expression, "the second death" (verse 14). No one understands this latter term literally as applying to a second physical death. It is commonly understood as referring to the eternal punishment of the wicked. Similarly, "the first resurrection" is a figurative expression, and this event (life in the intermediate state) is so called in order to distinguish it from the resurrection of the body which occurs later. Some, however, understand "the first resurrection" to refer to the regeneration of the soul, that is, to the new birth of the believer, which is followed by a period of sanctification in this life and is crowned by his being taken to heaven to reign with Christ during the period between death and the resurrection. In either case the "thousand years" is to be understood symbolically as relating to an indefinitely long period of time. For the Old Testament saints and for those who died in the early part of the Christian era this reign has already continued much longer than a literal one thousand years.

Chapter XII

A FINAL APOSTASY
AND REBELLION?

A question which confronts both Post- and Premillennialism is this: Is there to be a brief but world-wide apostasy and rebellion at the end of the Millennium? Does the large proportion of the human race, after enjoying the high privileges which come with life during the millennial era, turn violently against God and righteousness and attempt to overthrow the Kingdom that has been established?

That such is to be the case has usually been the assumption of Post- and Premillennialism alike. So far as Amillennialism is concerned a final rebellion does not present special difficulty, because it does not expect a future age of righteousness. Most Amillennialists, however, also have expected an apostasy. But on either post- or premillennial principles, and coming at the very height of the millennial reign, such a development does seem to be anti-climactic and to present a very unpleasant feature. Whether the millennial age is looked upon as the result and fruitage of a long and costly campaign of world evangelism, as the Postmillennialist believes, or whether it is looked upon as a divinely established kingdom with Christ ruling in person in Jerusalem, a general apostasy and rebellion in which the Devil is given a world-wide even though brief triumph seems to be entirely out of character. Much of the glory of the Kingdom would seem to be lost with such a rebellion.

The Scripture cited in this connection is Revelation 20:3, 7–10. After the statement that Satan is to be chained and cast into the abyss for a thousand years so that he should deceive the nations no more, we read: "After this he must be loosed for a little time . . . And when the thousand years are finished, Satan shall be loosed out of his prison, and shall come forth to deceive the nations which are in the four corners of the earth, Gog and Magog, to gather them together to the war: the number of whom is as the sand of the sea. And they went up over the breadth of the earth, and compassed the camp of the saints about, and the beloved city: and fire came down out of heaven, and devoured them. And the Devil that deceived them was cast into the lake of fire and brimstone, where are also the beast and the false prophet; and they shall be tormented day and night for ever and ever.''

This passage contains much figurative language and admittedly is difficult to interpret. However, as stated earlier, we believe that the binding of Satan referred to in verses 1–3, so that he can deceive the nations no more, means that the world is to be Christianized. These verses seem clearly to refer to the earth since John saw the angel *coming down out of heaven,* and the Devil was bound so that he should deceive the *nations* no more until the thousand years are finished. ''Nations'' relate to earthly life, not to heavenly life. We believe that verses 4–6 are parenthetical and that they refer to the intermediate state.

It is to be remembered in the first place that the Devil already is a defeated and fallen foe, and that he cannot tempt or injure mankind or do anything else except as he receives permission from God. Premillennialists have a tendency to underrate the power of God and to overrate the power of the Devil. Some talk as if the Devil were a formidable foe, ''the god of this world'' in a literal sense, contending on practically an equal footing with God, and winning many victories. We can never understand the course of this world's events unless we keep in mind that God is the absolute and unchallengeable Sovereign of all that exists, and that no event, good or bad, great or small, can take place without either His decretive or permissive will. That he does allow much evil that He could prevent if He chose, is an undeniable fact. But He limits it, controls it, and overrules it for His own glory and the greater good of His people. He often uses one evil person or power to punish another. The power that the Devil and evil men have in this world is like that which the cruel and arrogant king of Assyria exercised toward Israel, who, while pursuing his own plans, was in reality only the instrument of God for the chastisement of Israel (Is. 10:5-15). He was completely in the hands of God and could go as far as but no farther than God chose to allow him to go. This is the only adequate view of the course of history if we are to understand God's dealings with men.

All of this is clearly brought out in the story of Job. The Devil could not touch Job until given permission, and then could do so only within prescribed limits. In that instance God overruled the Devil's evil designs and made use of them to further the sanctification of His servant. By that means God tested Job's patience, humbled his pride, vanquished his self-confidence, and in the end led Job to trust more deeply in His grace. In the New Testament we read that "God spared not angels when they sinned [the Devil included], but cast them down to hell, and committed them to pits of darkness, to be reserved unto judgment" (II Peter 2:4). During the public ministry of Jesus the Devil and the demons were immediately subject to His commands. Hence any interpretation that we made of Revelation 20 must be made on the assumption that the Devil is at all times under God's absolute control and subject to His commands.*

This final "war," of course, has nothing to do with military maneuvers or military weapons, or even with geographical locations. It is the last phase of the spiritual warfare that has been raging between the seed of the woman and the seed of the serpent since the fall of man in the Garden of Eden. It has been shown, we believe, that the great battle described in Revelation 19:11-21 is not a military but a spiritual conflict which rages through the centuries. The war against the saints in Revelation 20:7-10 is of the same nature, although of much shorter duration.

* Inasmuch as new material relevant to this topic is being added in a new chapter on pages 388 and following (Revised Edition, 1983) it has become necessary to delete some material as contained on pages 69, 70, 73 and 75 of the original edition.

The Lord's people have a place of refuge and safety in "the camp of the saints," "the beloved city," and not one of them is lost. "The camp of the saints" and "the beloved city" of verse 9 quite clearly are figurative expressions referring to the Church, which is a source of spiritual strength and wisdom and safety for the saints. The regenerate souls in the true Church, as revealed in Revelation 7:3, 4, are sealed so that they cannot be hurt, that is, so that they cannot be led into apostasy by any of the Devil's works. No true saint apostatizes to the service of the Devil. All the time they are under divine protection, which is symbolized by the fire that comes down out of heaven and devours their enemies. The weapons used by Satan and his followers are false doctrines, heresies, lies, slander, etc., which are directed against the Lord's people. Those who are not born again Christians are easy victims of the Devil's wiles and become his followers. But true Christians are inwardly prepared and ready to meet any such attack and cannot be hurt by any of these things.

Earlier in the New Testament, when writing to the Christians inthe Church at Ephesus, Paul used similar language and expounded at length the idea that the Christian is inwardly prepared and secure against the attacks of the evil one. "Put on the whole armour of God," he said, "that ye may be able to stand against the wiles of the Devil." "For," he continues, "our wrestling is not against flesh and blood, but against principalities, against the spiritual hosts of wickedness in the heavenly places. Wherefore take up the whole armour of God, that ye may be able to withstand in the evil day, and having done all, to stand. Stand therefore, having girded your loins with truth, and having put on the breastplate of righteousness, and having shod your feet with the preparation of the gospel of peace; withal taking up the shield of faith wherewith ye shall be able to quench all the fiery darts of the evil one. And that the helmet of salvation, and the sword of the Spirit, which is the word of God: with all prayer and supplication praying at all seasons in the Spirit, and watching thereunto in all perseverance and supplication for all the saints" (Eph. 6:11-18). And to the Corinthians he wrote: "For though we walk in the flesh, we do not war according to the flesh (for the weapons of our warfare are not of the flesh, but mighty before God to the casting down of strongholds); casting down imaginations, and every high thing that is exalted against the knowledge of God, and bringing every thought into captivity to the obedience of Christ'' (II Cor. 10:3-5).

To assume that at the end of the Millennium the vast multitude of the saints of God are literally shut up in the city of Jerusalem by their enemies and rendered practically helpless is to assume the absurd. We must ever keep in mind that this is symbolical language, that what we are seeing is not the reality, but a vision, a great pageant, and that the material symbols are merely used to set forth spiritual truth.

In his recent book, *An Eschatology of Victory,* Rev. J. Marcellus Kik makes the following comment regarding the loosing of Satan and the warfare against the beloved city:

"Notice that Satan does not break out of the prison by his own power. He does not break his chains. He is loosed by the Lord . . . The names of Gog and Magog are used much as we might use the names of Hitler and Nazi after our experience in World War II. *Hitler* and *Nazi* bring before our minds cruel armies who wrought much damage. We might well term some future tyrant *Hitler* and some future nation *Nazi horde* without having Germans in mind. In Revelation the names of the old enemies are used to designate new ones. Gog and Magog represent future enemies of the Church whose names are as yet unknown. This type of interpretation is taught in Revelation 11:8, 'And their dead bodies shall lie in the street of the great city, which spiritually is called Sodom and Egypt, where also our Lord was crucified.' Sodom and Egypt are 'spiritualized.' Even so we 'spiritualize' Gog and Magog . . .

"It is difficult for some to conceive of the nature of the opposition. The language is so vivid that it is hard for us to realize that this is not a battle of arms—of sword and gun. Our Lord clearly implies that the battle for Christianity is not fought with carnal sword. It is a battle between the true Gospel and the false Gospel. It is a battle of truth against error. It is a battle of light against darkness. It is not a war against flesh and blood, 'but against principalities, against powers, against rulers of the darkness of the world, against spiritual wickedness in high places' . . .

"They compassed the camp of the saints about. The Church is likened to a military camp. This is a figure borrowed from the time of Moses and Joshua when the Church even externally presented the form of a military camp. The twelve tribes with their banners surrounded the Tabernacle on four sides. The camp was in the form of a square, of which the four sides were to be placed toward the four quarters of the compass. This was a type of the heavenly city as seen by Ezekiel 48:20 and the city four-square of Revelation 21:16. The camp and the City are but different figures of speech to describe the Church upon earth. The Church in heaven will never be surrounded by enemies such as are pictured to us in Revelation 20 . . .

"To others this is the literal city of Jerusalem. Just a little thinking will show how impossible this is. Imagine all the armies of the nations of the world laying siege to one city in Palestine! And you must picture modern armies equipped with missiles, bombs, and planes. The land of Palestine could not contain all the armies of the world. This is figurative language. This is the language of the Old Testament to express the enmity of the world against the Church'' (pp. 237-242).

It is of further interest in this connection to note that Dr. Warfield believed there will be no resurgence of evil at all at the end, but rather that at the return of Christ the present Kingdom —then perfected, with the conquering of the last enemy, death,— will be merged into the eternal kingdom. He understood the section Revelation 20:1-10 to refer to the intermediate state, and he believed that the "thousand years" was intended to describe the heavenly bliss of the saints in Paradise, in contrast with which the trial time of the Church on earth is described by the term "a little time" (vs. 3). This view made it possible for him to hold that there is no apostasy or rebellion at all at the close of the golden age of righteousness and peace. As a Postmillennialist he believed that the world is to be converted to Christianity before the return of Christ, but he based his view on Revelation 19:11-21 and on the intimations in Romans 11 and I Corinthians 15 rather than on Revelation 20:1-10. He says concerning Revelation 20:1-10:

"The picture that is brought before us here is the picture of the 'intermediate state'—of the saints of God gathered in heaven away from the confused noises and garments bathed in blood that characterizes the war upon earth, in order that they may securely await the end. The thousand years, thus, is the whole of this present dispensation, which again is placed before us in its entirety, but looked at now relatively not to what is passing on the earth but to what is enjoyed 'in paradise.' This, in fact, is the meaning of the symbol of a thousand years. For, this period between the events is, on earth, a broken time—three and a half years, a 'little time' (verse 3)—which, amid turmoil and trouble, the saints are encouraged to look upon as of short duration, soon to be over. To the saints in bliss it is, on the contrary, a long blessed period passing slowly and peacefully by, while they reign with Christ and enjoy the blessedness of holy communion with Him—'a thousand years.'

"Of course the passage (xx. 1-10) does not give us a direct description of 'the intermediate state.' We must bear in mind that the book we are reading is written in symbols and gives us a direct description of nothing that is set before us, but always a direct description of the symbol by which it is represented. In the preceding vision (xix. 11-21) we had no direct description of the triumph and progress of the Gospel, but only of a fierce and gruesome war: the single phrase that spoke of the slaying sword as 'proceeding out of the mouth' of the conqueror alone indicating that it was a conquest by means of persuading words. So here we are not to expect a direct description of the 'intermediate state' . . . It is a description in the form of a narrative:

the element of time and chronological succession belong to the symbol, not to the thing symbolized. The 'binding of Satan' is, therefore, in reality, not for a season, but with reference to a sphere; and his 'loosing' again is not after a period but in another sphere: it is not subsequence but exteriority that is suggested. There is, indeed, no literal 'binding of Satan' to be thought of at all: what happens, happens not to Satan but to the saints, and is only represented as happening to Satan for the purpose of the symbolical picture. What actually happens is that the saints described are removed from the sphere of Satan's assaults. The saints described are free from all access of Satan—he is bound with respect to them: outside of their charmed circle his horrid work goes on. This is indicated, indeed, in the very employment of the two symbols 'a thousand years' and 'a little time.' A 'thousand years' is the symbol of heavenly completeness and blessing; the 'little time' of earthly turmoil and evil. Those in the 'thousand years' are safe from Satan's assaults: those outside the thousand years are still enduring his attacks. And therefore he, though with respect to those in the thousand years bound, is not destroyed; and the vision accordingly requires to close with an account of his complete destruction, and of course this also must needs be presented in the narrative form of a release of Satan, the gathering of his hosts and their destruction from above" (Article, *The Millennium and the Apocalypse;* reprinted in *Biblical Doctrines,* pp. 649-651).*

We agree that Revelation 20:1-10 affords no real basis for believing that there is to be a final apostasy in the sense that a large proportion of earth's inhabitants turn against God, or that the safety of the saints is seriously threatened.

Furthermore, after we have been shown in the Revelation 19:11-21 how complete is Christ's victory and how thoroughly crushed are all His foes, we cannot believe that at the end God as the sovereign Ruler of the world—He of whom the Scriptures say, "The

---

* We shall have more information regarding Dr. Warfield's views in chapter 22, which includes an article added to the 1983 edition of this book.

king's heart is in the hand of Jehovah as the watercourses; he turneth it whithersoever he will" (Prov. 21:1); and, "He doeth according to his will in the army of heaven, and among the inhabitants of the earth; and none can stay his hand, or say unto him, What doest thou?" (Dan. 4:35)—will suddenly and purposefully throw away that victory and permit the Devil a worldwide triumph even for the briefest time. Once the hard-fought battle is over and such a magnificent victory won, we may be sure that it will be properly safeguarded, and that the Devil will never again be allowed to rise as a serious contender against God.

And this we believe is the consistent teaching of Scripture. Perhaps the most definite statement regarding the permanence of Messiah's kingdom is found in Daniel's interpretation of Nebuchadnezzar's dream, where, after indicating the successive world kingdoms that were to rise, Daniel said: "And in the days of those kings shall the God of heaven set up a kingdom which shall never be destroyed, nor shall the sovereignty thereof be left to another people; but it shall break in pieces and consume all these kingdoms, and it shall stand for ever" (2:44). Ezekiel pictures the ever-increasing blessings of Messiah's reign as a flow of healing waters that issue from under the threshold of the temple, first only ankle deep, then to the knees, then to the loins, then a great river that could not be passed through (47:1-5). Zechariah says of the Messianic Kingdom that "his dominion shall be from sea to sea, and from the River to the ends of the earth" (9:10). The kingdom prophecies in Isaiah and Micah teach a complete victory with never a reference to a final apostasy. Speaking through the Psalmist God said, "Ask of me, and I will give thee the nations for thine inheritance, And the uttermost parts of the earth for thy possession" (2:8).

The New Testament presents the same teaching. The healing stream pictured by Ezekiel finds fulfillment in the life-giving ministry of the Christian Church. The kingdom of heaven is said to be "like unto leaven," which a woman took, and hid in three measures of meal, till it was all leavened" (Matt. 13:33).

"The residue of men, and all the Gentiles" are to "seek after the Lord" (Acts 15:17). Christ is to sit at the right hand of the Father until all His enemies have been placed under His feet (Acts 2:35)—and there is no reason to believe that those enemies, having once been conquered, will ever again be permitted to rise up and renew the battle.

A striking contrast between the Millennium in which the Postmillennialist believes and that in which the Premillennialist believes is seen in the degree to which evil will be allowed to assert itself during that time and at its close. The Postmillennialist believes that as the Millennium becomes a reality evil will be reduced to a minimum. But the Premillennialist believes that while Satan is to be bound so that he can no longer deceive the nations, those nations nevertheless continue at heart enemies, ready to turn to Satan and to follow his leadership in a war against the saints the moment the thousand years are finished. According to the premillennial view evil is effectively held in check during the Millennium only by the rod-of-iron rule of Christ.

Premillennialists who are accustomed to think of the millennial age as an age of righteousness and peace may be surprised to know what three of their representative men who have been so influential in bringing the system to its present form (Dispensationalism) had to say on this subject. John N. Darby, whose influence at the beginning of the movement was so formative, says: "*Now* there are a faithful few, Satan being the prince and god of this world, going against the stream. *Then* Christ will be the prince of the world, and Satan bound, and obedience will be paid to Christ's manifested power even when men are not converted. When this obedience is not paid, excision takes place, so that all is peaceful and happy. It is a perfect government of the earth made good everywhere. When Satan is let loose and temptations come again, those not kept by grace follow him. I have an impression that piety will decline in the millennium; but it is founded on a figure, so that I do not insist on it; but the rest of what I have said is revealed. That men should fall when tempted, however sad, is nothing but what is very simple. It is the last effort of Satan" *(Collective Writings,* xi., p. 534).

James H. Brookes, in his *Maranatha,* presents an even darker picture. Says he: "That which is born of the flesh is flesh and though restrained during the Millennium it will manifest its inherent depravity at the first favorable opportunity, like a tiger long caged and curbed that will bound back to its native jungle with unquenchable thirst for blood when their iron bars are removed" (p. 540, Fifth Ed., 1878).

And Dr. G. Campbell Morgan says: "We have seen that the Golden Age is to be characterized by the direct government of Christ. Sin will still be in the earth; but it will be held in repression and summarily punished as soon as manifested. The nations which Christ will rule with a rod of iron will be to a large extent disloyal in heart; so that when Satan is loosed for a little season he will straightway deceive them. True, there will be everywhere those who refuse enlistment under his banners; but the picture here is that of an enormous apostasy, the most fearful even seen . . . There is no doubt that to some who have dreamed of the Millennium as a finality, the outlook afterward is disappointing; but ere the kingdom of Jesus Christ in all its glory can be ushered in, the unbelief and disloyalty which lurks in the hearts of men must be brought to a final head . . . All the nations will be under the government of the 'rod of iron,' and will be compelled to submit therefore. In heart, however, the great mass will be rebellious to the end, and will eagerly avail themselves of the opportunity of outwardly throwing off the yoke and entering upon actual conflict when it presents itself in the unloosing of Satan" *(God's Methods with Man,* pp. 132, 183).

Commenting on this view Dr. Allis observes that it is not an attractive one and then says: "it is not pleasing to think of the Messianic King, the Prince of Peace, sitting enthroned as it were on a smouldering volcano; of a reign of Messiah, peaceful on the surface but seething with hate and muttered rebellion;

of people yielding outward obedience because 'excision' is the inevitable consequence of disobedience and opposition, since the rod-of-iron rule can only mean the 'dashing in pieces' of the rebellious like a potter's vessel. When we read that 'the wolf shall dwell with the lamb,' we do not take this to mean that the wolf will be as eager as ever to devour the lamb and be restrained from doing so only by fear of the consequences. We naturally understand it to imply a change of nature; the ravening beast, whether the words be taken literally or figuratively, will no longer *desire* to devour the lamb. "They shall not hurt nor destroy' in all God's holy mountain, for the reason that they will not want to, not because they will be restrained by *force majeure* from doing what they will want to do."

He adds further that acccording to this view, "The enemies of Messiah will make a show of obedience to a rule which they hate. So we may say that, according to this view, the millennium will surpass all others as the age of hypocrisy and hypocrites. Men, many men, will submit only because they must; and these tiger-men will be waiting with ever growing impatience for the moment when defiance and resistance may offer at least the semblance of a successful issue" *(Prophecy and the Church,* p. 241).

What a Millennium the Premillennialist has! A thousand years of Jewish supremacy with Jerusalem as the capital, semi-heavenly and semi-earthly, saints in glorified resurrection bodies mingling with sinners in the flesh, a mixed state of mortals and immortals, and all of this climaxed by an unprecedented manifestation of evil at its close! Human life and the work of the world will go on during all that long period very much as now. Men and women will marry and children will be born; people with mortal bodies will live in houses and eat physical food and be subject to sickness and death although not to the same degree as at present. Conditions will be ideal but not heavenly; the earth will be abundantly fruitful; multitudes will honor and worship God while other multitudes will be sullen and resentful. Wicked men will be held in check by the rule of force. To a considerable extent Old Testament conditions will be re-established. "The middle wall of partition" between Jew and Gentile, which Christ has broken down "that he might create in himself of the two one new man, so making peace" (Eph. 2:14, 15), is to be built up again and made higher and stronger, and the Jews re-established as the chosen people. Such a Kingdom must of necessity be far inferior in glory to the final Kingdom.

Premillennialists insist that the latter part of Ezekiel, chapters 38 to 48, is to be taken with great literalness as having fulfillment in the millennial kingdom, and as foretelling a restored Israel in the land of Palestine. Thus the temple is to be rebuilt, animal sacrifices are again to be presented to make atonement for the sins of the people (45:15—46:15), the priests will officiate (46:2), the people of the earth will go up to Jerusalem for the appointed feasts (46:9), and Christ personally present and visible only to a comparatively small number of people will enter the temple by the eastern gate as the priests prepare His burnt-offerings and peace-offerings (46:2, 3). Notice that if these chapters are to be taken literally they do not say, as Premillennialists attempt to make them say, that the sacrifices will be only memorial in nature, but that they definitely are called "sin-offerings," "burnt-offerings," and "meal-offerings" (45:22, 25). A literalist has no right to give them any other meaning. We prefer to say that these predictions were fulfilled in part when Israel was restored to Palestine at the time of Ezra and Nehemiah and later, and that as regards any parts that did not find fulfillment at that time, Old Testament thought forms are employed to teach New Testament spiritual truths, truths which in that day could be expressed intelligently only through those forms with which the people were familiar.

Frankly, we have no desire for such a state as Premillennialism sets forth, but prefer at death to enter directly into the heavenly Kingdom. Surely it must be evident to anyone that such a state, though for the saints it may be marked by holiness of life, nevertheless leaves much to be desired, and that such a lesser state of things prolonged for a thousand years becomes not an increase but a decrease of blessedness, restraining rather than promoting the coming of the Kingdom of God in its fullness. There is in fact nothing to justify the prolongation of such a futile interval. For the departed saints who have been reigning with Christ a return to earthly life and earthly conditions would be, literally and figuratively, a great "come-down," a serious restriction of the glorious life that they now enjoy. The Premillennialist makes no adequate allowance for the far superior and radically different type of life enjoyed by the saints in Paradise and that to which they would be subjected if brought back to this earth. And as far as those who still are in the flesh are concerned, surely the Lord's physical presence, visible to but a comparatively small number of His people, would mean less than His spiritual presence now experienced by all His people in all parts of the world—unless we are to cease walking by faith and begin walking by sight.

Again we say, What a Millennium the Premillennialist has!— a Millennium preceded by seven years of unparalleled confusion and suffering and persecution during the "Great Tribulation" and under the reign of Antichrist, and ending with a universal revolt and war against which the saints and even Christ Himself seem to be helpless and from which they are rescued only by fire from heaven! We cannot refrain from asking, Does Christ desert His people at the end of the glorious millennial reign, that they should be shut up in Jerusalem and practically at the mercy of the enemy? Surely that cannot be! How is that strange turn of events to be explained?

And we must ask further, why, if such an important earthly interval lies ahead, why did not Christ and the apostles clearly predict that the temple would be rebuilt, the Levitical sacrifices and rituals re-established, the Aaronic priesthood restored, the Jews again appointed to be a separate and especially favored people, and Jerusalem again made the center of the world's worship in a thousand year Jewish kingdom? There can be but one answer: Such a scheme formed no part of their belief. Far from localizing worship in a temple in Jerusalem, Jesus said,

"The hour cometh, when neither in this mountain, nor in Jerusalem, shall ye worship the Father . . . The hour cometh, and now is, when the true worshippers shall worship the Father in spirit and truth: for such doth the Father seek to be his worshippers. God is a spirit: and they that worship him must worship in spirit and truth" (John 4:21-24).

Chapter XIII

PRINCIPLES OF INTERPRETATION

It is clear that each of the millennial views has been held and at the present time is held by men concerning whose sincerity and loyalty to the evangelical faith there can be no doubt. That believing Christians through the ages, using the same Bible and acknowledging it to be authoritative, have arrived at quite different conclusions appears to be due primarily to different methods of interpretation. Premillennialists place strong emphasis on literal interpretation and pride themselves on taking Scripture just as it is written. Post- and Amillennialists on the other hand, mindful of the fact that much of both the Old and New Testament unquestionably is given in figurative or symbolical language, have no objection on principle against figurative interpretation and readily accept that if the evidence indicates that it is preferable. This causes Premillennialists to charge that Post- and Amillenniallsts explain away or reject parts of the Bible. One premillennial writer says:

"Premillennialists insist that one general rule of interpretation should be applied to all areas of theology and that prophecy does not require spiritualization any more than other aspects of truth . . . History is history, not allegory. Facts are facts. Prophesied future events are just what they are prophesied" (Dr. John F. Walvoord, *Bibliotheca Sacra*, July-Sept., 1951, p. 272).

Another says: "Premillenarians hold to a literal interpretation of the sacred Scriptures, believing that the teachings of Christ and the Apostles are to be understood in a literal sense except in certain places where some other meaning is designated" (Jesse F. Silver, *The Lord's Return*, p. 204).

This general principle of interpretation has been expressed as, "Literal wherever possible" (H. Bonar), or "Literal unless absurd" (Govett). One does not have to read far in the Bible to discover that not everything can be taken literally. Silver refers to "certain places" where some "other meaning" is designated. But he gives no rule by which those certain places are to be recognized. We find no labels in the Scripture itself telling us, "Take this literally," or "Take that figuratively." Evidently the individual reader must use his own judgment, backed by as much experience and common sense as he can muster. And that, of course, will vary endlessly from individual to individual.

As an example of what he means by literal interpretation Silver says: "Every prophecy pointing to the first advent of Christ was literally fulfilled to the letter in every detail" (p. 209). That statement has been made in substance by various other Premillennialists. But it simply is not so. The very first Messianic prophecy in Scripture is found in Genesis 3:15, where, in pronouncing the curse upon the serpent God said, "He shall bruise thy head, and thou shalt bruise his heel." Now that prophecy certainly was not fulfilled literally by a man crushing the head of a snake, or by a snake biting the heel of a man. Rather it was fulfilled in a highly figurative sense when Christ gained a complete victory and triumphed over the Devil and all his forces of evil at the cross. The last prophecy in the Old Testament is found in Malachi 4:5, and reads as follows: "Behold, I will send you Elijah the prophet before the great and terrible day of Jehovah come." That prophecy likewise was not fulfilled literally. Christ Himself said that it was fulfilled in the person of John the Baptist (Matt. 11:14), who came in the spirit and power of Elijah.

Again, we have the prophecy of Isaiah: "The voice of one that crieth, Prepare ye in the wilderness the way of Jehovah; make level in the desert a highway for our God. Every valley shall be exalted, and every mountain and hill shall be made low: and the uneven shall be made level, and the rough places a plain: and the glory of Jehovah shall be revealed, and all flesh shall see it together; for the mouth of Jehovah hath spoken it" (Is. 40:3–5). This certainly was not fulfilled by a highway building program in Palestine, but rather in the work of John the Baptist who prepared the way for the public ministry of Jesus. John himself said, "For this is he that was spoken of through Isaiah the prophet, saying . . .", and then proceeded to quote these verses (Matt. 3:1–3; Luke 3:3–6).

The words of Isaiah 9:1,2, regarding the people of Zebulun and Naphtali, "The people that walked in darkness have seen a great light: they that dwelt in the land of the shadow of death, upon them hath the light shined," are fulfilled figuratively in the ministry of Jesus. For Matthew says: "Now when he heard that John was delivered up, he withdrew into Galilee; and leaving Nazareth, he came and dwelt in Capernaum, which is by the sea, in the border of Zebulun, and Naphtali: that it might be fulfilled which was spoken through the prophet, saying,

> The land of Zebulun and the land of Naphtali,
> Toward the sea, beyond the Jordan,
> Galilee of the Gentiles,
> The people that sat in darkness
> Saw a great light,
> And to them that sat in the region and shadow of death,
> To them did light spring up" (Matt. 4:15,16).

In these words Isaiah clearly was speaking of the spiritual darkness that exists wherever sin rules, and of the spiritual light that would be brought to those lands when the Messiah came.

And when Balaam attempted to pronounce a curse upon the people of Israel he pronounced instead a blessing, and said:

> "There shall come forth a star out of Jacob,
> And a sceptre shall rise out of Israel,
> And shall smite through all the corners of Moab
> And break down all the sons of tumult" (Nu. 24:17).

These words are commonly understood as embodying a Messianic prophecy, and as having had their fulfillment in the coming of Christ, who arose like a star out of Israel, and whose kingdom eventually is to embrace the whole world.

Many other Old Testament prophecies in figurative language might be cited, but surely these are sufficient to show that it simply is *not* true that "Every prophecy pointing to the first advent of Christ was literally fulfilled to the letter in every detail."

That a great deal of the Bible is given in figurative or symbolical language which by no stretch of the imagination can be taken literally should be apparent to every one. We spiritualize these statements because we regard this as the only way in which their true meaning can be brought out. To cite only a few further examples: In the midst of a very prosaic historical account of the deliverance of the children of Israel from Egypt the providential and protective power of God is set forth in these words: "Ye have seen what I did unto the Egyptians, and how I bare you on eagles' wings, and brought you unto myself" (Ex. 19:4). Palestine is described as "a land flowing with milk and honey" (Ex. 3:8). Read the 23rd or 91st Psalm and note the almost continuous use of figurative language.

The New Testament follows the same practice. To his disciples Jesus said, "Ye are the salt of the earth . . . Ye are the light of the world . . . Even so let your light shine before men; that they may see your good works, and glorify your Father who is in heaven" (Matt. 5:13–16). When instituting the Lord's Supper He said: "This is my body . . . This is my blood" (Matt. 26:26, 28). The writer recently heard a Roman Catholic priest argue quite convincingly that these words prove that in the Mass the bread and wine actually are changed into the flesh and blood of Christ. From the standpoint of literalism it would be impossible to refute that doctrine. Speaking to the elders of the Church in Ephesus Paul said: "I know that after my departing grievous wolves shall enter in among you, not sparing the flock" (Acts 20:29). To the Philippians he wrote: "Beware of the dogs, beware of the evil workers, beware of the concision" (3:2). And to the Galatians: "I have been crucified with Christ; and it is no longer I that live, but Christ liveth in me" (2:20). The word "blood" is used repeatedly in a figurative sense with reference to the suffering and death of Christ through which salvation was purchased on Calvary, e.g., ". . . in whom we have our redemption through his blood" (Eph. 1:7); ". . . the blood of an eternal covenant" (Heb. 13:20); ". . . and they washed their robes, and made them white in the blood of the Lamb" (Rev. 7:14; etc.). In spiritualizing certain Old Testament prophecies we are in good company, for the New Testament writers often do the same. In his discourse on the day of Pentecost Peter spiritualized the rather extended prophecy of Joel (Acts 2:16–21). James' discourse at the Jerusalem Conference spiritualized the prophecy of Amos (Acts 15:14–18). Literally thousands of such figurative and symbolic expressions are found throughout the Bible, usually without explanation. It is assumed that the reader will understand. Furthermore, foot washing is clearly commanded by Jesus (John 13:14), and is commended by Paul (I Tim. 5:10); and five times we have the command, "Salute one another with a holy kiss" (Rom. 16:16; I Cor. 16:20; II Cor. 13:12; I Thess. 5:26; and I Peter 5:14). Yet only a very few people take these literally.

To spiritualize certain prophecies or other statements does not mean that we explain them away. Sometimes their true meaning is to be found only in the unseen spiritual world. Premillennialists often materialize and literalize the prophecies to such an extent that they keep them on an earthly level and miss their true and deeper meaning. That is exactly what the Jews did in their interpretation of Messianic prophecy. They looked for literal fulfillments with an earthly kingdom and a political ruler, and the result was that they missed the redemptive element so completely that when the Messiah came they did not recognize Him but instead rejected and crucified Him. The fearful consequences of literalistic interpretation as it related to the first coming should put us on guard against making the same mistake in regard to the second coming.

The general principle of rigid literal interpretation leads to the conclusion that when Christ comes again He will re-establish the throne of David in the city of Jerusalem, and that He will reign in an earthly political kingdom of Jewish supremacy for one thousand years. According to that view the Jews are again to possess all of Palestine and the surrounding areas and are to live there, the temple is to be rebuilt, and the priesthood, temple ritual, animal sacrifices, feasts and fasts are to be reinstituted.

Premillennialists encounter real difficulty, however, and are forced to abandon their literalism when they come to the prophecies which predict that in the new kingdom all the nations of the earth are to go up to Jerusalem every year, and indeed every Sabbath: "And it shall come to pass that every one that is left of all the nations that came against Jerusalem shall go up from year to year to worship the King, Jehovah of hosts, and to keep the feast of tabernacles" (Zech. 14:16); "It shall come to pass, that from one new moon to another, and *from one sabbath to another,* shall *all flesh* come to worship before me, saith Jehovah" (Is. 66:23); and, "Thus saith the Lord Jehovah, No foreigner, *uncircumcised in heart* and *uncircumcised in flesh,* shall enter into my sanctuary, of any foreigners that are among the children of Israel" (Ezek. 44:9).

It soon becomes evident that such startling literalism goes a great deal farther than its advocates are willing, or indeed, able to carry it. Taken literally these predictions mean that the whole earth is to become *one great Israelitish nation and Church,* with but one temple, one form of worship, and one common law. Premillennialists do not want to acknowledge that weekly pilgrimages or universal circumcision is to become the rule during the Millennium. Since they cannot go through with the literal interpretation of their own millennial passages it becomes evident that their principle of literal interpretation is basically wrong.

Premillennialists also encounter difficulty with the Messianic and kingdom prophecies which involve the restoration of the historical conditions of Israel's national life, including her national enemies, not only the great powers of Assyria, Egypt, and Babylon, but the smaller nations of Moab, Ammon, Edom and Philistia, nations that have long since vanished from history without possibility of recall. Note especially: Micah 5:5,6 (following the prediction that the Messiah would be born in Bethlehem, vs. 2): "And this man [Messiah] shall be our peace. When the Assyrian shall come into our land, and when he shall tread in our palaces, then shall we raise up against him seven shepherds, and eight principal men. And they shall waste the land of Assyria with the sword, and the land of Nimrod in the entrances thereof: and he shall deliver us from the Assyrian." Similar references are found relating to Egypt, in Joel 3:19, and to Babylon in Revelation 18:1–24. In the Messianic prophecy found in Isaiah 11 regarding the relationship of the future kingdom to the smaller surrounding nations we read: "And they shall fly down upon the shoulders of the Philistines on the west; together shall they despoil the children of the east: they shall put forth their hand upon Edom and Moab; and the children of Ammon shall obey them" (vs. 14).

It would require a miracle of raising from the dead the nations referred to if these verses are to be literally fulfilled. We believe that George B. Fletcher gives the true interpretation when he says: "These verses are a prophecy of the conversion of the Gentiles (vs. 10), and of the return of the remnant according to the election of grace from among the Jews, that is, their return to God in Christ (vss. 11:16). This prophecy began to be fulfilled on the Day of Pentecost when 'Jews, devout men out of every nation under heaven,' were evangelized by the apostle Peter, and returned home to God in Christ, the mighty God. Under a figure of speech these Hebrew preachers are represented as flying from Jerusalem with eager activity upon Philistia to convert it, as an eagle pounces upon the shoulders of a sheep or other animal, its prey (see Acts 8:26-40, Philip's preaching to the Ethiopian eunuch; and 9:32-43, Peter's mission to Joppa)"—Pamphlet, *The Millennium*, p. 30). This one point alone, that the nations referred to have disappeared from the face of the earth and so could play no part in a future restoration of Israel, should be sufficient proof that the literalistic method of interpretation cannot be defended.

Rejecting the clearly enunciated Scripture principle that the Church has been established as the instrument through which Christ makes a *spiritual* conquest of the world—He is to sit at the right hand of God where He now is, the position of power and influence, until His enemies have been made the footstool of His feet (Mark 12:36; 16:19; Heb. 1:13)—Premillennialism substitutes the view that until He comes again the world is to grow progressively worse, and that at His coming He is to conquer the world and overthrow His enemies in the most gigantic and spectacular and sudden *military* conquest of all time. He is pictured as using overwhelming force in this conquest in that He rains fire and brimstone from heaven upon His enemies and thus utterly defeats Antichrist and all his hosts. Premillennialism seriously misunderstands the genius of Old Testament predictive prophecy in that it interprets in a literal, materialistic sense those foreviews of the Messianic age which can only be understood in a figurative sense.

In the following passage material objects and familiar ideas of the Old Testament era are used to set forth spiritual truth and to describe an era that had not yet dawned and which therefore could be described intelligently only in the thought-forms and language with which the people were familiar. "And it shall come to pass in the latter days, that the mountain of Jehovah's house shall be established on the top of the mountains, and shall be exalted above the hills; and all nations shall flow unto it. And many peoples shall go and say, Come ye, and let us go up to the mountain of Jehovah, to the house of the God of Jacob; and he will teach us of his ways, and we will walk in his paths: for out of Zion shall go forth the law, and the word of Jehovah from Jerusalem" (Is. 2:2,3).

These words are fulfilled in that the Gospel took its course out from Jerusalem as the disciples went under orders to evangelize all the world, with the Church over the centuries gradually coming into a position of world-wide prominence, gradually increasing in power and becoming more influential in the lives of men throughout the world until it stands out like a mountain on a plain. The attempt to assign specific meaning to each figure of the landscape not only mars the beauty of the picture but obscures the real meaning of the prophecy. When God says, "They shall not hurt nor destroy *in all my holy mountain*," let not the reader absurdly imagine that He had in mind only that insignificant elevation called Zion, in the southeast corner of the city of Jerusalem. "God's holy mountain," which at that time was the site of the temple and the center of the true religion, is the familiar and endeared name for *the Church* or Kingdom in the present Messianic age.

When we are told that God will "create Jerusalem a rejoicing, and her people a joy" (Is. 65:18), Jerusalem, the center of the theocracy and symbol of Old Testament Israel, is used to represent the New Testament Church. The writer of the Epistle to the Hebrews spiritualizes these passages and shows that their true fulfillment is found in the Christian Church when he says of believers: "For ye are not come unto a mount that might be touched, and that burned with fire . . . but ye are come unto mount Zion, and unto the city of the living God, the heavenly Jerusalem, and to innumerable hosts of angels and to the general assembly and church of the firstborn who are enrolled in heaven" (12:18–23); "Having then a great high priest, who hath passed through the heavens, Jesus the Son of God" (4:14); and, "We have such a high priest, who sat down on the right hand of the throne of the Majesty in the heavens, a minister of the sanctuary, and of the *true tabernacle, which the Lord pitched, not man*" (8:1,2). Paul, too, spiritualizes the term Jerusalem when he says that, "The Jerusalem that is above is free, which is our mother" (Gal. 4:26).

Isaiah says: "He shall smite the earth with the rod of his mouth; and with the breath of his lips shall he slay the wicked" (11:4). Similar language is found in Revelation 19:11–21, where Christ is pictured as the rider on the white horse, who slays His enemies with a sharp sword that proceeds "out of his mouth," that is, by the spoken word, the Gospel which is preached by His followers all over the world, and by which He makes a thorough conquest of His enemies. Isaiah says: "They shall beat their swords into plowshares, and their spears into pruning-hooks" (2:4)—fulfilled in the gradual elimination of wars as the world is Christianized and the energies and resources of the people are devoted to peaceful purposes. Again, he says: "And the wolf shall dwell with the lamb, and the leopard shall lie down with the kid; and the calf and the young lion and the fatling together; and a little child shall lead them . . . And the lion shall eat straw like the ox, and the sucking child shall play on the hole of the asp, and the weaned child shall put his hand on the adder's den. They shall not hurt nor destroy in all my holy mountain; for the earth shall be full of the knowledge of Jehovah, as the waters cover the sea" (11:6–9)—that is, forces naturally antagonistic and at enmity with each other shall be gradually subdued and reconciled with each other in a new relationship so that they co-operate harmoniously in Messiah's Kingdom. A fitting example of the wolf dwelling with the lamb is seen in the change that came over the vicious persecutor Saul of Tarsus, who was a wolf ravening and destroying, but who was so transformed by the Gospel of Christ that he became a lamb. After his conversion he lost his hatred for the Christians, and became instead their humble friend, confidant, defender. The lion eats straw like the ox when men who formerly were strong and cruel and wild by nature are so changed by the Gospel that they become gentle, meek, humble, and feed on the word of life along with those who are members of Christ's Church.

One writer has this to say about Isaiah's prophecy:

"Since we have here a description of Christ's kingdom which is not composed of beasts, wolves, serpents, lions, etc., but of men, we must understand that 'in all My (God's) holy mountain,' that is, the Church of Christ ('Zion'), the peace that is to reign is of such a nature that those people who formerly were like wolves, bloodthirsty lions, insidious adders will by the grace of God put off their old nature, cease to harm one another, and peacefully dwell together as the lambs of Christ and feed on the green pasture of the Gospel. Of this change of nature St. Paul speaks in plain words (II Cor. 5:17), 'If any man be in Christ, he is a new creature; old things are passed away; behold, all things are become new.' Not only the ferocious persecutor Saul who became the Gospel-preaching, soul-seeking Paul is an example (I Tim. 1:13), but the entire history of Christian missions abounds with such examples" (L. A. Heerboth, booklet, *The Millennium and the Bible,* p. 12).

When Ezekiel says that Israel is to be restored to her land forever (37:24-28), he indicates clearly that those words are not to be taken literally. He says: "And my servant David shall be king over them . . . David my servant shall be their prince for ever" (vss. 24,25). Jeremiah likewise says that David is to be their king (30:9). If we take that literally, then David must be raised from the dead to be the millennial king in Palestine,—David, and not Christ. The literalists say that David is here used as a symbol for Christ. But that is not what the Bible says. To take David as a symbol for Christ would be to "spiritualize" the prophecy away. If the other parts of the prophecy are literal this must be too.

To take these descriptions literally is to miss their real beauty and their great spiritual import. The literalistic premillennial interpretation of many Old Testament passages is, as Rutgers points out, "even beneath the level of certain passages in the Old Testament itself, which transcend the particular, local color and open up the higher spiritual, ethical and universal. These carnal, materialistic notions," he very appropriately adds, "are (but) the 'swaddling clothes' of Judaism" (*Premillennialism in America,* p. 255).

We have indicated earlier that one of the errors of Premillennialism is that it fails to understand that *the Church is New*

Testament Israel. It persists in thinking of "Israel" as composed only of the physical descendants of Abraham. Dispensationalism carries this principle to an almost unprecedented extreme, and insists that in all cases Israel must mean fleshly Israel, or the Jews, that it can never mean the Church, and that the kingdom prophecies of the Old Testament must be fulfilled to the Jews literally. And since some of these were not fulfilled before the nation of Israel passed out of existence, they tell us that Israel must be re-established in Palestine and these fulfilled in a future age.

But the fact of the matter is that the spiritual relationship is more important than, and takes precedence over, the physical. Paul stated that quite clearly when he said: "Know therefore that they that are of faith, the same are sons of Abraham"; and again, "If ye are Christ's, then are ye Abraham's seed, heirs according to promise" (Gal. 3:7,29). And Christ himself placed the spiritual above the physical when he said, "Whosoever shall do the will of my Father who is in heaven, he is my brother, and sister, and mother" (Matt. 12:50). The Epistle to the Hebrews is one sustained argument that the old forms and ceremonies and relationships have passed away forever, and that all nations and races now stand as equals before God.

The Old Testament Sacrificial System

The writer of the Epistle to the Hebrews has much to say about the endless repetition and the futility of the ancient sacrifices. He shows that their only value was to symbolize and point forward to the one true sacrifice that was to be made by Christ. "We have been sanctified," he said, "through the offering of the body of Jesus Christ *once for all*. And every priest indeed standeth day by day ministering and offering oftentimes the same sacrifices which can never take away sins; but he, when he had offered one sacrifice for sin for ever, sat down on the right hand of God; henceforth expecting till his enemies be made the footstool of his feet. For by one offering he hath perfected for ever them that are sanctified" (Heb. 10:10–14).

Rev. Harold Dekker, one of the speakers on The Back to God Hour radio program, says concerning the futility of the animal sacrifices and the finality of Christ's sacrifice as set forth in this passage:

"Continually, day by day, year after year, God's people made their sacrifices according to the Old Testament law. The writer calls to mind the mountains of herbs and grain and meal offerings which had been brought before the Lord, the rivers of blood which had flowed from millions of sheep and goats and droves of cattle. And then he raises the question, Why the constant repetition? Why the endless pilgrimages to Jerusalem? Why the interminable fires upon Israel's altars? Why the shedding of blood? The reason, says the inspired writer, is that none of these brought lasting relief to troubled consciences. So on and on went the sacrifices." But of Christ's sacrifice on Calvary he says: "He was surely the sacrifice to end all sacrifices. Let the blood now dry on the horns of the altar. Let the ovens that bake meal offerings now be cooled. Let the sacrificial animals go back to pasture. Final atonement is accomplished! Let all men everywhere now look to the one sacrifice of Christ finished on the cross!"

In its doctrine of an earthly Kingdom with a restored temple, priesthood and sacrificial system, Premillennialism is a recrudescence of Judaism. Snowden has set this forth quite convincingly, and we quote him at length:

"It is one of the plainest universal teachings of the New Testament that the sacrifices of the Mosaic economy were fulfilled in Christ and were then done away as vanishing shadows that prefigured the substance, or as morning stars that heralded the rising of the sun and were then lost in its light." Paul's warnings against a return to these are cited: "How turn ye back to the weak and beggarly rudiments, wherewith ye desire to be in bondage over again? Ye observe days, and months, and seasons, and years"; "For freedom did Christ set us free: stand fast, therefore, and be not entangled again in a yoke of bondage" (Gal. 4:9,10; 5:1). "The Epistle to the Hebrews," says Snowden, "is one long and conclusive argument that the old ordinances are fulfilled and done away in Christ, 'who needeth not daily, like those high priests, to offer up sacrifice, first for his own sins, and then for the sins of the people; for this he did once for all, when he offered up himself' (7:27).

"Who would ever have expected that in the face of all this teaching and of these earnest efforts to rid the Christian Church of these old ordinances that had served their day as the withered and empty husk has served the corn, there would arise among believers in later times a school of interpreters who would teach that the whole Mosaic system, with its temple and central seat of worship and its seasons and feasts and sacrifices, its passover and its unleavened bread, its daily peace offerings and bloody burnt-offerings and sin offerings, its altar streaming with blood and its smoke and incense, was to be restored in Jerusalem after **the second coming of Christ?** Who would have believed this incredible thing? And yet this very thing has come to pass and now is . . .

"This doctrine is first rooted in the logic of the system. It is a cardinal principle of Premillennialism that the prophecies of the Messianic kingdom in the Old Testament apply, not to the first but to the second coming of Christ and to the millennial kingdom He will inaugurate. It is a further principle of this system that these prophecies must be interpreted in a literal sense in accordance with its teaching that the Bible means what it says, and to abandon this mode of interpretation in its application to these prophecies would be to concede the principle of figurative interpretation and this again would wreck the system.

"Premillennialism is therefore required by its own logic to take the prophecy of Ezekiel, chapters 40–48, in which an idealized vision of the temple is set forth, including the passover and all the bloody offerings which are expressly commanded (45:21–25), and transfer it bodily and literally to the millennial kingdom in Jerusalem after the second coming of Christ. And this system must do the same thing with all similar prophecies. Isaiah declares: 'And they shall bring all your children out of all the nations for an oblation unto Jehovah, upon horses, and in chariots, and in litters, and upon mules, and upon dromedaries, to my holy mountain Jerusalem, saith Jehovah, as the children of Israel bring their oblation in a clean vessel into the house of Jehovah. [Here we notice that the means of conveyance have long since been outmoded and belong to a distant age. Surely they would not be appropriate for the very advanced and prosperous kingdom that Premillennialists expect in the millennium]. And it shall come to pass, that from one new moon to another, and from one sabbath to another, shall all flesh come to worship before me, saith Jehovah' (66:20,23). Zechariah prophesies: 'And it shall come to pass, that every one that is left of all the nations that came up against Jerusalem shall go up from year to year to worship the king, and to keep the feast of tabernacles' (14:16); 'and all they that sacrifice shall come.'

"The inescapable logic of Premillennialism requires that all these and similar prophecies be literally fulfilled in Jerusalem. This is 'judaizing Christianity' with a vengeance. And this is revolting; and some premillennialists do revolt at it. David Brown quotes Increase Mather, a premillenarian, as saying, 'And a most loathsome work they do perform, both to God and man, that dig up the ceremonies out of that grave where Jesus Christ buried them above sixteen hundred years ago'" (*The Coming of the Lord,* pp. 206–209).

Let there be no doubt but that Dispensationalism does teach the re-establishment of Judaism following the Church age. Lewis Sperry Chafer, late President of Dallas Theological Seminary, says that after the Church age has run its course there is to be "the regathering of Israel and the restoration of Judaism" (*Dispensationalism,* **p. 46**). And Merrill F. Unger, also of Dallas Theological Seminary, says: "At the second advent Christ will restore the Judaistic system with far greater glory and spirituality than it ever had in the Old Testament period until its complete dissipation with the destructon of Herod's temple in 70 A. D. The heart and center of re-established Judaism will be the millennial temple, in connection with which Judaism will enjoy its final state of development" (*Bibliotheca Sacra,* Jan.-March, 1950).

Only to a literalist does the re-establishment of the sacrificial system and temple ritual seem sensible. To a Post- or Amillennialist it is too materialistic. Premillennial logic, however, does not permit these sacrifices to be "spiritualized." To do so would remove a cornerstone from the system, and, if consistently carried out would lead straight to conclusions that they are most anxious to avoid.

Some Premillennialists say that the sacrifices to be offered in the Millennium will only be "memorials" of the work that Christ accomplished on the cross. Scofield gives this explanation when he says: "Doubtless these offerings will be memorial, looking back to the cross, as the offerings under the old covenant were anticipatory, looking forward to the cross" (p. 890). This explanation is also given by G. Campbell Morgan in his book, *God's Methods with Man* (p. 118). But that explanation contradicts the premillennial principle of literal interpretation of prophecy and cannot be allowed. Ezekiel says plainly that "the priests," "the sons of Zadok," shall again serve, that they shall be given "a young bullock for a *sin-offering.*" He says further: "And thou shalt take the blood thereof, and put it on the four horns of it [the altar], and on the four corners of the ledge, and upon the border round about: thus shalt thou cleanse it and *make atonement* for it" (40:46; 43:19,20). Those who are so insistent that "the Bible means what it says" cannot be allowed to "spiritualize and allegorize" statements such as these when found in sections which they themselves say describe the restoration of the Jews in Palestine during the millennial era. Ezekiel chapters 40–48 is at least twenty times more extensive and detailed than is Revelation 20:1–10, which Premillennialists say must be taken literally. So those who insist on literal interpretation find here a program for the restoration of the Levitical ritual and priesthood, despite the fact that Galatians and Hebrews each makes it plain that the temple, the human priesthood and the ritual have been abolished forever.

In any event, the re-institution of a sacrificial system could not do other than dishonor the sacrifice that Christ made on Calvary, which the Scripture represents as a "once for all" sacrifice (Heb. 7:27). The New Testament has absolutely nothing to say about such memorial sacrifices, nor anything about rebuilding the temple. Furthermore, all memorials are unnecessary when the one to be memorialized is present in person, as Christ will be after His Second Coming. We may also add that one feature of Roman Catholicism that we find particularly offensive is its doctrine that in the Mass the sacrifice of Christ is repeated, that the bread and wine actually are changed into His flesh and blood —"the unbloody repetition of the Mass," as it is called.

Concerning the subject of animal sacrifices during the Millennium Allis says:

"The thought is abhorrent that after Christ comes, the memory of His atoning work will be kept alive in the hearts of believers by a return to the animal sacrifices of the Mosaic law, the performance of which is so emphatically condemned in passages which speak with unmistakable plainness on this very subject. Here is unquestionably the Achilles' heel of the Dispensational system of interpretation. Its literalistic and Old Testament emphasis leads almost inevitably, if not inevitably, to a doctrine of the millennium which makes it definitely Jewish and represents a turning back from the glory of the gospel to those typical rites and ceremonies which prepared the way for it, and having served that necessary purpose have lost for ever their validity and propriety" (*Prophecy and the Church*, p. 248).

Snowden's conclusion regarding this phase of Premillennialism is also worth quoting. He says:

"Enough and more than enough has been said to prove that Premillennialism is a recrudescence of Judaism. It is Judaistic in its method of establishing the kingdom, and above all, in its restoration of the sacrifices after the second coming of Christ. This is indeed renouncing the logic of Paul and 'turning back to the weak and beggarly rudiments' and putting our necks again under the Mosaic yoke of 'bondage.' This is turning the clock of religious development back two or three thousand years. It is putting the altar back in Jerusalem and going back to 'the blood of bulls and goats.' If any premillenarians pause at this or say that they do not hold it, we must repeat that we are not dealing with individuals but with the logic and literature of the system, and there can be no doubt whither the logic leads and what the representative writers teach.

"Truly old forms of religions die hard. Judaism has strange tenacity and still clings to the Christan Church . . . Judaism is a withered husk; the corn has gone out of it. Jerusalem is a splendid memory. The eagle, once it gets out, can never be crowded back into its shell. Christianity has taken its flight from Mount Zion and never will it officially be back there. Jesus Himself swept the kingdom off that mountain-top as its central seat and released it to go into all the world and make disciples of all nations that men everywhere may worship the Father in Spirit and in truth . . .

"Paul with one stroke of his pen 'spiritualized' the whole Old Testament economy when he wrote, 'And if ye are Christ's then are ye Abraham's seed, heirs according to promise' (Gal. 3:29). Peter also 'spiritualized' the Old Testament and buried the Jewish eschatology when he wrote. 'Ye also, as living stones, are built up a spiritual house, to be a holy priesthood, to offer up spiritual sacrifices, acceptable to God through Jesus Christ' (I Peter 2:5). This is the way the New Testament throughout spiritualizes the Old. This is 'the glorious liberty of the children of God' (Rom. 8:21); and when we read these premillenarian interpretations and arguments we hear Paul's earnest and eloquent voice ringing across all these centuries and bidding us, 'stand fast therefore in the liberty wherewith Christ made you free, and be not entangled again with the yoke of bondage' (Gal. 5:1)" (*The Coming of the Lord*, pp. 217–219).

It is admittedly difficult in many instances to determine whether statements in Scripture should be taken literally or figuratively. As regards prophecy, that often cannot be determined until after the fulfillment. Most of the Bible, however, particularly the historical and the more didactic portions, clearly is to be understood literally, although some figurative expressions are found in these. But that many other portions must be understood figuratively is also clearly evident. Even the Premillennialists must take many expressions figuratively or they become nonsense. Since the Bible gives no hard and fast rule for determining what is literal and what is figurative we must study the nature of the material, the historical setting and style and purpose of the writer, and then fall back on what for lack of a better name we may call "sanctified common sense." Naturally the conclusions will vary somewhat from individual to individual, for we do not all think alike nor see alike.

It should hardly be necessary to point out that true Postmillennialism is supernaturalistic through and through. Pre- and Amillennialists sometimes represent this system as though it taught the conversion of the world through merely humanistic and evolutionary processes. Present day Modernism does set forth a program of world betterment by natural rather than supernatural means, and opponents sometimes represent that as Postmillennialism. But by no stretch of the imagination does such a system have any moral right to be called Postmillennialism. That is not the sense in which the term has been used historically, yet comments of that kind have given rise to much unjust criticism. Representative postmillennial theologians, such as Augustine, Brown, Hodge, Dabney and Warfield, have been consistent supernaturalists and have believed in a fully inspired and authoritative Bible and in the regenerating work of the Holy Spirit as the only means by which an individual can be brought to salvation.

On the other hand the distinguishing feature of present day Modernism by which it is to be identified wherever it shows itself is its more or less consistent denial of the supernatural, i.e., denial of the plenary inspiration of the Scriptures, the Trinity, the Deity of Christ, blood atonement, miracles, final judgment, heaven and hell. It is concerned primarily with this life, and it proposes to reform the world through education, social and economic progress, improved health programs, better relations between capital and labor, etc. Those things are good as far as they go and, wherever possible, should be encouraged. But they are only the by-products of true Christianity.

The fact that different views concerning the Second Coming of Christ and the Millennium have been held and are held should not discourage anyone from making an earnest search for the truth. This situation in the field of Theology is no different from that in the field of Medicine, in which eminent doctors hold differing views as to how certain diseases should be treated or how the human body should be cared for. We have, for instance, medical doctors, chiropractors, osteopaths, surgeons, dietetic specialists, physical exercise enthusiasts, etc. But that does not prevent us from believing in health nor from seeking the best methods to preserve health; nor does it save us from suffering the consequences if we choose wrongly. Nor is the situation in the realm of politics and statesmanship any different. We have various political parties, Republican, Democrat, Socialist, Labor, Communist, etc., each advocating different principles as to how the nation should be governed, and particularly at election time we hear very conflicting opinions. There are various theories of education and of church government. In each of these spheres it is our duty to search diligently for the truth and so far as possible to separate truth from error. Our beliefs concerning the manner and time of the Second Coming of Christ will not change that event by one iota, but what we believe concerning those matters will very definitely affect our lives and conduct while we are waiting for that event.

It is to be regretted that these differences of opinion even among those who accept the Bible as the inspired and authoritative word of God cannot always be dealt with by unprejudiced exegesis and friendly discussion rather than made the basis for quarrels or tests of orthodoxy. As a general rule Premillennialists, basing their views on a more literal interpretation of Scripture, have a tendency to feel that those who do not accept their system hold a lower view of Scripture and that they are not consistently Christian. One might easily receive the impression from reading premillennial literature that only they believe fully in the Lord's return. It has even reached such a state in some dispensational circles that if one questions the personal reign of Christ in an earthly kingdom he is met with a question such as, "Then you do not believe that Christ is to return?" An examination of Bible institute catalogues reveals that most of them restrict faculty members to the premillennial view. Some are reluctant to graduate a student, or at least will give him a lower grade, if he does not accept that view. Prophetic conference literature presents a one-sided futurism and encourages the inference that opposing views are not evangelical. Some make a hobby of Premillennialism, finding it with remarkable ingenuity in almost every prophecy and vision and promise from Genesis to Revelation, and giving it undue prominence in their preaching—Gray places the number of New Testament references to the coming of Christ at a minimum of 300, and Morgan says that on an average one verse in each 25 in the New Testament refers to it. The differences between Post-, A-, and Premillennialists, which should be treated as comparative non-essentials, actually divide the churches and becomes a serious impediment to Christian fellowship. Unquestionably the vagaries of dispensational extremists, not merely in such sects as Jehovah's Witnesses, Millennial Dawnists, and some Pentecostal and Holiness groups, but also in the conventional evangelical churches, have divided Christians into antagonistic groups and have done much harm to the cause of Christianity.

In discussing these problems, then, two important facts should be kept in mind: (1) Evangelical Post-, A-, and Premillennialists agree that the Bible is the word of God, fully inspired and authoritative. They differ not in regard to the nature of Scripture authority, but in regard to what they understand Scripture to teach. And, (2) the three system agree that there was a First Advent, and that there will be a Second Advent, which will be personal, visible, glorious, and as objective as was the Ascension from the Mount of Olives.

It should be added that while the Church has debated and reached conclusions and has embodied these conclusions in her creeds as regards all of the other great doctrines of the faith, the subject of Eschatology still remains in dispute as to the manner of Christ's return and the kind of kingdom that He is setting up or will set up in this world. For this reason the Church in practically all of her branches has refused to make any one of the millennial interpretations an article of the creed, and has preferred rather to accept as Christian brethren all those who believe in the *fact* of Christ's Coming. Hence, while personally we may have very definite views concerning the manner and time of His coming, it would seem that our motto should be: "In essentials, unity; in non-essentials, liberty; in all things, charity."

THE NATURE AND PURPOSE OF PROPHECY

Also in connection with the subject of interpretation something should be said about the basic nature of prophecy. Premillennialists regard prophecy as *history written beforehand.* We prefer to say, however, that the primary purpose of prophecy is to inspire faith in those who see its fulfillment, and only secondarily to inform us of what is going to happen in the future. At the time of fulfillment the observer looks back to the author of the prophecy and is led to acknowledge that he could have spoken only by inspiration, and that his message therefore is authoritative and trustworthy. Prophecy thus comes under the general category of miracle, and its primary purpose is to accredit a message or a messenger. This was the purpose set forth when Jesus said: "I have told you before it come to pass, that, when it is come to pass, ye may believe" (John 14:29); and again, "From henceforth I tell you before it come to pass, that, when it is come to pass, ye may believe that I am he" (John 13:19). Here the primary purpose of prophecy, like that of a miracle in the physical realm, is to inspire faith. It is in effect a delayed miracle.

As proof that this is the correct principle we find that most of the Old Testament prophecies concerning the First Coming of Christ were so vague and enigmatic that they could not possibly have been understood until after their fulfillment. While some were in language that was easy to understand, such as that He would be born in Bethlehem, that He would be born of a virgin, and that He would heal the sick and afflicted, the meaning of the more important ones relating to the nature of His work of redemption and to the nature of the Kingdom that He was to establish could not be understood until after their accomplishment. As examples of the latter we may cite: the protevangelium, given in Genesis 3:16, "And I will put enmity between thee and the woman, and between thy seed and her seed: he shall bruise thy head, and thou shalt bruise his heel"; the extensive prophecy concerning the suffering of Messiah as found in Isaiah 53; various prophecies concerning the nature of the Kingdom that was to be established, as found in Isaiah, chapters 2, 11, 66; the nature of the work of atonement as prefigured in the priesthood, ritual and sacrifices; and the promise made to David that the throne of his kingdom was to be established for ever, involving, as we see in the light of the New Testament, a long line of merely human kings and then a transition to the Messiah who is the true King of Israel. The manner in which the events connected with the crucifixion of Christ as predicted in the Old Testament would be fulfilled could not have been understood until their fulfillment, e.g., that His hands and feet would be pierced (Ps. 22:16); that the soldiers would part His garments among them and cast lots for His robe (Ps. 22:18; John 19:24); that not a bone of His body would be broken (Ex. 12:46; John 19:36); His resurrection (Ps. 16:10; Acts 2:27); and even the death and burial of His betrayer, Judas Iscariot (Ps. 69:25; 109:8; Acts 1:19,20). It was clearly impossible for any Old Testament Jew to draw from these prophecies a plan of the life of the coming Messiah.

The promise given to Abraham that his seed should be very numerous and that through his seed all the nations of the earth should be blessed, finds its primary fulfillment, not in the totality of his physical descendants as at first sight would seem to have been indicated, nor even in the descendants through Jacob who stood in a special relationship to God, but in those who are his spiritual descendants (Gal. 3:7,29); and the seed through which all the nations of the earth were to be blessed was not his descendants in general, but one individual, which is Christ: "Now to Abraham were the promises spoken, and to his seed. He saith not, And to seeds, as of many; but as of one, And to thy seed, which is Christ" (Gal. 3:16). Who could have understood that before it was fulfilled?

Concerning this feature of predictive prophecy Campbell has well said:

"The enigmatic form of prophecy precludes the possibility of the merely human actors in the fulfillment being aware that they are participating in the predicted event. It permits the prescience and power of God to appear, while in no way encroaching on the free agency of man. The advent of Christ, His character, ministry, sufferings, death, and enthronement in glory, are all predicted in the Hebrew prophets in such a manner that no one living prior to their fulfillment was able to read their meaning clearly; and yet the diligent reader today who studies the ancient records in the light of the fulfillment cannot fail to see that he has before his eyes clear testimony to the importance and the supernatural origin of the records in which the predictions appear. The disciples of Jesus probably knew well enough what the prophets had spoken; but their familiarity with the written word did not of itself enable them to see the nature or character of the kingdom over which Messiah would reign. Not until they were compelled by contemporary events did they lay aside their racial preconceptions and recognize the glorious vision of all nations of men united in one universal brotherhood under the risen and glorified Christ" (*Israel and the New Covenant*, p. 170).

It should be further evident that as the Old Testament prophets used figures of speech with which their people were familiar, that is, language borrowed from the vocabulary of the old economy, such as the land, the temple, the sacrifices, etc., to describe the glories of the Messianic era, so no doubt the New Testament uses terms with which we are familiar to describe the future state which we as yet are able to grasp only faintly. We are told enough to make it clear that great and glorious events lie ahead; but the manner in which those events are to be accomplished, and the details concerning the future course of the Kingdom both on earth and in heaven are left largely unexplained. In all probability the realities of the future state will be as different from our ideas concerning them as the realities of the present era have proved to be different from the ideas of the Old Testament Jews.

We must keep in mind that it was the mechanical, literalistic method of interpreting prophecy that led the Jews at the time of Christ to expect a Messiah who would conquer their enemies and set up an earthly political kingdom in Jerusalem. Fastening their eyes on the very letter of Scripture, they became tragically blind to its real meaning and spirit, with the result that when Christ "came unto his own," "they that were his own received him not" (John 1:11), but rejected and crucified Him. This same literalistic principle can also have tragic results in our day, in that it arouses hopes that are false and disappointing. This is particularly true in regard to the view that the Jews still are to be looked upon as God's favored people, that Palestine belongs to them as a matter of Divine right, and that prophecy foretells a glorious kingdom for them in Palestine. It is productive of even more serious results in the Church when it is employed to teach that Christ is to set up a one thousand year political kingdom in this world, and so to divert attention from the real purpose of the Church, which is to evangelize the world during this present age. Nearly a century ago Dr. Charles Hodge warned against the unnatural insistence of Premillennialists on literalism as an *ignis fatuus,* as he called it, a false or misleading fire which "leads those who follow it, they know not whither." That method proved disastrous for the Jews who tried to predict the details of Christ's First Coming. Most likely it will not work any better for those who attempt to set forth in detail the order of events for His Second Coming.

As a matter of fact no Premillennialist can carry out the principle of literal interpretation consistently. No one has yet devised a sure method for distinguishing between the figurative and the literal. Many statements in Scripture clearly are figurative, and the Premillennialist must spiritualize them no matter how critical he may be of Post- or Amillennialism. No one can take literally the statement that the saints in Paradise have "washed their robes and made them white in the blood of the Lamb" (Rev. 7:14); or that the victorious saint is to be made a "pillar" in the temple of God (Rev. 3:12); or that the Devil, who is a spirit, can be bound with a chain and shut up in a deep pit for a thousand years (Rev. 20:2,3). We do not take literally Christ's words, "This is my body," and "This is my blood," although these two sentences are composed of very plain, short, simple words. Roman Catholics do take those words literally, and get their doctrines of Transubstantiation and the Mass. It is inconsistent for Premillennialists to pick and choose in deciding what statements they will take literally and what ones they will take figuratively while at the same time criticizing Post- and Amillennialists for accepting figurative or symbolical interpretations when those seem preferable. If figurative or symbolical interpretation is wrong in principle it should not be resorted to at all. Otherwise Premillennialists do precisely what they accuse Post- and Amillennialists of doing,—take Scripture literally where that seems preferable, and spiritualize where that seems preferable.

Another principle of interpretation is that when a prophecy or promise has been fulfilled once, there is no valid reason why it must be fulfilled again, or repeatedly. A present day condition involving this principle relates to the State of Israel. Some tell us that since Palestine and the surrounding lands were promised to Abraham and to the Children of Israel, and that since those lands never were fully occupied, or because they later were lost, they now rightfully belong to the Israelis. But in Joshua 21:43,45, we read: "So Jehovah gave unto Israel all the land, which he sware to give unto their fathers; and they possessed it, and dwelt therein. . . . There failed not aught of any good thing which Jehovah had spoken unto the house of Israel: all came to pass." In I Kings 4:21 we read: "And Solomon ruled over all the kingdoms from the River unto the land of the Philistines, and unto the border of Egypt: they brought tribute, and served Solomon all the days of his life." And II Chr. 9:26 tells us: "And he (Solomon) ruled over all the kings from the River unto the land of the Philistines, and to the border of Egypt." Hence we conclude that those promises have been amply fulfilled, and that they do not apply to the present day State of Israel.

II.

Amillennialism

Chapter I

INTRODUCTION

The definition of Amillennialism as previously cited is:

"Amillennialism is that view of the Last Things which holds that the Bible does not predict a 'Millennium' or period of world-wide peace and righteousness on this earth before the end of the world."

The author of this definition, Dr. J. G. Vos, has observed further by way of explanation that,

"Amillennialism teaches that there will be a parallel and contemporaneous development of good and evil—God's kingdom and Satan's kingdom—in this world, which will continue until the second coming of Christ. At the second coming of Christ the resurrection and judgment will take place, followed by the eternal order of things—the absolute, perfect Kingdom of God, in which there will be no sin, suffering nor death" (*Blue Banner Faith and Life*, Jan.-March, 1951).

Amillennialists see no Scriptural evidence for a Millennium on either post- or premillennial principles. Some Amillennialists understand the term to relate to the entire Christian era or Church age, that is, to the period between the first and second advent of Christ. Others understand it to relate to a particular part of this period. Still others, more consistently it seems to us, apply it to the intermediate state. The term is thus used sometimes in a broad, sometimes in a narrow, sense. In the broad sense it denies that the thousand years means that during the Church age there is to be either a period of righteousness and peace as set forth by Postmillennialism, or a personal reign of Christ on earth with the saints as set forth by Premillennialism. In the narrow sense it holds that the thousand years has reference not to anything that happens on earth, but to the reign of the saints with Christ in the intermediate state.

With the broad sense of the term in mind, Dr. Berkhof says:

"Some premillennialists have spoken of *Amillennialism* as a new view and as one of the most recent novelties, but this is certainly not in accord with the testimony of history. The name is new indeed, but the view to which it is applied is as old as Christianity. It had at least as many advocates as Chiliasm among the Church Fathers of the second and third centuries, supposed to have been the heyday of Chiliasm. It has ever since been the view most widely accepted, is the only view that is either expressed or implied in the great historical Confessions of the Church, and has always been the prevalent view in Reformed circles" (*Systematic Theology*, p. 708).

While not necessarily agreeing that Amillennialism is the only view expressed or implied in the Confessions, nor that it has always been the prevalent view in Reformed circles, Post-millennialism having been at least for a considerable time the prevailing view in American Reformed theology, we believe this analysis is essentially correct. Similarly, Dr. John F. Walvoord, a Premillennialist and editor of the magazine *Bibliotheca Sacra*, acknowledges that,

"Reformed eschatology has been predominantly amillennial. Most if not all of the leaders of the Protestant Reformation were amillennial in their eschatology, following the teachings of Augustine" (Issue of Jan.–March, 1951).

In regard to Augustine the fact of the matter is that in his teaching there are elements of both Post- and Amillennialism. He is, therefore, claimed by both schools. Dr. Allis has brought this out clearly, and in the following comments has given quite a full and accurate outline of the Augustinian eschatology. Says he:

"The view which has been most widely held by opponents of Millenarianism is associated with the name of Augustine. He taught that the millennium is to be interpreted spiritually as fulfilled in the Christian Church. He held that the binding of Satan took place during the earthly ministry of our Lord (Luke 10:18), that the first resurrection is the new birth of the believer (John 5:25), and that the millennium must correspond therefore to the inter-adventual period or Church age. This involved the interpretation of Revelation 20:1–6 as a 'recapitulation' of the preceding chapters instead of as describing a new age following chronologically on the events set forth in chapter 19. Living in the first half of the first millennium of the Church's history, Augustine naturally took the 1000 years of Revelation 20 literally; and he expected the second advent to take place at the end of that period. But since he somewhat inconsistently identified the millennium with what then remained of the sixth chiliad of human history, he believed that this period might end about A. D. 650 with a great outburst of evil, the revolt of Gog, which would be followed by the coming of Christ in judgment . . .

"It is to be noted that all forms of the Augustinian view, by which we mean, all views which discover the millennium in the inter-adventual period or in some part of it, whether that part be past, present, or future, may properly be called both *a*millennial and *post*millennial. They are amillennial in the sense that they all deny that after the present dispensation has been terminated by the resurrection and rapture of the saints, there is to be a reign of Christ on earth with the saints for 1000 years before the last judgment. But since they identify the millennium with the whole, or with some part, of the present gospel age, they may also be called postmillennial. In this sense Augustine was a postmillennnialist. But while this is true, the word 'postmillennial' has come to be so identified with the name of Whitby that as used by very many writers on the subject it applies exclusively to that view which regards the millennium as a golden age of the Church which is wholly future, perhaps still remote, and which is to precede the second advent" (*Prophecy and the Church*, pp. 3, 4).

We have said that in the narrow sense of the term Amillennialism holds that the thousand years has reference to the intermediate state. This view was set forth most clearly by a German theologian Kliefoth (1874). He held that Revelation 20 follows chronologically after Revelation 19. But, not finding what he believed to be Scriptural support for a Millennium on earth, he concluded that the reign of the saints with Christ could only relate to the intermediate state. Since the term has been used in two senses, some confusion was bound to arise. But at any rate we have seen that it is in reality an ancient system. It evidently is in the narrow sense that some Premillennialists have understood it, e.g., Chafer and Gaebelein, who have referred to it rather contemptuously as a new and novel system.

Amillennialism has been most fully developed by the Dutch

theologians, Drs. Abraham Kuyper, Herman Bavinck, and others. On the continent of Europe even to the present day it can justly be called the "Standard Reformed and Lutheran theology." On the other hand the outstanding American theologians of the later nineteenth and early twentieth century have been Postmillennialists. In comparatively recent years, particularly since 1930, a considerable number of American theologians have produced scholarly books setting forth the amillennial position, as has been indicated earlier in this study. Practically all of these books, however, have been concerned primarily with the refutation of Premillennialism, and have given comparatively little space to the development of the amillennial position. During this same period, particularly since the appearance of the *Scofield Reference Bible* there has been an almost endless flow of premillennial and dispensational books and articles far surpassing in volume either the post- or amillennial writings.

At the present time Amillennialism is the official view of the conservative Missouri Synod Lutheran Church, which has a membership of more than 2,000,000 and sponsors a world-wide "Lutheran Hour" radio program. It is also the view of the equally conservative Christian Reformed Church, likewise sponsoring an extensive radio program known as the "Back To God Hour," and by the Orthodox Presbyterian Church.

Chapter II

STATEMENTS BY REPRESENTATIVE AMILLENNIALISTS

Perhaps the best way to set forth the doctrinal position of Amillennialism is to let its leading advocates speak for themselves. This we shall do in considerable detail. Probably the most representative spokesman in the United States is Dr. Louis Berkhof, for 38 years a professor in Calvin Seminary and author of a very excellent *Systematic Theology* (1941). He says:

"There are very large numbers who do not believe that the Bible warrants the expectation of a millennium, and it has become customary of late to speak of them as *Amillennialists*. The Amillennial view is, as the name indicates, purely negative. It holds that there is no sufficient ground for the expectation of a millennium, and is firmly convinced that the Bible favors the idea that the present dispensation of the Kingdom of God will be followed *immediately* by the Kingdom of God in its consummate and eternal form. It is mindful of the fact that the Kingdom of Jesus Christ is represented as an eternal and not as a temporal kingdom (Is. 9:7; Dan. 7:14; Luke 1:33; Heb. 1:8; 12:28; II Peter 1:11; Rev. 11:15); and that to enter the Kingdom of the future is to enter upon one's eternal state (Matt. 7:21,22), to enter life (Matt. 18:8,9), and to be saved (Mark 10:25,26)" (p. 708).

Here we notice particularly his statements that the amillennial view is "purely negative," that any idea of a millennium on either post- or premillennial grounds is ruled out as without Scripture support, that one phase of the Kingdom is acknowledged as being in existence during the present dispensation, and that the present dispensation is to be followed immediately by the Kingdom in its consummate and eternal form.

One of the most comprehensive statements is found in Prof.

Floyd E. Hamilton's book, *The Basis of Millennial Faith* (1942).
He says:

"The name itself is unfortunate in that it would seem to
indicate that its advocates do not believe in the thousand year
period of Revelation 20. The name literally means 'no millennium,' while as a matter of fact its advocates believe that the
millennium is a spiritual or heavenly millennium, rather than an
earthly one of a literal reign of Christ on earth before the final
judgment. From one point of view it might be called a variety
of postmillennialism, since it believes that the spiritual or heavenly millennium precedes the Second Coming of Christ. The
only mention in the Bible of a kingdom of Christ limited to a
1000 years is in the 20th chapter of the Revelation where it is
said that the 'souls' are seen reigning with Christ during the 1000
years. The amillennialist interprets this as indicating *the spiritual
reign with Christ of the disembodied spirits in heaven,* during
the 1000 years. A thousand, the number of perfection or completion, is held to be the symbolic reference to the perfect period,
or *the complete period between the two comings of Christ*
(italics ours).

"The picture of eschatological events, without any discussion
at present of supporting Scripture passages, is as follows. Like
the premillennialist we view the world as a mixture of good and
evil up to the time of the Rapture. We have no hope or expectation that the whole world will grow better until it is all converted
to Christianity. We expect that wars will continue right up to
the time of the end when Christ comes to set things right. We
expect the elect to be gathered out of an evil world, though we
believe that the command of Christ to preach the gospel to the
whole world must be obeyed, and that it is our duty to endeavor
to establish a Christian society so far as it is in our power to do
so, but while we have the obligation to do this, we by no means
expect that the whole of society will be Christianized. In fact,
we expect the forces of evil to grow more and more violent in
their opposition to Christianity and Christians. This in no way
excuses us from the attempt to propagate the Christian principles
as well as the gospel in the world.

"At the close of the present age we expect the forces of evil
to head up in a powerful combination of political, economic and

religious power led by the Antichrist. At the close of the reign of the Antichrist or Man of Sin, he institutes a terrible persecution against the Christian Church (not against the Jews as some premillennialists assert). In this terrible tribulation vast numbers of Christians are killed, but at the climax, when the hosts of Satan seem to be on the point of complete victory, during the battle of Armageddon, Christ appears in the Shekinah glory, the resurrection of all men takes place, and the transfigured bodies of the dead and living saints are caught up to welcome their Saviour. Then, as a terrible out-pouring of the wrath of God occurs, smiting the unbelieving nations of the world into destruction, the Jewish people look 'on Him whom they pierced,' repent and believe instantly in their Messiah . . . They too are transfigured with the living Church of Christ, and join in the rapture of the united body of the elect church of Christ of all ages. This completes the number of the elect, and from that point onward there is no more salvation for men . . . After the Judgment, the eternal kingdom of God is established in the new heavens and on the new earth . . . It will continue through all eternity" (pp. 35-37).

Dr. Robert Strong, a minister in the Southern Presbyterian Church, in a series of articles on Amillennialism, says:

"The amillennialist sees no ground in Scripture for holding to a millennium of righteousness before the Lord's coming, and he sees the possibility of such a millennium after the second advent expressly excluded in the New Testament teaching. Amillennialism agrees with premillennialism that the Scriptures do not promise the conversion of the world through the preaching of the gospel. It agrees with postmillennialism that the coming of Christ ushers in the last judgment and the eternal state. Briefly outlined, the amillennial view is that, preceding the coming of Christ, there will be a widespread apostasy from the true faith, climaxed by the manifestations of the personal antichrist. Thus the final great rebellion against Christ will be overthrown at the personal appearing of the Son of God, who will come from heaven to take unto Himself His own people and to demolish the forces of Antichrist. The wicked dead will be raised to judgment. The earth and its works will be overwhelmed in fire and a new heavens and a new earth will appear in which only righteousness will dwell" (*The Presbyterian Guardian*, Jan. 10, 1942).

Dr. Rutgers holds that the Millennium includes both the present age and the intermediate state, and traces the origin of this view to Augustine. In the writings of Augustine, says Rutgers,

"The thousand years is conceived of symbolically, the saints of the church militant on earth and those who have departed are now reigning with Christ and in this sense we are now living in the midst of the millennium, the church-age is identified with the millennial age. (cp. Civitae Dei) ... Augustine has moulded and directed theological thinking in general, has offered an interpretation of the kingdom of God, the church, the millennial imagery of the Apocalypse which held undisputed sway for more than a thousand years and even after all the enlightenment of modern times, with highly technicalized terminology and specialized study, maintains his hold. He was followed by all the great Latin Fathers, Leo the Great, Gregory the Great, Albertus Magnus, Thomas Acquinas, etc. Chiliasm was thus banished, rejected by the church, and arose centuries later only in schismatic and sectarian movements, where it periodically flourishes up to the present day. In its crude and unscriptural form it never was countenanced by the governing faith of the church" (*Premillennialism In America*, p. 71 (1930).

One of the clearest statements of the amillennial position is found in Dr. George L. Murray's *Millennial Studies* (1948). He believes that the binding of Satan was accomplished by Christ in His work of atonement at the time of His first advent, referred to in Matthew 12:29—"How can one enter into the house of the strong man, and spoil his goods, except he first bind the strong man? And then he will spoil his house." This binding is understood to have restricted Satan not in every way but only in regard to his work of deceiving the nations, so that he no longer is able to prevent the Gospel being proclaimed to them. Previous to that time only the Jews knew the way of salvation, and all other nations were held in heathen darkness. But since that time the Gospel has been carried to the entire world. Concerning Revelation 20:1–10 Dr. Murray says:

"We believe that God led the Seer of Patmos to present here a brief summary of the entire Gospel dispensation, from the first advent of Him who claimed to have come down from heaven, until the second advent, when the kingdom which He founded shall be established in all its glory" (p. 176).

Concerning the thousand years he says:

"We believe that the figure of one thousand years presents a definite period of time, measured by and known to God Himself. It is the cycle of time extending from our Lord's first advent to the day of His return. It consists of the period during which the souls of the departed saints reign with Christ. That is what they are doing now. This heavenly reign of theirs is described as 'the first resurrection.' It is with regard to this phrase that many people have become confused, for they think that a resurrection must mean the raising of the body. To be sure, that is the sense in which we generally use the word, but the New Testament speaks very definitely and in many places of the raising of those who have been dead in trespasses and sins to a newness of life . . . When this regenerated soul leaves the body and goes to be with Christ, the spiritual resurrection has reached its culmination, for then the redeemed soul lives and reigns with Christ. This is the first resurrection . . . The so-called millennial reign of the saints and martyrs with Christ is a present reality. The figure of a thousand years represents the period during which they are to reign and live with Him, leading up to His return with them" (Pp. 184–186).

Dr. Albertus Pieters believed that the thousand years, understood symbolically, related to a comparatively tranquil period in church history, that this period began "at the point in history when paganism ceased to be a menace to the Christian Church." He adds that,

"If looked at from the standpoint of the Roman empire, this was at the accession of Constantine the Great. If the barbaric nations to the north are included in the view, it comes some centuries later, in the time of Charlemagne. The thousand years are taken to mean a period of great length . . . At the end of the period there will be a revival of the conflict with paganism" (*Studies In the Revelation of St. John,* p. 305).

Kliefoth was one of the first to hold that the Millennium related not to an earthly state at all, but to the reign of the souls of the blessed dead with Christ in the intermediate state. This, as we have pointed out, is Amillennialism in the strictest sense of the word, for it conceives of the Millennium as something entirely apart from this world.

From the foregoing it should be clear that an exact definition of Amillennialism is rather difficult to formulate. Different and to some extent conflicting views are set forth by those who call themselves by that name. The word literally means "no millennium." Some relate the Millennium to a part or all of the Church age. Others relate it to the reign of the saints with Christ in the intermediate state. Nearly all understand the term symbolically. As against Premillennialism they hold that there is to be no personal reign of Christ on earth with the saints. As against Postmillennialism they deny that the world is to be Christianized during this dispensation, although some have an element of Postmillennialism in their system in that they hold that Christ comes after the Millennium, symbolically understood. Most of the books written by Amillennialists have Premillennialism as their special targets, understandably so since Amillennialism rejects the 1000 year earthly kingdom set forth by Premillennialism and agrees with Postmillennialism that Christ's coming marks the end of earthly history. In all of these books the positive statement regarding Amillennialism is very brief. This, of course, is understandable if, as Dr. Berkhof says, the system is "purely negative." Only a few brief paragraphs are needed to show what a system is not.

The tenets of Amillennialism, like those of Premillennialism, allow its holders to maintain that the second coming of Christ is "imminent," since they see the Millennium either as the present church age or as the intermediate state which may come to an end at any time. Also, as with the Premillennialists, they usually are inclined to take a pessimistic view of the future of the Church, holding either that conditions will continue until the end much as they now are or that they will grow progressively worse. Dr. Murray, for instance, after a reference to the loosing of Satan for a little while toward the close of the Gospel age adds: "We wonder if we are not witnessing this in our own day." (1948). *Millennial Studies,* p. 186. Amillennialism agrees with Premillennialism in teaching that a personal Antichrist is to appear shortly before the return of Christ. Dr. Strong says of Christ at His coming that "He consumes Antichrist and his rebel followers in a fiery overthrow that engulfs also the world" (*The Presbyterian Guardian,* June 10, 1942).

Chapter III

THE KINGDOM PROPHECIES

Much of what we would say in refutation of Amillennialism has already been said in setting forth the postmillennial position and does not need to be repeated here. We must say, however, that we understand the Bible to teach very definitely that the world is to be converted to Christianity before Christ returns, and that the amillennial position, which makes no provision for a Christianized world, leaves a whole continent of prophecies unexplained, many of which then become quite meaningless. The kingdom prophecies of the Old Testament, as well as various statements in the Psalms and in the New Testament, often in highly figurative language, surely foretell a future golden age of some kind. We are bound to say that in this regard we agree with the Premillennialists, as against the Amillennialists, that there is to be a Millennium, that there is in fact yet something great in store for the human race before this world order ends. But since we believe that the premillennial notion of an earthly kingdom after the return of Christ is in error, we are convinced that these prophecies and promises must find fulfillment before that event. What shall we say, for instance, to the following?

Isaiah 2:2–4: "And it shall come to pass in the latter days, that the mountain of Jehovah's house shall be established on the top of the mountains, and shall be exalted above the hills; and all nations shall flow unto it. And many nations shall go and say, Come ye, and let us go up to the mountain of Jehovah, to the house of the God of Jacob; and he will teach us of his ways, and we will walk in his paths: for out of Zion shall go forth the law, and the word of Jehovah from Jerusalem. And he will judge between the nations, and will decide concerning many peoples; and they shall beat their swords into plowshares, and their spears into pruning hooks; nation shall not lift up sword against nation, neither shall they learn war any more."

Micah 4:1–5. Here the prophecy of Isaiah 2:2–4 is repeated in almost identical words, to which the prophet adds: "And they shall sit every man under his vine and under his fig-tree; and none shall make them afraid: for the mouth of Jehovah of hosts hath spoken it. For all the peoples walk every one in the name of his god; and we will walk in the name of Jehovah our God for ever and ever."

Here, in figurative language and under Old Testament terminology of Mount Zion and the house of Jehovah,—which was the only terminology that the people to whom this prophecy was given would have been able to understand—was predicted the world-wide conquest and dominion of the Church, a Christianized people, dwelling securely, free from the devastations of war, and doing righteously. In other places in Scripture the mountain of Jehovah's house is spiritualized to mean the Church. See particularly Hebrews 12:22, where, speaking of the Church it is said: "But ye are come unto mount Zion, and unto the city of the living God, the heavenly Jerusalem . . ." In Isaiah 2 we are taught that the Church is to be prominent, like a house on the top of a mountain, or like a mountain on a plain, and that its guidance will be sought willingly in all phases of human life—in the spiritual, social, economic and political realms. The statement that "all peoples shall flow unto it" must mean that people all over the world are to be Christian, and that they will seek to know God's will as it is made known to them through His Word. Their beating their swords into plowshares, and their spears into pruning hooks, is clearly figurative language, a figure appropriate for the time in which this prophecy was given, but to be fulfilled in a far distant age in which the nations would not spend their energies and substance in destructive wars,—"Nation shall not lift up sword against nation, neither shall they learn war any more." To "sit every man under his vine and under his fig tree" is again a figure appropriate to that day and age, a symbol of contented peaceful home life, pointing forward to a time of world-wide righteousness on which alone true peace can be based.

Isaiah 11:1–10: "And there shall come forth a shoot out of the stock of Jesse, and a branch out of his roots shall bear fruit. And the Spirit of Jehovah shall rest upon him, the spirit of wisdom and understanding, the spirit of counsel and might, the spirit of knowledge and of the fear of Jehovah. And his delight shall be in the fear of Jehovah; and he shall not judge after the sight of his eyes, neither decide after the hearing of his ears; but with righteousness shall he judge the poor, and decide with equity for the meek of the earth; and he shall smite the earth with the rod of his mouth; and with the breath of his lips shall he slay the wicked. And righteousness shall be the girdle of his waist, and faithfulness the girdle of his loins.

"And the wolf shall dwell with the lamb, and the leopard shall lie down with the kid; and the calf and the young lion and the fatling together; and a little child shall lead them. And the cow and the bear shall feed; their young ones shall lie down together; and the lion shall eat straw like the ox. And the sucking child shall play on the hole of the asp, and the weaned child shall put his hand on the adder's den. They shall not hurt nor destroy in all my holy mountain; for the earth shall be full of the knowledge of Jehovah, as the waters cover the sea.

"And it shall come to pass in that day, that the root of Jesse, that standeth for an ensign of the peoples, unto him shall the nations seek; and his resting place shall be glorious."

In Isaiah 11:9 the statement that "the earth shall be full of the knowledge of Jehovah, as the waters cover the sea," clearly foretells a time when righteousness shall be triumphant over all the earth. This fits perfectly into the postmillennial system. It does not fit into the amillennial system. Amillennialists take it to be a description of the final heavenly kingdom, and so place it after the resurrection and judgment. But there is no sufficient reason for assigning it to the heavenly kingdom except that it does not fit into their scheme of things for this world. Verses 1–5 are clearly a prediction of the coming Messiah. Verses 6–9 foretell the nature of the change that is to be wrought in Messiah's kingdom. Verse 10 is another Messianic prediction, declaring that the Messiah shall be "an ensign of the peoples," and that "unto him shall the nations seek." That clearly speaks of this world, not of the next. Isaiah 11:9 loses its force when taken in any other than a postmillennial sense. Similarly, swords and plowshares, and spears and pruning hooks, spoken of in Isaiah 2:4, cannot be thought of as having any place in heaven. This is, of course, figurative language. It foretells an age of peace, contentment and safety right here on this earth.

Isaiah 42:1–4: "Behold, my servant, whom I uphold; my chosen, in whom my soul delighteth: I have put my Spirit upon him; he will bring forth justice to the Gentiles. He will not cry, nor lift up his voice, nor cause it to be heard in the street. A bruised reed will he not break, and a dimly burning wick will he not quench: he will bring forth justice in truth. He will not fail nor be discouraged, till he have set justice in the earth; and the isles shall wait for his law."

Isaiah 65:17–25: "For, behold, I create a new heavens and a new earth; and the former things shall not be remembered, nor come into mind. But be ye glad and rejoice for ever in that which I create; for, behold, I create Jerusalem a rejoicing, and her people a joy. And I will rejoice in Jerusalem, and joy in my people; and there shall be heard in her no more the voice of weeping and the voice of crying. There shall be no more thence an infant of days, nor an old man that hath not filled his days; for the child shall die a hundred years old, and the sinner being a hundred years old shall be accursed. And they shall build houses, and inhabit them; and they shall plant vineyards, and eat the fruit of them. They shall not build, and another inhabit; they shall not plant, and another eat; for as the days of a tree shall be the days of my people, and my chosen shall long enjoy the work of their hands. They shall not labor in vain, nor bring forth for calamity; for they are the seed of the blessed of Jehovah, and their offspring with them. And it shall come to pass that, before they call, I will answer; and while they are yet speaking, I will hear. The wolf and the lamb shall feed together, and the lion shall eat straw like the ox; and dust shall be the serpent's food. They shall not hurt nor destroy in all my holy mountain, saith Jehovah."

Jeremiah 31:31–34: "Behold, the days come, saith Jehovah, that I will make a new covenant with the house of Israel, and with the house of Judah: not according to the covenant that I made with their fathers in the day that I took them by the hand to bring them out of the land of Egypt; which my covenant they brake, although I was a husband unto them, saith Jehovah. But this is the covenant that I will make with the house of Israel after those days, saith Jehovah: I will put my law in their inward parts, and in their heart will I write it; and I will be their God, and they shall be my people. And they shall teach no more every man his neighbor, and every man his brother, saying, Know Jehovah; for they shall all know me, from the least of them unto the greatest of them, saith Jehovah: for I will forgive their iniquity, and their sins will I remember no more."

Joel 2:28: "And it shall come to pass afterward, that I will pour out my Spirit upon all flesh."

Malachi 1:11: "And from the rising of the sun even unto the going down of the same my name shall be great among the Gentiles."

These are very great and precious promises, and certainly they point forward to conditions that have not yet been enjoyed on this earth. They are in fact so far-reaching and expansive that they stagger the imagination. Some amillennialists, finding no place in their system for these conditions, attempt to carry them over into the eternal state. But references to the "nations" (Is. 2:2,4); judging the people with righteousness (Is. 11:4); people dying at the age of one hundred years (Is. 65:20); etc., point unmistakably to this world. Of necessity much Old Testament prophecy, designed for fulfillment in an age that had not yet dawned, had to be given in figurative language. Had our present day terminology been used it would have been unintelligible to the people of that day. The "shoot out of the stock of Jesse," and "the root of Jesse that standeth for an ensign of the peoples" (Is. 11:1–10), quite clearly refer to the coming Messiah. "The mountain of Jehovah's house," "exalted above the hills," or Mount Zion, from which "shall go forth the law, and the word of Jehovah" to the nations (Is. 2:2–4), is the New Testament Church which, divinely established and as the custodian of the Gospel, is the true successor to Old Testament Israel. Today it is carrying the Gospel to all the world, and is exerting a marvelously great influence for good wherever it goes. Compare again (Heb. 12:22,23), "But ye are come [present tense, not future] unto mount Zion, and unto the city of the living God, the heavenly Jerusalem, and to innumerable host of angels, to the general assembly and church of the firstborn who are enrolled in heaven . . ." The wolf dwelling with the lamb, the leopard lying down with the kid, the young child putting its hand unhurt into the adder's den (Is. 11:6,8), evidently means that peoples and forces now hostile and antagonistic and at enmity with each other shall be converted and so changed by Christianity that they shall live and work together harmoniously in Messiah's kingdom. Messiah smiting the earth with the rod of His mouth, and slaying the wicked with the breath of His lips (Is. 11:4), is clearly parallel with Revelation 19:15,21, where the Rider of the white horse wins an overwhelming victory over all His enemies by means of the sword that proceeds out of His mouth. The words,"dust shall be the serpent's food," Is. 65:25, symbolizes the complete and ignominious defeat of Satan,—whose mouth would be mashed in the ground and filled with dust as his head was crushed under the heel of the Seed of the woman (Gen. 3:15); who was cast down to the earth (Rev. 12:9); all the enemies of Christ, and Satan foremost among them, are to be put under His feet (I Cor. 15:25); and, Paul writing to the Christians in Rome uses the same figure to describe either the victory of the Christian over sin or a particular triumph of the church in Rome over some evil persecuting force of that day when he says, "And the God of peace shall bruise Satan under your feet shortly" (Rom. 16:20). A similar statement is found in the Messianic 72nd Psalm, which describes Christ's conquest of the world: "And his enemies shall lick the dust," vs. 9.

Chapter IV

THE BINDING OF SATAN

The usual amillennial interpretation of Revelation 20:2 is that the "binding" of Satan took place at the first advent, and that it was accomplished when Christ triumphed over him at the cross. In other words, the atonement is said to have been the effective means for the binding of Satan, and on that basis the Millennium is said to have begun with the first advent and to continue until the second. The Scripture cited to prove this is Matthew 12:29: "How can one enter into the house of the strong man, and spoil his goods, except he first bind the strong man? and then he will spoil his house."

We believe, however, that while the satisfaction which Christ, acting as the sinner's substitute, made to Divine justice (which was the real substance of the atonement) was accomplished at that time, the binding of the Devil spoken of in Revelation 20:2 was not an event that was accomplished at any one particular time, but that it is a long, continuing action, now in process of accomplishment, and that while the Devil has been bound in some respects he has not yet been bound in others. The statement that he is to be bound and cast into the abyss so that he can no longer deceive the *nations,* teaches that this restraint is to be placed on him during the course of this present world, that is, during the Gospel age, while the nations still are in existence. It cannot relate to the intermediate state, as some say, nor to the eternal state, as others say, for in neither of those cases will the nations have any meaning. Furthermore, the angel who was to bind Satan was seen "coming down out of heaven," to the earth (Rev. 20:1). The Amillennialist cannot avail himself of the explanation given by the Premillennialist, that this restraint on Satan is to occur during the personal reign of Christ on earth, for he does not believe in such a reign. Nor is there much force in the usual amillennial explanation that since the first advent of Christ the Devil is bound in the sense that he can no longer prevent the proclamation of the Gospel to the nations and so hold them captive as he did in pre-Christian times. That explanation is too narrow and limited. Had that been the effect of the binding of Satan, there should have been no further resistance to the spread of the Gospel after the crucifixion of Christ. Once the atonement was made, it should have been possible to have carried the good news to all the nations without restraint. But we find instead that the Devil's resistance has continued very vigorously, and that even today, nineteen centuries later, some nations still remain almost completely closed, and that many others have received only a very inadequate and superficial witness.

The amillennial interpretation that the binding of Satan took place at the first advent of Christ seems rather far-fetched and unconvincing. It is open to the objection that if that is the meaning of the "binding" of Satan, then the "loosing" spoken of in Revelation 20:3,7, which is the opposite of binding, must mean the reversing of the work of Christ, that is, the annulment of the atonement, or at least a time when it becomes ineffective. But that is impossible even for a little time. We prefer to take Matthew 12:29 as a simple statement of the superiority of Christ over the Devil, and the casting out of the demon recorded in this same context as a proof of the Deity of Christ. In fact, God was as able in Old Testament times as in New Testament times to set free from the bondage of sin those whom He pleased and as many as He pleased. An atonement was necessary in order that sinners might be saved, but its future accomplishment was so sure that salvation was possible even before it was accomplished. The knowledge of salvation was extended to the nation of Israel, and multitudes were saved. Had God so willed he could have extended it to all other nations as well. Jonah was sent to preach to the city of Nineveh, and provision was made for any Gentiles who wished to join with Israel. The Devil had no inherent rights over mankind to begin with, nor any power to tempt or afflict or hold human souls in bondage except as God gave him permission. He was already a fallen creature and under condemnation for sin. Calvin rightly says that the Devil "cannot attempt anything but by the Divine will."

Furthermore, the satisfaction that Christ rendered by His suffering and death was not in any sense made to the Devil, but was made to satisfy Divine justice. The Devil had no right of ownership over human beings, but was from the beginning a usurper. The law that God Himself had established, on the basis of which He proposed to govern the universe, was that sin should be punished with suffering and death. Having made that law and proclaimed it to all intelligent creatures, He could not, after Adam sinned, merely pardon that sin without an atonement. His honor was at stake, and the law had to be enforced as He had said that it would be. The sinner must suffer—or if he is to be spared that suffering God Himself must take the sinner's place as his Substitute and pay that penalty Himself. Consequently, in taking the sinner's place before the Divine law and meeting its full demands in His own person, Christ was rendering satisfaction to Divine justice.

That the Devil was a defeated and conquered foe long before the work of Christ on the cross is shown by the apostle Peter when he says that "God spared not angels when they sinned, but cast them down to hell, and committed them to pits of darkness, to be reserved unto judgment" (II Peter 2:4). Consequently, the fallen angels, Satan included, had already been cast down to hell and committed to pits of darkness entirely apart from Christ's work of redemption for men. We must, therefore, reject the view that the binding of Satan referred to in Revelation 20:2 was accomplished by Christ's triumph over him at the cross. We hold rather that the binding of Satan is a process continuing through this dispensation as evil is more and more suppressed, as the world is more and more Christianized, and as there is therefore less and less occasion for God to use the Devil as an instrument in the punishing of sinners.

Chapter V

PARABLE OF THE
WHEAT AND THE TARES

The Scripture most generally referred to by Amillennialists as proof of their position is the Parable of the Wheat and the Tares (Matt. 13:24–30,36–43). Here it is pointed out that the two grow together until the harvest, which is the end of the world. This is taken to mean not only that good and evil continue to exist side by side, which is the real meaning of the parable, but that the proportion between the two remains practically constant as do the stalks in a field. Postmillennialists readily agree that as long as the world continues there will be some evil mixed with the good. Their view of a generally Christianized world does not mean that all individuals will become Christians nor that all evil will be eliminated. In a field of wheat and tares the same proportion does continue through the season, none of the wheat becoming tares, nor any of the tares becoming wheat. But as regards human beings, as one generation follows another, and even within each generation, there is constant change. In fact, theologically speaking, all the members of the human race come into this world as fallen creatures, that is, all are born "tares." But as the Gospel is proclaimed, and as the Holy Spirit does His work of regenerating souls, many, very many, are brought from the realm of darkness to the realm of light. Tares are constantly being transformed into wheat. What that proportion is, and how it varies from generation to generation, is a matter of God's own choosing. The way at least is open and, in view of the many promises of future blessing, we may expect to see an ever-increasing proportion of the world's inhabitants brought from sin to holiness. The biology of grace can effect a transmutation of the species that the biology of nature cannot. Indeed, the transfer of souls from a state of sin to a state of holiness is the primary purpose of this Gospel age. God is now "bringing many sons unto glory" (Heb. 2:10). The Great Commission that Christ gave to His Church is: "Go ye therefore, and make disciples of all the nations . . ." We are not merely to witness to, but to *make disciples* of, all the nations. And as that work is efficiently and effectively carried out first individuals and then nations are Christianized.

When Christ was on earth the proportion of wheat to tares was comparatively small. Through the years it has increased greatly. As the kingdom is carried forward and this process is continued there is no reason why the wheat should not become the overwhelmingly greater proportion. Christ has provided an atonement which is infinite in value—*sufficient* for the redemption of the entire world, *efficient* for as many as God sees fit to call to Himself. And since, as Paul tells us, this system of redemption was designed to show forth "the exceeding riches of his grace" (Eph. 2:7), we may expect that the final number of the redeemed will be incredibly large, in comparison with which that of the lost will be comparatively insignificant. In strong language the writer of the Epistle to the Hebrews tells us, "Since then the children are sharers in flesh and blood, he also himself in like manner partook of the same; that through death he might bring to naught him that had the power of death, that is, the Devil; and might deliver all them who through fear of death were all their lifetime subject to bondage" (Heb. 2:14,15). Mankind is now divided into two great classes, the *regenerate* and the *unregenerate;* and the Holy Spirit is constantly taking those whom He chooses from the unregenerate and making them regenerate.

Nor can the parable of the wheat and the tares be made to fit into the premillennial scheme, which holds that first all believers are transfigured and removed in the Rapture; for the Lord says, "In the time of harvest I will say to the reapers, Gather up *first the tares,* and bind them in bundles to burn them; but gather the wheat into my barn" (Matt. 13.30). If the evil are gathered first, as Christ says they are, where then can be found those hosts of evil ones over whom Christ is to rule with a rod of iron in the millennial Kingdom? The Scofield Bible attempts to escape this dilemma by saying that while the tares are gathered into bundles for burning, this does not imply immediate judgment, that the tares are set aside for burning but first the wheat is gathered into the barn (p. 1016). But surely this is an evasive explanation. A decisive answer to that is found in the words of Christ Himself in this same context: "The Son of man shall send forth his angels, and they shall gather out of his kingdom all things that cause stumbling, and then that do iniquity, and shall cast them into the furnace of fire: there shall be the weeping and the gnashing of teeth. *Then* shall the righteous shine forth as the sun in the kingdom of their Father" (Matt. 13:41–43)— a division which we believe is made only at the end of the world, at the time of the final judgment.

Chapter VI

FURTHER CONSIDERATIONS

The Parable of the Leaven and that of the Mustard Seed, which describe the Kingdom as beginning very small and growing until the whole lump is leavened, or until the little seed has become a tree (Matt. 13:31–33), teach quite clearly the expanding nature of the Kingdom. Amillennialism acknowledges that these parables teach that the Kingdom of God does make a great development in this world and that it exerts many and great uplifting influences. But it nullifies that to a considerable extent by its teaching that the kingdom of evil also makes a great development, that the two kingdoms have a parallel development, and that the relative strength between the two may remain approximately as it now is until the end. Nor is there any force in the premillennial objection that leaven always symbolizes evil and so cannot here have the meaning that we give it. For in this parable it is specifically said that *the kingdom of heaven* is like leaven. Concerning this general subject Dr. Snowden has well written:

"The leaven is especially suggestive of growth as it works its way from atom to atom through the meal until it pervades the whole mass. Because the parables of the Leaven and the Mustard Seed especially embarrass the premillenarian view that the kingdom of God is not to be gradually established as a growth by the spread of the gospel but is to be suddenly set up at the coming of Christ, some premillenarians hold that the leaven does not represent the kingdom, as the parable itself says it does, but the spirit of evil, as it does in some other Scripture passages; and that the birds in the mustard-tree are unclean birds of sin. But this interpretation is far-fetched and forced. Trench, who was a premillenarian, repudiates both of these perversions and points out that it is no more strange that leaven should in one passage of Scripture represent good and in another

131

evil than that a lion should in one place (Rev. 5:5) represent Christ and in another (I Peter 5:8) the Devil (*The Parables of Our Lord,* p. 113). 'Leaven here,' affirms Dr. G. Campbell Morgan, 'as everywhere else in Scripture, is a type not of good but of evil; and if you will carefully search your Bible, you will find that in no single instance is there variation from this principle' (*God's Methods With Man,* pp. 56, 57). Well, we did 'carefully search' our Bible, evidently more carefully than Dr. Morgan searched his, and found two 'variations from this principle'; 'With cakes of leavened bread he shall offer his oblation with the sacrifice of his peace-offerings' (Lev. 7:13); 'Ye shall bring out of your habitations two wave-loaves of two tenth parts of an ephah: they shall be of fine flour, they shall be baken of leaven, for first-fruits unto Jehovah' (Lev. 23:17). We may therefore dismiss the eccentric notion as unworthy of serious consideration. The point of all these four parables [he had earlier cited the parable of the Secret Growth of the Seed (Mark 4:26–29), and the parable of the Sower (Matt. 13:1–23)] is that the kingdom of heaven is a growth and not a cataclysm; it is an unfolding seed and not exploding dynamite" (*The Coming of the Lord,* pp. 73, 74).

Post- and Amillennialists agree that the final separation between the good and the bad comes at the end of the world. They further agree, in opposition to Premillennialists, that Christ's coming is in the most absolute sense a consummate coming, that all evangelistic effort then ceases, and that there is no place at all in the teaching of Scripture for a thousand year earthly Kingdom. They cite Romans 2:5–10, which declares that "in the day of wrath and revelation of the righteous judgment of God," Christ, to whom all judgment has been given (John 5:22,27), will, at His coming, "render to every man according to his works: to them that by patience in well-doing seek for glory and honor and incorruption, eternal life: but unto them that are factious, and obey not the truth, but obey unrighteousness, shall be wrath and indignation, tribulation and anguish, upon every soul of man that worketh evil, of the Jew first, and also of the Greek; but glory and honor and peace to every man that worketh good, to the Jew first, and also to the Greek." That, they believe, describes the great crisis at the end of the world as a closely unified event into which it is manifestly impossible to intrude an era of a thousand years between the coming of Christ and the final judgment.

A Scripture often quoted by both A- and Premillennialists against the postmillennial position is Matthew 24:37–39: "And as were the days of Noah, so shall be the coming of the Son of man. For as in those days which were before the flood they were eating and drinking, marrying and giving in marriage, until the day that Noah entered into the ark, and they knew not until the flood came, and took them all away; so shall be the coming of the Son of man." It is alleged that this verse teaches that when Christ returns the world is to be in a very bad state morally.

We would point out, however, that eating and drinking, marrying and giving in marriage, are not things that in themselves are morally wrong, and there is no reason why they should be understood here in a bad sense. They are the perfectly normal pursuits of everyday life. This Scripture teaches that in Noah's day the warnings had been given, life was proceeding as usual, and then, suddenly, destruction took them unawares. Those words were a warning to the people to whom Christ spoke, as they are a warning to us. Our time, too, may come very unexpectedly. We are to be ready at all times. Verse 42 makes this clear: "Watch therefore; for ye know not on what day your Lord cometh." That warning is appropriate whether it is understood as applying to the coming of the Lord for the individual at death, or His return at the end of the age. Christians as well as non-Christians need to be admonished to watch. There is no necessary implication here that the world is to grow progressively worse.

Historical perspective and simple observation of world conditions should make it clear to everyone that the world is getting better. If we compare conditions today with those that existed at the time of Christ we see that there has been marvelous progress. When we look back to that period what a picture of spiritual darkness and desolation we behold! The ignorance and superstition that abounded, particularly the abominations and vices that were practiced in connection with the pagan festivals, stagger the imagination. Slavery, polygamy, the low position accorded women and children, political oppression and poverty were commonplace. All the nations except Israel lived in heathen darkness, and even in Israel there was very limited spiritual knowledge, much oppression and wrong-doing and, compared with that which we enjoy, very primitive living conditions. Between that time and the present there has been great advance in every realm. Even in most of those nations where false religions still predominate, moral and social and economic conditions have been greatly improved through the indirect influence of Christianity. In practically every country a foundation has now been laid through economic contacts and an understanding of the language that should make possible a much greater extension of Christianity, an extension waiting only for the Church to claim those promises and resources that have been given to her for that purpose. Surely one must be very blind to progress and unappreciative of the benefits of Christian civilization to insist that life throughout the world today is not on an immeasurably higher plane than it was nineteen centuries ago.

While we hold that the world is becoming better, that does not mean that there is steady progress. Individual nations and the world at large have their periods of evangelical advance and recession. As in business and in economic development there are periods of prosperity and periods of depression. But over the long term there is progress. Look at a chart of our national income, for instance, or at a chart of the New York Stock Exchange covering the last fifty years. There are waves of advances, waves of declines, waves within waves, some sharp and pronounced, others small and of short duration. From the standpoint of the moment we cannot always judge accurately the direction of the economic trend. But over all there has been a great advance. And so it has been with the course of Christianity in the world. The Church made a great advance during the first three centuries of the Christian era, then followed a time of recession. Another great advance was made in Augustine's day, which in turn was followed by nearly a thousand years of stagnation known as the Dark Ages. Then came the glorious Protestant Reformation under Luther, Calvin, Zwingli and Knox, during which evangelical Christianity again came into its own and won whole nations. Later came the revival in England under Whitfield and Wesley, and in America a much greater advance in theological doctrine and in the relationship between Church and State. The world over the pagan religions quite clearly have had their day and are disintegrating. No one of them can meet the open competition of Christianity. Nor can any one of them stand up under the glaring light of present day science and education. Christianity is clearly the religion of the future. Admittedly Christians have not taken their religion as seriously nor practiced it as consistently as they should have. But theirs is *the* system of truth, the only one that through the ages has had God's blessing upon it. We may rest assured that in time it will emerge triumphant and rule the world.

Pre- and Amillennialists sometimes make the claim that the course of recent world history, particularly the events of World Wars I and II, disprove the postmillennial claim that the world is getting better. Prof. Hamilton, for instance, writing in 1942 while World War II was in progress, said:

"The events of the past thirty years have revealed the fallacy of such reasoning. World War I shattered the hopes of the advocates of peace through international cooperation, in the Hague Peace Conference. The failure of the League of Nations and the breaking of World War II, have given the final death blow to any hopes of the ushering in of an era of universal peace and joy through the interplay of forces now in action in the world" (*The Basis of Millennial Faith*, p. 33).

This type of criticism is found more often in premillennial books. In the first place, however, true Postmillennialism does not depend on Peace Conferences or Leagues of Nations or any other merely humanitarian forces to bring about a better world, but upon the effective proclamation of the Gospel and the regenerating power of the Holy Spirit to change individuals, which in turn does lead to higher moral and spiritual and social standards which are reflected throughout the whole range of life.

In the second place this type of criticism is based on too short a view of history. It seems largely blind to the progress that has been made in both Church and State. Moreover, it assumes that the end of the world will come in the comparatively near future, and that there is, therefore, but little time left in which the postmillennial system can come to fruition. But there is no substantial ground for assuming that the end is near. The world has continued for nearly 2,000 years since Christ came the first time. It may, for all we know, continue another 2,000 or 200,000 years. One thing that the Bible makes clear is that we do not know even approximately when the end is to come. Let us remember that in every generation there have been those who thought they saw signs which indicated that the end was near, signs which to them were just as convincing as any that are seen today. But they have all been mistaken. If the end is to be in the very remote future there is nothing in the Bible to contradict that. God works on a scale that is beyond our comprehension, and we must not be too anxious to limit Him as to the time that yet remains for this world.

Furthermore, as we look back over the course of history there are numerous periods which must have looked far more discouraging to the people of those days than the present looks to even the most pessimistic among us. To mention only a few: the period of persecution under the Roman emperors, the pillaging of the Roman Empire and the fall of Rome, the Mohammedan invasions of both eastern and western Europe, the Thirty Years' War in Germany, St. Bartholomew's Massacre and the almost complete extermination of the Protestants in France, the Inquisition in Spain and Italy, the French Revolution with all its cruelties, the horrors of the Napoleonic wars, etc. In each instance there was much suffering and much destruction of life and property. But after each disaster the Church rallied and reached new heights. Repeatedly the prophets of doom were proved to have been in error. We do not understand how anyone can take a long range view of history and deny that across the centuries there has been and continues to be great progress, and that the trend is definitely toward a better world. Let us not be in too much of a hurry. The postmillennial idea of a Christianized world has not yet been disproved. We are convinced that Bible students in general have been inclined to take too short a view of history and too ready to conclude that we are in the final stages of the Church age.

III.

Premillennialism

Chapter I

HISTORIC PREMILLENNIALISM

"PREMILLENNIALISM is that view of the Last Things which holds that the second coming of Christ will be followed by a period of world-wide peace and righteousness, before the end of the world, called 'the Millennium' or 'the Kingdom of God', during which Christ will reign as King in person on this earth. (Premillennialists are divided into various groups by their different views of the order of events associated with the second coming of Christ, but they all agree in holding that there will be a millennium on earth *after* the second coming of Christ but *before* the end of the world)" (Dr. J. G. Vos, *Blue Banner Faith and Life*, Jan.-March, 1951).

We propose to discuss first those beliefs which belong to the *essence* of Premillennialism as that system has been held by various scholars throughout most of the Church age, and then to discuss those distinctive beliefs that in large measure have come to characterize present day American Premillennialism, which in general is known as Dispensationalism.

Unfortunately Premillennialism has never developed an official creed, either in former generations or in present day discussion. A movement that has enlisted such a large following and which purports to set forth the divine plan in such detail surely should have an authoritative statement, not only for its own use but also that others at least may know what it teaches and what it does not teach. If such a statement were available there would be much less occasion for Premillennialists to complain that their system is so often misrepresented. As it is, we are forced to rely primarily on the statements of so-called "representative" Premillennialists or Dispensationalists, although these differ endlessly and sometimes violently among themselves. No doubt it is because of this difference of opinion that they never have been able to work out an authoritative statement. Consequently it is not always possible to set forth precisely what the system does teach. This lack of agreement proves that their detailed programs are after all not so certain and that they are in fact of rather doubtful value. In view of all the books and articles that have been written, the charts prepared, and the time spent in "prophetic conferences," it would seem that a fair degree of unity should have been achieved, and that some representative conference should have set these views down in authoritative statement.

The nearest thing approaching a creed is the set of Notes found in the *Scofield Reference Bible*. But this system differs considerably from Historic Premillennialism. It is known as "Dispensationalism" because it divides all history into seven dispensations or periods in which man is tested in regard to certain principles of obedience. It had its origin in the teachings of John N. Darby and some of his companions in the Plymouth Brethren group, in England, about 1830. It is, therefore, of comparatively recent date. The teachings of this school have long since ceased to have any important influence in England or on the continent of Europe, but they have been popularized in the United States by the writings of James H. Brookes, W. E. Blackstone, Arno C. Gaebelein, Lewis Sperry Chafer, and above all by the *Scofield Reference Bible*. These dispensational views have been just as vigorously opposed by other Premillennialists such as Alexander Reese, whom we take to be the best representative of Historic Premillennialism, and whose book, *The Approaching Advent of Christ* (1940), is a classic that should be read by everyone who wants to know the difference between Historic Premillennialism and Dispensationalism; also by Dean Alford, H. Grattan Guinness, Nathaniel West, Theodor Zahn, and more recently, George E. Ladd.

The chief passages in the New Testament to which Premillennialists appeal are: Matt. 24:3–44; Acts 3:19–21; I Cor. 15:20–28; I Thess. 4:13–18; and Rev. 20:1–10; and in the Old Testament: Isaiah 2:2–4; 11:1–11; 65:17–25; Ezekiel, chs. 40–48; Daniel 2:42–45; 7:23–25; 9:24–27; and Micah 4:1–8.

As regards the second coming of Christ the primary difference between Historic Premillennialism and Dispensationalism relates to the question whether or not the Church goes through the Tribulation, that is, whether the Rapture occurs at the beginning or at the close of the Tribulation. Historic Premillennialism holds that the Christians who constitute the Church go through the Tribulation and are exposed to its afflictions, at the end of which Christ comes with great power and glory to raise the righteous dead and to rapture the saints who are caught up to meet Him in the air but who almost immediately return with Him as He comes to destroy the forces of Antichrist in the battle of Armageddon and establish His Kingdom. Dispensationalism, on the other hand, holds that the Rapture occurs before the Tribulation, that Christ may come at any moment without warning signs, that at His coming the righteous dead are raised and that they together with the living saints are caught away in a secret Rapture to meet the Lord in the air, where they remain for a period of seven years. During that time the Antichrist rules on the earth and the dreadful woes spoken of in the Book of Revelation, chapters 4 through 19, fall on the inhabitants of the earth. Notice, according to this view, nothing in Revelation chapters 4 through 19 has yet been fulfilled; all of it belongs to the future, and will not even begin to happen until after the Rapture. One chief advantage of Historic Premillennialism is that it does not find it necessary to crowd all of these events into the short space of seven years as does Dispensationalism. At the end of that period Christ and the saints return to earth, Antichrist and his forces, who are persecuting the Jews and have them shut up in Jerusalem, will be destroyed in the battle of Armageddon, and the millennial Kingdom will be set up on the earth. The Jews are to be converted at the mere sight of their Messiah and, as the Lord's "brethren," are to have a very prominent and favored place in the Kingdom.

A further distinctive doctrine of Dispensationalism is that when Christ was on earth at the time of the first advent He offered the Kingdom to the Jews but they rejected it; it was then withdrawn until the time of His second coming, and the Church, an institution altogether new and not foreseen nor predicted by the Old Testament prophets, was established instead as a temporary substitute for the Kingdom. Dispensationalists are thus double "Pre-s"—Pre-tribulation Pre-millennialists, with the added distinctive tenets regarding the Church and the Jews.

The premillennial system is considerably more complicated

than either the post- or amillennial system and, consequently, it has also been attended with greater diversity of opinion among its advocates. But despite these differences it has been characteristic of both schools of Premillennialism to hold:

1. That the Kingdom of God is not now in the world, and that it will not be instituted until Christ returns.

2. That it is not the purpose of the present gospel age to convert the world to Christianity, but rather to preach the gospel as a witness to the nations and so to warn them of and make them justly subject to judgment; also to gather out of all nations God's elect, the Church saints.

3. That the world is growing worse and will continue to grow worse until Christ comes to establish His Kingdom.

4. That immediately preceding the return of Christ there is to be a period of general apostasy and wickedness.

5. That we are now in the latter stages of the Church age and that the return of Christ is near, probably to occur within the lifetime of the present generation.

6. That at Christ's coming the righteous dead of all ages are to be raised in the "first resurrection."

7. That the resurrected dead together with the transfigured living saints who are then on the earth are to be caught up to meet the Lord in the air.

8. That the judgment of all the righteous then takes place, which judgment consists primarily in the assignment of rewards.

9. That before and during the tribulation period the Jews are to be restored to the land of Palestine.

10. That at the mere sight of their Messiah the Jews are to turn to Him in a national conversion and true repentance.

11. That Christ at His coming destroys the Antichrist and all his forces in the battle of Armageddon.

12. That after the battle of Armageddon Christ establishes a world-wide Kingdom with Jerusalem as its capital, in which He and the resurrected and transfigured saints rule for a thousand years in righteousness, peace and prosperity.

13. That during this reign the city of Jerusalem and the temple are to be rebuilt, the feasts and fasts and the priesthood, ritual and sacrificial system reinstituted, though performed in a Christian spirit and by Christian worshippers.

14. That the golden age also is to be characterized by the removal of the curse from nature so that the desert shall blossom as the rose and the wild ferocious nature of the beasts shall be changed.

15. That during the Millennium great numbers of the Gentiles will turn to God and be incorporated into the Kingdom.

16. That while many remain unconverted and rebellious at heart they are not destroyed, but are held in check by the rod-of-iron rule of Christ.

17. That during the Millennium Satan is to be bound, cast into the abyss, and so shut away from the earth.

18. That at the close of the Millennium Satan is to be loosed for a short time.

19. That the Millennium is to be followed by a short but violent outbreak of wickedness and rebellion headed by Satan which all but overwhelms the saints and the holy city of Jerusalem.

20. That the forces of wickedness are to be destroyed by fire which is cast down upon them from heaven.

21. That the wicked dead of all ages are then to be raised in the "second resurrection," judged, and with the Devil and the wicked angels cast into hell.

22. That heaven and hell are then introduced in their fullness, with the new heavens and the new earth as the future home of the redeemed, which will constitute the eternal state.

Historic Premillennialism holds that the coming of Christ will be preceded by certain recognizable signs, such as the preaching of the Gospel to all the nations, the apostasy, wars, famines, earthquakes, the appearance of the Antichrist or Man of Sin, and the Great Tribulation. Many think that they see some of these signs at the present time. Dispensationalists, on the other hand, hold that there will be no further signs, all the prophecies relating to events before the coming of Christ having now been fulfilled, and that the return of Christ therefore may occur literally at "any moment"—even for the righteous their heavenward movement being the first indication they have that Christ has come.

Dispensationalism thus sets forth a secret coming of Christ *for* His saints, which they term the Rapture, and a visible coming of Christ seven years later *with* His saints, which they term the Revelation. It also holds that in addition to the judgment of individuals, which occurs in the sky following the Rapture, there is a judgment of nations, the "Sheep and Goats" judgment of Matthew 25:31–46, when Christ and the saints return to earth. The nations are then judged on the basis of the treatment they have accorded the Jews, the Lord's "brethren," during the Great Tribulation, the righteous nations entering the millennial Kingdom, while the evil nations are consigned to punishment.

The Jews are given a much more prominent place in the scheme of things in the dispensational system than in the historic premillennial system, some writers in the latter system treating the distinction between Jews and Gentiles as comparatively unimportant. Dispensationalism holds that the millennial Kingdom will be predominantly Jewish, with Christian Gentiles in a subordinate position, and the Gentile nations in effect vassals of the Jewish Kingdom in Palestine. Since the establishment of the nation of Israel in Palestine there is general agreement among dispensational writers that the Jews are to return to Palestine in unbelief and then be converted at the appearance of Christ. But in the past many have held that they would be converted and then return.

Historic Premillennialism holds that the entire New Testament is applicable to this age, while Dispensationalism holds that much of the Gospels, including particularly the Sermon on the Mount, was not designed for the Church age but is Israelitish or Kingdom truth and will find its primary application during the Kingdom age.

Within each group there are numerous further points of disagreement regarding details. There is, for instance, no agreement as to whether death befalls any of the believers during the Millennium, although it is agreed that it does befall unbelievers. There is no agreement as to the relationship that shall exist between the resurrected and transformed saints with glorified, resurrection bodies, and those who still are in the flesh, particularly those who are unbelievers. Many believe that the means to be used for the conversion of the world after the Rapture will be other than the preaching of the Gospel, e.g., the personal appearance of Christ, the great judgments that fall on the earth, etc.

It is not clear whether during the millennial reign the risen saints dwell on earth, or in heaven, or alternate between the two. There is also difference of opinion regarding the propagation of the race during the Millennium, the extent to which and the manner in which sin will be suppressed or controlled, whether the Jews only or the whole Church will reign with Christ during the Millennium, and many other points in this highly complicated theory.

As we attempt to understand the premillennial system, particularly as it is set forth in Dispensationalism, it is not without some misgivings that we grope our way through a bewildering maze of dispensations, covenants, second comings, resurrections, judgments, etc. Present day Dispensationalism, which is the popular form in the United States, sets forth seven dispensations; eight covenants (the Edenic covenant before the fall, and after the fall one each with Adam, Noah, Abraham, **Moses, and David**), the Palestinian covenant (Deut. 30), and the New Covenant instituted by Christ (*Scofield Bible*, p. 6); two second comings (a coming of Christ *for* His people at the Rapture, and a coming *with* His people seven years later at the Revelation); at least three and perhaps four resurrections (the resurrection of the righteous dead at the Rapture, a resurrection of the martyrs who died during the Great Tribulation which occurs at the Revelation, a resurrection of the wicked dead at the end of the Millennium, and a resurrection of the righteous who die during the Millennium if such there be); and from four to seven judgments (the judgment of the righteous immediately following the Rapture, the "sheep and goats" judgment of the nations at the Revelation, the judgment of the wicked at the end of the millennium, and a judgment of angels,—presumably also a judgment of the righteous who live during the Millennium. Scofield adds a judgment of the believer's sins at the cross in the person of Christ, a judgment of self in the believer (conscience), and a judgment of Israel).

A second Rapture also will be needed for the righteous who are alive at the end of the Millennium, in order that their earthly bodies may be changed. Even this does not exhaust the possibilities of the system, for according to some there will be two eternally separate peoples of God, the Church permanently in heaven and Israel permanently on the earth. The Bible is written in language that ordinary people can understand, but this intricate, complex, imaginative system presents an interpretation that surely never would have been thought of except in defense of a theory. How refreshing to turn back to the straightforward postmillennial system, which teaches one second coming, one Rapture, one general and universal resurrection, one general and universal judgment, and one unified people of God inhabiting the new heavens and the new earth!

In the study of Eschatology there are two extremes that we should try to avoid—on the one hand the uncritical, credulous type of mind that accepts these things without adequate evidence as to their truth or falsity; and on the other the rationalistic type of mind that rejects this or any other system which gives a prominent place to the supernatural. David Brown has analyzed this problem well in the following paragraphs. He says:

"There are certain types of mind which, either from constitutional temperament, or the peculiar school of theology to which they are attached, have tendencies in the direction of premillennialism so strong, that they are ready to embrace it almost immediately, with love, souls that burn with love for Christ—who with the mother of Sisera, cry through the lattice, 'Why is his chariot so long in coming? Why tarry the wheels of his chariot?'" These people he refers to as "honest and warm-hearted," sincerely looking for Christ's return.

"There are next," he says, "the curious and restless spirits who feed upon the future. They are in their very element when settling the order in which the events shall occur, separating the felicities of the kingdom into its terrestrial and celestial departments respectively, sorting the multiplied particulars relating to the Ezekiel and Apocalyptic cities—and such like studies. For such minds, whose appetite for the marvelous is the predominant feature of their mental character, and who live in a sort of unreal world—for these, the confused and shadowy grandeur of a kingdom of glory upon earth, with all that relates to its introduction, its establishment, its administration, and its connection with the final and unchanging state, opens up a subject of surpassing interest and reveling delight—the very good which their peculiar temperament craves and feeds on.

"And, to mention no more, there are those who seem to have

a constitutional tendency to materialize the objects of faith, and can scarcely conceive of them save as more or less implicated with this terrestrial platform. Such minds, it is superfluous to observe, will have a natural affinity with a system which brings the glory of the resurrection-state into immediate and active communion with sublunary affairs, and represents the reign of those who neither marry nor are given in marriage, but are as the angels of God in heaven, as consisting in a mysterious rule over men in the flesh, who eat and drink, buy and sell, plant and build, marry wives, and are given in marriage. To set about proving to persons of this cast of mind that Premillennialism will not stand the test of Scripture, is like attempting to rob them of a jewel, or to pluck the sun out of the heavens. To such minds, any other view of the subject is perfectly bald and repulsive, while theirs is enriched with a glory that excelleth. To them it carries the force of intuitive perception; they *feel*—they *know* it to be true."

On the other hand Brown warns against an unreasonable, anti-premillennial tendency on the part of those who do not have the patience to make a careful exegetical investigation into the real meaning of the text, particularly the type that tends to tone down the supernatural element in the Scriptures. "Such minds," he says, "turn away from Premillennialism just as instinctively as the others are attracted to it. The bare statement of its principles carries to their minds its own refutation—not so much from its preconceived unscripturalness as from the absurdity which it seems to carry on the face of it. They have hardly patience to listen to it. It requires an effort to sit without a smile under a grave exposition and defense of it. If they undertake to refute it, it is a task the irksomeness of which they are unable to conceal, and their unfitness for which can scarcely fail to appear. Let us try to avoid both extremes, investigating reverently the mind of the Spirit" (*The Second Advent*, pp. 8, 9).

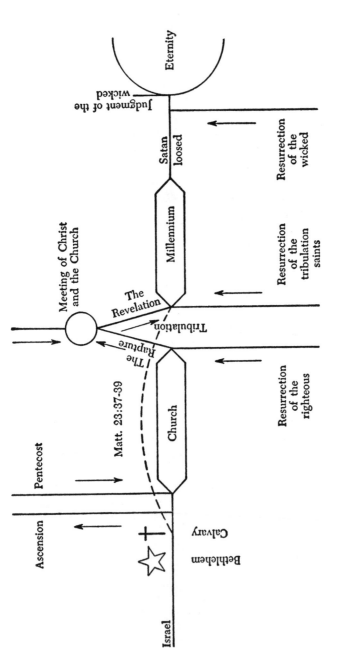

The above diagram, taken with slight modification from William E. Blackstone's book, *Jesus Is Coming* (page 72), should help to fix more clearly in mind the order of events according to the Dispensational scheme. Five of the dispensations run their course before Pentecost: Innocence, Conscience, Human Government, Promise, and Law. Grace continues through the Church Age, Kingdom during the Millennium. A similar chart for Historic Premillennialism would differ only in that the Tribulation would be included in the Church Age, there would be but one resurrection of the righteous, and the Rapture or meeting of Christ and the saints in the air would be followed almost immediately by the return of Christ with the saints to establish the millennial kingdom on earth.

Chapter II

DISPENSATIONALISM

The Seven Dispensations

Earlier in this work we have cited the definition of Dispensationalism given by Dr. J. G. Vos, which is as follows:

"Dispensationalism is that false system of Bible interpretation represented by the writings of J. N. Darby and the Scofield Reference Bible, which divides the history of mankind into seven distinct periods or 'dispensations,' and affirms that in each period God deals with the human race on the basis of some one specific principle. (Dispensationalism denies the spiritual identity of Israel and the Church, and tends to set 'grace' and 'law' against each other as mutually exclusive principles.)"

Dr. Scofield says that, "A dispensation is a period of time during which man is tested in respect to obedience to some *specific* revelation of the will of God" (p. 5).

The dispensations are said to be seven in number. In each succeeding dispensation there is a radical change of character and governing principles so that God deals with man on a plan different from that of any preceding dispensation. Each is thus complete and sufficient in itself and is not to be confused with the principle operative in any preceding dispensation.

No Scripture proof is given for the number seven. Why the number should be set at seven is difficult to understand, unless it be that seven is the Biblical number often used to express the idea of perfection and completeness. We must say, however, that the number is wholly fanciful and arbitrary, and that one could argue just as plausibly for other dispensations, or combine some of these.

According to the Scofield Bible the dispensations are as follows:

1. Innocence—the period in Eden, from the creation of Adam and Eve until the Fall.
2. Conscience—from the Fall until the Flood. Conscience is defined as the knowledge of right and wrong, and in this period it became man's guide. No Scripture proof is given to show why this period as contrasted with the others should be characterized as pre-eminently that of Conscience.
3. Human Government—from the Flood until the call of Abraham. Again no reason is given, nor is any apparent, for this designation. If this term had been applied to the time of Moses there would have been at least an apparent reason, for at that time much of the civil and religious life of Israel was placed under human administrators.
4. Promise—from the call of Abraham to the giving of the Law on Mount Sinai. Special promises were given at this time to Abraham, Isaac, Jacob and Moses; but these were essentially the same as the all-embracing promise of redemption given in Gen. 3:15 immediately after the Fall.
5. Law—from the giving of the Law on Mount Sinai through most of the public ministry of Christ. The Gospels are assigned primarily to the era of Law rather than that of Grace, despite the fact that Christ said, "The law and the prophets were until John," Luke 16:16; and John wrote, "For the law was given through Moses; grace and truth came through Jesus Christ" (John 1:17).
6. Grace—from the closing days of the public ministry of Christ until the Second Coming. This is the period of the Church. It is free from Law as a means of salvation, and lives exclusively in the realm of Grace.
7. Kingdom—the Millennium, a one thousand year period, from the return of Christ until the end of His reign on earth.

It is interesting to compare with this the system worked out by Blackstone in *Jesus Is Coming* (chart p. 225). Briefly it is as follows:

1. Innocence—from Eden to the Expulsion.
2. Freedom—from the Expulsion to the Flood, 1655 years.
3. Government—from the Flood to Sodom, 431 years.
4. Pilgrim—from Sodom to the Red Sea, 427 years.

5. Israel—from the Red Sea to the Ascension, 1491 years.
6. Mystery—the Church Age, from the Descent of the Holy Spirit at Pentecost to the Rapture (already over nineteen centuries).
7. Manifestation—the kingdom, from the Descent of Christ at the "Revelation," 1000 years, to be followed by the New Heavens and the New Earth.

It is significant that these systems, worked out by two of the leading advocates of Dispensationalism, differ in considerable detail. Not all Dispensationalists are agreed on the number of dispensations. Some list only four. Others list as many as eight. But due to the popularity of the Scofield Bible seven is the number most generally accepted. This difference of opinion regarding the number, and the difference in time as to when they begin and end, is good evidence that the system does not have solid Scriptural support, that it is in fact only a speculative theory.

This division of history into dispensations is felt by non-dispensationalists to be quite arbitrary and without Scriptural support. The titles are to be criticized as particularly inappropriate since five of the seven as outlined by Scofield—Conscience, Human Government, Promise, Law, and Grace—characterize every age of human history. Five of these are past, having had their fulfillment in the Old Testament period. We are now in the sixth, that of Grace. The seventh, Kingdom, is to follow during the Millennium. Extreme Dispensationalists say that the Sermon on the Mount and most of the Gospels belong to the Kingdom. The Book of Revelation after the third chapter also is said to belong to the future. Thus only part of the Gospels and the Pauline Epistles are said to be intended for the Christian of today.

The distinctive feature of this system is that each dispensation represents a different principle in God's dealings with men. The dispensations are regarded not as stages in one single organic development, but as distinct and mutually exclusive, or even as opposed to each other. In each there is a new revelation of God's will, and in each God tests man's obedience in a new and different way. God starts each dispensation out all right, and man is thus given repeated opportunities to solve his problems of sin and government. But in each dispensation he fails to meet the test, and each ends in moral bankruptcy and in a judgment. God intervenes only when man has proved himself unequal to the task.

To appeal to Augustine's words, "Distinguish the ages, and the Scriptures harmonize," to justify Dispensationalism, as Scofield does (p. iii), is entirely unwarranted, for the simple reason that Augustine knew nothing of such divisions as are set forth in this system. Nor was Augustine a Premillennialist in the first place. He was in fact strongly opposed to that system.

The importance which Dispensationalists attach to these divisions is set forth by George D. Beckwith when he says:

"To study the Bible dispensationally is all-important, if one would learn how to divide aright the Word of Truth. [Scofield also uses this expression]. God's plan of redemption in the Bible cannot be fully understood except through an understanding of these dispensations" (*God's Prophetic Plan*, p. 22).

We are reminded, however, of the words of Dr. Allis, who says:

"The slogan of Dispensationalists, 'rightly dividing the word of truth,' is itself a misinterpretation. This exhortation does not mean to divide up Scripture into dispensations and set each one at variance with the others, but so to interpret it that by a study of each and every part, the glorious unity and harmony of the whole shall be exhibited and the correctness of the exposition of the one part be established by its perfect agreement with every other part of Scripture as the God-inspired word" (*The Evangelical Quarterly*, London, Jan. 1936). And Dr. Murray says that dividing the plan of salvation into dispensations "Is not 'rightly dividing the word of truth,' but wrongly dividing the Word of God."

This practice of dividing the Bible into parts, and setting one part over against the others, means, for instance, that in the dispensation of law there was no grace, and that during the dispensation of grace there is no law. Dr. Scofield says that during the dispensation of promise, Abraham and his descendants were under a covenant of grace, but that "Israel rashly accepted the law . . . At Sinai they exchanged grace for law" (*Scofield Bible*, p. 20). The inference is that under law they *became righteous* by doing righteously, while under grace we are declared to be righteous because of the righteousness of Christ imputed to us.

Scofield does not actually say that the Jews were saved by their own good works in obeying the law of God, but that is implied in the sharp contrast between the covenant of law and that of grace, and the exchange of the one for the other.

The plan of salvation as set forth in the Bible is one organic whole, revealing a marvelous and profound unity. It cannot be split up into contradictory parts, much less into seven mutually exclusive dispensations. Dr. William Masselink properly says: "There is but one mediator for the New Testament as for the Old. There is no other name given under heaven whereby we must be saved than the name of Jesus, and neither is there any other foundation laid. The way of the Cross leads home, in the Old Testament as well as in the New. This is told us in the sacrifices and symbols of the Old Testament as well as in the New Testament fulfillment" (*Why Thousand Years?* p. 67).

To say that the Mosaic dispensation was a dispensation under law from which grace was excluded is clearly erroneous. Rather, in the Mosaic dispensation the outward emphasis was upon law, but that was designed to serve a two-fold purpose, namely, that the law might serve as a guide and rule of life in showing the Israelites what was right, and that by showing them how utterly impossible it was for them to earn salvation by a perfect keeping of the law they should be convinced of the need of a Saviour. In other words, as Paul expresses it, the law was a tutor to bring them to Christ (Gal. 3:24). Ever since the first promise of salvation, the Protevangelium, given in Genesis 3:15, salvation has been by grace, not by works. The law in itself was a means of grace, designed to show how far short all human righteousness fell, and so to point the worshippers to One who would provide righteousness for them. Through the blood sacrifice, in which the life of an innocent and faultless victim was substituted for that of the sinner, it served as a means to educate them concerning the future atonement that would be provided for sins. Hence the Mosaic dispensation of law and the Gospel dispensation of grace are not mutually exclusive or contradictory, but supplementary, each a part of one unified system revealed throughout the Bible.

Dr. Berkhof points out that there are serious objections to the dispensational view and lists the following:

"(a) The word 'dispensation' (*oikonomia*), which is a Scriptural term (cf. Luke 16:2–4; I Cor. 9:17; Eph. 1:10; 3:2,9; Col. 1:25; I Tim. 1:4) is here used in an un-Scriptural sense. It denotes a stewardship, an arrangement, or an administration, but never a testing time or a time of probation.

"(b) The distinctions are clearly arbitrary. This is evident already from the fact that dispensationalists themselves sometimes speak of them as overlapping. The second dispensation is called the dispensation of conscience, but according to Paul conscience was still the monitor of the Gentiles in his day (Rom. 2:14,15). The third is known as the dispensation of human government, but the specific command in it which was disobeyed and therefore rendered man liable to judgment, was not the command to rule the world for God—of which there is no trace—but the command to replenish the earth. The fourth is designated the dispensation of promise and is supposed to terminate with the giving of the law, but Paul says that the law did not disannul the promise, and that this was still in effect in his own day (Rom. 4:13–17; Gal. 3:15–29). The so-called dispensation of the law is replete with glorious promises, and the so-called dispensation of grace did not abrogate the law as a rule of life . . .

"(c) According to the usual representation of this theory man is on probation right along. He failed in the first test and thus missed the reward of eternal life, but God was compassionate and in mercy gave him a new trial. Repeated failures led to repeated manifestations of the mercy of God in the introduction of new trials, which, however, kept man on probation all the time . . . This representation is contrary to Scripture, which does not represent fallen man as still on probation, but as an utter failure, totally unable to render obedience to God, and as absolutely dependent on the grace of God for salvation.

"(d) This theory is also divisive in tendency, dismembering the organism of Scripture with disastrous results. Those parts of Scripture that belong to any one of the dispensations are addressed to, and have normative significance for, the people of that dispensation, and for no one else . . . The Bible is divided into two books, the Book of the kingdom, comprising the Old Testament and part of the New, addressed to Israel; and the Book of the Church, consisting of the remainder of the New Testament, addressed to us. Since the dispensations do not intermingle, it follows that in the dispensation of the law there is no revelation of the grace of God, and in the dispensation of grace there is no revelation of the law as binding on the New Testament people of God. If space permitted, it would not be difficult to prove that this is an entirely untenable position" (*Systematic Theology*, pp. 290, 291).

Instead of setting forth God's dealings with man under seven dispensations, the Bible sets forth two covenants,—the Covenant of Works, and the Covenant of Grace. It then divides the Covenant of Grace into two dispensations or administrations, (1) that of the Old Testament, and (2) that of the New Testament.

In the Covenant of Works Adam, in the Garden of Eden, was placed under a test of pure obedience to God's command. If he had been obedient he would have gained eternal life for himself and for all his posterity since he acted in a representative capacity. This test, however, ended in disobedience and brought eternal death to him and his posterity except as God's grace intervened to provide redemption.

The Old Testament dispensation was the first stage of the process by which God proposed to redeem man from sin through a Saviour. This, all of it after the Fall in the Garden of Eden, belonged to the Covenant of Grace. It looked forward to a future atonement and was based largely on promises given to the patriarchs, the keeping of the law of Moses, and on rituals and sacrifices which had no real value in themselves but which foretold the coming of the Messiah. The law was a constant reminder of the demands of the Covenant of Works, which was perfect obedience, and was designed to teach man the hopelessness of trying to earn salvation by good works. Through this period salvation was limited to God's chosen race, the Israelites, and to individuals who were brought into this group. During the Old Testament dispensation the Covenant of Grace was revealed in four stages:

(1) The **sentence on the serpent (Gen. 3:15)**: "I will put enmity between thee and the woman, and between thy seed and her seed: he shall bruise thy head, and thou shalt bruise his heel." Here in the curse pronounced upon Satan there is found an indirect promise of redemption for man. There is no formal covenant, but God places Himself on the side of man in the

struggle with Satan. That redemption would be costly and painful, as was symbolized by the bruising of the heel of the woman's seed; but it would mean total defeat for Satan, as was symbolized by the crushing of the head of the serpent. This is generally recognized as the first Messianic prophecy. (2) The Covenant with Noah (Gen. 8:20–9:17). In Genesis 9:9 we read: "And I, behold, I establish my covenant with you, and with your seed after you . . ." In this covenant God promises that He will not again destroy the earth with a flood, and that the regular succession of seedtime and harvest, cold and heat, summer and winter, day and night, shall not cease. (3) The Covenant with Abraham (Gen. 12:1–3). Here we read: "Now Jehovah said unto Abraham, Get thee out of thy country, and from thy kindred, and from thy father's house, unto the land that I will show thee: and I will make of thee a great nation, and I will bless thee, and make thy name great; and be thou a blessing: and I will bless them that bless thee, and him that curseth thee will I curse: and in thee shall all the families of the earth be blessed." Abraham and his family are set aside as a definitely marked body of believers, with the promise that in him and his seed all the families of the earth shall be blessed. This has been called by some "the beginning of an institutional Church." (4) The Sinaitic Covenant. This was a national covenant, made with all of the descendants of Jacob who had come out of Egypt. Church and State were so closely linked that they could not be separated. Membership in the one automatically meant membership in the other. An elaborate body of moral, civil and religious laws was given. As Berkhof says concerning this covenant: "A separate priesthood was instituted, and a *continuous* preaching of the gospel in symbols and types was introduced. These symbols and types appear under two different aspects: as the demands of God imposed on the people; and as a divine message of salvation to the people. The Jews lost sight of the latter aspect, and fixed their attention exclusively on the former. They regarded the covenant ever increasingly, but mistakenly, as a covenant of works, and saw in the symbols and types a mere appendage to this" (*Systematic Theology*, p. 298). While there were many legal aspects to this covenant, it was definitely not a "covenant of works" through which Israel might merit life by keeping the law. Scofield is in error when, in accordance with his assignment of this period to the dispensation of Law, he speaks of this as a "conditional Mosaic covenant of works" (p. 95), in which the test was legal obedience as the condition of salvation. God's purpose, however, was not that Israel should merit salvation by keeping the law. That had become impossible since the fall. Rather it showed the Israelites their inability to keep the law as God had demanded.

The New Testament Covenant of Grace, or the New Testament Dispensation, is that in which we now are. The Messiah has now come, and through His suffering and death has paid the price for man's redemption so that God now deals with men on the basis of an accomplished atonement. All that remains now is to apply that atonement in the salvation of individual souls. The distinction between Jew and Gentile has been broken down, never to be re-established since the condition which prompted that distinction in the first place is never to be re-established. The dispensational idea of a Jewish remnant which does not accept Christ as Messiah but which during the Tribulation preaches another gospel, that of the "kingdom," is false and comes under Paul's condemnation in Galatians 1:8: "But though we, or an angel from heaven, should preach unto you any gospel other than that which we preached unto you, let him be anathema." This dispensation continues until the second coming of Christ, which is followed immediately by the general resurrection and the general judgment and the introduction of the eternal state.

Thus in all ages God's dealings with men have been through a covenant relationship. The word "covenant" occurs many times in both the Old and the New Testament, and the religion of the Bible is better described as a covenant religion, not a religion of dispensations as set forth in present day Dispensationalism. Adam in the Garden of Eden was in covenant relationship with God, in a Covenant of Works, and was on test not merely for himself but as the federal head and representative of all his posterity, that is, for all humanity. But that covenant was speedily broken. It was followed by the Covenant of Grace. "Salvation by a covenant!" says Dr. Masselink, "The thought is charming for we were lost by a covenant. Father Adam represented the whole human race in the Covenant of Works. Had Adam kept the covenant he and all his children would have been blessed. Alas, our foundation was too frail. Adam fell and the whole human race fell with him. Some have inquired, 'Is it just?' Do not raise the question for it is the only way of Redemption. The devils [evil spirits] when they fell, fell each one for himself, and so they could never rise again; but we fell by our representative. Here then was the way to restore us again. As we sinned representatively, it was also possible for us to satisfy the law by a representative. Here was the opening for the way of salvation! By a second covenant head man can be redeemed, and therefore Jesus Christ comes as the second Adam and God makes the covenant with Him. O, matchless mystery of Divine love and mercy!" (*Why Thousand Years?* p. 46).

It is important to keep in mind that Premillennialism and Dispensationalism are not synonymous terms. Premillennialism is the broader term, and includes all those who believe that Christ returns *before* the millennium and that He will rule personally on earth for a thousand years. Dispensationalism on the other hand includes only those Premillennialists who follow Darby and Scofield in dividing the divine plan into dispensations during each of which God deals with the human race on the basis of some specific principle. Thus all Dispensationalists are Premillennialists, but not all Premillennialists are Dispensationalists. At the present time, however, the great majority of Premillennialists, particularly in the United States, are Dispensationalists. Most of the Bible institutes, as well as the minority of theological seminaries that teach Premillennialism, are dispensational. There is a logical connection between Premillennialism and Dispensationalism. Most of those who take Premillennialism seriously and become enthusiastic about it go on to adopt Dispensationalism. But, conversely, we believe that most of those who become convinced of the errors of Dispensationalism proceed to throw Premillennialism overboard too.

Chapter III

THE RAPTURE

The best definition of the Rapture that we have found is that given by Dr. Robert Strong, who says:

"By the Rapture is meant the sudden and possibly secret coming of Christ in the air to catch away from the earth the resurrected bodies of those who have died in the faith and with them the living saints" (*The Presbyterian Guardian.* Feb. 25, 1942).

The word "Rapture," like the word "Trinity," is not found in the Bible, but the idea that it expresses is clearly taught in two of Paul's epistles. In I Thessalonians 4:13-17 we read:

"But we would not have you ignorant, brethren, concerning them that fall asleep; that ye sorrow not, even as the rest, who have no hope. For if we believe that Jesus died and rose again, even so them also that are fallen asleep in Jesus will God bring with him. For this we say unto you by the word of the Lord, that we that are alive, that are left unto the coming of the Lord, shall in no wise precede them that are fallen asleep. For the Lord himself shall descend from heaven with a shout, with the voice of the archangel, and with the trump of God: and the dead in Christ shall rise first; then we that are alive, that are left, shall together with them be caught up in the clouds, to meet the Lord in the air: and so shall we ever be with the Lord."

And in I Corinthians 15:51-53 we read:

"Behold, I tell you a mystery: we all shall not sleep, but we shall all be changed, in a moment, in the twinkling of an eye, at the last trump; for the trumpet shall sound, and the dead shall be raised incorruptible, and we shall be changed. For this corruptible must put on incorruption, and this mortal must put on immortality."

Here we are told that as regards the saints two great miracles are to occur at the Lord's coming,—first, that the dead in Christ are to rise; and, second, that the living saints are to be changed, transformed, transfigured, "in a moment, in the twinkling of an eye," so that they do not go through the process of death; and then both groups together are to be caught up to meet the Lord in the air. Notice that it is not the Rapture, not the taking away of the saints, but *the translation of the living saints* that is to be accomplished suddenly,—"we all shall not sleep, but we shall all be changed, in a moment, in the twinkling of an eye."

And how marvelously magnificent that change shall be! When Christ shall appear, we shall be like Him, remade in His heavenly image and His celestial likeness! "When Christ, who is our life, shall be manifested, then shall ye also with him be manifested in glory" (Col. 3:4).

Thus one generation of believers is to be taken out of the world without dying. In all human history, so far as the record goes, only two persons have been taken out of the world in that manner. Concerning Enoch we read: "And Enoch walked with God: and he was not; for God took him," Gen. 5:24; and in Heb. 11:5: "By faith Enoch was translated that he should not see death; and he was not found, because God translated him." And regarding Elijah we read: "Behold, there appeared a chariot of fire, and horses of fire, which parted them [Elijah and Elisha] both asunder; and Elijah went up by a whirlwind into heaven" (II Kings 2:11).

Historic Premillennialism holds that there is to be but one return of Christ, that is, but one "second coming," and that this occurs immediately before the establishment of the millennial Kingdom. It differs from Dispensationalism in that it holds that the Church is to go through the Tribulation, which it believes is foretold in Matthew 24. It holds that the return of Christ will be heralded by certain signs, such as wars and unrest among nations, an apostasy from the faith (some think that the present wave of Modernism in the Church fulfills that condition), the return of the Jews to Palestine, and the appearance of the Antichrist. It holds further that the Tribulation is to be of indeterminate, although of comparatively short, duration. At the end of that period the saints, both the living and the dead, are to be caught up to meet the Lord in the air, and almost immediately thereafter Christ and His people return to the earth for the millennial reign. This was standard premillennial doctrine until the rise of the Plymouth Brethren movement, in England, under the leadership of John N. Darby.

Post- and Amillennialists too believe that the Rapture comes at the end of the present world order, although Postmillennialists believe that it is preceded by the Millennium, while Amillennialists believe there is to be no Millennium in the usual sense of the term, some holding that the term relates to the entire Church age, while others hold that it relates to the intermediate state.

Dispensationalists, on the other hand, hold that the Rapture occurs before the Tribulation, that the Church therefore does not go through the Tribulation, that Christ's coming is without further signs and literally may occur "at any moment," and that following the Rapture Christ and His people are to be in the air for a period of seven years (the seventieth week of Daniel's prophecy) while the Tribulation is in progress on the earth. Dispensationalism further holds that while the saints are with Christ in the air during this period there occurs the judgment of the saints, which consists primarily in the assignment of rewards, and the marriage feast of the Lamb. At the end of this seven year period Christ and the saints return to the earth, and the millennial kingdom is instituted. Thus the first resurrection, the Rapture, and the first judgment take place more than a thousand years before the end of the world.

Dispensationalism splits the second coming of Christ into two parts, the Rapture, which is His coming for the saints, and the Revelation, which is His coming with the saints, this latter being also His coming for Israel and the world. It holds that no predicted event remains to be fulfilled before it occurs. Not even those to be raptured are to have any further sign or indication that the event is near. "Nothing is given us in Scripture so definite as to form a sign of or date for the Rapture," says Blackstone. And then he adds: "We are to be always watching and waiting for it, and expecting it at any moment" (*Jesus Is Coming*, p. 207).

According to the dispensational theory Christ comes only part way to the earth at this time, and so is not seen by unbelievers who are left. Rev. Jesse F. Silver, another dispensational writer, says: "Quickly and invisibly, unperceived by the world, the Lord will come as a thief in the night and catch away His waiting saints" (*The Lord's Return*, p. 260). Thus all will be silent, secret, mysterious. According to the Scofield Bible the saints of both the Old and New Testament are included (p. 1228).

However, there seems to be an inconsistency at this point in the dispensational theory, for while in most cases they are so careful to distinguish between Jews and Gentiles and to keep them separate, here they have the Old Testament saints, the great majority of whom are Jews, rising at the time of the Rapture with the Church saints, the large majority of whom are Gentiles. On the other hand, the Revelation, or Christ's coming at the end of the tribulation period, is said to be for the Jews, as well as for the Gentile nations. According to the Dispensationalists the Church did not even exist during Old Testament times. The question arises, therefore, How can those Jews, long after their death, be incorporated into the Church to which they never belonged?

Another inconsistency appears in connection with the removal of the Church at that particular time. In Revelation 21:9 the Church is declared to be "the bride, the wife of the Lamb." Dispensationalists say that the removal of the Church at the time of the Rapture is for the purpose of being united with Christ in the wedding of the Lamb. Yet they admit that the number of the saved will not be complete until the end of the Millennium. Hence the wedding occurs before the bride is complete. Some members of the Church evidently will miss their own wedding! Surely this is a strange inconsistency. It is also inconsistent with a further element of their theory which, as we shall see later, holds that in the eternal kingdom the Church saints are to constitute a heavenly people, while Israel constitutes an earthly people, the two to be kept permanently separate and distinct. Reese insists that the Dispensationalists wreck their system by placing the resurrection of the Old Testament saints at the time of the Rapture.

Three terms are used in Scripture with reference to Christ's return. They are: The Coming (Gr. *parousia*); the Appearing (*epiphany*); and the Revelation (*apocalypse*). See particularly: John 14:3; I Cor. 15:23; I Thess. 3:13; 4:13–17; Jude 14; Acts 1:11; Matt. 16:27; 24:30; Mark 8:38; Luke 9:26; II Thess. 1:7. We believe that these three terms are used interchangeably as suits the convenience of the writers, and that they have essentially the same meaning. Historic Premillennialists, too, take these as synonymous or at least as closely related terms. Dispensationalists, however, take the "Coming" as referring to the Rapture, which they place seven years before the "Appearing" or the "Revelation," and as being for the Church only. But it is hard to get these distinctions from the above references.

It is to be noted particularly concerning Paul's teaching in I Thessalonians 4:13–17, which is the primary passage cited by Dispensationalists as the basis for their doctrine, that:

(1) The term "rapture" is not a Scripture word at all, but rather is a term invented to express an idea that has become prominent in millennial discussions.

(2) The teaching concerning the Rapture of believers was not first given here by Paul as a new revelation, but by Christ Himself some twenty years earlier when He said, "I will come again, and will receive you unto myself; that where I am there ye may be also" (John 14:3).

(3) The new revelation given by Paul did not have to do directly with the Rapture at all, but was given to reassure those who had lost loved ones and who were afraid that those would not be able to share the glory of the Lord's return. It also informed them that the saints who survive until the Lord's coming will have no precedence or advantage whatever over the saints who have died. And,

(4) The real message of comfort to be found in Paul's words is not that there is to be a Rapture, but that at the Lord's coming all the saints whether living or dead will live together with the Lord and be forever with Him.

Dr. Allis, an acknowledged authority in the field of linguistics, has given the following analysis of the terms used in connection with the Lord's return, showing that the distinctions made by Dispensationalists are not tenable:

"(a) 'Coming' (parousia) is used by Paul 14 times, 8 of which refer to the coming of Christ. I Thessalonians 4:15, which speaks of the catching up of believers, clearly refers to the rapture; likewise II Thessalonians 2:1, which speaks of our 'gathering together with him.' On the other hand, I Thessalonians 3:13 speaks of the 'coming of our Lord Jesus with all his saints.' If 'saints' means or includes the Church, as all Dispensationalists believe, this verse speaks quite as plainly of the appearing. In II Thessalonians 2:8, which clearly refers to the appearing, since it speaks of the slaying of Antichrist, the expression used is 'the manifestation' (or 'brightness,' epiphany) of His 'coming' (parousia). Consequently, we must recognize that Paul uses *coming* both of the rapture and of the appearing and even combines the two expressions in II Thessalonians 2:8 to describe what is apparently one and the same event.

"(b) 'Revelation' (apocalypse) is used 13 times by Paul. In I Corinthians 1:7 it is used of the rapture. It is what the Christian waits for. In II Thessalonians 1:7 the reference is as plainly to the appearing, the coming in glory."

"(c) 'Appearing' (epiphany). This word is used only by Paul. In I Timothy 6:14, the reference to the rapture seems unmistakable. In II Timothy 4:1,8 the allusions to judgment as in Titus 2:13 to glory favor the reference to the appearing . . .

"Paul uses all three words and he uses them ambiguously. Particularly clear is the fact that he uses *parousia* both of the rapture and of the appearing . . . How is this to be explained, if he had been told by the Lord that there was an important difference between these two events? . . .

"The question which confronts us is this. If the distinction between the rapture and the appearing is of as great moment as Dispensationalists assert, how are we to explain Paul's failure to distinguish clearly between them? And the failure of other writers, Peter, James, and John, to do the same? Paul was a logician. He was able to draw sharp distinctions. If he had wanted, or regarded it important, to distinguish between these events, he could have done so very easily. Why did he use language which Dispensationalists must admit to be confusing? Feinberg recently made the following surprising statement regarding the three words we have been discussing: 'We conclude, then, that from a study of the Greek words themselves the distinction between the coming of the Lord for His saints and with His saints is not to be gleaned' (*Premillennialism or Amillennialism?*, p. 207). Such an admission raises the question whether the distinction itself is valid. If the distinction is of importance, Paul's ambiguous language is, we may say it reverently, inexcusable.

If the distinction is negligible, accuracy of statement would be quite unnecessary. We conclude, therefore, that the language of the New Testament and especially of Paul not merely fails to prove the distinction insisted on by Dispensationalists but rather by its very ambiguity indicates clearly and unmistakably that no such distinction exists" (*Prophecy and the Church*, pp. 181–185).

If Christians are to be removed from the earth *before* the Epiphany, that is, before the Appearing or Revelation of Christ, then the Scriptures cannot anywhere state or imply that they are to remain on the earth until the Appearing or the Revelation. If so much as one passage can be pointed out which teaches that believers are to remain on the earth until the Epiphany, the whole argument for a secret Rapture is disproved, and the dispensational system falls with it. That the Rapture and the Revelation are contemporaneous events, or nearly so, and that Christ at His coming will be visible to all people in all His power and glory, is indicated in numerous passages. Witness particularly the following:

I Timothy 6:13,14: "I charge thee . . . that thou keep the commandment, without spot, without reproach, until the appearing of our Lord Jesus Christ." But how can Christians "keep the commandment . . . until the appearing" if they are raptured seven years before the appearing? The appearing of Christ is here set forth as the event which terminates the service of Christians on earth. Hence they cannot be raptured before that time.

II Timothy 4:8: "Henceforth there is laid up for me the crown of righteousness, which the Lord, the righteous judge, shall give to me at that day; and not to me only, but also to all them that have loved his appearing." Here Paul sets his hope on the glorious appearing, not on a dispensational rapture which occurs seven years before the appearing of Christ, and that because of the reward that the righteous Judge shall give to him at that time. His teaching is the same as that of Christ, who said, "Thou shalt be recompensed in the resurrection of the just" (Luke 14:14). The glorious appearing of Christ, the resurrection of the saints, and the rewarding of the saints all occur at the same time.

Titus 2:13: "Looking for the blessed hope and appearing of the glory of the great God and our Saviour Jesus Christ." Here

the blessed hope (which is the coming of Christ) and the appearing are the same. In the original Greek the two substantives *hope*
and *appearing* are closely united with the common article. They
are not two separate events, as if it read, "looking for the blessed
hope and the appearing," but simply, "looking for the blessed
hope and appearing." The one explains the other. "The blessed
hope" of Christians *is* "the glorious appearing" of our great God
and Saviour Jesus Christ.

I Peter 5:4: "And when the chief shepherd shall be manifested, ye shall receive the crown of glory that fadeth not away."
Here Peter says that the crowning and rewarding of the saints
takes place at the manifestation, which is the same as the coming,
of Christ.

I Corinthians 1:7: "Waiting for the revelation of our Lord
Jesus Christ; who shall also confirm you unto the end, that ye
be unreprovable in the day of the Lord Jesus Christ." Here the
event that Christians are encouraged to wait for is not the secret
Rapture but the Revelation of Christ.

I Peter 1:13: "Wherefore girding up the loins of your mind,
be sober and set your hope perfectly on the grace that is to be
brought unto you *at the revelation* of Jesus Christ."

I Peter 4:13: "Insomuch as ye are partakers of Christ's sufferings, rejoice; that at the *revelation* of his glory also ye may rejoice
with exceeding joy."

II Thessalonians 1:7–10: "And to you that are afflicted rest
with us, at the revelation of the Lord Jesus from heaven with
the angels of his power in flaming fire, rendering vengeance to
them that know not God, and to them that obey not the gospel
of our Lord Jesus: who shall suffer punishment, even eternal destruction from the face of the Lord and from the glory of his
might, when he shall come to be glorified in his saints, and to be
marveled at in all them that believed." Here Christians are said
to receive relief from suffering and tribulation at the time the
Lord comes with His angels in flaming fire and for judgment on
evildoers. Concerning this passage Rev. William J. Grier says:

"We may notice that when the Saviour comes for the deliverance of His troubled saints, he comes 'in flaming fire'—no secret
rapture here! But it is even more important still to notice how
the reward of the righteous and the punishment of the wicked

are interwoven with each other *as to time*, and made to follow, both of them, immediately on the coming of the Lord. Surely this passage should make perfectly clear that there is no secret rapture to be followed at an interval of seven years by an open revelation of the Lord and His glory to the world. Surely it is perfectly clear also that since the coming of the Lord brings upon the wicked 'eternal destruction away from the face of the Lord,' there are no wicked who will survive His coming to be ruled over in a millennium to follow. But there must be wicked people surviving, according to the premillennial scheme" (*The Momentous Event*, p. 55).

And in I Thessalonians 5:1–4, which follows immediately after the passage from which Dispensationalists think to derive their doctrine of a secret Rapture (4:16,17), Paul's words make it clear that he is not talking about a seven year Rapture at all, but rather the *day of the Lord* or *Judgment Day*. These verses read: "But concerning the times and the seasons, brethren, ye have no need that aught be written you. For yourselves know perfectly that the *day of the Lord* so cometh as a thief in the night. When they are saying, peace and safety, then sudden destruction cometh upon them, as travail upon a woman with child; and they shall in no wise escape. But ye, brethren, are not in darkness, that that day should overtake you as a thief." This passage shows that instead of the righteous being taken away before the Judgment Day, they are here right up until the time the wicked receive their punishment, at which time the righteous receive their reward.

Concerning this passage, Grier says: "Paul associates the second coming with the resurrection and the ensuing glory of the saints *and* the sudden destruction of the wicked. Without the shadow of a doubt, that day has its reference to both parties: —believers are to look for it (I Thess. 5:4–10), for *then* they shall obtain salvation in all its fullness (vs. 9), *then* they shall 'live together with him' (vs. 10); while that *same* day will bring the false security of unbelievers to an end in their 'sudden destruction'" (*The Momentous Event*, p. 54).

Surely Paul would not have written these words if he had been looking for a secret Rapture. There is nothing here to indicate that Christians are to be raptured away seven years before the day of judgment. Rather, they are to receive relief from tribulation and suffering "at the *revelation* of the Lord Jesus from heaven with the angels of his power in flaming fire, rendering vengeance to them that know not God, and to them that obey not the gospel."

From these numerous references it should be clear to everyone that what is called the appearing or the revelation of Christ must coincide with His coming at the Resurrection. The Coming, the Appearing, and the Revelation of Christ are but different aspects of the same event. Hence we conclude that nowhere in Scripture does it teach a secret or pre-tribulation Rapture. Christ's coming *for* the saints and His coming *with* the saints are one and the same event and take place at the same time.

Once this is clearly seen the dispensational scheme falls away like a house of cards. For when their doctrine of a secret Rapture is shown to be contrary to Scripture, various other doctrines of their system are also left without support.

A further valuable contribution to our study of the use of words is made by H. C. Heffren. He says:

"Our quest for the answer to the events yet to be leads us back to the 24th chapter of Matthew. The question in verse 3 engages our attention. 'Tell us, when shall these things be? and what shall be the sign of thy coming, and of the end of the world?' The word 'end' is translated from the Greek word '*sunteleia*,' meaning *full end*. According to Young's Analytical Concordance 'sunteleia' is only used six times in the New Testament. It always designates the Judgment Day, that is, the end of the world.

"Before His ascension Jesus gave His disciples the well known command, 'Go ye, therefore and teach all nations . . . and lo, I am with you always, even unto the 'sunteleia (full end) of the world' (Matt. 28:19,20). Jesus would not have commanded His Church to preach the Gospel until the Judgment Day (*sunteleia*) if a rapture preceded the event; nor if the final phase of evangelizing the world were to be given to the Jews before the final end. The fact is that Jesus did not provide any channel for disseminating the gospel other than the Church. When that task is done, the gospel preached to all the world, then the end comes. But the Church must be in the world till the full end of the age in order for Christ to be with us as long as He promised to be.

"Christ gives a detailed account of the sequence of events at the end of the age in Matthew 13:24–52. The passage is too long to quote in full, but it should be carefully studied. In Matthew 13:39 we read: 'The enemy that sowed them is the Devil; the harvest is the 'sunteleia' (full end) of the world; and the reapers are the angels' (verse 40): 'As therefore the tares are gathered and burned in the fire; so shall it be in the 'sunteleia' (full end) of the world; the angels shall come forth and sever the wicked from among the just.' The use of the Greek word 'sunteleia' in each of these verses absolutely precludes the possibility of the righteous being taken out of the world before the full end of the age. Both the righteous and the wicked grow together until the end of the age" (*The Sign of His Coming*, p. 35).

We note that the Greek word *apokalupsis*, revelation, carries with it the idea of suddenness and unexpectedness, as though a curtain were withdrawn and the Lord stood revealed. But there would be nothing sudden or unexpected about it if a seven year warning of its approach had been given by such a tremendously startling event as the Rapture. Grier has well said: "There could be no such surprise about the second advent, if the premillenarian scheme were true, for once the 'day of Christ' (rapture) came, the seven-year period of Antichrist and the great tribulation would follow. The seven-year period, once begun, would revolve its course till its close, when 'the day of the Lord,' or 'the revelation' would follow. But the good Greek students tell us that the word 'revelation' (*apokalupsis*) has intimately associated with it the very idea of suddenness and unexpectedness; yet according to the ordinary premillennial scheme, it can neither be sudden nor unexpected" (*The Momentous Event*, p. 45).

The notion that the resurrection of the righteous is to occur a thousand years before the end of the world is contradicted by Jesus who, on four different occasions, said that He would raise up those who believe in Him *at the last day* (John 6:39,40,44,54). Clearly there can be no other days after the last day.

The parables of our Lord also teach that the final separation comes at the end of the world, not at a seven year rapture preceding the Millennium. In the parable of the Wheat and the Tares we are told that these grow together until the time of harvest, and that the lord of the harvest will then say to the reapers, "Gather up *first* the *tares,* and bind them in bundles to burn them, but gather the wheat into my barn" (Matt.13:30). The dispensational doctrine, however, says that seven years before the time of harvest the wheat portion of the crop is first to be gathered out, leaving only the tares. Again, in the parable of the Drag-net, we are told that "The kingdom of heaven is like unto a net, that was cast into the sea, and gathered of every kind: which, when it was filled, they drew up on the beach; and they sat down, and gathered the good into vessels, but the bad they cast away. So shall it be in the end of the world: the angels shall come forth, and sever the wicked from among the righteous, and shall cast them into the furnace of fire: there shall be the weeping and the gnashing of teeth" (Matt. 13:47–50).

In these parables the separation comes "in the end of the world," not a thousand years before the end, as all kinds of Premillennialism teach. And in so far as there is a difference in time, the wicked are taken out from among the righteous, not the righteous from among the wicked. If the dispensational theory were true, namely, that the Church is raptured out of the world, there would be left only the tares.

There is not a word in the Epistles of Paul to indicate that the coming of Christ shall be a secret affair. On the other hand he speaks of the coming as a "revelation": "Waiting for the revelation of our Lord Jesus Christ" (I Cor. 1:7). In writing to the Thessalonians he describes it as "the revelation of the Lord Jesus from heaven with the angels of his power in flaming fire, rendering vengeance to them that know not God, and to them that obey not the gospel of our Lord Jesus: who shall suffer punishment, even eternal destruction from the face of the Lord and from the glory of his might, when he shall come to be glorified in his saints, and to be marvelled at in all them that believed" (II Thess. 1:7–10). Surely by no stretch of the imagination can this coming be secret. Rather it is described as occurring in flaming fire, abundantly visible to all the world, through which He renders vengeance to the wicked at the same time that He is glorified in His saints and marveled at by all them that believe.

And where is there anything to indicate that the Rapture is silent, or secret, or unseen? Paul says that His coming occurs "at the last trump: for the trumpet shall sound, and the dead shall be raised incorruptible . . ." (I Cor. 15:52); and that "The Lord himself shall descend from heaven, with a shout, with the voice of the archangel, and with the trump of God" (I Thess. 4:16). Surely there is nothing secret about a rapture that is heralded by a shout, the voice of the archangel, and the trump of God, and which is seen by every eye! How could it be stated more clearly that *all men everywhere* are to see and hear that event? Surely this latter verse is a strange one on which to found a doctrine of a secret Rapture! It would seem rather to be just about the noisiest verse in the entire Bible! Nor does either of these verses say that the saints shall remain where they meet with the Lord in the sky for a period of seven years. That idea is without the slightest support anywhere in Scripture. Alexander Reese well says:

"The suggestion of Darby, backed by vigorous efforts of Kelly and others, to prove from this magnificent passage in I Thessalonians 4, that a secret coming, a resurrection and a secret rapture, are supported, followed by the rise and reign of Antichrist, is among the sorriest in the whole history of freak exegesis" (*The Approaching Advent of Christ,* p. 146).

It may be pointed out further concerning the Second Coming, which Dispensationalists divide into two parts, that some attempt is made to preserve at least a semblance of unity by referring to these as two different phases of the same coming. But the fact remains that Dispensationalists really do set forth two different comings, separated in time by a period of seven years, each having its own concommitants, each serving a different purpose and bearing a different name, the first being known as the Rapture and relating to the Church saints only, while the second is known as the Revelation and has reference to the entire world. These comings clearly are not the same.

We are prompted to say that those who hold the Rapture to be the next event on the prophetic calendar, and to look for it to occur "at any moment," are in this regard like those Jews in Christ's day who, we are told, "supposed that the kingdom of God was immediately to appear" (Luke 19:11). To offset that view Christ gave the parable of the pounds, in which a certain nobleman "went into a far country, to receive for himself a kingdom, and to return." By that parable He taught that His coming in glory was still some considerable distance in the future, perhaps even in the remote future.

We may point out further that the apostle Paul could not have looked for the Lord's return at any moment, for he had been assigned a great task that would in any event require much time, perhaps all of his natural life; for God had said to him, "I will send thee far hence unto the Gentiles" (Acts 22:21). Nor could the apostle Peter have understood the command to watch for the Lord's coming to mean that he was to expect it momentarily; for the Lord had told him that he was to live to old age and die by martyrdom (John 21:18,19).

The doctrine of an any moment Rapture, and particularly that of a secret Rapture, lends itself to the dramatic and the sensational. In treating this subject, on which even its proponents can find but little revealed in Scripture, the human mind can give full reign to its imaginative powers. The event is supposed to occur in absolute secrecy. Consternation and confusion reign among those who are left behind when they wake up to discover that all the Christians have suddenly vanished. Bewildering and terrifying scenes follow as families are separated and all the best neighbors are gone. They search everywhere, but cannot find them. Industries and utilities are immobilized. Hearts are filled with fear and dread. One Dispensationalist describes it this way:

"One of these days, as sure as this is the Word of God, those who have pled with you, who have warned you, who have prayed for you, will be missing. The preacher will be gone, mother will be gone, wife will be gone, and baby's crib will be found empty. Oh, what an awakening that is going to be! Imagine getting up some morning and your wife is not there, and you call for her, but there is no answer. You go downstairs, but she is not there. You call upstairs to daughter asking where mother is, but no answer from daughter. Daughter too is gone. You ring the police, but the line is busy. Hundreds and thousands are calling up, jamming the telephone lines. You rush out of doors and bump into the pal of last night's wild party. He is white as a sheet. He is out of breath, and he stammers a few words, and bawls out, 'My wife is gone. My brother is gone, and I don't know where they are.' Down the street runs a woman shrieking at the top of her voice,

'Someone has kidnapped my baby!' and in a moment the streets are full of people, weeping, crying and howling over the disappearance of loved ones. What has happened? The Lord has come, like a thief in the night. He has quietly stolen away those who trusted him, like Enoch, and no one is left behind to warn you any more, to pray or show you the way" (Rev. Richard W. De-Haan, Radio Bible Class, November, 1954).

Another says:

"When Christ comes the invisible Church will be caught up out of the midst of the visible. It will be a secret rapture—quiet, noiseless, sudden as the step of a thief in the night. All that the world will know will be that multitudes at once have gone. The extras will advertise in the streets, 'Universal Consternation—Remarkable Disappearances.' Such and such ministers are missing. Such and such business men are not to be found. Such and such women of high and low position have left their places vacant. The next Sunday the fashionable churches will show certain of their seats empty. In smaller, more devout churches, the majority will be gone—only a remnant left. For some days nothing else can be talked about. Excitement will be tremendous. Then reaction will set in. Philosophers and rationalistic ministers will begin to account for the phenomenon on scientific principles. The world will resume its occupations. Gradually the breaches in the churches will be closed up. Only a few here and there will wake up and say, 'It is too late! I am left out. My godly relatives have gone—the Spirit of God has departed. The reign of evil has begun. We have slept away our day of grace!" (Dr. George Sayles Bishop, *The Doctrines of Grace*, p. 341).

It is important that we realize how little emphasis is placed on the doctrine of the Rapture in Scripture. Paul makes but a passing reference to it in the two passages that we have quoted, with no mention at all of the 7-year feature which the Dispensationalists stress so strongly and on which they base so much of their distinctive doctrine. Scripture presents the Rapture as but a fleeting event, in a sense only the mechanical means by which we are introduced into the blessed hope, and places the emphasis on the heavenly glory that shall follow. Certainly there is no proof that the Church will remain in the air above the earth for seven years, or for any other length of time. The words, "So shall we ever be with the Lord," I Thessalonians 4:17, indicate that when the saints are caught up they enter immediately into the eternal heavenly state. Dispensationalists have made a fetish of that which is only an incident in the coming of Christ. Fortunately, many of them have abandoned the theory when they realized how destitute of Scriptural support it really was, and how prone to encourage other errors regarding the second coming.

Chapter IV

THE GREAT TRIBULATION

In the writings of John N. Darby four passages are cited as teaching an "unequalled tribulation," through which he says the Jews, Gentiles, and the professing Church will pass, but from which the true Church will be exempt. These are:

Jeremiah 30:7, "Alas! for the day is great, so that none is like it: it is even the time of Jacob's trouble; but he shall be saved out of it."

Daniel 12:1, "And at that time shall Michael stand up, the great prince who standeth for the children of thy people; and there shall be a time of trouble, such as never was since there was a nation even to that same time: and at that time thy people shall be delivered, every one that shall be found written in the book."

Matthew 24:21, "For then shall be great tribulation, such as hath not been from the beginning of the world until now, no, nor ever shall be."

Mark 13:19, "For those days shall be tribulation, such as there hath not been the like from the beginning of the creation which God created until now, and never shall be."

In the King James Version of the Bible the word "tribulation" occurs 25 times. Twenty of these are found in the New Testament. Christ is recorded as having used the word on three different occasions (assuming that Matthew 24 and Mark 13 record the same event), and on two of these, Matthew 13:21 and John 16:33, it is clear that He is talking, not about a climactic period of destruction and suffering at the end of the age, but about the ordinary sufferings and trials which come to those who follow Him. The first of these (Matt. 13:21), has to do with the Parable of the Sower, in which He says that the one who is sown upon the rocky places "hath not root in himself, but endureth for a while; and when tribulation and persecution ariseth because of the word, straightway he stumbleth." In the second passage (John 16:33), He says to the disciples, "In the world ye have tribulation: but be of good cheer; I have overcome the world." On the other occasions where Jesus spoke of "tribulation" (Matt. 24:21,29, and Mark 13:24—the American Standard Version uses the word also in Mark 13:19), the context makes it clear that He has reference to the events that would accompany the destruction of the temple and the city of Jerusalem, events which occurred within the lifetime of that generation.

The apostle Paul uses the word 12 times. In ten of those he was speaking of the sufferings which come upon Christians in the ordinary course of life. These references are: Acts 14:22; Rom. 5:3 (here mentioned twice); 8:35; 12:12; II Cor. 1:4; 2:4; Eph. 3:13; I Thess. 3:4; and II Thess. 1:4. In the other two places (Rom. 2:9 and II Thess. 1:6), he is referring to the fate of the wicked, but in neither of these places is he speaking about a period of time. In one of these he is speaking of "the day of wrath," and in the other of "the revelation of the Lord Jesus from heaven."

In the Book of Revelation the word "tribulation" occurs five times. In three of these (Rev. 1:9; 2:9; and 2:10), the words are directed to Christians and refer to events in this life. The fourth instance has to do with people who "have washed their robes and made them white in the blood of the Lamb" (7:14). And the fifth is an instance in which Christ says that He will cast "into great tribulation" certain ones in the church in Thyatira who commit great sins.

In the Old Testament the word is used four times. In Deuteronomy 4:30 Moses warns the Jews that if they are disobedient they shall "perish" and shall be "scattered among the nations," but adds that if when they are in "tribulation" they seek God He will not forsake them. In this case the word refers to the sufferings of the Jewish people. In Judges 10:14 the reference is to sufferings of Israel in the time of the Judges, sufferings from which they wanted to be delivered. In I Samuel 10:19 Samuel refers to past sufferings of the Jews, from which they had already been delivered. And in I Sam. 26:24 David refers to his own personal sufferings, from which he hopes for deliverance.

Hence our conclusion must be: *Nowhere in the Bible is the word "tribulation" used in connection with a seven year period at the end of the age,* either while the Church is still on the earth, as Historic Premillennialism holds, or after the Church has been removed from the earth, as Dispensationalism holds. Instead, it is used to describe: (1) the sufferings of Christians during this present age; (2) the sufferings inflicted upon worldly rejectors of Christ; and (3) the sufferings especially prophesied for the Jewish nation at various times in its past history. The most general use is to describe the sufferings of Christians during this present age.

In regard to the four verses commonly cited by Premillennialists to prove this doctrine we make the following observations:

In Jeremiah 30:7, in which a day is referred to as "great" and is described as "the time of Jacob's trouble," the word "great" need not be understood in an intensive sense but can also be used in the sense of long duration, great in length, and this sense is indicated by the word "time" which follows. Old Testament scholars tell us that this prophecy was uttered before the destruction of Jerusalem by Nebuchadnezzar, which occurred in 587 B. C. It seems extremely improbable that Jeremiah at that time could have been referring to a brief period of three and one-half years which even yet is wholly future. What he refers to as the time of Jacob's trouble seems more naturally to refer to that long period of affliction that befell the Jewish people beginning with the destruction of their city Jerusalem and which indeed continues even through the present time. Following the fall of Jerusalem the Jews were in captivity in Babylon for 70 years; and then when they were given permission to return to Palestine only a small minority did so, and they never again had a truly free and prosperous nation. The destruction of Jerusalem by the Romans in 70 A. D., and the dispersal of the Jewish people throughout the world through the past nineteen centuries has been but a continuation of "the time of Jacob's trouble."

That this is the correct interpretation is indicated by the fact that the name Jacob in verse 7 must be interpreted in harmony with the name David in verse 9, where we read: "But they shall serve Jehovah their God, and David their king, whom I will raise up unto them." We do not understand this to mean that David in person is again to reign in Jerusalem as he did centuries ago, but rather in a higher and typical sense as referring to the Messiah, who was the true son of David and who would be the true ruler, not of the Jewish people as such, but of His own people throughout the world. In harmony with this, a higher and typical meaning is also assigned to the word Jacob, and the time of Jacob's trouble may be thought of as paralleled by what Paul terms "the times of the Gentiles," which indeed is a time of trouble for Jacob. In this sense the day is "great," not so much in the intensity of its suffering but in the duration of its length.

Daniel 12:1, quoted above, is too obscure to justify its being used as a basis for a doctrine. It speaks of "a time of trouble, such as never was since there was a nation even to that same time," and says that "at that time thy people shall be delivered." This verse has received various interpretations. The "wilful king" who is spoken of in 11:36, and who evidently figures in these experiences, has been designated by some as Antiochus Epiphanes, by others as Herod the Great, or as the Pope or the Papacy, and as a future Antichrist. There is at least no proof that a time of this kind is wholly future. The reference to "thy people," as seen from the Old Testament viewpoint, can be regarded as referring exclusively to Israel, although the New Testament often gives a larger meaning and scope to Old Testament prophecies which at first appearance seem to be restricted to Israel,—as witness the expansion of the "seed" of Abraham to include all true believers in Christ (Gal. 3:7,29), and in this immediate context in Daniel (12:2) the resurrection and the fullness of the new life in heaven is prefigured in the statement that "many of them that sleep in the dust of the earth shall awake, some to everlasting life, and some to shame and everlasting contempt."

Matthew 24:21f., also quoted above, is cited by Pretribulationists as a proof-text, on the assumption that at this time the Church will have been raptured and will therefore not be on the earth during the tribulation. But if the "elect" referred to in the next verse, for whose sake these days shall be shortened, *are* the Church saints who are still on earth, as seems to be the clear meaning of the words, then this passage becomes one of the clearest of all proofs that the Church saints *do* pass through the tribulation. It is hard to see how "the elect" can refer to any others. It is expressly for their sake that those days will be shortened.

Mark 13:19f., describes the same event as does Matt. 24:21, and so does not need further discussion.

We may cite further Revelation 7:14, which reads: "These are they that come out of the great tribulation, and they washed their robes, and made them white in the blood of the Lamb." This group which is described in verses 9–17, clearly represents those who have departed, the blessed dead, the Church Triumphant, for in verse 15 it is said, "Therefore are they before the throne of God; and they serve him day and night in his temple." This group, therefore, is seen in heaven, not on earth. Concerning the "great tribulation" through which they have passed, Dr. Allis says:

"Dispensationalists tell us that this great tribulation is a wholly future period, a brief period of only three and a half years but one of intense trial. But the New Testament represents tribulation as the lot of all true Christians. Since it is quite clear that the word rendered 'great' can be understood extensively as well as intensively, it is quite as arbitrary to insist that it must have reference to a period which is almost negligible in extent and which is entirely future, when we think of the terrible and extended persecutions which the Church has already been through, as it is to insist that this must be the meaning of Jeremiah 30:7. If it is to be the lot of Christians generally that through 'many tribulations' they are to enter into the kingdom, it is quite appropriate to refer to this entire period as 'the great tribulation.' And such an interpretation is favored by the language used to describe those who shall have passed through it. To restrict language which is perfectly applicable to believers, at least to many believers, of all ages, to a special group living in a restricted period is arbitrary. To say that the redeemed (or at least the martyrs) of nearly two millenniums, the Church saints, are not included among them seems so improbable that it would require to justify it far more conclusive evidence than any which Pretribulationists have been able to produce. The vision seems clearly to describe the heavenly felicity of all the redeemed of every age and of every race" (*Prophecy and the Church*, p. 215):

The Church To Go Through The Tribulation?

All classes of Premillennialists agree that there is to be a period of great tribulation at the end of the present age. The question on which they divide is: Will the Church go through the Tribulation? Historic Premillennialists hold that the Church does go through the Tribulation, while Dispensationalists hold that it is raptured at the beginning of that period. Both agree that the world is growing progressively worse, and that this process is to be climaxed during the Tribulation by a seven year reign of a personal Antichrist. Those who hold to Historic Premillennialism point out that the Church has suffered tribulation throughout the ages and that it will continue to suffer until the coming of Christ, and that on principle there is no reason why the last generation of Christians should be spared what all previous generations have endured.

The question really comes down to this: Is the Tribulation the wrath of man, or is it the wrath of God? Historic Premillennialists say that the Antichrist is a man, and that the Church has no promise of deliverance from the wrath of man, but only a promise of grace to endure it. Dispensationalists hold on the other hand that the Tribulation is the wrath of God, poured out upon an apostate world, and that since there is no condemnation to those who are in Christ (Rom. 8:1), and since those who believe on Christ do not come into judgment but have passed out of death into life (John 5:24), the true Church is taken out of the world before the woes begin. They say that Christ comes *for* His saints at the beginning of the Tribulation, that all believers therefore are caught up and taken away, and that only unbelievers are left to go through the Tribulation. "What a fearful prospect it is," they say, "if the Church is to be in this Tribulation, as all the woes described in Revelation, chapters 4 through 19, are poured out upon the earth!" "How can we suppose it possible," they ask, "that God would permit any part of this terrible suffering to fall on His redeemed and believing people? Is it not more fitting, more in accord with His dealings in grace toward men, that they should be removed to be with Him before this trouble sets in?"

But where, we may ask, is there Scripture to support that view? Sufferings and trials are no strange lot for the people of God. They are, in fact, specifically set forth in Scripture as the disciplinary means in this world through which faith and patience are developed. "These things have I spoken unto you, that in me ye may have peace. In the world ye have tribulation: but be of good cheer; I have overcome the world," said Jesus to His disciples (John 16:33). At Lystra Paul, the greatest of the Lord's servants, was stoned and dragged out of the city for dead, but on regaining consciousness he went back into that same city and continued his work, making many disciples, "confirming the souls of the disciples, exhorting them to continue in the faith, and that through many tribulations we must enter into the kingdom of God" (Acts 14:22). The writer of the Epistle to the Hebrews says: "My son, regard not lightly the chastening of the Lord, nor faint when thou art reproved of him; for whom the Lord loveth he chasteneth, and scourgeth every son whom he receiveth. It is for chastening that ye endure; God dealeth with you as with sons; for what son is there whom his father chasteneth not? But if ye are without chastening, whereof all have been made partakers, then are ye bastards, and not sons. Furthermore, we had the fathers of our flesh to chasten us, and we gave them reverence: shall we not much more be in subjection unto the Father of spirits, and live? For they indeed for a few days chastened us as seemed good to them; but he for our profit, that we may be partakers of his holiness. All chastening seemeth for the moment to be not joyous but grievous; but afterward it yieldeth peaceable fruit unto them that have been exercised thereby, even the fruit of righteousness" (12:5–11).

Christians are repeatedly warned that in this world theirs is not to be a life of luxury and ease, but rather one of trials and suffering. Paul wrote of the afflictions that Christians are to suffer before the coming of Christ (II Thess. 1:4f). Peter wrote of the "fiery trials" which Christians undergo (I Peter 4:12). And John wrote of the "tribulation" which he shared with others (Rev. 1:9), and of "tribulation" in the church in Smyrna (Rev. 2:9,10). It is to be remembered that for the Christian this tribulation is not punishment but chastening, designed for his advancement and growth in grace. In proportion as the Church is zealous in proclaiming the Gospel, she is sure to suffer persecution at the hands of those who reject it. There is nothing in Scripture to indicate that the Christian, who through many tribulations is to enter into the kingdom of God, will be exempt from such suffering.

Dispensationalists divide the Tribulation into two parts. The entire period is said to be of seven years duration—the 70th week of Daniel's prophecy (9:24–27). During the first part of this period the Jews return to Palestine, make a covenant with the Antichrist, rebuild the temple, reinstitute the sacrifices and rituals, and carry on a world-wide campaign of evangelism which results in the conversion of great numbers of people. In the middle of the week Antichrist breaks the covenant, reveals his true character as the Man of Sin, abolishes the sacrifice, sets up his own image in the temple and demands worship. This the Jews refuse to give him. Terrible persecutions then break out against the Jews (Rev. 13:14,15). The Tribulation proper thus occurs primarily during only the last three and a half years of the period. A place of refuge for the Jews is found in the wilderness countries beyond the Jordan, in Edom, Moab, and Ammon. William E. Blackstone, author of *Jesus Is Coming*, believed this so strongly that he had cases of Bibles hidden away in the caves of those regions, so that the Jews might find them in the time of their distress. This, they say, is "the time of Jacob's trouble," referred to in Jeremiah 30:7. During this time all of the woes foretold in Revelation chapters 4 through 19 are fulfilled. The Great Tribulation affects also, of course, all existing Gentile nations and the apostate church.

Scofield refers to the Great Tribulation as "a final catastrophe of civilization, everything poured into one awful maelstrom of destruction and suffering—the great tribulation" (Article, reprinted in *Bibliotheca Sacra*, Oct.-Dec., 1951, p. 486). Dr. John Walvoord, President of Dallas Theological Seminary, says concerning the Tribulation that, "The Book of Revelation describes it as an outpouring of the wrath of God upon an unbelieving world (Rev. 6:17), a time when apostasy and sin reach unprecedented blasphemy. It is a period which brings death to most of the world's population and destruction to civilization. Nothing like it has ever happened before" (Article in *Christian Life*, Feb. 1955). Dr. Lewis Sperry Chafer refers to it as a "Protestant purgatory": "No one saved by Christ . . . will be left behind for a supposed Protestant purgatory" (*Bibliotheca Sacra*, Jan.-March, 1952).

At the end of the seven year period Christ returns with His saints, defeats and destroys the Antichrist and his armies in the battle of Armageddon, thus ending "the times of the Gentiles," and sets up an earthly kingdom in Jerusalem, over which He rules personally for 1000 years.

If it be asked, Where in Scripture is there authority for a seven year period such as Dispensationalism sets forth as elapsing between the Rapture and the Revelation, the answer must be: There is none. It is a period of time imported by inference from Daniel's prophecy of the 70 weeks, it being assumed that each of these weeks is a period of 7 years, and being further assumed that the 70th week has not yet been fulfilled. According to this theory "prophetic time" ceased to run when the Jews rejected Christ as their King at His first Advent, and will not be counted again until He returns in the Rapture.

Since Dispensationalists hold the "any moment" theory of the Rapture, and yet must provide time for a number of predicted events which they say are to occur before the appearing of Christ —such as the apostasy, the appearance and reign of the Antichrist, the Great Tribulation, the return of the Jews to Palestine and their conversion—they find the 70th week of Daniel's prophecy a very convenient parenthesis of 7 years during which these events are to occur. They then divide the coming of Christ into two parts, the unseen coming at the beginning of this period *for* His saints, and His visible and public coming at the end of this period *with* His saints. According to this view the events predicted in the Book of Revelation, chapters 4 through 19, have not yet been fulfilled and will not begin to have their fulfillment until the Rapture, but then will be rushed through in jig-time and fulfilled during the seven year tribulation, and largely during the last three and one-half years in a veritable phantasmagoria of horrors.

The correct interpretation of Daniel's prophecy is, we believe, that the events of the 70th week were fulfilled during the public ministry of Christ in Palestine, including the completion and abolition of the Old Covenant. After a further period of grace, some 37 years later, the final break-up of the Jewish economy came with the destruction of the temple and the city of Jerusalem and the final dispersion of the Jewish people.

It is interesting to notice that Dr. Scofield thought the First World War would result in the emergence of the *ten kingdoms* in the region of the old Roman empire, allegedly foretold in Daniel, and that Antichrist and Armageddon soon would follow. Speaking before the annual Philadelphia (Prophetic) Bible Conference in 1914, shortly after the outbreak of the war, he said concerning the ten kingdoms:

"Very likely that may be the arrangement in which there will come a pause in the World War now going on. Certainly, at no distant period those who are at war now will come to a condition of exhaustion. . . If there comes a cessation and a readjustment of some sort in that ancient-battle-land, the Roman Empire, this is the form in which it will settle down for the moment. And then there will arise Daniel's 'little horn,' a man of base birth but of mighty genius, a greater Napoleon. He overcomes three of these ten kingdoms and becomes the federal head of all of them, a world emperor for a moment."

He continued: "Now, while the earth is in that condition and the Beast, the little horn of Daniel, the abomination of desolation, the man of sin, the beast of the sea, is grasping and holding this power, the great tribulation is running its course. In the meantime a comparatively large number of Jews have been permitted, encouraged even, to return to Jerusalem and set up again their temple worship as best they can. If it be objected that all this takes a long time, let it be remembered that right on the site of the temple of Solomon there is now a building, the mosque of Omar, that in its divisions, in its structural arrangement, could be turned in probably one week into a very fair temporary temple for the restoration of the Jewish worship." Imagine that, if you can—the Most Holy God of heaven and earth, who in Old Testament times was so extremely particular that no element of paganism should enter the temple worship, now accepting the full ritual of worship in a pagan temple! Scofield thought further that during the tribulation period the armies of the ten nations would come against the believing Jewish remnant in Jerusalem, ". . . of which," he said, "Scripture has so much to say. . . It is very plain here in the prophetic word." He spoke with much assurance and went into considerable detail describing the events that were to occur just before the battle of Armageddon and the "Revelation" of Christ. "The word is plain enough," he said, "if you will just let it say what it means and believe that it does say what it means" (Reprinted in *Bibliotheca Sacra*, Jan.-March, 1952).

We would add that the Word may be plain enough, but that it certainly did not mean what Dr. Scofield thought it meant, as has been proved by the course of events since that time. We can point to scores of such interpretations given by Premillennialists with great confidence during both the First and Second World War. Yet they still assure us that the world is now in its last stages, that the "signs" indicate that the end is near.

THE HOLY SPIRIT TO BE ABSENT DURING THE TRIBULATION

It is standard premillennial doctrine that as the Holy Spirit was given at Pentecost, at which time the Church was especially equipped for its work of world evangelism, so at the Rapture with the departure of the Church the Holy Spirit is withdrawn from the world. This is usually explained to mean not that the Holy Spirit is withdrawn altogether, but that He is present only in a very limited way, as He was before Pentecost. He dwells in the Church, and when the Church is removed He too is removed. Says Dr. Walvoord: "The Church indwelt by the Holy Spirit is removed from the earth, then, the man of sin is revealed; with his appearance the tribulation begins. While the Holy Spirit continues to be omnipotent, His work will be similar to the period before Pentecost, but with His restraint withheld" (Article in *Christian Life*, Feb., 1955). And the period before Pentecost, we remember, was a period in which all the nations of the world except Israel were under the reign of heathenism.

Another of the strange doctrines of Dispensationalism is that, despite the fact that the Holy Spirit is to be absent during the Tribulation, a Jewish remnant (some say the 144,000 of Revelation 7) turns to God and is sealed, and then goes through the world preaching the Gospel of the Kingdom minus the Cross. These are Jews who are looking for the Messiah, but who have only a partial understanding of the Gospel and who therefore cannot be regarded as Christians in the proper sense of the word. Strange as it may seem, however, their work proves far more effective than anything that the Church has been able to accomplish in all the nineteen centuries of its existence. This great success is achieved without the special regenerating and enlightening power of the Holy Spirit as that power was manifested in the hearts of believers at Pentecost and afterward. Dr. David L. Cooper, President of the Biblical Research Society, says: "The greatest revival of all the ages will occur in the Tribulation— after the Church has been removed from the earth by the Rapture" (Pamphlet, *God's Torchbearers*, p. 34).

The Jews, so this theory holds, are to be converted at the mere sight of Christ their Messiah on the Mount of Olives, and through their testimony whole nations are to be converted. We must point out, however, that people were not converted at the mere sight of Jesus at the time of His first advent, and that it is the particular work of the Holy Spirit to regenerate the soul and give it new vision and so *enable* it to turn to Christ. The mere presence of Christ often had the effect of hardening His enemies rather than converting them. There is manifested here on the part of Dispensationalism a lack of understanding of the process of redemption. For in the system of redemption set forth in the Scriptures Christ's work is not to convert people, but to provide an objective atonement so that there shall be a basis on which the Holy Spirit can bring souls to faith and repentance and therefore a Gospel to preach. Man is not merely sick, but "dead" in trespasses and sins (Eph. 2:1), and before he can believe and turn to God he must be regenerated, or as the Scripture expresses it, "born anew," or from above (John 3:3). And that is the particular work of the Holy Spirit. Hence it is simply preposterous to believe that during the Tribulation un-Christian or anti-Christian Jews without the Pentecostal presence and power of the Holy Spirit can accomplish the evangelization of the world after the Church has been removed—or, as the Scofield Bible puts it, after "the Holy Spirit in the church" is "taken out of the way" (p. 1272). What a fearful blow that is to the Cross and at the Church which is founded upon it! It is simply unthinkable that the salvation of the world can be accomplished without the aid of the Holy Spirit. So important is His presence and His work that Christ said: "It is expedient for you that I go away; for if I go not away, the Comforter will not come unto you" (John 16:7). Dispensationalism thus sets forth, among other things, the doctrine of a "second chance" or second opportunity for salvation in a later dispensation on the part of those who are living at the time of the Rapture—which is generally regarded as a peculiar doctrine of Russellism. But the Bible teaches that "*Now is the acceptable time; behold, now is the day of salvation*" (II Cor. 6:2). When the Holy Spirit is taken out of the world the only possible means of approach to God is severed. The fact of the matter is that the coming of Christ ushers in the day of judgment, and closes forever the door to any future repentance. Those who do not accept the present Gospel offer are lost forever.

Alexander Reese, a Premillennialist but not a Dispensationalist, ridicules the notion of such "a prodigious tour of the world in 1,260 days, an army of half-converted Jews, still in their sins. Preachers without life," he says, "without forgiveness, and without the Holy Spirit in the soul, will do in 1,260 days what the whole Christian Church has been unable to do in 1,900 years— evangelize the world, and convert the 'overwhelming majority' of the inhabitants of the world to God. This declaration of Scofield's works out at about a million converts a day; and this at a time when, *ex hypothesi*, the Holy Spirit is in heaven, and the Antichrist is raging here below" (*The Approaching Advent of Christ*, p. 269).

And Hamilton, an Amillennialist, says: "How could they be regenerated if there were no Holy Spirit present to give them the New Birth? This whole theory is thoroughly unscriptural throughout, since it would by inference deny that man is dead in sins and thus contradict Ephesians 2:1" (*The Basis of Millennial Faith*, p. 77).

IDENTIFYING THE TIME OF THE GREAT TRIBULATION

The New Testament passages bearing most fully and directly on the Great Tribulation are: Matt. 24:1–31; Mark 13:1–37; and Luke 19:41–44; 21:5–36. However, a very remarkable prophecy spoken by Moses and found in Deuteronomy 28 throws much light on this subject. It set forth on the one hand the great blessings that would attend Israel as a nation if they remained true to God and kept His covenant, and on the other the fearful consequences that would follow if they broke the covenant. Said Moses:

"And it shall come to pass, if thou shalt hearken diligently

unto the voice of Jehovah thy God, to observe to do all his commandments which I command thee this day, that Jehovah thy
God will set thee on high above all the nations of the earth . . .
Blessed shalt thou be in the city, and blessed shalt thou be in the
field. Blessed shalt be the fruit of thy body, and the fruit of thy
ground, and the fruit of thy beasts, and the increase of thy
cattle, and the young of thy flock . . . Jehovah will cause thine
enemies that rise up against thee to be smitten before thee:
they shall come out against thee one way, and shall flee before
thee seven ways . . . Jehovah will establish thee for a holy people
unto himself, as he hath sworn unto thee: if thou shalt keep
the commandments of Jehovah thy God, and walk in his ways.
And all the peoples of the earth shall see that thou art called by
the name of Jehovah; and they shall be afraid of thee . . . And
Jehovah will make thee the head, and not the tail; and thou
shalt be above only, and thou shalt not be beneath; . . . thou
shalt not turn aside from any of the words which I command you
this day, to the right hand, or to the left, to go after other gods
to serve them" (vss. 1–14).

Over against this promise of marvelous blessing if Israel remained true there was set forth the utterly terrible consequences
of disobedience:

"But it shall come to pass, if thou wilt not hearken unto
the voice of Jehovah thy God, to observe to do all his commandments and his statutes which I command thee this day, that
all these curses shall come upon thee, and overtake thee. Cursed
shalt thou be in the city, and cursed shalt thou be in the field . . .
Cursed shall be the fruit of thy body, and the fruit of thy ground,
the increase of thy cattle, and the young of thy flock . . .
Jehovah will cause thee to be smitten before thine enemies;
thou shalt go out one way against them, and shalt flee seven
ways before them: and thou shalt be tossed to and fro among
all the kingdoms of the earth . . . Jehovah will bring a nation
against thee from far, from the end of the earth, as the eagle
flieth; a nation whose tongue thou shalt not understand . . .
And they shall besiege thee in all thy gates, until thy high and
fortified walls come down, wherein thou trustedst, . . . And
thou shalt eat the fruit of thine own body, the flesh of thy sons
and of thy daughters, whom Jehovah thy God hath given thee,

in the siege and in the distress wherewith thine enemies shall distress thee. The man that is tender among you, and very delicate, his eye shall be evil toward his brother, and toward the wife of his bosom, and toward the remnant of his children whom he hath remaining; so that he will not give to any of them of the flesh of his children whom he shall eat, because he hath nothing left him, in the siege and in the distress wherewith thine enemy shall distress thee in all thy gates. The tender and delicate woman among you, who would not adventure to set the sole of her foot upon the ground for delicateness and tenderness, her eye shall be evil toward the husband of her bosom, and toward her son, and toward her daughter, and toward her young one that cometh out from between her feet, and toward her children whom she shall bear; for she shall eat them for want of all things secretly, in the siege and in the distress wherewith thine enemy shall distress thee . . . And Jehovah will scatter thee among all peoples, from the one end of the earth unto the other end of the earth; and there thou shalt serve other gods, which thou hast not known, thou nor thy fathers, even wood and stone . . . And Jehovah will bring thee into Egypt again with ships, by the way whereof I said unto thee, Thou shalt see it no more again: and there ye shall sell yourselves unto your enemies for bondsmen and for bondswomen, and no man shall buy you" (vss. 15–68).

These words were spoken nearly fifteen centuries before the time of Christ. In Daniel 9:24–27 there is found another remarkable prophecy to the same effect:

". . . And the people of the prince that shall come shall destroy the city and the sanctuary; and the end thereof shall be with a flood, and even unto the end shall be war: desolations are determined. And he shall make a firm covenant with many for one week: and in the midst of the week he shall cause the sacrifice and the oblation to cease; and upon the wing of abomination shall come one that maketh desolate; and even unto the full end, and that determined, shall wrath be poured out upon the desolate."

Now let us compare with these prophecies of Moses and Daniel the words of Christ spoken to His disciples concerning the coming destruction of Jerusalem and the great tribulation that He said would befall the people. In Matthew 24 we read:

"And Jesus went out from the temple, and was going on his way; and his disciples came to him to show him the buildings of the temple. But he answered and said unto them, See ye not all these things? Verily I say unto you, There shall not be left here one stone upon another, that shall not be thrown down . . . Then shall they deliver you up unto tribulation, and shall kill you: and ye shall be hated of all the nations for my name's sake. And then shall many stumble, and shall deliver up one another, and shall hate one another. And many false prophets shall arise, and shall lead many astray. And because iniquity shall be multiplied, the love of the many shall wax cold. But he that endureth to the end, the same shall be saved. And this gospel of the kingdom shall be preached in the whole world for a testimony unto all the nations; and then shall the end come. When therefore ye see the abomination of desolation, which was spoken of through Daniel the prophet, standing in the holy place (let him that readeth understand), then let them that are in Judaea flee unto the mountains: let him that is on the housetop not go down to take out the things that are in his house: and let him that is in the field not return back to take his cloak. But woe to them that are with child and to them that give suck in those days! And pray ye that your flight be not in the winter, neither on a sabbath: for then shall be great tribulation, such as hath not been from the beginning of the world until now, no, nor ever shall be. And except those days had been shortened, no flesh would have been saved: But for the elect's sake those days shall be shortened" (vss. 1,2,9–22).

The awful climax of suffering toward which the city and the nation were rapidly building was also reflected in the strong words of Jesus as He was being led out to be crucified, recorded in Luke 23:28–30.

"Daughters of Jerusalem, weep not for me, but weep for yourselves, and for your children. For behold the days are coming, in which they shall say, Blessed are the barren, and the wombs that never bare, and the breasts that never gave suck. Then shall they begin to say to the mountains, Fall on us; and to the hills, Cover us."

That Jesus was speaking of the siege of Jerusalem, which

was then only a few years in the future, is made clear in the parallel passages (Matt. 24:1–34 and Luke 21:20–36). And that His words referred especially to that generation is placed beyond all doubt when in Matthew 24:34 and Luke 21:32 He said: "This generation shall not pass away, till all these things be accomplished." Those who picture a future tribulation of awful proportions should remember that Christ Himself said that the greatest tribulation of all time was to occur at the siege of Jerusalem.

That the "great tribulation" of which Christ spoke did not refer to an event at the end of the age is made clear by the fact that after saying that such suffering had not been known since the beginning of the world, He goes on to say, "No, nor ever shall be." It would have been pointless to have added that comment if it was to occur at the end of the age, for then of course no time would have been left for such an occurrence. This is also borne out by the fact that Jesus told the Christians to pray "that your flight be not in the winter, neither on a sabbath" (vs. 20). They were to pray that no natural causes might hinder their flight from the scene of horror, and that it would not happen on a sabbath when according to Jewish law they could travel only a short distance. These provisions indicate a local, not a world-wide, event. Nor can they apply to the Second Coming, for then true believers are to be taken directly to be with Christ. There will be no reason at all then for them to flee to the mountains.

Nor do the words, "And this gospel of the kingdom shall be preached in the whole world for a testimony unto all the nations; and then shall the end come" (Matt. 24:14), mean that those events are to occur at the end of the age. This language is similar to that used to describe the events that occurred on the day of Pentecost, where we read: "Now there were dwelling at Jerusalem Jews, devout men, from every nation under heaven" (Acts 2:5)—and then the nations represented are named: Parthia, Media, Mesopotamia, Cappadocia, Egypt, Rome, Arabia, etc.— not the entire world, but the world as known to the Jews of that day. Mark, too, uses similar language when he says that after the ascension of Christ the disciples "went forth, and preached everywhere, the Lord working with them, and confirming the word by the signs that followed" (16:20). In writing to the Romans about the year 58 A.D., Paul said, "I thank my God through Jesus Christ for you all, that your faith is proclaimed throughout the whole world (1:8); "unto all the nations" (16:26); and in the letter to the Colossians he used the most expansive language concerning the preaching of the gospel that had already occurred (A.D. 63), ". . . the gospel which ye heard, which was preached in all creation under heaven" (1:23). Hence Christ referred not to a preaching of the gospel in our day, or near the end of the age, but to a preaching that was to occur before the destruction of Jerusalem in the year A.D. 70.

Likewise, the end referred to by Matthew—"and then shall the end come" (vs. 14)—refers not to the end of the world, but to the end of the Old Testament economy, with its temple and priesthood, its ritual and sacrifice, the final break-up of the Jewish nation and the dispersal of the people, which, as the events proved, was just at hand. It is hard for us at this distance to realize what a revolutionary change that was, as the old order which had been in existence for fifteen centuries and which had set the Jews apart from all of the surrounding nations, came to its final climax and was abolished. In Old Testament times the message of salvation was confined to the one little nation of Israel; but before the destruction of Jerusalem in the year 70 A.D., the distinction between Jew and Gentile had been abolished and a new era had dawned in which the gospel was being preached to all nations without distinction of race or color. For the Jews who had grown up under the old order it meant the end of a way of life as they had known it, and the launching out into a new way, in effect, a new world.

There has been much conjecture and much misunderstanding regarding what Matthew meant by "the abomination of desolation." Verses 15 and 16 read: "When therefore ye shall see the abomination of desolation, which was spoken of through Daniel the prophet, standing in the holy place (let him that readeth understand), then let them that are in Judaea flee unto the mountains." Some, as Blackstone, have thought that this meant "an idol placed in the holy of holies of the temple during the reign of Antichrist" (*Jesus Is Coming*, p. 187). That, of course, is only a conjecture, a private opinion entirely without Scriptural support. An image in the holy of holies could not have been seen by the people, for only the high priest was allowed to enter that sacred place, and then only once each year. Jesus spoke of some public event that the people could "see," something that the Christians could recognize as the appointed sign when they were to flee immediately to the mountains.

The explanation of the sign is to be found, we believe, in the difference in wording between Matthew's account and that given by Luke. Luke says: "And when ye see Jerusalem compassed with armies, then know that her desolation is at hand. Then let them that are in Judaea flee unto the mountains . . ." (21:20,21). A foreign, pagan army on the sacred soil of Palestine would be an abomination; and the desolating work of invading armies is well known. Hence this is a reference to the soon coming invasion of Palestine by the Romans. It is generally assumed on the part of Bible scholars that the Gospel of Matthew was written primarily for the Jews, who were familiar with Old Testament prophecy and who therefore would recognize this expression as a reference to invading armies, but that the Gospel of Luke was written more particularly for Gentiles who were not acquainted with prophecy; hence Luke says plainly, "When ye see Jerusalem compassed with armies . . ." The cup of iniquity of the Jewish nation was just about full (Matt. 23:32). Upon the generation then living would come "all the righteous blood shed on the earth, from the blood of Abel the righteous unto the blood of Zachariah son of Barachiah, whom ye slew between the sanctuary and the alter" (Matt. 23:35). This prophecy is repeated in Matthew 24:34, where Jesus says: "Verily I say unto you, This generation shall not pass away, till all these things be accomplished."

Concerning this last statement and the meaning of the word "generation," Dr. Murray says:

"The meaning of this sentence seems quite obvious, but it is difficult to see how 'all these things' were really fulfilled during the lifetime of that generation. Some interpreters have tried to overcome this obstacle by substituting the idea of race, nation, stock or family, for generation. They insist that what Jesus really meant was that the Jews, as a race, would not pass away until these things should be fulfilled. The Scofield Reference Bible states that the Greek word *genea* translated *generation* means 'race, kind, family, stock or breed' (p. 1034). To this Dr. Scofield adds parenthetically, 'so all lexicons.' It may be that some lexicons support this opinion, but certainly not 'all lexicons.' We have before us Thayer's Greek-English Lexicon of the New Testament, a very able and reliable work in this field. On page 112 of this volume it is distinctly stated that the word *genea* translated *generation* in Matthew 23:36 and Matthew 24:34 means 'the Jewish race at one and the same period' or 'the whole multitude of men at the same time.' This interpretation seems both obvious and reasonable."

He continues: "It may be profitable and convincing to the reader to see how the word *generation* is used in other parts of Matthew's Gospel. In Matthew 1:17 we read, 'so all the generations from Abraham to David were fourteen generations; and from David unto the carrying away to Babylon are fourteen generations; and from the carrying away to Babylon unto the Christ are fourteen generations.' Here one finds the same Greek word used, but no one would suggest that it be translated 'fourteen races, kinds, families, stocks or breeds.' In Matthew 11:16 Jesus said, 'But whereunto shall I liken this generation?' It is plain to anyone that He is speaking of the people then living and describing their attitude toward John the Baptist and Himself. Again in Matthew 12:39–43 Jesus speaks of an adulterous generation and says that the men of Nineveh and the queen of the south shall rise against it. The men of Nineveh repented at the preaching of Jonah, and a greater than Jonah preached to that generation. The queen of the south came from the uttermost parts of the earth to hear the wisdom of Solomon, and a greater than Solomon was available to that generation. In each case Jesus Christ is using the word *generation* to describe His contemporaries, and we question seriously if in any of the four Gospels the word is used with any other meaning. This, then, should convince us beyond a doubt that our Lord is not speaking of a race, but that He is speaking of a people living at that time when He says: 'Verily I say unto you, This generation shall not pass, till all these things be fulfilled' . . . We take the position that Matthew 24:34, in which our Lord speaks of the generation then living, is the time text of the chapter and that our Lord's predictions up to that point have to do with the destruction of

Jerusalem, which took place in the year 70 A. D. All His predictions concerning that notable event are clear and definite" (*Millennial Studies*, pp. 109, 110).

THE SIEGE AND DESTRUCTION OF JERUSALEM

What, then, were the events that occurred during the siege of Jerusalem and the final break-up of the Jewish nation, the events concerning which Christ said, "For then shall be *great tribulation*, such as hath not been from the beginning of the world until now, no, nor ever shall be"?

The climax came in the year 70 A. D., at Passover time with people from all over the nation gathered in Jerusalem, when in a spasm of maniacal fervor which undoubtedly was as sincere as it was hopelessly impossible of accomplishment the Jews decided to cast off the Roman yoke. The city was crowded with people from all parts of Palestine. Our primary source of information is the famous history written by Josephus, who as we have said was a Jew and an eye-witness of the destruction of Jerusalem. His works, *The Antiquities of the Jews*, and *The Wars of the Jews*, have been preserved. They are considered reliable by competent historians, and his account of the long and fiercely contested siege and fall of the city corresponds to such a time of tribulation as Christ said would befall the city. He was an educated Pharisee and had been appointed governor of Galilee. After a valiant defense against the Roman army in Galilee before the siege of Jerusalem began, he was forced to surrender. However, he succeeded in ingratiating himself with the Roman general Titus, who was impressed with his ability and his sincerity and who used him as a mediator between himself and the Jews during the latter part of the campaign. It was in this capacity that he was present at the siege of Jerusalem. He was later given his freedom, and went to Rome where his literary work was done. He was not a Christian, and so cannot be accused of having written with any idea of favoring the Christians.

Concerning his fellow-Jews Josephus said: "I shall therefore speak my mind here at once briefly: That neither did any other city ever suffer such miseries, nor did any age ever breed a generation more fruitful of wickedness than this was, from the beginning of the world." *Wars of the Jews*, Book V, Chapter 10:5. He says that 1,100,000 people perished during the long and fiercely contested siege, and that 97,000 survivors were sold as slaves (VI, 9:3). The temple was destroyed and the city was razed to the ground. "Now this vast multitude," he says, "was indeed collected out of remote places, but the entire nation was now shut up by fate as in prison, and the Roman army encompassed the city when it was crowded with inhabitants. Accordingly the multitude of those that perished therein exceeded all the destructions that either man or God ever brought upon the world" (VI, 9:4).

It was by that event that the national existence of the Jews came to an end. Since that time the exiles have been scattered all over the world, with no national unity until very recent times when a small minority of them set up a new government in Palestine (1948). During all those years, however, they maintained their racial existence despite many hardships and much persecution. In long continued suffering their lot is unparalleled in the experience of any other people.

We take no pleasure in recording the terribleness of the siege, and we include such an account only with reluctance in order to show what actually did happen and how literally this fulfilled the prophecy that Christ made concerning the great tribulation. In order to understand what actually happened it is necessary to keep in mind that during the siege the greater part of the suffering and horror was caused by the Jews themselves. Their feeling that they were the chosen people and that they would be rescued by divine intervention, that indeed God would have to intervene in order to protect His temple, caused them to neglect to do those things which under normal conditions would have been considered good military tactics and sound judgment. When they were in such extremity and were daily expecting a mighty deliverance it became extremely easy for false prophets and false Christs to impose upon them, as Christ had said they would. As conditions grew steadily worse and it finally dawned upon them that no divine help was coming the sense of abandonment and despair led to such crimes against each other as otherwise never would have been perpetrated or tolerated. The besieged people broke into three vicious rival factions which fought each other, and robbed and tortured and slaughtered those who refused to join their factions. Unmentionable crimes were committed, and the aged and women and children suffered so much from this internal war that they longed for the Romans to come and deliver them. Even the temple became a battleground in this internecine warfare and hundreds of dead bodies were strewn throughout its chambers. This caused Josephus to write: "O most wretched city, what misery so great as this didst thou suffer from the Romans, when they came to purify thee from thy intestine hatred! For thou couldst be no longer a place fit for God, nor couldst thou long continue in being, after thou hadst been a sepulchre for the bodies of thy own people, and hadst made the holy house itself a burying-place in this civil war of thine" (V, 1:3).

The account by Josephus continues:

"The madness of the seditious did also increase together with the famine, and both these miseries were every day inflamed more and more . . . Many there were indeed, who sold what they had for one measure; it was of wheat, if they were of the richer sort; but of barley, if they were poorer. When these had so done, they shut themselves up in the inmost rooms of their houses, and ate the corn they had gotten . . . The famine was too hard for all other passions, and it is destructive to nothing so much as to modesty; for what was otherwise worthy of reverence was in this case despised; insomuch that children pulled the very morsels that their fathers were eating out of their mouths, and what was still more to be pitied, so did the mothers do as to their infants; and when those that were most dear were perishing under their hands, they were not ashamed to take from them the very last drops that might preserve their lives; and while they ate after this manner, yet were they not concealed in so doing; but the seditious everywhere came upon them immediately, and snatched away from them what they had gotten from others; for when they saw any house shut up, this was to them a signal that the people within had gotten some food; whereupon they broke down the doors, and ran in, and took of what they were eating, almost out of their very throats, and this by force; the old men, who held their food fast, were beaten; and if the women hid what they had within their hands, their hair was torn for so doing; nor was there any commiseration shown either to the aged or to the infants, but they lifted up children from the ground as they hung upon the morsels they had gotten, and shook them down upon the floor. But still they were more barbarously cruel to those that had prevented their coming in, and had actually swallowed down what they were going to seize upon, as if they had been unjustly defrauded of their right. They also invented terrible methods of torture to discover where any food was . . ." (V, 10:2, 3).

"Now the seditious at first gave orders that the dead should be buried out of the public treasury, as not enduring the stench of their dead bodies. But afterward, when they could not do that, they had them cast down from the walls into the valley beneath. However, when Titus, in going his rounds among these valleys, saw them full of dead bodies, and the thick putrefaction, called God to witness that this was not his doing; and such was the sad case of the city itself."

Josephus records an event concerning a wealthy and cultured woman which will show that the language of Jesus was not too extravagant when He foretold the terrible tribulation that would befall the city. This woman at first had much food, but was robbed until she had nothing left. She cursed the villains who robbed her, but to no avail. Josephus continues: "She then attempted a most unnatural thing: and snatching up her son, who was a child sucking at her breast, she said, 'O thou miserable infant! for whom shall I preserve thee in this war, this famine, this sedition? As to the war with the Romans, if they preserve our lives, we must be slaves. This famine also will destroy us, even before that slavery comes upon us. Yet are these seditious rogues more terrible than both the other. Come on; be thou my food, and be thou a fury to these seditious varlets, and a by-word to the world, which is all that is now wanting to complete the calamities of the Jews.' And as soon as she had said this, she slew her son, and roasted him, and ate the one-half of him, and kept the other half by her concealed. Upon this the seditious came presently, and smelling the horrid scent of this food, they threatened her that they would cut her throat immediately if she did not show them what food she had gotten already. She replied that she had saved a very fine portion of it for them, and withal uncovered what was left of her son. Hereupon they were seized with a horror and amazement of mind, and stood astonished at the sight, when she said to them, 'This is mine own son, and what hath been done was my own doing! Come, eat of this food; for I have eaten of it myself. Do you not pretend to be either more tender than a woman, or more compassionate than a mother; but if you be so scrupulous, and do abominate this my sacrifice, as I have eaten the one-half, let the rest be reserved for me.' After which those men went out trembling, being never so much affrighted at any thing as they were at this, and with some difficulty they left the rest of that meat to the mother" (VI, 3:4).

Josephus says that in the latter stages of the siege the Romans, angered at what they considered the unduly long and stubborn resistance of the city, crucified Jews until they could no longer find wood to make crosses. Concerning those who tried to escape from the city he says: "When they were going to be taken, they were forced to defend themselves, for fear of being punished; but after they had fought, they thought it too late to make any supplication for mercy; so they were first whipped, and tormented with all sorts of tortures before they died, and were then crucified before the walls of the city. This miserable procedure made Titus greatly to pity them, while they caught every day five hundred Jews; nay, some days they caught more; yet did it not appear to be safer for him to let those taken by force go their way; and to set a guard over so many, he saw would be to make such as guarded them useless to him . . . So the soldiers, out of the wrath and hatred they bore the Jews, nailed those they caught, one after one way, and another after another, to the crosses, by way of jest; when their multitude was so great that room was wanting for the crosses, and crosses wanting for the bodies" (V, 11:1).

He continues: "Now the number of those that were carried captive during this whole war was collected to be ninety-seven thousand; as was the number of those that perished in the whole siege eleven hundred thousand, the greater part of whom were indeed of the same nation, but not belonging to the city itself; for they were come up from all the country to the feast of unleavened bread and were on a sudden shut up by an army" (VI, 9:3).

Some of those who tried to escape from the city swallowed pieces of gold before leaving, in order to take it with them. Says Josephus: "Yet did another plague seize upon those that vere thus preserved, for the deserters used to swallow pieces of gold. But when this contrivance was discovered in one instance the fame of it filled the several camps, that the deserters came to them full of gold, so the multitude of the Arabians with the Syrians, cut up those who came as supplicants, and searched their inwards. Nor does it seem to me that any misery befell the Jews that was more terrible than this, since in one night's time about two thousand of those deserters were thus massacred."

As the Romans fought their way into the city and the last pockets of resistance were overcome further horrors were inflicted on the people. The temple was burned and torn down, thus fulfilling the words of Jesus, "There shall not be left here one stone upon another that shall not be thrown down" (Matt. 24:2). As a final gesture of contempt the Romans even plowed the ground where the city stood. The entire surviving remnant of the people was sold into slavery.

Jesus had wept over the city because He foresaw the judgment that was coming upon it. It was His foreknowledge of that event, as He was led out of the city to be crucified, that caused Him to say to the women of Jerusalem: "Daughters of Jerusalem, weep not for me, but weep for yourselves, and for your children" (Luke 23:28).

In accordance with our view that Matthew 24 foretold the coming destruction of Jerusalem, and not a future tribulation of the end-time, the words of Jesus in verse 28 have special significance: "Wheresoever the carcass is, there will the eagles be gathered together." The eagle was then the symbol of Roman power, as it is today the symbol of American power, and as the lion is of British power. It was carried by the different units of the Roman army. It was over the governor's palace. Wherever Roman authority was exercised there the eagle was in evidence. Hence the reference in the words of Jesus was readily understood. It found its fulfillment in that in the year 70 A. D., the Roman eagles gathered at the city of Jerusalem and devoured the carcass of apostate Judaism.

One of the most remarkable events in connection with the fall of Jerusalem was the escape of the Christians from the city before the siege began. Nearly forty years earlier Jesus had foretold this destruction and had made provision for the escape of His people. He had given them a sign by which they were to know when to flee, and had said, "But when ye see Jerusalem compassed with armies, then know that her desolation is at hand" (Luke 21:20); and again, "When therefore ye see the abomination of desolation, which was spoken of through Daniel the prophet, standing in the holy place (let him that readeth understand), then let them that are in Judea flee unto the mountains . . . for then shall be great tribulation, such as hath not been from the beginning of the world until now, no, nor ever shall be" (Matt. 24:15,21). History informs us that the Christians took the invasion of the Roman armies as the appointed sign and made their escape to Pella, a village east of the Jordan about 15 miles south of the Sea of Galilee, and that none of them perished. Thousands of Jews from the other parts of the country fled into Asia Minor, Egypt, and various parts of Europe. In the year 135 A. D., after another incipient revolt, the Emperor Hadrian completed the work of driving practically all Jews out of Palestine.

It is a far cry from Moses to Josephus. Yet that which God speaking through Moses said would come upon a disobedient people (Deut. 28), had its fulfillment in detail and was recorded by an historian who, without thought of what God had promised, simply reported what he saw with his own eyes. Truly that was "the time of Jacob's trouble" (Jer. 30:7), as it was also the Great Tribulation of Daniel's prophecy and of Matthew 24. It fulfilled our Lord's prophecy,—and the point that really proves the argument beyond all successful contradiction is the statement that "This generation shall not pass away, till all these things be accomplished" (Matt. 24:34). It was also clearly predicted that believers were to escape that great tribulation, not as the Dispensationalists tell us, by being raptured into the air, but by fleeing for their lives to the mountains, which they did. Premillennialists of both schools relate the prophecy concerning a Great Tribulation to a future period, holding that it occurs at the very end of the age, and so are blind to the fact that it already has been fulfilled literally in the year 70 A. D. It is significant that while the gospels of Matthew, Mark and Luke, which were written before the destruction of Jerusalem, contain prophecies regarding the Great Tribulation, the Gospel of John, which was written in the year 95 A. D., or 25 years after that event, makes no mention of it at all. Had the prophecy related to the end of the age John undoubtedly would have mentioned such an important event. The fact that he omitted any reference to it is a strong indication that he regarded it as fulfilled. Clearly the Great Tribulation of which Jesus spoke is a matter of history. Surely that tribulation was horrible enough, and surely we do not need to put the poor Jews or humanity at large through another and, if possible, even greater tribulation at the end of the age.

We call attention also to the completely disproportionate emphasis that the premillennial system places on the Book of Revelation. For according to that interpretation chapters 4 through 19, a total of 16 chapters, are used to describe the comparatively short seven year Tribulation, while *only six verses* in chapter 20 are used to describe the glorious one thousand year reign of Christ upon the earth, with all the great and mighty events that undoubtedly would happen during that time. Such a method of interpretation is absurd on the face of it. The order should at least be reversed.

There have been, of course, other periods of tribulation or suffering in which greater numbers of people were involved, and which continued for longer periods of time. But considering the physical, moral and religious aspects, suffering never reached a greater degree of awfulness and intensity than in the siege of Jerusalem. Nor have so many people ever perished in the fall of any other city. We think of the atomic bomb that was dropped on Hiroshima as causing the greatest mass horror of anything in modern times. Yet only about one-tenth as many people were killed in Hiroshima as in the fall of Jerusalem. Add to the slaughter of such a great number the bestiality of Jew to Jew and of Roman to Jew and the anguish of a people who knew they were forsaken of God, and we see the justification for Christ's words, "For then shall be great tribulation, such as hath not been from the beginning of the world until now, no, nor ever shall be."

FURTHER CONSIDERATIONS

But while we reject the idea of a Great Tribulation at the end of the age, and hold that the one spoken of by Moses and Daniel and in the Gospels had its fulfillment in the destruction of Jerusalem, we nevertheless find that there are many tribulations, that

the life of a Christian in this present world is in a sense a continuing tribulation. We have cited Christ's words, "In the world
ye have tribulation: but be of good cheer; I have overcome
the world" (John 16:33); and Paul's admonition that "through
many tribulations we must enter into the kingdom of God" (Acts
14:22). In the first chapter of the Revelation John addresses himself to his readers as follows: "I John, your brother and partaker
with you in the tribulation and kingdom and patience which are
in Jesus . . ." (1:9). In other words, the tribulation was then
in progress, and John and the Christians to whom he was writing
were partakers in it—as also are we and all Christians who have
lived and suffered for their faith since that time. Concerning the
saints in the intermediate state John wrote: "These are they that
come out of the great tribulation, and they washed their robes,
and made them white in the blood of the Lamb" (7:14). Philip
Mauro has well said: "The 'tribulation saints' of the futurist
system are altogether an imaginary company; and we, the Lord's
people of this dispensation, are the true 'tribulation saints.'" The
dispensational system, in teaching that believers are not to pass
through the great tribulation but are to be raptured away from
it, merely helps to close the eyes of the saints to the real meaning
and importance of the tribulation through which they now are
passing.

One reason that it is so difficult for some people to realize
that the Great Tribulation had its fulfillment in the siege and fall
of Jerusalem is that they do not fully appreciate what a tremendously important event and what a landmark in history the
break-up and abolition of the Old Testament economy really
was. For a period of 1500 years God had worked with and
through the Jewish people exclusively in matters pertaining
to salvation. This had set Israel off very sharply from all of the
other nations. The law as given on Mount Sinai had rigidly
regulated the form of their religion and thinking and conduct.
They had been God's chosen people to the exclusion of all others,
except as some few individuals came into the nation and accepted
their religion. But with the advent of Messiah all of that was
ended. The passing away of the old order was an event of such
great significance that in speaking of it Jesus in Matthew 24

uses language which if read hurriedly or carelessly can be misunderstood as describing events at the end of the world.

It should be added that Amillennialists and some Postmillennialists also teach that there is to be a tribulation period immediately preceding the close of the present age, although they do not go to the extreme of the Dispensationalists who assert that all of the Book of Revelation from chapter 4 to 19 inclusive is a description of that period. Dr. Berkhof, for instance, says that the passages in Matthew, Mark and Luke ". . . undoubtedly found a partial fulfillment in the days preceding the destruction of Jerusalem, but will evidently have a fulfillment in the future in a tribulation far surpassing anything that has ever been experienced (Matt. 24:21; Mark 13:19). Paul also speaks of the great apostasy in II Thessalonians 2:3; I Timothy 4:1; II Timothy 3:13. He already saw something of that spirit of apostasy in his own day, but clearly wants to impress upon his readers that it will assume much greater proportions in the last days" (*Systematic Theology*, p. 700).

Dr. Murray also looks for tribulation at the end, but not the Great Tribulation of the Dispensationalists. He says:

"For the sake of better understanding, it might be plainly stated that we do not deny that there shall be great tribulation toward the end of the Gospel age. Those who have spiritual discernment can already hear the rumblings which betoken the loosening of an avalanche of apostasy. As it gains momentum, life will become increasingly difficult for those who remain steadfast in the faith, and loyal to Jesus Christ. Some of them are already paying a price for their devotion to Him."

"The present church," he continues, "is gradually, but surely, concentrating its endeavors on carnal organization which shall presumably embrace all of Christendom. The indications of ecclesiastical regimentation are everywhere in evidence. The question of questions is whether the world organization shall be under the direction of Christ, or of Antichrist. The history of ecclesiastical mergers does not justify the hope of world revival under a world church. The alternative is world-wide apostasy" (*Millennial Studies*, p. 130).

We have already given our reasons for believing that the references in Matthew, Mark and Luke relate to the destruction of Jerusalem. We do not believe that any further events are needed for their completion. Similarly, Paul's references to "later times," in which "some shall fall away from the faith" (I Tim. 4:1), and his statement that "in the last days grievous times shall come" (II Tim. 3:1), applied primarily to problems of his own day, as is shown by his admonition to Timothy to "put the brethren in mind of these things" (I Tim. 4:6), and in his second epistle, after enumerating the things that he has in mind he admonishes Timothy, "From these also turn away" (3:5). And surely the sufferings that were endured by the Christians during the first centuries under the Roman emperors, by the Protestants during the Spanish and Italian inquisitions, and by the Huguenots in France, resulting as they did in the death of thousands and in the torture and exile of countless other thousands, make present day indications of any coming tribulation insignificant by comparison. And while it is to be admitted that today there is too much ecclesiastical regimentation, the moves that have been made toward establishing a world church do not indicate to us that we are heading into a tribulation period of the end-time. Surely the world church that existed at the time of the Reformation must have looked far more imposing and domineering and dangerous to Luther and Calvin and the other evangelicals of that day than does anything that we see now. Also the Established Church in the days of John Wesley, with its dead formalism and lack of spiritual life, must have looked the same way to Wesley and his followers. As regimentation develops in the established churches, invariably smaller groups break off and grow, and in time revival comes. We believe that the Great Tribulation is long since past. We also believe that the indications of spiritual growth throughout the Church today are much more promising than they have been in any previous period of history.

Chapter V

THE ANTICHRIST

One of the distinguishing marks of Premillennialism is that its adherents all believe in the appearing of a personal Antichrist shortly before the coming of Christ. This character is thought to be a wicked secular or ecclesiastical ruler who is referred to by that name in the First and Second Epistles of John, who in the Book of Revelation is termed the Beast or the False Prophet, and who is the same as the Man of Sin described by Paul in II Thessalonians 2:3,4. It is said that he is to live in the very last days of the present dispensation, and that he will be exalting himself on the earth at the time Christ returns to set up His millennial kingdom.

Premillennialism usually holds too that the Roman empire is to be revived, and that the Antichrist is to be the king or dictator of this realm. His kingdom is said to include ten nations (Dan. 7:7,20) in central and southern Europe, western Asia, northern Africa, and England. He is not to be revealed as such until after the Rapture of the Church, although he may be the ruler in his kingdom before that time. He is to have more power than has ever before been exercised by any king or dictator. The unbelieving Jews in Palestine are to make a covenant with him, but after three and one-half years he breaks the covenant and institutes a fierce persecution against them. When the Jews are shut up in Jerusalem and are about to be overwhelmed, Christ returns, destroys the Antichrist and his armies in the battle of Armageddon, delivers the Jews, and sets up His millennial kingdom. Some say, however, that the Jews are first to be attacked by a king who invades Palestine from the north, usually said to be the king of Russia, that they appeal to the Roman dictator for help and enter into an agreement with him. According to this view the Roman dictator goes to the aid of the Jews. The armies are drawn up on the plains of Esdraelon, the scene of so many past battles, and in the ensuing battle the Antichrist is victorious. This, however, leads on shortly afterward to a war against the Jews, which is climaxed by the battle of Armageddon. At that moment Christ returns, overthrows the Antichrist, delivers the Jewish people, and sets up His millennial kingdom. In either event the Antichrist still is in the future, and will not be manifested until the Church has been removed at the Rapture.

Many Post- and Amillennialists also believe that a personal Antichrist is to appear in the last days. Some hold that he will be a political ruler. Others identify him with the Pope or the line of popes. Such was the belief of the Reformers, and it continues to be held in the Lutheran Church even to the present day. All of these likewise believe that he will be destroyed at the coming of Christ.

In view of the rather elaborate programs that have been built up around the person and work of the Antichrist it may come somewhat as a surprise to find that there are but four verses in Scripture in which the word "antichrist" occurs. Other alleged references, such as the "man of sin" mentioned by Paul, the beast or the false prophet mentioned by John in Revelation, and the "little horn" mentioned in Daniel 7, are such only by inference. The verses that mention Antichrist are as follows:

I John 2:18: "Little children, it is the last hour: and as ye heard that antichrist cometh, even now have there arisen many antichrists; whereby we know that it is the last hour."

I John 2:22, "Who is the liar but he that denieth that Jesus is the Christ? This is the antichrist, even he that denieth the Father and the Son."

I John 4:3, "And every spirit that confesseth not Jesus is not of God: and this is the spirit of the antichrist, whereof ye have heard that it cometh: and now it is in the world already."

II John 7, "For many deceivers are gone forth into the world, even they that confess not that Jesus Christ cometh in the flesh. This is the deceiver and the antichrist."

In the first place we notice that the word "antichrist" as here used by John is applied to many persons existing in the first century. He says clearly that "even now have there arisen *many* antichrists." And concerning these he says: "They went out from us, but they were not of us; for if they had been of us, they would have continued with us: but they went out, that they might be made manifest that they all are not of us" (I John 2:19).

In other words, the antichrists of John's day were Christian apostates, those who had forsaken the Church and who were teaching false views concerning our Lord's person. The distinguishing mark of the antichrist, or an antichrist, says John, whether an individual or a class of individuals, is the denial of the essential deity of Christ. Those who so denied Him reduced Him to a mere man, perhaps a great and good man, but still only a man. The denial of His deity was especially heinous, because on that fact depended the entire fabric of man's salvation and of God's redemptive plan. To strike at the deity of Christ is to strike at the very heart of the Christian system. Hence such deniers are branded as liars, deceivers, false prophets, and antichrists. I John 2:19 makes it clear that they were men who had gone out from the disciples, that is, apostates and heretics who had deserted the Church and were opposing it.

In this same context John also contrasts "the spirit of truth, and the spirit of error" (I John 4:6), indicating that in some instances the spirit of antichrist is not necessarily personal. Briefly, we may say that anyone who opposes Christ and His kingdom, any opposition to the person and work of Christ, is antichrist and anti-Christian. This spirit is at work in the world today, and it was already at work in John's day. Notice, too, that the American Standard and King James versions do not capitalize the word "antichrist," indicating at least that in the opinion of the translators it was not the name of one particular individual.

In the main, however, the antichrists of whom John wrote were those who denied the true deity or the true humanity of Christ. The Scriptures teach clearly and repeatedly that Christ is truly God and that He is also truly man, One who had come from heaven, who lived a perfectly normal life among men for a period of thirty-three years, who really died, arose from the dead, ascended to heaven, and who will come again in His glorified resurrection body. There were, says John, many who denied that teaching in his day. He does not point them out as atheists, or infidels, or pagans, but as false prophets, liars, deceivers, those who had been within the Church but who now were denying its doctrines. In John's day and in every generation since there have been "many antichrists." As John uses the term every person or thing that is opposed to Christ is antichrist. Certainly it is not confined, if indeed it has any reference at all, to one particular person who is to appear in aggravated form just before the coming of Christ. Too much is read into these verses when that meaning is placed upon them.

The fantastic lengths to which some Premillennialists go, however, and the detailed events which they believe they are able to foretell, are well illustrated in the following exposition by George W. Beckwith:

"The dictator will increase his activities rapidly during the tribulation period after he breaks the covenant with the Jews. He will carry his conquest into Egypt (Dan. 11:42,43). This will be the start of his last campaign . . .The king of the south will come against him, and the beast will conquer. He will conquer all of the Mediterranean countries except Edom, Moab, and Ammon (Dan. 11:41). These nations will be a place of refuge for the remnant of the Jews.

"The Northern Confederacy," he continues, "also is preparing for conquest while the beast of the Roman federation is conquering around the Mediterranean sea with his eye on Palestine. Russia and Germany, as well as all the other countries of the earth, also have their eyes on Palestine.

"The Northern Confederacy is described in Ezekiel 38:8,9. 'In the latter years thou shalt come into the land that is brought back from the sword, and is gathered out of many people, against the mountains of Israel, which have been always waste: but it is brought forth out of the nations, and they shall dwell safely all of them. Thou shalt ascend and come like a storm, thou shalt be like a cloud to cover the land, thou, and all thy bands, and many people with thee' . . .

"The antichrist will be troubled by tidings out of the East and out of the North. With his federation of ten nations, he will meet the Northern Confederacy, with Gog as their head, in the valley of Esdraelon. Both of these confederations will seek the wealth of Palestine. The antichrist will be the conqueror. He will become the head of the armies of all nations. This will lead him to the battle of Armageddon, to war against God's chosen people, the Jews. This war therefore will be fought by the combined armies of the Gentile nations under the leadership of the antichrist against the Jews. Then will occur the Revelation of Jesus Christ as the Rider of the white horse from heaven. The result of Christ's coming on His white horse from heaven to battle against the antichrist will be that the hosts of the antichrist will be slaughtered in great numbers. The dead will be buried in the valley of Himmon-Gog. The house of Israel will be seven months burying the dead of the armies of the antichrist.

"Thus will end the power of the antichrist, the king of the Revived Roman Empire . . . Christ will come with all His hosts of heaven, at the time of His Revelation, to the Mount of Olives, to put a stop to the work of the antichrist, to judge the nations and to usher in His kingdom" (*God's Prophetic Plan*, pp. 104–106).

We have no need to enter into a detailed refutation of such an elaborate theory. It is a fundamental rule of exegesis that every passage must be understood in the light of its context. Yet not one single reference in Daniel or Ezekiel or Paul or the Book of Revelation which Premillennialists allege refers to the Antichrist is connected in any way with the verses in the epistles of John that mention antichrist. All is based on inference. Let the reader search for himself and see how far-fetched that connection is. We make bold to say that this picture of Antichrist as a world ruler who persecutes the Jews during an alleged tribulation period and then leads the armies of the Gentiles against the Jews in Palestine is pure fiction, without so much as one clear supporting verse in all Scripture.

Nor do we find any adequate support for the view generally accepted by Amillennialists and some Postmillennialists, that the Antichrist will emerge as a powerful political or religious leader shortly before the coming of Christ. That too impresses us as built largely on inference, and as in fact contrary to other Scripture which teaches the future glorious state of the Church and its victorious sweep before the end comes.

II Thess. 2:3—The Man of Sin

The verse most often cited as teaching that an Antichrist is to appear shortly before the end is II Thessalonians 2:3. This verse speaks of a "man of sin" and of a "falling away" or apostasy, and with its context reads as follows:

"Now we beseech you, brethren, touching the coming of our Lord Jesus Christ, and our gathering together unto him; to the end that ye be not quickly shaken from your mind, nor yet be troubled, either by spirit, or by word, or by epistle as from us, as that the day of the Lord is just at hand; let no man beguile you in any wise: for it will not be, *except the falling away come first, and the man of sin be revealed, the son of perdition,* he that opposeth and exalteth himself against all that is called God or that is worshipped; so that he sitteth in the temple of God, setting himself forth as God. Remember ye not, that, when I was yet with you, I told you these things? And now ye know that which restraineth, to the end that he may be revealed in his own season. For the mystery of lawlessness doth already work: only there is one that restraineth now, until he be taken out of the way. And then shall be revealed the lawless one, whom the Lord Jesus shall slay with the breath of his mouth, and bring to naught by the manifestation of his coming; even he, whose coming is according to the working of Satan with all power and signs and lying wonders, and with all deceit of unrighteousness for them that perish; because they received not the love of the truth, that they should be saved" (vss. 1–10).

There have been many attempts down through the ages to identify the Man of Sin or the Antichrist. The early Christians believed him to be the persecuting Roman emperor. It was noted by the Christians that the name Nero, *Neron Kesar,* written in Hebrew letters, had the numerical value of 666 (cf. Rev. 13:18). Mohammed, the false prophet, or his successors in the Caliphate, were thought by some to be the Antichrist. The Reformers believed that both of these prophecies, John's references to the Antichrist and Paul's references to the Man of Sin, were fulfilled in the Roman Pope, or in the succession of the popes, and that the "falling away" found its fulfillment in the corrupt condition of the medieval Church. Luther publicly burned the Pope's decree of excommunication, calling it "the execrable bull of Antichrist." The Reformers wrote this view into their commentaries and creeds. Strengthening this view was the fact that the Latin title of the Pope, *Vicarius Filii Dei,* Vicar of the Son of God, had the numerical value of 666.

V —	5	F		D —	500
I —	1	I —	1	E	
C —	100	L —	50	I —	1
A		I —	1		
R		I —	1	Total —	666
I —	1				
U —	5				
S					

Intriguing though this scheme may be, we do not believe that the papacy is the specific agency intended by either John or Paul. We are told that the Man of Sin "opposeth and exalteth himself against all that is called God or that is worshipped; so that he sitteth in the temple of God, setting himself forth as God" (vs. 4). He therefore is not a religious figure at all. He is not only opposed to the true God, but to every form of true worship and even to the idea of God. He is notoriously anti-religious. This cannot be said of the Pope of Rome, or of the succession of the popes; for they very definitely have been religious figures.

There have been still other candidates for the title of Antichrist or Man of Sin. Napoleon, the "Tyrant," the scourge of Europe, was thought by some in his day to be the one spoken of. At the time of the First World War some leveled this charge against the Kaiser. Between the wars and during the first part of the Second World War Mussolini and his "restored Roman empire" was set forth by many as a likely candidate for this role. Numerous articles were written and sermons preached to that effect. Typical of those who advocated this view was Dr. John R. Rice, who in a book, *World-Wide War and the Bible*, published in 1940, in answer to the question, "Is Mussolini the Antichrist?" said:

"He may be. I know of no reason why he should not fit the description of this terrible Man of Sin. He is an Italian. He is evidently an atheist. He once debated for atheism. He has the ruthless disposition, the ruling genius. He has an obsession to restore the Roman Empire. Furthermore, he is already in power in Rome. If Christ called His saints today, and if every saved person should be taken out to meet Christ, then soon Mussolini might have a mandate over Palestine, make the promised treaty with the Jews, and in three and one-half years attain world-wide power and then reign another three and one-half years, forty-two months, over the whole world. Mussolini is somewhat past fifty, neither too young nor too old for the brief but meteoric rule of the terrible Man of Sin. The Man of Sin must be a ruler in Rome, and Mussolini might be the man."

It was particularly this latter fact, that Mussolini was a Roman, that misled many Premillennialists, for they insist that the Antichrist when he comes will be a ruler in Rome. But since his sudden and ignominious fall we hear nothing more about Mussolini and his restored Roman empire.

It should also be clear that the Man of Sin is not Satan, for while Paul's description breathes a satanic atmosphere, it is said that his coming is "according to the working of Satan." That is, he is like Satan, but he is not Satan.

The usual amillennial view identifies the Man of Sin and the Antichrist, and holds further that the rise of the Antichrist and an apostasy immediately precede the return of Christ. Hamilton says concerning II Thessalonians 2:1–10:

"This declares that there will be a 'falling away,' that the man of sin will arise and that he will deceive the unbelievers before the coming of Christ to destroy him with the breath of His mouth. The world will not be converted before the coming of Christ, but on the contrary there will be a great apostasy before the coming of Christ" (*The Basis of Millennial Faith*, p. 105).

It should be clear, however, that Paul was not writing about a personage and event of the remote future, some abstract figure who would not manifest himself until nineteen or more centuries later and who therefore could not have been of any interest to the hard-pressed Christians in the early Church. Rather he was writing of a person and an event of his day, for he says, "The mystery of lawlessness doth already work" (vs. 7). In other words, the apostasy was happening then. Similarly, his statement that "he sitteth in the temple of God, setting himself forth as God" (vs. 4), contemplates the temple as still standing, and therefore prior to its fall in 70 A. D.

The best opinion, we believe, identifies the Man of Sin with the Roman emperor, or the line of emperors of that time. The apostasy or "falling away" (vs. 3) was then the Jewish apostasy, which would not reach its climax until the destruction of Jerusalem and the dispersal of the Jewish people. The Jews had rejected their Messiah, they had crucified the Lord of Glory, and now they were persecuting His followers to the death. This view as regards the apostasy is confirmed by Paul himself in I Thessalonians 2:15,16, where he says that the Jews "killed the Lord Jesus and the prophets, and drove out us, and please not God, and are contrary to all men; forbidding us to speak to the Gentiles that they might be saved; to fill up their sins always;" and then he adds, "But wrath is come upon them to the uttermost." In other words, Judaism was then, as it has been in every age since, bitterly anti-Christian. It is contrary to God's plan and purpose and so is subject to His wrath.

Probably the most accurate analysis of these expressions, the "Man of Sin" and the "falling away" or apostasy, is that given by Dr. Warfield. He says:

"We cannot fail to observe that in his description of the Man of Sin, the Apostle has a contemporary, or nearly contemporary, in mind. The withholding power is already present. Although the Man of Sin is not yet revealed, as a mystery his essential 'lawlessness' is already working—'only until the present restrainer is removed from the midst.' He expects him to sit in 'the temple of God,' which perhaps most naturally refers to the literal temple in Jerusalem . . . and if we compare the description which the Apostle gives of him with our Lord's address on the Mount of Olives (Matt. 24), to which Paul makes obvious allusion, it becomes at once in the highest degree probable that in the words, 'he that exalteth himself against all that is called God, or is worshipped, so that he sitteth in the sanctuary of God showing himself that he is God,' Paul can have nothing else in view than what our Lord described as 'the abomination of desolation which was spoken of by Daniel the prophet, standing in the holy place' (Matt. 24:15); and this our Lord connects immediately with the beleaguering of Jerusalem (cf. Luke 21:20). This obvious parallel, however, not only places the revelation of the Man of Sin in the near future, but goes far toward leading us to his exact identification. Our Lord's words not only connect him with the siege of Jerusalem, but place him distinctly among the besiegers; and led by the implication of the original setting of the phrase (in Dan. 11:36) which Paul uses, we cannot go far wrong in identifying him with the Roman emperor.

"Whether a single emperor was thought of or the line of emperors, is a more difficult question. The latter hypothesis will best satisfy the conditions of the problem; and we believe that the line of emperors, considered as the embodiment of persecuting power, is the revelation of iniquity hidden under the name of the Man of Sin. With this is connected in the description certain other traits of Roman imperialism—more especially the rage for deification, which, in the person of Caligula, had already given a foretaste of what was to come. It was Nero, then, the first persecutor of the Church—and Vespasian the miracle-worker —and Titus, who introduced his divine-self and his idolatrous insignia into the Holy of Holies, perhaps with a direct anti-Christian intent—and Domitian—and the whole line of human monsters whom the world was worshipping as gods, on which, as a nerve-cord of evil, these hideous ganglia gathered—these and such as these it was that Paul had in mind when he penned this hideous description of the son of perdition, every item of which was fulfilled in the terrible story of the emperors of Rome.

"The restraining power, on this hypothesis, appears to be the Jewish state. For the continued existence of the Jewish state was both graciously and naturally a protection to Christianity, and hence a restraint on the revelation of the persecuting power. Graciously, it was God's plan to develop Christianity under the protection of Judaism for a short set time, with the double purpose of keeping the door of salvation open to the Jews until all of their elect of that generation should be gathered in and the apostasy of the nation should be rendered doubly and trebly without excuse, and of hiding the tender infancy of the Church within the canopy of a protecting sheath until it should grow strong enough to withstand all storms. Naturally, the effect of the continuance of Judaism was to conceal Christianity from notice through a confusion of it with Judaism—to save it thus from being declared an illicit religion—and to enable it to grow strong under the protection accorded Jewish worship. So soon as the Jewish apostasy was complete and Jerusalem given over to the Gentiles—God deserting the temple which was no longer His temple to the fury of the enemies, of those who were now His enemies—the separation of Christianity from Judaism, which had already begun, became evident to every eye; the conflict between the new faith and heathenism culminating in and now alive almost only in the Emperor-worship, became intense; and the persecuting power of the empire was inevitably let loose. Thus the continued existence of Judaism was in the truest sense a restraint on the persecution of Christians, and its destruction gave the signal for the lawless one to be revealed in his time . . .

"Finally, in this interpretation, the apostasy is obviously the great apostasy of the Jews, gradually filling up all these years and hastening to its completion in their destruction. That the Apostle certainly had this rapidly completing apostasy in his mind in the severe arraignment that he makes of the Jews in I Thessalonians 2:14–16, which reached its climax in the declaration that they were continually filling up more and more full the measure of their sins, until already the measure of God's wrath was prematurely filled up against them and was hanging over them like some laden thunder-cloud ready to burst and overwhelm them—adds an additional reason for supposing his reference to be to this apostasy—above all others, 'the' apostasy—in this passage.

". . . As a matter of mere fact the growing apostasy of the Jews was completed—the abomination of desolation had been set up in the sanctuary—Jerusalem and the temple, and the whole Jewish state was in ruins—Christianity stood naked before her enemies—and the persecuting sword of Divus Caesar was unsheathed and Paul had himself felt it keenness: all the prophecy had been fulfilled before two decades had passed away" (*Biblical and Theological Studies*, pp. 472–475).

One further point needs to be cleared up. After saying that "the mystery of lawlessness doth already work; only there is one that restraineth now, until he is taken out of the way," Paul adds: "And then shall be revealed the lawless one, whom the Lord Jesus shall slay with the breath of his mouth, and bring to naught by the manifestation of his coming" (Vs. 8). We believe that this refers not to Christ's final coming, as so many assume, but to His coming in judgment on the Roman emperor or on the line of emperors, in the same way that He came in judgment on Jerusalem and the nation of Israel. In the Old Testament God's judgment on Egypt was foretold in these words: "Behold Jehovah rideth upon a swift cloud, and cometh unto Egypt: and the idols of Egypt shall tremble at his presence; and the heart of Egypt shall melt in the midst of it" (Is. 19:1); and His judgment on Samaria and Jerusalem was foretold in similar language: "For, behold, Jehovah cometh forth out of his place, and will come down, and tread upon the high places of the earth" (Micah 1:3). Paul was a student of the Old Testament and was quite familiar with its prophetic phraseology. Hence it should not be thought strange that he should sometimes express himself in their spirit and style, as present day speakers sometimes employ the spirit and style of the New Testament to express their messages. When he says that the Lord Jesus will "bring to naught" the lawless one "by the brightness of his coming," anyone who is well versed in Old Testament prophecy will not understand him as having reference to the Second Coming of Christ, but rather as predicting in figurative language the Lord's coming in judgment on the lawless person. The Old Testament has numerous such phrases in its prophetic portions.

Hence the present day premillennial interpretation, and to a lesser extent the amillennial interpretation, of John's references to "antichrist," and Paul's brief reference to a "man of sin," is a typical example of how an obscure reference can be blown up to fantastic proportions and given an interpretation that misses the writer's meaning completely. John's references to "antichrist," not always with clear indication as to whether he had in mind a personal or an impersonal agency, and his statement that "even now have there arisen many antichrists," shows how scanty is the Scriptural evidence for this alleged evil character of the endtime. We are convinced that nothing in any one of John's references requires the embodiment of this anti-Christian influence in a single individual, but rather that the term is applied to false teachers who denied the incarnation. Similarly, we are convinced that Paul's statement that "the mystery of lawlessness doth already work," indicates quite clearly that he was writing of something that related to the problems of his day, not about some mythical figure of the future, who after a lapse of nineteen centuries still has not appeared, and the mention of whose appearance therefore could have had no conceivable value for the people to whom he was writing. The Christians in the early Church needed practical information and encouragement that would prepare them for the fiery trials and suffering that were just ahead. A careful reading of Paul's words should convince an open-minded Bible student that the Antichrist and the apostasy are long since past. Few seem to realize how frail is the foundation on which their doctrine of an Antichrist rests. This, incidentally, if it is the true interpretation as we believe it is, clears another important obstacle out of the way for the post-millennial doctrine that the world is to be converted to Christianity before the end comes, and that when Christ returns He comes to a world in which His cause has already been magnificently victorious.

Chapter VI

THE KINGDOM
POSTPONEMENT THEORY

We have said earlier that one of the distinctive doctrines of Dispensationalism as contrasted with Historic Premillennialism is that it holds that Christ at His first advent intended to establish an earthly Kingdom with Himself as King and with the Jews in favored positions, but that after He had preached "the gospel of the Kingdom" during most of His public ministry the Jews rejected the Kingdom as He had offered it to them and so made necessary its postponement until His Second Coming, and that in the meantime and as an interlude between the two phases of the Kingdom He established the Church. We also pointed out that according to this theory the Church was not foreseen nor predicted by the Old Testament prophets and that it was first revealed to the Apostle Paul.

It is an integral part of this theory that prophetic time (that is, time during which the Old Testament prophecies are being fulfilled) ceased to run with the rejection of the King. Says one writer, "The prophetic clock stopped at Calvary. Not one tick has been heard since." He adds further that "From the moment Christ bowed His head and yielded up His spirit to the Father, all the glories of the kingdom spoken of by Old Testament seers and prophets have been held in abeyance" (Dr. H. A. Ironside, for a number of years pastor Moody Memorial Church, Chicago; *The Mysteries of God*, p. 54). And Dr. Scofield says: "When Christ appeared to the Jewish people, the next thing, in the order of revelation as it then stood, should have been the setting up of the Davidic kingdom. In the knowledge of God, not yet disclosed, lay the rejection of the kingdom (and King), the long period of the mystery-form of the kingdom, the world-wide preaching of the cross, and the out-calling of the Church. But this was as yet locked up in the secret counsels of God (Matt. 13:11,17; Eph. 3:3–10)" (p. 998). In another connection he says: "The kingdom of heaven, announced as 'at hand' by John the Baptist, by the King Himself, and by the twelve, and attested by mighty works, has been morally rejected. The rejected King now turns from the rejecting *nation* and offers, not the *kingdom*, but rest and service to such as are conscious of need" (p. 1011). And again: "The kingdom in its outward form as covenanted to David, and described to the prophets, had been rejected by the Jews; so that during this present age it would not come with observation but in the hearts of men. Meantime the kingdom was actually in the midst of the Pharisees in the person of the King and His disciples. Ultimately the Kingdom of heaven *will* come with outward show" (p. 1100).

We remember that Jesus said: "The kingdom of God cometh not with observation" (Luke 17:20). But here Scofield in effect says, "Ultimately it will come with observation."

The same teaching is put forth by Blackstone: "He (Jesus) would have set up the kingdom but they rejected and crucified Him." And again: "The kingdom did come 'nigh' when Christ came, and had they received Him, it would have been manifested, but now it is in abeyance, or waiting until He comes again" (*Jesus Is Coming*, pp. 87,88).

In opposition to all of this we shall undertake to prove that no earthly kingdom was offered to the Jews, that nothing in the Divine plan was postponed, and that the Christian Church is the fulfillment of that to which the Old Testament prophets, and indeed the entire Old Testament economy, looked forward.

In the first place, it is not the New Testament dispensation of Grace, but the Old Testament dispensation of Law, that actually was parenthetical and temporary. The promise made to Abraham, "In thee shall all the families of the earth be blessed" (Gen. 12:3), as well as the earlier promises to Adam and Noah, had a universalistic tendency. This was temporarily laid aside at Sinai, and the narrower form under which Israel was singled out for special favor came into being, and the universalistic tendency was not again manifested until the work of Christ broke down the middle wall of partition that separated Jew and Gentile. Ritualism and legalism came to an end with the crucifixion of Christ, and salvation was made equally available for all nations and races. The New Testament age or Church age is therefore no parenthesis, no side issue, but the original divine purpose to which the Old Testament had led step by step.

The dispensational theory holds that "prophetic time" is not counted, (1) when Israel is out of the land, or (2) when Israel is in apostasy. Hence we have the view that the kingdom prophecies are not being fulfilled during the Church age when Israel either is out of the land, or is in apostasy, or both, and that the Church is only an interlude between a Jewish kingdom that is past and a Jewish kingdom that is future. The First Advent of Christ, according to this theory brought Israel up to the 70th week of Daniel's prophecy (9:24-27). With the Second Advent, that is, at the Rapture, prophetic time again will begin to run, and the seven years of the Great Tribulation will complete the seventieth week. That in turn will be followed by the establishment of the millennial kingdom on earth.

But there are no grounds either in reason or in Scripture for inserting a parenthesis of many centuries duration between the 69th and 70th week of Daniel's prophecy, a parenthesis which strangely has already extended nearly four times as long as the entire period of the 70 weeks themselves. In this prophecy it is quite evident that the weeks refer to years. The Jews had just completed 70 years captivity in Babylon—years that had run consecutively. Daniel understood from the prophecies that the time was at an end, and he besought God earnestly in prayer for their deliverance. It was revealed to him that 7 times 70 were determined to complete God's dealings with Israel as a nation—for their return to their own land, the rebuilding of Jerusalem and the temple, and until Messiah should come and accomplish His work of redemption. Certainly the natural inference is that in this prophecy time runs concurrently as it does in any other prophecy.

If in our present day social affairs or business contracts we attempted to insert hidden parentheses of days or months or years we would get into trouble immediately. Suppose that a traveling companion asks me how far it is from New York to Denver, and I inform him that it is 70 miles. We travel that distance, and beyond, but haven't reached Denver. So he says to me, "You said it was 70 miles from New York to Denver. But we have already traveled more than that and we still haven't come to Denver." Then I explained to him, "Oh, but there is a parenthesis in there of 2,000 miles that I didn't tell you about. You see, the speedometer is set so that it registers only the first 69 miles, which is country through which I enjoy traveling, then it doesn't register again until we enter the last mile going into Denver." Or suppose that when a note comes due at the bank I inform the banker that there is a five year parenthesis between the dates that hasn't yet run its course. Now if we attempted such chicanery what would be the result? Such trifling would, of course, be condemned as puerile and dishonest. In all of our dealings we assume that the 70th mile follows immediately after the 69th mile, and that the 70th week follows immediately after the 69th week. Nowhere in Scripture is a specified number of time-units, making up a described period of time, set forth as meaning anything but continuous and consecutive time. Likewise, the 70 weeks in Daniel's prophecy are 70 links in a chain, each holding to the others, a definite measure of the remaining time allotted to the nation of Israel before the coming of the Messiah.

In harmony with this, in another of Daniel's prophecies, that in which he interpreted Nebuchadnezzar's dream (2:31–45), he informed the king that the great image of diverse parts that he had seen represented four successive world kingdoms that were to follow in precise order, with a fifth kingdom of a diverse kind to be set up during the days of the kings that would then be reigning, a kingdom which would increase until it filled the whole earth and which would never be destroyed. The head of gold represented the Babylonian, which was then present; the arms of silver the Medo-Persian; the thighs of brass that of Greece, and the legs of iron and feet of iron mixed with clay, the Roman. On this interpretation the dream was chronologically complete from the Babylonian to the Roman empire, and in the days of this last empire the God of heaven did set up a new kingdom different from all the others, which was the Church. That, historically, is exactly what happened. On the other hand, when the Church age is arbitrarily inserted between the 69th and 70th week, the last political empire and the one that God sets up are separated by a long interval of time. In that case the events of the 70th week are left as still future, and a revived Roman empire is needed in order to make possible the fulfillment of the prophecy.

Concerning the idea that there can be such periods of time that are not counted Dr. Allis says:

"According to Dispensational principles, the Babylonian captivity was to an almost unique degree 'time out.' Israel was not in the land; Israel was not governed by God. Yet this period was definitely defined prophetically as 70 years (Jer. 25:11). The same is true of the Egyptian bondage which is described prophetically as 400 years (Gen. 15:13) and historically more precisely as 430 years (Ex. 12:40). If this theory were correct, these should be 'uncounted' intervals. It may also be noted that Dispensationalists who endeavor to explain the 480 years between the Exodus and the beginning of the work on the temple (I Kings 6:1) by reckoning the periods of bondage during the time of the Judges as 'time out,' do not treat the '40 years' of wanderings when Israel was both outside the land and rejected by God as also representing such an uncounted period. This is both inconsistent and arbitrary; and it shows the weakness of the 'Jewish time' theory" (*Prophecy and the Church*, p. 308).

Dispensationalists hold that it was the earthly Jewish kingdom to which John the Baptist and Jesus referred when they said, "The kingdom of heaven is at hand." That means, of course, that the coming of Christ from heaven was primarily a mission to the Jews. In fact Scofield says this in so many words: "The mission of Jesus was, *primarily*, to the Jews. He was 'made under the law' and was 'a minister of the circumcision for the truth of God'" (p. 989). Had the Jews accepted their Messiah, so the theory runs, the Kingdom would have been set up in Jerusalem at that time. And since the Kingdom is *eternal*, the cross would not have been necessary, and atonement for sin would have been made some other way—presumably through animal sacrifices, as during the Old Testament kingdom. According to this view Christ's atonement for the sins of the world became necessary only because His original plan miscarried.

The primary purpose of Christ at His first coming, then, according to Dispensationalism, was to fulfill the glowing predictions of the prophets concerning the future rule of the house of David. The necessary prerequisite, however, for the establishment of the Kingdom, in the preaching of John the Baptist and in that of Jesus, was repentance. But this the Jews refused. Moreover, they not only refused to repent, but actually accused Christ of being in league with the Devil. With the kingdom that He sought to establish thus rejected Christ decided to postpone its establishment until His Second Coming, and instead founded the Church as an institution which through the intervening period would gather both Jews and Gentiles into the heavenly body. Scofield even points out what he terms "the pivotal point in the ministry of Jesus," which he says is Matthew 11:28, "Come unto me, all ye that labor and are heavily laden, and I will give you rest." He affirms that at that point the Kingdom is taken from "Israel nationally and given to the Gentiles" (p. 1029), and that the public entry into Jerusalem (Matt. 21:1–11) was "the King's final and official offer of Himself" to the Jewish nation (p. 1028). The Kingdom thus made way for the Church, which was a distinct and separate entity which can never be merged with the Kingdom, neither in time nor in eternity. And the message is no longer "the gospel of the Kingdom," but "the gospel of the grace of God." Of this Church Christ is said to be not the King but the Divine Head. Thus a new institution of which the prophets had not spoken, and of which they knew nothing, came into being. "The Church corporately," says Scofield, "is not in the vision of the Old Testament prophets" (corporately means "as a body") (p. 711).

The complete refutation of this view, however, is found in Old Testament prophecy itself, which foretold in detail the suffering and crucifixion and death of the Messiah (cf. particularly Is. 53 and Psalm 22). Furthermore, the suffering and death of the Messiah and the purely substitutionary nature of that sacrifice was the essential lesson foretold and taught daily under the Levitical law in the sacrifice of the lamb, in which the life of an innocent and faultless victim was given in place of that of the sinner. There can be no getting around the fact that this was consistently held before the people as God's method of redemption.

Furthermore, the idea that the Divine plan could have been to any degree whatever defeated and thwarted by evil men is utterly contrary to what the Bible teaches concerning the sovereignty of God—"He doeth according to his will in the army of heaven and among the inhabitants of the earth; and none can stay his hand, or say unto him, What doest thou?" (Dan. 4:35); "I know that thou canst do all things, And that no purpose of thine can be restrained" (Job 42:2); "The counsel of Jehovah standeth fast forever, The thoughts of his heart to all generations" (Ps. 33:11); "Jehovah of hosts hath sworn, saying, Surely as I have thought, so shall it come to pass; and as I have purposed, so shall it stand" (Is. 14:24); "In whom we were made a heritage, having been foreordained according to the purpose of him who worketh all things after the counsel of his will" (Eph. 1:11); "All authority hath been given unto me (Christ) in heaven and on earth" (Matt. 28:18). Many more verses of similar import could be cited. How ridiculous, then, to think that puny, sinful man can rise up against God and compel Him to change His plans! The idea that unregenerate man can frustrate the purposes of God is so contrary to clear Scripture teaching and to all right ideas of God that it is almost unbelievable that it could be seriously put forth by any who claim to be students of the Word. We have mentioned earlier that opposition to Premillennialism has come mainly from theologians in the Reformed churches. It is primarily this fact, that sinful man cannot thwart the plans of Almighty God, that makes Premillennialism, particularly in its dispensational form, so unacceptable to Reformed Theology.

Had Christ offered the Jews a political kingdom in the pomp and glory of David and Solomon, as Dispensationalism affirms that He did, they most certainly would have accepted and would have rallied to His standard. That was the very thing they wanted and were expecting. But that is what He clearly refused to offer. After the feeding of the five thousand great numbers of people came to Him for this very purpose. But we read: "Jesus therefore perceiving that they were about to come and take him by force, to make him king, withdrew again into the mountain himself alone" (John 6:15). And the following day, after the multitude had followed Him to the other side of the Sea of Galilee, He declared to them plainly that He was not a political Messiah or miracle bread-king, but a spiritual Ruler, the Messiah who had come down from heaven to give His life for the world (John 6:22–71). Interpreting the promised Davidic kingdom in earthly, carnal and materialistic terms, they rejected the true Davidic kingdom which Jesus offered them, which was spiritual and universal, and they were greatly offended because He so pointedly refused to give them the kind of kingdom that they wanted.

That the Kingdom that Jesus preached is a present reality, the outward manifestation of which is the Church, and that Christ is now reigning on David's throne, is taught in Peter's great Pentecostal sermon. There he declared: "Brethren, I say unto you freely of the patriarch David, that he both died and was buried, and that his tomb is with us unto this day. Being therefore a prophet, and knowing that God hath sworn with an oath to him, that of the fruit of his loins he would set one upon his throne; he foreseeing this [the events on the day of Pentecost, when about 3,000 were converted] spake of the resurrection of the Christ, that neither was he left unto Hades, nor did his flesh see corruption. This Jesus did God raise up, whereof we all are witnesses. Being therefore by the right hand of God exalted, and having received of the Father the promise of the Holy Spirit, he hath poured forth this, which ye see and hear. For David ascended not into the heavens: but he saith himself,

The Lord said unto my Lord,
Sit thou on my right hand,
Till I make thine enemies the footstool of thy feet."

Then Peter adds: "Let all the house of Israel know assuredly, that God hath made him both Lord and Christ, this Jesus whom ye crucified" (Acts 2:29–36).

Here Peter recalls the great promise made to David, that his Son would sit on his throne. And as fulfillment of that promise Peter points to Christ's resurrection from the dead and His exaltation to the right hand of God, the position of power and influence, from which position and in the exercise of His kingship He has poured forth this Pentecostal blessing. David did not himself ascend into the heavens, but he predicted that God the Father would make his Greater Son, here also acknowledged as his Lord, the Ruler in the Kingdom until all His enemies have been made the footstool of His feet. What we now see in the effective forward moving of the Church, says Peter, is the proof that the promise has been fulfilled, that Christ is now on David's throne directing the affairs of His Kingdom. The promise as originally given to David is found in II Samuel 7:12–15, and contains the assurance that the throne of his kingdom shall be established for ever.

Another great promise concerning the tabernacle of David is found in Amos 9:11,12 and reads as follows: "In that day I will raise up the tabernacle of David that is fallen, and close up the breaches thereof; and I will raise up its ruins, and I will build it as in the days of old; that they may possess the remnant of Edom, and all the nations that are called by my name, saith Jehovah that doeth this." And in Acts 15 this prophecy is quoted by James and interpreted as having its fulfillment in the great missionary expansion of the New Testament era, that is, during the Church age, in which the Gentiles are being brought into the Church on an equality with the Jews without being required to submit to Jewish rituals and ceremonies. And this on-going of the work of the Church, this extension of the Kingdom of Christ, is to continue until the remote parts of the earth, here described as "the remnant of Edom, and all the nations that are called by my name," are brought under His rule.

That the Kingdom is a present reality, that it therefore has not been postponed, is taught in a number of Scripture passages. In the song offered to the Lamb, recorded in Revelation 5:9,10, we read: "Worthy art thou to take the book, and to open the seals thereof: for thou wast slain, and didst purchase unto God with thy blood men of every tribe, and tongue, and people, and nation, and madest them to be unto our God a kingdom and priests; *and they reign upon the earth.*" Christ Himself said, "The kingdom of God is within you" (Luke 17:21). The Apostle Paul throughout his ministry preached this message of the presently existing Kingdom; and at the very close of his ministry, when he was a prisoner in Rome, he still was "preaching the kingdom of God, and teaching the things concerning the Lord Jesus Christ" (Acts 28:31). John's message to the first century Christians, "*And he made us to be a kingdom,* to be priests unto his God and Father; to him be the glory and the dominion for ever and ever" (Rev. 1:6), proves beyond doubt that the Kingdom is in the world. Nothing has been postponed. The Kingdom is here, and we are it, says John.

What a striking contrast there is between the dispensational idea of the Kingdom, on the one hand, with Christ as an earthly King, once rejected but yet to set up His throne in the city of Jerusalem, and on the other the Scriptural idea that Christ did establish His Kingdom as planned, that His Kingdom is a spiritual Kingdom in the hearts of men, the Church being the outward and visible manifestation of that Kingdom during this age as the nation of Israel was in Old Testament times, that Christ is now ruling from His throne in Heaven directing the program of His advancing Kingdom, and that He is to go on conquering and to conquer until the whole world has been brought into subjection to Him!

Chapter VII

THE PARENTHESIS
CHURCH THEORY

In its doctrine of the Church Dispensationalism holds that the Jewish rejection of the Kingdom caused Jesus to postpone the Kingdom until the Second Advent and to establish the Church as an interlude between the two advents, and that the Church was in no sense a fulfillment of the Old Testament prophecies and promises but something entirely new and revealed for the first time to the Apostle Paul. According to that view Judaism remains intact as one of the true and acceptable forms of worshipping God, runs a predicted course, and does not give way before nor merge into the New Testament Church as held by Post- and Amillennialists. Commenting on the dispensational idea that the Church was substituted for the Kingdom, and writing in criticism of that view, Dr. Hendriksen says:

"There are those who maintain that the Church is a mere parenthesis, an afterthought in God's program of redemption, a valley invisible to Old Testament prophets who never even dreamed about it; that, in dealing with the Church, history has left the main highway and is making a detour; and that God ignores the flight of time until He deals again with the Jews. In the sight of God, so runs the argument, the Jews are all-important. Hebrew time is the Lord's time. Israel is like a scheduled train which has been put on a side-track temporarily but will be put back on the main track again as soon as the *unscheduled* (!) Gentile-Special has passed through" (Booklet, *And So All Israel Shall Be Saved*, p. 7).

The dispensational view holds that the Church Age will come to an end in the Rapture which, it is alleged, is the first stage of the Second Advent, the miraculous, silent, secret removal of all true believers to meet the Lord in the air. Seven years after the Rapture there occurs the Revelation, which is the public, visible return of Christ and His people to the earth. Thus the key point of the dispensational system may be said to be the mystery-parenthesis doctrine of the Church, which is that the Christian Church is a stop-gap between two phases of an earthly Jewish kingdom, one past and the other future. The particular feature of this system that we now wish to examine is that which holds that the Church is only an interlude, a "parenthesis in history," as it has been called, and that it is to remain eternally separate from that Kingdom.

The key text on which this view of the Church is based is Ephesians 3:3–7:

"How that by revelation was made known unto me the mystery, as I wrote before in few words, whereby, when ye read, ye can perceive my understanding in the mystery of Christ; which in other generations was not made known unto the sons of men, as it hath now been revealed unto his holy apostles and prophets in the Spirit; to wit, that the Gentiles are fellow-heirs, and fellow-members of the body, and fellow-partakers of the promise in Christ Jesus through the gospel, whereof I was made a minister, according to the gift of the grace of God which was given me according to the working of his power."

But while this is the primary passage relied on by Dispensationalists to prove their doctrine of the Church, a careful reading will show that the "mystery" is not the Church, not even a Gentile Church, but the fact that in the Church the Gentiles are to enjoy, and actually do enjoy, a status of *complete and absolute equality* with the Jews. They belong to the same body, and they have the same access to God through prayer and the atonement purchased by Christ as do the Jews.

The "mystery" that Paul speaks of was not completely unknown in Old Testament times, but was not as well known as it now is. It was not unknown to Abraham, for the promise first given to him was that "in thee shall all the families of the earth be blessed" (Gen. 12:3). Speaking through the prophet Isaiah, God declared His reason for having chosen Israel: "I will give thee for a light to the Gentiles, that thou mayest be my salvation unto the ends of the earth" (49:6). Speaking through the prophet

Joel He said: "And it shall come to pass afterward, that I will pour out my Spirit upon all flesh . . . And it shall come to pass that whosoever shall call on the name of Jehovah shall be delivered" (2:28,32). Various other prophets wrote to the same effect. Thus future blessing to the Gentiles, and even equality between Jew and Gentile, was predicted in the Old Testament, but it was not revealed so clearly as in the New Testament.

Nor was the revelation that the Gospel was for the Gentiles as well as for the Jews a revelation to Paul only, nor even given first to Paul. Peter had already been sent to preach to the Gentiles in the house of Cornelius, and in the Jerusalem council he rose up and said: "Brethren, ye know that a good while ago God made choice among you, that by my mouth the Gentiles should hear the word of the gospel, and believe. And God, who knoweth the heart, bear them witness, giving them the Holy Spirit, *even as he did unto us;* and he made *no distinction* between us and them, cleansing their hearts by faith" (Acts 15:7-9). Notice, that he does not say a word about Paul, nor about any special revelation having been made to Paul, but appeals instead to his own experience, which for him had been almost as revolutionary as Paul's experience on the road to Damascus. And Paul, making his defense before king Agrippa, said: "Having therefore obtained the help that is from God, I stand unto this day testifying both to small and great, *saying nothing but what the prophets and Moses did say should come* [thus what he was preaching concerning the Church *was* predicted in the Old Testament]; how that the Christ must suffer, and how that he first by the resurrection of the dead should proclaim light both to the people and to the Gentiles" (Acts 26:22,23).

In regard to the word "mystery" and the meaning given to it by Dispensationalists, Dr. Allis says:

"The word 'mystery' occurs 29 times in the New Testament, most of which are in Paul's epistles, 6 being in Ephesians. It is important, therefore, to observe how the word is used, especially by Paul. Paul speaks of several mysteries: 'the mystery of God, and of the Father, and of Christ' (Col. 2:2), 'of Christ (Col. 4:3), 'of the gospel' (Eph. 6:19), 'of his will' (Eph. 1:9), 'of the faith' (I Tim. 3:9), 'of godliness' (I Tim. 3:16), 'of iniquity' (II Thess. 2:7). These passages show that to describe a person or subject as a mystery does not necessarily imply that he or it was entirely unknown. It might be known, yet still be a mystery because not fully known. God was known in Israel—that was Israel's pre-eminence. To know God was Israel's duty. Yet Paul speaks of 'the mystery of God.' Christ was God 'manifest in the flesh.' He had been on earth and the facts of His earthly life were known. Yet Paul speaks of the 'mystery of Christ.' Especially noteworthy is I Timothy 3:16 where Paul speaks of the 'mystery of godliness' and then refers to events in the earthly life of Christ which were known to and had been witnessed by Christians who were in Christ before him. Consequently, according to Paul, a mystery may be a truth which can only be understood by believers or a truth only partly known to them, but not necessarily something entirely new or utterly unknown. Was the Church a mystery in the latter sense? . . .

"It is significant that Paul never uses the expression, 'the mystery of the Church.' He does not tell us that the Church is a mystery. What he is concerned to tell us is, that something about the Church is a mystery. This he states with great plain-ness and very emphatically. The mystery is, that the Gentiles are to enjoy, actually do enjoy, a status of complete equality with the Jews in the Christian Church. They are 'fellow-heirs, fellow-members of the body, and fellow-partakers of the promise in Christ Jesus through the gospel.' The word rendered 'fellow' is the preposition 'with' ('with-heirs,' etc.), which indicates close association or identification. They are co-heirs with the Jews; they belong to the same body; they share equally with the Jews in 'the promise in Christ Jesus through the gospel.' This is the doctrine which Paul preached with great earnestness (e.g., Rom. 1:14, 3:22, 10:12; I Cor. 12:13; Gal. 3:28f.; Eph. 2:12f.). This important feature of the Christian Church was the mystery. But it was not a mystery in the sense that no inkling of it had ever been given. For by insisting that the Abrahamic covenant in-cluded all who were of a like faith with Abraham (Rom. iv) Paul had already made it clear that the rights of the Gentiles for which he was contending were theirs by virtue of the covenant. It was a mystery in the sense that, like other teachings which were spoken of as such, it was not fully revealed in the Old Testament and was completely hidden from the carnal mind.

A doctrine which was so hated by Jews that they were ready to kill those who preached it (Luke 4:16f.; Acts 22:21f.) and which was unknown to Gentiles, might well be called a mystery. But, we repeat, it was not the Church itself, but this doctrine regarding the Church which was the mystery" (*Prophecy and the Church*, pp. 90–92).

And concerning the same subject Dr. Murray says:

"If the Church remained a hidden mystery until its discovery by Paul, one feels like asking what Jesus Christ meant and what Peter would have understood by the phrase, 'Upon this rock I will build my church' (Matt. 16:18). It is not quite enough for us that the Scofield Reference Bible has in the preface to Ephesians three, 'The Church a mystery hidden from past ages' (*Scofield Reference Bible*, p. 1252). There ought to be something stronger and more conclusive than a Scofield footnote to convince people that the Church which Peter knew and the Church which Paul discovered were not the same . . . How alien to traditional Christianity is this dividing of the redeemed of the Lord into different entities known as *body* and *bride, the bride* and *the friends of the bridegroom* according to the period in which they lived, as though salvation were offered on different terms! *This is not rightly dividing the Word of Truth, but wrongly dividing the Church of God* (italics added). It is putting asunder what God hath joined together" (*Millennial Studies*, p. 34).

As regards the relationship of the Jews to the Gentiles, even a cursory reading of the Bible, either Old Testament or New, reveals that the Jews were chosen not merely for their own sake, but in order that they might be the divinely appointed means for bringing God's message of salvation to the entire world. But so completely did they misunderstand their mission that they generally did not realize that the Gentiles were to have any part in the Divine purpose. They were reluctant even to think of the Gentiles as being of any concern at all to God. This has been well expressed by Dr. Allis:

"For centuries the Jews had looked upon themselves as in a unique sense the people of God; and nothing gave them more grievous offense than the teaching that sinners, unbelieving 'dogs,' of the Gentiles, were to share with them in the blessings of Messiah's kingdom, especially the idea that they would be in any sense their equals in it. But this was also, as we have seen, an old truth which was taught at least in germ in the Abrahamic covenant. The blessing of the nations is one of the prominent features in that covenant. All that was intended or involved in that blessing was not at once made clear. The law was given to Israel. The kingship was Davidic. The Messiah was to come of David's line. Yet in the Psalms and in the Prophets, especially in Isaiah, we are given occasional glimpses of the world-wide scope of this promise to the fathers. A Jew must have had his eyes holden by Jewish prejudice who could not learn from Isaiah 19:23–25 that the future had wonderful things in store for the Gentiles, even for those nations at whose hand Israel had suffered the most. Yet there were other prophecies which seemed to declare with equal clearness that the pre-eminence of the Jews was to continue world without end. Consequently, the statements of the prophets might be regarded as ambiguous, and the carnally minded Jews would naturally interpret them all in terms of their selfish, nationalistic desires and expectations. Clearly, the equality of Gentile with Jew was predicted in the Old Testament. But it was not there made known, 'as it hath now been revealed' to the Apostles and prophets of the Lord" (*Prophecy and the Church*, p. 95).

We hold, therefore, that the Church in which the Gentiles play such an important part is no unforeseen interlude or parenthesis in history but the true and lawful successor of Old Testament Israel, that Judaism served its divinely appointed purpose in preparing the way for the coming of the Messiah and the establishment of the Church, that having served that purpose its mission was accomplished and it was abolished and should never have been revived, and that now Jews and Gentiles in the Church stand on absolutely the same plane with identically the same needs and rights and privileges.

Just at this point many people stumble, for they assume that when we say that the Gentiles have the same rights and privileges as the Jews we are taking something from the Jews that is their exclusive possession. The only thing taken from the Jews was their privilege as a nation of being God's representative in bringing His Gospel to all the earth. That purpose came to an end and was abolished, and originally was intended to be abolished, with the coming of the Messiah and the accomplishment of His work of Redemption. But we repeat that individually nothing has been taken away from the Jews, that under the New Testament dispensation believing Jews retain all of the rights and privileges of access to God and blessing by Him that they possessed in the Old Testament dispensation, and that in point of fact both Jews and Gentiles now enjoy much freer access and a much closer relationship with Him than ever was possible through the Old Testament priesthood and sacrificial system. Even Dr. A. C. Gaebelein, who defends the dispensational position, acknowledges that Christian Jews "possess now something infinitely more glorious than the nation will possess when the Lord comes to restore His ancient people" (*Unsearchable Riches*, p. 30). Dispensationalists generally acknowledge that in the New Testament dispensation the Jews stand on a plane of equality with the Gentiles; yet, with strange inconsistency they teach that after Christ returns there will be a restoration of Judaism with its rituals and ceremonies, and a setting up again of the middle wall of partition between Jew and Gentile.

In reply to the charge that we are "robbing Israel" when we claim for the Church the Old Testament promises and blessings that originally were spoken to Israel, Dr. Allis says:

"It is this [dispensational] attitude, we believe, that deserves to be characterized by the word 'robbery.' It robs Israel of her true destiny and glory by excluding her from the Church of God. By insisting that her heritage is earthly, it robs her of that better portion which is heavenly" (*Prophecy and the Church*, p. 280).

Also in this connection it is appropriate to point out that the Christian Church was not originally a Gentile Church, but a purely Jewish Church. All of the early disciples were Jews. It began as a Jewish organization, and so it continued in the main for the first two or three decades. Then gradually Gentiles were admitted. It was not until after Peter's vision on the housetop and his mission to the house of the Roman centurion Cornelius that he realized that the Gentiles too were to be admitted on terms of equality with the Jews. We can almost hear the gasp of wonder as he said to Cornelius: "Of a truth I perceive that God is no respecter of persons: but in every nation he that feareth him, and worketh righteousness, is acceptable to him" (Acts

10:35). Paul and Barnabas also first preached primarily in the synagogues and to Jews, and it was not until after opposition arose to them that they turned to the Gentiles. In Acts 13:45,46 we read: "But when the Jews saw the multitudes, they were filled with jealousy, and contradicted the things which were spoken by Paul, and blasphemed. And Paul and Barnabas spoke out boldly, and said, It was necessary that the word of God should first he spoken to you. Seeing ye thrust it from you, and judge yourselves unworthy of eternal life, lo, we turn to the Gentiles."

Chapter VIII

THE CHURCH IN
OLD TESTAMENT PROPHECY

Dispensationalism is insistent that the Church was not foreseen by the Old Testament prophets. The reason it was not foreseen, they tell us, is because it was not in the original plan of God, but is an expedient to which Christ resorted when His plan to establish the kingdom was rejected. One of the clearest refutations of that view, however, is the fact that on the day of Pentecost Peter, speaking to the great crowd in Jerusalem, explained the wonderful things that they were seeing (what they were seeing was the Christian Church in its corporate witness) by saying: "But this is that which hath been spoken through the prophet Joel." And then he proceeded to quote:

> "And it shall come to pass in the last days, saith God,
> I will pour forth of my Spirit upon all flesh:
> And your sons and your daughters shall prophecy,
> And your young men shall see visions,
> And your old men shall dream dreams:
> Yea and on my servants and on my handmaidens in those days
> Will I pour forth of my Spirit; and they shall prophecy.
> And I will show wonders in the heaven above,
> And signs on the earth beneath;
> Blood, and fire, and vapor of smoke:
> The sun shall be turned into darkness,
> And the moon into blood,
> Before the day of the Lord come,
> That great and notable day:
> And it shall be, that whosoever shall call on the name of the Lord shall be saved" (Acts 2:17-21; Joel 2:28-32).

In Acts 3:24 we read that after the healing of the lame man at the door of the temple, Peter said: "Yea and all the prophets from Samuel and them that followed after, as many as have spoken, they also told of these days."

To those in the new Church Peter wrote: "Concerning which salvation the prophets sought and searched diligently, who prophesied of the grace that should come unto you; searching what time or what manner of time the Spirit of Christ which was in them did point unto, when it testified beforehand the sufferings of Christ, and the glories that should follow them. To whom it was revealed, that not unto themselves, but unto you, did they minister these things, which now have been announced unto you through them that preach the gospel unto you" (I Peter 1:9–12).

As a means of testing the truth or falsity of the dispensational doctrine regarding the Church the 15th chapter of Acts is one of the most important in the New Testament. This is because the Jerusalem Conference, which is reported there, dealt with the question which had arisen at Antioch regarding the status of Gentiles in the Church, whether or not they were under obligation to keep the Mosaic law. It therefore concerned the nature of the Church and the relation of Gentile and Jew in it. To settle that question James quoted from the Old Testament prophet Amos (9:11,12). In Acts 15:13–18 we read:

"And after they had held their peace, James answered, saying, Brethren, hearken unto me: Symeon hath rehearsed how first God visited the Gentiles, to take out of them a people for his name. And to this agree the words of the prophets; for it is written,

After these things I will return,
And I will build again the tabernacle of David, which is fallen,
And I will build again the ruins thereof,
And I will set it up:
That the residue of men may seek after the Lord,
And all the Gentiles upon whom my name is called,
Saith the Lord, who maketh these things known from of old."

Here in the first general assembly of the Church at Jerusalem James, speaking by inspiration, appeals directly to Old Testament prophecy as having predicted this influx of the Gentiles into the Kingdom. The prophecy concerning the rebuilding of the tabernacle of David is interpreted as having its fulfillment in the rise and expansion of the New Testament Church into all the nations, and on this basis he proceeds to give it as his judgment that circumcision is not to be required of the Gentiles, but only that they refrain from the pollution of idols, from fornication, and from the eating of things that had been strangled and from blood (vss. 19,20), which conclusion was accepted as authoritative by the other apostles. Dr. Scofield says that "Dispensationally this is the most important passage in the New Testament" (p. 1169). However, he interprets it as applying to the future and says that these words "describe the final gathering of Israel." In other words he says that the prophecy quoted by James actually had no direct bearing on the question under debate by the Council. We take our stand with James and maintain that the prophecy did apply definitely and directly to the problem under discussion, namely, the status of the Gentiles in the Church. Furthermore, we insist that here we have clear and direct refutation of the dispensationalist claim that the Church and its attendant problems arising in the New Testament age were not foreseen nor predicated by the Old Testament prophets.

Similarly, Paul justifies his action in turning from the Jews to the Gentiles by an appeal to Old Testament prophecy. In Acts 13:46,47 we read: "And Paul and Barnabas spoke out boldly, and said, It was necessary that the word of God should first be spoken to you. Seeing that ye thrust it from you, and judge yourselves unworthy of eternal life, lo, we turn to the Gentiles. For so hath the Lord commanded us, saying, I have set thee for a light of the Gentiles, That thou shouldest be for salvation unto the uttermost part of the earth." The fact of the matter is that the calling of the Gentiles into the Church was one very important feature in Old Testament prophecy. It is mentioned repeatedly.

When on trial before king Agrippa Paul defended his work in the Church and declared most emphatically that he had said "nothing but what the prophets and Moses did say should come; how that the Christ must suffer, and how that he first by the resurrection of the dead should proclaim light both to the people and to the Gentiles" (Acts 26:22,23). In the midst of his defense he turned to his judge and said, 'King Agrippa, believest thou the prophets?" (Acts 26:27). The conclusion is inescapable that this is the way Paul understood the prophecies, that his interpretation was that the crucifixion and resurrection of Christ and the following work of the Church in which he was so thoroughly absorbed was precisely the thing foretold by the Old Testament prophets. This was the new age to which the prophets had looked forward, and he justifies his work as being just that which had been predicted. Speaking to the Jews in Rome, when they had appointed him a day, Paul "expounded the matter, *testifying the kingdom* of God, and persuading them concerning Jesus, *both from the law of Moses and from the prophets,* from morning till evening" (Acts 28:23). And at the close of the book of Acts we read of Paul's work in the city of Rome at the very end of his ministry: "And he abode two whole years in his own hired dwelling, and received all that went in unto him, *preaching the kingdom of God,* and teaching the things concerning the Lord Jesus Christ with all boldness, none forbidding him" (Acts 28:30,31). Thus throughout his ministry Paul preached the Kingdom of God as manifested in the Church and as the very thing that had been predicted by the Old Testament prophets. Hence the Kingdom is not merely a future hope but a present reality manifested in the Church, although like the grain of mustard seed and like the leaven in the meal, very small in its early stages.

Had the Kingdom been postponed, it would have been impossible for Paul to have preached it as a present reality. Likewise it would have been impossible for him to have persuaded orthodox Jews from the Old Testament that Jesus was the Christ and that the Christian Church which he proclaimed was the fulfillment of those prophecies. The message of the Apostolic Church was not an expedient to which it was driven as a result of frustration by the Jews. Rather it was "the gospel of God, which he promised afore through the prophets in the holy scriptures" (Rom. 1:1,2). In the light of the many references that have been cited it is vain to insist that the Church and its work is "not in the vision of the Old Testament prophets." We cannot do other than brand the dispensational parenthesis view as false.

The Jewish leaders, steeped in their man-made traditions,

completely misunderstood the nature of the Messianic Kingdom. Looking for and desiring only a kingdom of this earth, and unable to understand the higher spiritual kingdom that Jesus preached, they rejected the Messiah and caused Him to be crucified. That was the sin for which they received such heavy punishment.

It should be remembered, of course, that Christ lived under the Old Testament dispensation. He submitted to the ordinances, and kept the feasts, the fasts, and the whole ceremonial law. The Church as a distinct organization was not established until after the close of His public ministry. Consequently, He said very little about the Church, but a great deal about the Kingdom. Yet the New Testament doctrine regarding the Church was latent in His teaching about the Kingdom. As He proclaimed a spiritual Kingdom which was in many ways the antithesis of the earthly kingdom that the Jews were expecting, He was in reality describing the Church which would be founded on the finished work of His redemption.

Our position is that the true or invisible Church is the whole body of the elect of all ages. The visible manifestation of this body in Old Testament times was the nation of Israel, and in New Testament times it is the Christian Church in all its various denominations and branches which truly look to Christ as Saviour. Old Testament Israel, as the congregation of God's people set aside from the Gentiles, was the forerunner of and developed into the Christian Church in which the earthly distinction between Jew and Gentile disappears never to be re-instituted. To re-instate the old distinction between Jew and Gentile after the New Testament era has dawned would be to reverse the forward march of the Kingdom, and would be as illogical and useless as to go back to candle or lamp light after the sun has risen.

Naturally there were some differences between the group which constituted the Lord's people in the Old Testament dispensation and that in the New. The Old was prophetic, looking forward to the coming of the Messiah and His work of redemption; the New is historical, looking back to that accomplished work. The Old was largely national, being limited to the people of Israel and some few individuals who came into that company; the New is universal, designed for and open to men of all nations and races. Furthermore, at Pentecost the Holy Spirit was poured out upon the Church so that it now possesses a much more advanced revelation and a degree of spiritual power for appealing to and bringing in the unsaved such as never was possessed by Old Testament Israel. But these differences are not of great importance. They relate to methods of administration, not to fundamental principles. Each group was a covenant people. Salvation was on the same basis, namely, grace. Never has man been able to earn salvation or to make himself acceptable to God by doing good works. In both dispensations salvation was by blood atonement vicariously suffered, of which the Old Testament saints had the promise and shadow as set forth in the temple rituals and sacrifices and looked forward to its accomplishment, while the New Testament saints have the knowledge of its accomplishment as they look back to Calvary. The rituals and sacrifices were, of course, of no value at all in themselves. Their whole importance lay in the fact that they pointed forward to and prefigured a coming Redeemer and His work of atonement.

From the time of Abraham on God has had a continuing group of believers. Stephen speaks of "the church in the wilderness" (Acts 7:38), by which he certainly says that this same group existed in early Old Testament times. Dr. Hodge expresses it well when he says: "There is no authorized definition of the Church which does not include the people of God under the Mosaic Law." And Masselink says more fully:

"The unity of the New Testament Church with that of the Old is clearly brought out in the Biblical word that is used for 'church.' The Greek word *ekklesia* designates the Church as those 'called out' of the world. The Church is not part of the world but is separated from it. This same thought is contained in Genesis 3:15 when God speaks of the enmity that shall exist between the seed of the woman and the seed of the serpent. It is also expressed in the call of Abraham in Ur of the Chaldees . . . In the letter to the Galatians Paul argues that the Gentile Christians belong to the same covenant that was made with Abraham the father of all believers. The organic unity between the Old Testament Church and the New Testament Church is clearly expressed. This unity must not be disregarded as is done by the Chiliasts. The Hebrews were called out of the nations of the earth to be a peculiar people of God. To them were committed the oracles of God. They received the blessings of adoption as children of God together with the covenant promises. They were called out of the world for a church purpose; namely, to be witnesses of God among the nations" (*Why Thousand Years?* p. 65).

Dr. Allis says:

"The common doctrine of Protestants is that there is only one true Christian Church. It is the Church which is built upon 'the foundation of the apostles and prophets, Jesus Christ Himself being the chief cornerstone' (Eph. 2:20). As a visible body it may have many forms and divisions; and there may be many tares among the wheat. As an invisible body it consists of the elect, of all those who truly believe in Christ as Saviour and belong to Him. The Church was founded at Pentecost. It was originally wholly Jewish and is proved by this very fact to be the continuation and successor of the Old Testament Church. Gentiles were early received into it and soon came to constitute a majority in it; and the teaching that the middle wall of partition between the two was completely broken down was especially, but not exclusively, committed to Paul who was in a pre-eminent sense the apostle to the Gentiles. But no one emphasized more strongly than did Paul the vital oneness of the New Testament Church with the Old Testament Church. The Gentile branches were grafted into the good olive tree that they might enjoy its fatness, the fulness of the blessing promised to all the spiritual heirs of the Abrahamic covenant" (*Prophecy and the Church,* p. 166).

In regard to the meaning of the Greek word, *ekklesia,* translated "church," it is well to keep in mind that in the Septuagint, which was a Greek translation of the Old Testament and which was in common use in Palestine in Jesus' day, the word *ekklesia* is used about 70 times to render the Hebrew word *qahal,* assembly, or congregation. This translation was made in Alexandria, Egypt, about 150 B. C., by a group of 70 scholars, whence it received its name. Consequently the Jewish people were familiar with this rendering and naturally would have connected the New Testament Church with the assembly or congregation of Israel as it had existed in Old Testament times.

It is perfectly obvious, of course, that the Church did not come to maturity until the Holy Spirit was poured out upon it at Pentecost. Whereas the Old Testament saints saw only the shadow of things to come, as those were made known to them through the words of the prophets, the sacrifices and the rituals, the New Testament saints walk in the full light of revelation and know the Christ who has provided that redemption. Furthermore, the New Testament Church has a separate and visible form all its own, while the Old Testament Church was bound up with the Israelitish nation although it was not identical with it. The New Testament Church is universal in its outreach, while the Old Testament Church was limited to the nation of Israel. The Levitical law prescribed in detail both the worship and the civil life of ancient Israel, telling the people what they could do and what they could not do, while we who are in the New Testament Church are free from those restrictions and are governed not by laws but by basic moral and spiritual principles. Hence the glory of the Church under the new dispensation is far greater than it was under the old. But regardless of the differences the Church in the new dispensation is the continuation of that in the old, so that we who are Gentiles are, as Paul tells us, "no more strangers and sojourners, but fellow-citizens with the saints, and of the household of God, being built upon the foundation of the apostles and prophets, Christ himself being the chief corner stone; in whom each several building, fitly framed together, groweth into a holy temple in the Lord" (Eph. 2:19–21).

We have referred to Paul's use of the figure of the olive tree to illustrate the continuity between believers in Israel and believers in the New Testament Church. The people of Israel were the olive tree, but because of unbelief many of them, like dead branches, were broken off. Others were not broken off, but continued in their native tree. In place of the branches that were broken off, branches from a wild olive tree were grafted in, and "became partakers with them of the root and the fatness of the olive tree" (Rom. 11:17). Those who are grafted in are warned, "Glory not over the branches: but if thou gloriest, it is not thou that beareth the root, but the root thee" (vs. 18). Thus the life of the olive tree, which is God's people, continues unbroken. Israel and the Christian Church are not two distinct olive trees, but one. A clearer illustration of the continuity of Old Testament Israel over into the New Testament Church could hardly be imagined.

Another serious defect in dispensational teaching is its doctrine that many portions of the Bible are not meant for the Church age at all, that is, not for Christians, but that they are intended for a future Jewish-led kingdom. This follows from their belief that most of Christ's ministry was taken up with preaching designed to prepare Israel for the Kingdom, but that when it became evident that the Jews would not accept the Kingdom the Church was substituted. This means that the Lord's prayer, the Sermon on the Mount, the Kingdom parables, the Great Tribulation, the Book of Revelation chapters 4 through 19, and some say, most of the New Testament except the Pauline Epistles, are "Jewish" and "legal" and therefore do not concern the Church. We point out, however, that Paul certainly did not make this distinction between the gospel of Grace and the gospel of the Kingdom of God. Rather, he identified the two, for late in his ministry he said to the elders from Ephesus: "For I hold not my life of any account as dear unto myself, so that I may accomplish my course, and the ministry which I received from the Lord Jesus, to testify *the gospel of the grace of God.* And now, behold, I know that ye all, among whom I went about *preaching the kingdom,* shall see my face no more" (Acts 20:24,25).

Thus Dispensationalists would put us back under the Old Testament economy, with a millennial kingdom that is primarily Jewish and earthly. The boundaries of revived Israel would then be either those of the days of Solomon when it extended from the Egyptian border to the Euphrates River, or those of the rectangular state described in Ezekiel's prophecy. The Dispensationalist holds further that the temple will be rebuilt and that the Levitical sacrifices of bulls and goats will be renewed as described in Ezekiel 40–48. We must say that this view is essentially Jewish, in contrast with the view of Historic Premillennialism which, despite its other faults, is to be acknowledged as essentially Christian.

After this survey of the Church in both Testaments we cannot but agree with Dr. Pieters when he says:

"The point at which Dr. Scofield comes most definitely into

conflict with the historic Christian faith, as otherwise held by all branches of the Church, both ancient and modern, is his doctrine of the Church in its relation to the Old Testament Israel. While in his Premillennialism he has a certain degree of support from the post-apostolic age, there is no such support in this matter. This he himself recognizes, for his announcement of his position is as follows: 'Especially it is necessary to exclude the notion—a legacy of Protestant thought from post-apostolic and Roman Catholic theology—that the Church is the true Israel, and that the New Testament foreview of the kingdom is fulfilled in the Church.'"

To this latter comment Pieters replies:

"Here he says that the doctrine he opposes was taught by the Roman Catholic Church. Certainly it was, and by the Greek Church, and by all the Protestant churches, and by any sort of church of whatever name up to the time of John N. Darby, who was born in 1800 and died in 1882, a leader of the sect called the 'Plymouth Brethren'" (A Candid Examination of the Scofield Bible, p. 23).

Dr. H. A. Ironside, a dispensationalist and an ardent disciple of Scofield, acknowledges that the dispensational doctrine of the Church is of comparatively recent origin. Says he:

"In fact, until brought to the fore through the writings and preaching of a distinguished ex-clergyman, Mr. J. N. Darby, in the early part of the last century, it is scarcely to be found in a single book or sermon throughout a period of 1600 years! If any doubt this statement, let them search, as the writer has in a measure done, the remarks of the so-called Fathers, both pre- and post-Nicene, the theological treatises of the scholastic divines, Roman Catholic writers of all shades of thought; the literature of the Reformation; the sermons and expositions of the Puritans, and the general theological works of the day. He will find the 'mystery' conspicuous by its absence" (Mysteries of God, p. 50).

Hence our conclusion must be that the Church was foretold by the prophets. Far from being a mere interlude or parenthesis in Kingdom history, an expedient to which Christ resorted when His plans were rejected by the Jews, the Church is in reality the culmination and fruitage of the Old Testament Kingdom. It is related to Old Testament Israel as the fruit is related to the flower. The organizational continuity between Israel and the Church is not the same, but the spiritual continuity is the same. The Church is, therefore, the instrument of God in all ages for the up-building of the Kingdom. This means further that any of the prophecies or promises made to Old Testament Israel which were not fulfilled before Israel ceased to be a nation, have either lapsed because Israel failed to meet the conditions, or they have now become the property of the Church, which is the true and legal successor to Israel, and so find their fulfillment on a higher and spiritual plane. In other words, with the coming of Christ and the establishment of the Christian Church no Old Testament prophecy or promise remains which relates either to a future Jewish nation or to the Jewish people as such.

Chapter IX

THE COMING OF CHRIST

We have pointed out that the distinctive feature of Premillennialism as regards the Second Coming of Christ is that the Coming precedes the Millennium. Historic Premillennialism has held that certain predicted events are to precede the Coming and that these would be signs that the Coming was near. There has not always been agreement, however, as to what these events would be. Events usually mentioned are: wars, famines, earthquakes, political turmoil and unrest among the nations, the increase of knowledge and new inventions, the preaching of the Gospel to all the nations although there has been no agreement as to how intensive and effective that preaching must be, the return of the Jews to Palestine, and particularly the setting up of a Jewish national government in Palestine. Historic Premillennialism has held that the Church will go through the Tribulation and that the events of Revelation chapters 4 through 19 are to be fulfilled before the return of Christ.

On the other hand Dispensationalism has insisted on the "any moment" Coming, which means that no predicted events remain to be fulfilled, and that there are therefore no signs to herald the Coming. Dispensationalists place the events of Revelation chapters 4 through 19 after the Rapture, and hold that they will occupy a period of seven years.

Premillennialists of both schools represent the Coming as near. They are never tired of quoting: "Watch therefore, for ye know not the day nor the hour" (Matt. 25:13); "The coming of the Lord is at hand" (James 5:8); "For yet a very little while, He that cometh shall come, and shall not tarry" (Heb. 10:37); "Yea: I come quickly" (Rev. 22:20; etc.). They insist that only on the basis of their doctrine of the near return of Christ can justice be done to the warnings in Scripture that we are to be always ready, expect, and watch for the return of Christ. They object to Postmillennialism on the ground that those who believe that Christ is not to come until after the Millennium cannot expect or watch for His Coming during their lifetime.

It is true that Postmillennialists normally do not expect the Second Coming during their lifetime. And in this regard they are in good company, for neither did the apostle Paul expect the Lord's return within his lifetime. For to the elders from Ephesus he said, "I know that after my departing grievous wolves shall enter in among you, not sparing the flock" (Acts 20:29). And again, "For I am already being offered, and the time of my departure is come. I have fought the good fight, I have finished the course, I have kept the faith . . ." (II Tim. 4:6,7).

That the warnings of Christ's Coming are not to be taken in the sense in which Premillennialists take them, as though the Second Coming is to occur soon as measured by the calendar, is proved by the fact that these words were spoken or written over nineteen centuries ago, and the Second Coming has not occurred yet. These words undoubtedly are intended to mean to us the same thing that they meant to the first century Christians. If they were intended to teach that Christ was to return in a short time they have long since been proved false. And that we cannot admit. Men sometimes attempt to encourage false hopes, as in behalf of those who are incurably sick or deeply discouraged; but such counsel is hardly consistent with common honesty, and certainly such counsel could not have had any place in the teaching of Christ. If Christ had reference to His Second Coming but did not know whether or not it would occur within their lifetime, then at best He could have warned them that His Coming *might* occur within that time. Honesty would have required that qualification. But the fact is that He gave them a practical warning against an event or events which it was implied would happen within their lifetime, not a speculative warning against something that might or might not happen during that time.

And just what should be the psychical state of mind of those who are watching for the Second Coming of Christ? Are they to "jab their noses against the window panes, looking for Him?" Or are they to stand gazing into the sky in the hope of seeing Him appear at any moment in the clouds? Some have done just that. We venture to say, however, that the correct way to watch is to go steadily about our work, accomplishing the tasks that are before us, so that when He comes He will find us so occupied. "Who then is the faithful and wise servant, whom his lord hath set over his household, to give them their food in due season? Blessed is that servant whom his lord when he cometh shall find so doing. Verily I say unto you, that he will set him over all that he hath" (Matt. 24:45–47).

The time of Christ's final Coming was entirely uncertain, and even He Himself in His human nature did not know when that would happen—"But of that day and hour knoweth no one, not even the angels in heaven, neither the Son, but the Father only," Matt. 24:36. So far as His words were concerned that Coming might have been soon, or it might have been in the far distant future,—as we now see that it was. The disciples were told to be always ready, but there were no clear indications as to what form His coming would take. There were some indications His final Coming might occur only after a considerable delay. On one occasion when the disciples (somewhat like the present day Premillennialists) "supposed that the kingdom of God was immediately to appear" (Luke 19:11), He gave them the parable of the nobleman who went into "a far country" to receive a kingdom—an event which would take considerable time to accomplish. In the parable of the talents it was "after a long time" that the Lord of those servants came to make a reckoning with them (Matt. 25:19). In the parable of the ten virgins the bridegroom after a long delay came at midnight, at the most unexpected hour (Matt. 25:6).

Immediately before the ascension of Christ the disciples asked, "Lord, dost thou at this time restore the kingdom to Israel?" But His reply was: "It is not for you to know times and seasons, which the Father hath set within his own authority. But ye shall receive power, when the Holy Spirit is come upon you: and ye shall be my witnesses both in Jerusalem, and in all Judaea and Samaria, and unto the uttermost part of the earth" (Acts 1:6–8). And more important and perhaps more clearly than anywhere else, in the Great Commission the disciples were commanded: "Go ye therefore, and make disciples of all the nations, baptizing them into the name of the Father and of the Son and of the Holy Spirit: teaching them to observe all things whatsoever

I commanded you: and lo, I am with you always, even unto the end of the world" (Matt. 28:19,20).

The task of presenting an effective witness to all the earth (and we cannot believe that anything less than an effective witness will satisfy this command), and the task of making disciples of all the nations (and again, we cannot believe that anything less that the Christianizing of these nations is the task assigned to the Church), this task, we say, is far from completed even in our day. In these passages Jesus repressed all expectation of the disciples for a restoration of the kingdom to Israel in their day and taught them that after His departure they would have other work which in the very nature of the case would be more than could be accomplished within their lifetime. Surely as the apostles came to realize the magnitude of the task that was to be accomplished in the Christian era these considerations were sufficient to discourage any idea of an immediate or speedy return of Christ. True, they did not immediately understand the import of these words, nor the magnitude of the task that was assigned to them. But after Pentecost they did understand. And though the Church began to grow, yet during their lifetime the heathenism of the empire scarcely felt the impact of the stone which was mysteriously cut out without hands (Dan. 2:34), and the darkness that covered the earth had scarcely begun to be dissipated by the beams of the Sun of Righteousness (Mal. 4:2). But a start had been made, and in due time the divinely appointed results would appear.

Another class of passages, those which announce the judicial transfer of the Kingdom of God from the Jews to the Gentiles, teaches the same lesson. "The kingdom of God shall be taken away from you, and shall be given to a nation bringing forth the fruits thereof" (Matt. 21:43), said Jesus to the Jews; and again, "And Jerusalem shall be trodden down of the Gentiles, until the times of the Gentiles be fulfilled" (Luke 21:24). Paul wrote: "A hardening in part hath befallen Israel, until the fulness of the Gentiles be come in; and so all Israel shall be saved" (Rom. 11: 25,26). Even a primitive Christian might be expected to understand that the duration of the Kingdom in Gentile hands might reasonably be expected to be in proportion to the time that it had previously been in Jewish hands. The old dispensation was the time of the fullness of the Jews, and it had lasted some fifteen centuries; the new dispensation, the New Testament era, which was to extend from Pentecost until the end of the world, was the time of "the fullness of the Gentiles." And the "all Israel" which is to be saved includes not merely some part of the Jewish people (it is very clear that not *all* Jews are saved), but the sum total of the elect, God's people composed of both Jews and Gentiles, "the Israel of God," that Paul refers to in Galations 6:16.

Just in proportion as the early Christians understood the teaching of Jesus they could not have expected His early return. The course of history through the past nineteen centuries demonstrates the truth of this statement. We can only marvel that after all this time, through which the Premillennialists have steadily insisted that the return of Christ was "near" or "imminent," only to be proved wrong generation after generation and century after century, there still should be those who with great earnestness and often with a considerable show of learning insist on that selfsame tenet. Such belief has been founded, not on knowledge, but on ignorance. There is an old saying to the effect that "The only thing that people learn from history is that people do not learn anything from history." How true that has been in regard to the doctrine of the speedy or imminent return of Christ!

Various Ways In Which Christ Comes

In reply to the objection that we cannot watch for the coming of Christ unless we think of His Second Coming as imminent, it is important to keep in mind that the word "come" or "coming" is used in different senses. There are various ways in which Christ comes. Unless we recognize this we only involve ourselves in error. Premillennialism fails to do justice to the *manifold* comings of Christ. It is so absorbed with the final and so-called Second Coming that it stubbornly refuses even to acknowledge that there are others. The present writer has read numerous premillennial books which treat at length the final Coming but which either ignore or scoff at the idea that there are other ways in which Christ comes. We agree that there will be one great, final, visible, glorious, personal Coming. But we find that Scripture teaches there are also other ways in which He comes.

In both the Old and the New Testament the providential

presence and activity of God in human affairs is represented as a coming of God or of Christ. We cite the following:

1. THE COMING OF CHRIST TO THE CHRISTIAN AT DEATH.

This is a coming which so far as affording opportunity to watch is concerned is fully the equivalent of the Second Coming. There is a coming of Christ for the believer at the time of his death, and we know that for each of us that event is in the comparatively near future. We believe this was the primary sense intended when Jesus said, "Watch therefore, for ye know not the day nor the hour" (Matt. 25:13); "Watch, therefore: for ye know not on what day your Lord cometh . . . Therefore be ye also ready: for in an hour that ye think not the Son of man cometh" (Matt. 24:42,44). That coming, like the sword of Damocles which was suspended by only a hair, hangs over the head of every mortal. In many instances it has fallen with startling suddenness. For the Christian it means translation into the very presence of Christ. The present writer recalls a statement made years ago by his college Bible teacher, Dr. J. B. Work, who said: "The Lord is coming for me when I die; and the end of the world for me is when I leave it." That, we believe, is the coming of Christ and the end of the world that we have most need to be prepared for.

The warnings quoted from Matthew 24:42,44 and 25:13 were spoken with great earnestness, and were intended as intensely practical warnings to the first disciples. They likewise have been of great practical value to those who have lived in all succeeding generations and are as practical for our generation as for that one to which they were spoken. For the great majority of people who pass through this world it is this coming rather than the great final Coming that should be their primary concern. If these warnings had related only to the final Coming they would have been not only useless but a source of confusion to those to whom they were first spoken, for the disciples would then have been encouraged to look for an event which in reality was not to occur until the remote future.

Many years ago David Brown wrote:

"The death of an individual is, to all practical purposes, the coming of Christ to that individual. It is his summons to appear before the judgment seat of Christ. It is for him the close of time, and the opening of an unchanging eternity, as truly as the second advent will be to mankind at large." He warned, however, against identifying the two events too closely and pointed out that Christ's coming for the believer at death is in nowise a substitute for the final coming. "The death of believers," he said, "however changed in its character, in virtue of their union with Christ, is, intrinsically considered, not joyous, but grievous—not attractive, but repulsive. It is disruptive of a tie which the Creator formed for perpetuity—the unnatural and abhorrent divorce of parties made for sweet and uninterrupted fellowship. True, there is no curse in it for the believer; but it is the memorial of the curse, telling of sin, and breach of the first covenant, and legal wrath. All of the ideas, therefore, which death as such is fitted to suggest, even in connection with the better covenant, are of a humiliating kind. Whatever is associated with it of a joyous nature is derived from other considerations, by which its intrinsic gloominess is, in the case of believers, relieved. But the Redeemer's second appearing is, to the believer, an event of unmingled joyousness, whether as respects the honor of his Lord, which will then be majestically vindicated before the world, or his own redemption, which will then be complete" (*The Second Advent* pp. 21,22).

2. THE COMING OF GOD OR OF CHRIST IN JUDGMENT.

In the Olivet discourse recorded in Matthew 24 we have in figurative language a prediction of Christ's coming in judgment on the apostate nation of Israel, which coming occurred in the year 70 A. D. Said He: "But immediately after the tribulation of those days [we have already seen that the "tribulation" referred to the horrors connected with the siege and fall of Jerusalem], the sun shall be darkened, and the moon shall not give her light, and the stars shall fall from heaven, and the powers of the heaven shall be shaken: and then shall appear the sign of the Son of man in heaven: and then shall all the tribes of the earth mourn, and they shall see the Son of man coming in the clouds of heaven with power and great glory" (vss. 29,30). And in verse 34 we have the time of this coming fixed very definitely: "Verily I say unto you, This generation shall not pass away, till all these things be accomplished."

The use of pictorial language has caused many to believe that this could refer only to the end of the world. But the fact was that those events would be so horrible, so beyond the powers of the human mind to grasp, that ordinary prosaic language could not convey their awfulness. For the Jews who would survive the fall of Jerusalem, who would find their sacred temple in ruins, their nation destroyed, their families scattered or killed, and themselves or their countrymen slaves in a foreign land and in the depths of despair, it would seem as if the very elements of nature had been changed, as if they were in a different world, so great would be the contrast with their former condition.

The reference to "the sign of the Son of man in heaven," has caused the commentators no little trouble. It is perhaps best understood to mean that not the sign, but the Son of man, the ascended Lord, is in heaven, that the sign appears on the earth and is seen by the disciples, that it was in fact the event that took place on the day of Pentecost, which was in the truest sense a visible and tangible sign to the disciples by which they were enlightened regarding the real nature and purpose of Christ's Kingdom and through which they were given the power to speak other languages and so were equipped to be His ministers to the various nations of the earth.

In Mark 14:61,62 we have a declaration similar to that recorded by Matthew. At the trial of Jesus before Caiaphas and the Sanhedrin the high priest asked Him, "Art thou the Christ, the Son of the Blessed?" and Jesus answered, "I am: and ye shall see the Son of man sitting at the right hand or Power, and coming with the clouds of heaven." Since this event was to occur within the lifetime of the members of the Sanhedrin, these events are best referred to His coming at the destruction of Jerusalem.

Coming with clouds, or coming on the clouds of heaven, was a familar Old Testament expression for His coming in judgment. The words of judgment on Egypt spoken through the prophet Isaiah are: "Behold, Jehovah rideth upon a swift cloud, and cometh unto Egypt . . . And I will stir up the Egyptians against the Egyptians; and they shall fight every one against his brother, and every one against his neighbor; city against city and kingdom against kingdom . . . And I will give over the Egyptians into the hands of a cruel lord; and a fierce king shall rule over them, saith the Lord, Jehovah of hosts" (19:1–4). In Psalm 104:3 we read of Him "Who walketh upon the wings of the wind; who maketh the clouds his chariot." And the prophet Nahum says: "The clouds are the dust of his feet" (1:3).

Pictorial language is used to portray the judgment of God upon Babylon and upon Edom. Concerning Babylon it was said: "Behold, the day of Jehovah cometh, cruel, with wrath and fierce anger; to make the land a desolation, and to destroy the sinners thereof out of it. For the stars of heaven and the constellations thereof shall not give their light; the sun shall be darkened in its going forth, and the moon shall not cause its light to shine" (Is. 13:9,10). Judgment on Edom is similarly declared: "And all the hosts of heaven shall be dissolved, and the heavens shall be rolled together as a scroll; and all their host shall fade away, as the leaf fadeth from the fig-tree. For my sword hath drunk its fill in heaven: behold, it shall come down upon Edom, and upon the people of my curse, to judgment" (Is. 34:4,5).

Also in the Old Testament God's judgment on Jerusalem and Samaria was described in similar language: "For, behold, Jehovah cometh forth out of his place, and will come down, and will tread upon the high places of the earth. And the mountains shall be melted under him, and the valleys shall be cleft, as wax before the fire, as waters that are poured down a steep place. For the transgression of Jacob is all this, and for the sins of the house of Israel" (Micah 1:3–5).

Concerning the events of Matthew 24:29,30, as read in the light of Isaiah's and Micah's prophecies, Rev. J. Marcellus Kik, whose exposition of this 24th chapter of Matthew is the best that we have found, has well said:

"The prophet Isaiah definitely refers the darkening of the sun, moon and stars to the judgment of God against Babylon. The language can only refer to Babylon. Babylon in all its shining beauty and its marvelous glory was to be totally eclipsed. Hence the use of such highly figurative language. If the Holy Spirit speaking through the prophet Isaiah uses such figurative language to describe the downfall of a heathen nation like Babylon, *how much more* would not such language be used to describe the downfall of the chosen nation of Israel? . . . Surely, no one will maintain that when the judgment of God came upon

Idumea [Edom] that the hosts of heaven were dissolved and the heavens were rolled together as a scroll and that all the stars fell down as leaves falling from a vine! Surely, no one will maintain that a literal sword came down from heaven upon Idumea. Surely, everyone recognizes this as figurative language to describe a sudden and total judgment against Idumea. If the Holy Spirit speaking through the prophet Isaiah uses such figurative language to describe the downfall of such an insignificant nation as Idumea, *how much more* would not such language be used to describe the downfall of the Jewish nation!" (*Matthew Twenty-Four*, p. 66).

Also concerning those events Mr. Kik says:

"If the sun, moon, and stars refer to the Jewish nation and its prerogatives, then we have seen the fulfillment of this prophecy. The Jewish nation has been darkened and no longer shines for God. This has been true ever since the tribulation of those days. God in His righteous wrath has removed the Jewish nation from His heavens. The sun of Judaism has been darkened: as the moon it no longer reflects the Light of God; bright stars, as were the prophets, no longer shine in the Israel of the flesh" (p. 65).

Parenthetically, we may add that verse 31 has caused many to believe that these events can refer only to the Second Coming of Christ. It reads: "And he shall send forth his angels with a great sound of the trumpet, and they shall gather together his elect from the four winds, from one end of heaven to the other." In the Greek the term translated "angel" is "aggelos." This, however, does not always mean heavenly spirits. In various other New Testament passages it is translated "messenger." See: Matt. 11:10; Luke 7:24,27; 9:52; Mark 1:2; and James 2:25. In these passages John the Baptist, the messengers that John the Baptist sent to Jesus, the disciples of Jesus, and the messengers who were sent to Rahab, are called "aggeloi," or "angels." Consequently the term in Matthew 24:31 does not necessarily mean "angels" in the commonly accepted sense. We think that here it can better be translated "messengers," indicating that the messengers of Christ, that is, His ministers, are sent forth to preach the Gospel and to gather in His elect from all parts of the earth. That, in fact, is what His ministers started doing almost immediately after His ascension, and they have continued that work until the present day.

3. The Coming of Christ to the Disciples After His Resurrection.

This was a literal coming, or we may say, a literal return. In His last discourse He said: "I will not leave you desolate: I come unto you"; and, "Ye heard how I said to you, I go away, and I come unto you" (John 14:18,28). And again, "A little while, and ye behold me no more; and again a little while, and ye shall see me" (John 16:16). The disciples were perplexed at those words, for they had not yet understood what He meant when He told them that He must be killed and that He would rise on the third day. As the event proved, His resurrection and His appearances to the disciples was a glorious coming again, by which He "was declared [proved] to be the Son of God with power" (Rom. 1:4), a coming which restored and strengthened the bewildered disciples. When during His public ministry Jesus first disclosed that He was to be crucified He said: "Verily I say unto you, There are some of them that stand here, who shall in no wise taste of death, till they see the Son of man coming in his kingdom" (Matt. 16:28). Because this coming was to take place within the lifetime of the disciples it can be referred to His coming to them after His resurrection. At that time the crucifixion had taken place, and the atonement had been made. The Kingdom, therefore, was firmly established on its proper basis and had been launched upon its world-wide mission. Hence the disciples during their lifetime truly saw Him "coming in his kingdom."

4. The Coming of Christ on the Day of Pentecost.

Peter explained the events of the day of Pentecost by saying: "This is that which hath been spoken through the prophet Joel." And then he proceeded to quote: "And it shall be in the last days, saith God, I will pour forth of my Spirit upon all flesh . . ." (Acts 2:16–21). The attendant gifts are named: prophecy, visions, the showing of wonders, signs, etc. And that this was the work of Christ providentially manifesting His presence in human affairs, Peter makes clear in verse 33: "Being therefore by the right hand of God exalted, and having received of the Father the promise of the Holy Spirit, he hath poured forth this, which ye see and hear."

In the events of Pentecost Christ, the Messianic King, came to His people with a great out-pouring of His Spirit, an impressive manifestation of His power, which enlightened and equipped the apostles to be world evangelists, and which in the initial launching of the Church resulted in the conversion of about 3,000 souls in one day (vs. 41).

5. THE COMING OF CHRIST TO THE CHURCHES OF ASIA MINOR.

This was a coming in blessing or in judgment in the early part of the Christian era. To the church in Ephesus the Lord gave this warning: "Remember therefore whence thou art fallen, and repent and do the first works; or else I come to thee, and will remove thy candlestick out of its place, except thou repent" (Rev. 2:5). To the Church in Pergamum He said: "Repent therefore; or else I come to thee quickly, and I will make war against them [the Nicolaitans] with the sword of my mouth" (Rev. 2:16). To the church in Laodicea He said: "Behold, I stand at the door and knock: if any man hear my voice and open the door, I will come in to him, and will sup with him, and he with me" (Rev. 3:20). This, of course, was not a visible coming, but it was nevertheless a very real coming. Similar warnings were given to the other churches. Christ did come to each of those early churches, not with outward appearance, but in His providential care and control; and each of the predictions was fulfilled. He came sometimes in deliverance and to give rewards, and sometimes in judgment.

6. THE COMING OF CHRIST TO VARIOUS CITIES IN PALESTINE DURING HIS PUBLIC MINISTRY.

When the twelve disciples were sent out on a preaching mission Jesus said to them: "But when they persecute you in this city, flee into the next; for verily I say unto you, Ye shall not have gone through the cities of Israel, till the Son of man be come" (Matt. 10:23). He evidently meant that He Himself would visit those same cities shortly, for we are told that soon after He "appointed seventy others, and sent them two and two before his face into every city and place, whither he himself was about to come" (Luke 10:1).

These passages illustrate again how some references that are generally understood as referring to the Lord's final return are legitimately capable of quite a different interpretation. Dr. Scofield says that the passage in Matt. 10:23 relates to "the preaching of the remnant in the tribulation preceding the return of Christ in glory" (p. 1009). Another ardent Premillennialist, Dr. G. Campbell Morgan, wrote that "This coming of the Son of man" can be explained only in terms of judgment, which judgment fell on Jerusalem in 70 A.D. (*The Gospel According to Matthew,* p. 106). We feel compelled to reject both of those views. It was clearly the purpose of Jesus to preach the Gospel in the various cities of Israel. Matthew tells us that "Jesus went about all the cities and villages, teaching in their synagogues, and preaching the gospel of the kingdom, and healing all manner of disease and all manner of sickness" (9:35). And Luke records that on another occasion Jesus said: "I must preach the good tidings of the kingdom of God to the other cities also: for therefore was I sent" (4:43). We give it as our opinion that the interpretations of Matthew 10:23 by the writers just quoted illustrate the tendency to read the Lord's final return into passages which in reality have quite a different meaning.

7. THE COMING OF CHRIST TO BELIEVERS.

There is a coming of Christ to individual believers, and a presence of Christ through the Spirit with believers, in all ages. In John 14:21,23 we read: "He that hath my commandments, and keepeth them, he it is that loveth me: and he that loveth me shall be loved of my Father, and I will love him, and will manifest myself unto him . . . If a man love me, he will keep my word: and my Father will love him, and we will come unto him, and make our abode with him." And again: "Where two or three are gathered together in my name, there am I in the midst of them" (Matt. 18:20).

8. THE FINAL, PERSONAL, VISIBLE, GLORIOUS COMING OF CHRIST AT THE END OF THE AGE.

Apart from the preliminary and limited comings of Christ there is to be a final, world-wide Coming in which He will manifest Himself as visibly and personally as when He ascended from the Mount of Olives. Premillennialists often assume that any-one who acknowledges the preliminary comings does not believe in a final and climactic Coming. But that conclusion does not follow. The Scriptures clearly represent Christ as coming in some manifestations to the people of His own generation and to later generations; and they just as clearly set forth His Coming in glory and judgment at the end of the age.

It is worthy of note that the New Testament never speaks of the return of Christ as His "second coming"—no doubt for this reason, that He comes in various ways and at all periods of world history. During the Old Testament era God came to men on numerous occasions—to Abraham when He announced that Sodom would be destroyed; to Jacob as he wrestled with the Angel; to Moses at the burning bush and on Mount Sinai; to Manoah and his wife when He announced that a son Samson would be born; to the boy Samuel in the temple; etc. An ap-pearance such as these is called a "theophany." The "Angel of Jehovah" who made these appearances was in time revealed as the Christ of the New Testament, the second person of the Trin-ity, who in all ages has been the Mediator between God and man. Time and again the providential presence or activity of God in human affairs is spoken of as God's coming to or meeting with His people. The Old Testament representations throw much light on the New Testament teaching, and we are prepared to find that the coming of Christ is not limited to His final, climac-tic Coming. Quite naturally a certain amount of misunderstand-ing has arisen because the New Testament does not draw a sharp distinction between the partial, preliminary comings and the final Coming.

Some further points which are often overlooked are brought out by Dr. Craig in the following paragraph:

"It is the thought of the Lord's return as *absolutely certain* rather than the thought of it as imminent that dominates the New Testament. Moreover, if we are to appreciate the emphasis that the New Testament places on this 'Blessed Hope' we must remember that it is the hope not only of the saints on earth but also of all those who in the ages past have entered into their rest. It is the hope, therefore, of Abraham and Isaiah and Paul no less than of those of us who still labor on the earth. Hence, assuming that we die before the final return of our Lord, we will continue to long for it until it actually takes place. That is to say, all the saints, whether they are in heaven or on earth, are looking for that blessed hope and the glorious appearing of our great God and Saviour Jesus Christ. And the reason for this is to be found in the fact that the saints do not attain their full blessedness until the Second Advent. Unquestionably the blessed dead are in a state of bliss as compared with what they experienced on earth: none the less 'better things' are in store for them, and these better things will not be theirs until at His coming Jesus will give them their resurrection bodies and say unto them, 'Come ye blessed of my Father, inherit the kingdom prepared for you from the foundation of the world" (*Jesus As He Was And Is*, p. 286).

Chapter X

THE RESURRECTION

The distinctive feature of Premillennialism as it relates to the Resurrection is that there is to be not one general Resurrection as set forth in Post- and Amillennialism, but two or more limited resurrections, separated by at least a thousand years between the first and the last. Historic Premillennialism holds that the first resurrection is that of the saints, both Old and New Testament saints, who are raised at the Coming of Christ and who are to reign with Him through the Millennium, and that a thousand years later, at the end of the Millennium, there occurs the resurrection of the wicked of all ages, who are raised for judgment and condemnation.

Dispensationalism requires three or perhaps four resurrections to meet the demands of its system. According to this system the first, that of the saints, occurs at the Rapture. This is followed seven years later, at the Revelation, by the resurrection of other saints who have died or been put to death during the Great Tribulation. Both Historic Premillennialism and Dispensationalism logically call for a resurrection at the end of the Millennium of the righteous who have died during that time—presumably there will be some death of the righteous as well as of the wicked during the Millennium, for we read, "The child shall die a hundred years old, and the sinner being a hundred years old shall be accursed" (Is. 65:20). Dr. Scofield neglected to give any pronouncement regarding this point, and no other authoritative voice has been able to do so. Also, Dispensationalism holds that there is to be a resurrection of the wicked of all ages at the end of the Millennium, that being the fourth needed to meet the requirements of this system.

Revelation 20:4-6.

The premillennial view is based primarily on three Scripture references. The first is Revelation 20:4-6, which is the chief and only direct support for the doctrine of two or more resurrections. It reads as follows:

"And I saw thrones, and they sat upon them, and judgment was given unto them: and I saw the souls of them that had been beheaded for the testimony of Jesus, and for the word of God, and such as worshipped not the beast, neither his image, and received not the mark upon their forehead and upon their hand; and they lived, and reigned with Christ a thousand years. The rest of the dead lived not until the thousand years should be finished. This is the first resurrection. Blessed and holy is he that hath part in the first resurrection: over these the second death hath no power: but they shall be priests of God and of Christ, and shall reign with him a thousand years."

In our discussion of Postmillennialism we have given what we believe to be the correct interpretation of this passage, which is that it is not a description of a physical resurrection at all, but rather a figurative descripiton of the righteous dead in the intermediate state, or, as some prefer to take it, that it relates to the regeneration of the soul, which change carries over into the intermediate state as its chief sphere of activity. We have noted that there is no reference in these verses to the Jews, nor to Jerusalem, nor to an earthly kingdom of any kind, all of which are important elements in the premillennial scheme. Furthermore, John saw the "souls," not the bodies, of those who were reigning with Christ. And most important of all, we noted that in verse 6 "the first resurrection" is set in contrast with "the second death," which clearly cannot be a second physical death, but which in verse 14 is set forth as the state of eternal punishment of the wicked: "And death and hades were cast into the lake of fire. This is the second death, even the lake of fire." Since in this passage the second death is not a physical death, there is no reason to believe that the first resurrection is a physical resurrection. Clearly both are figurative expressions.

In support of the view that "the first resurrection" finds its fulfillment in the regeneration of the soul, we find various Scripture passages which use similar language. In Colossians 2:12 we read: ". . . wherein ye were also raised with him through faith in the working of God, who raised him from the dead." Here the new birth is directly called being "raised with him." In Colossians 3:1 we read: "If then ye were raised together with Christ [past tense], seek the things that are above, where Christ is, seated on the right hand of God." In Ephesians 2:5 we are told that God "made us alive together with Christ." In Romans 6:13 there is the command, "present yourselves unto God as alive from the dead." In Romans 6:4 our "walk in newness of life" is compared with His resurrection. In John 11:25,26 this new life of the soul is said to continue on into eternity without interruption: "I am the resurrection, and the life: he that believeth on me, though he die, yet shall he live; and whosoever liveth and believeth on me shall never die." In these verses the change that is brought about by regeneration, in which the soul is brought from spiritual death to spiritual life, is set forth as in one sense a resurrection, and is likened to or compared with the resurrection of Christ.

Concerning the premillennial doctrine of two resurrections Dr. Berkhof says:

"The only Scriptural basis for this theory is Revelation 20:1–6, after an Old Testament content has been poured into it. This is a very precarious basis for various reasons. (1) The passage occurs in a highly symbolical book and is admittedly very obscure, as may be inferred from the different interpretations of it. (2) The literal interpretation of this passage, as given by Premillenarians, leads to a view that finds no support elsewhere in Scripture, but is even contradicted by the rest of the New Testament. This is a fatal objection. Sound exegesis requires that the obscure passages of Scripture be read in the light of the clearer ones, and not *vice versa*. (3) Even the literal interpretation of the Premillenarians is not consistently literal, for it makes the chain in verse 1 and consequently also the binding in verse 2 figurative, often conceives of the thousand years as a long but undefined period, and changes the souls of verse 4 into resurrection saints. (4) The passage, strictly speaking, does not say that the classes referred to (the martyr saints and those who did not worship the beast) were raised from the dead, but simply that they lived and reigned with Christ. And this living and reigning with Christ is said to constitute the first resurrection. (5) There is absolutely no indication in these verses that Christ and His saints are seen ruling on the earth. In the light of such passages as Revelation 4:4; 6:9, it is far more likely that the scene is laid in heaven. (6) It also deserves notice that the passage makes no mention whatever of Palestine, of Jerusalem, of the temple, and of the Jews, the natural citizens of the millennial kingdom. There is not a single hint that these are in any way concerned with this reign of a thousand years" (*Systematic Theology*, p. 715).

Interesting and instructive also is the view of Prof. Hamilton, who believes that the first resurrection has reference to the regeneration of the soul and that it continues through the intermediate state. Says he:

"The first resurrection is the new birth of the believer which is crowned by his being taken to heaven to be with Christ in His reign during the interadventual period. This eternal life which is the present possession of the believer, and is not interrupted by the death of the body, is the first resurrection and participation in it is the millennial reign." He continues:

"In John 5:24–29 we have two resurrections brought together in the same paragraph. 'He that heareth my word, and believeth him that sent me, hath eternal life, and cometh not into judgment, but is passed out of death into life. Verily, verily I say unto you, the hour cometh and now is, when the dead shall hear the voice of the Son of God; and they that hear shall live . . . Marvel not at this: for the hour cometh in which all that are in the tombs shall hear his voice, and shall come forth, they that have done good, unto the resurrection of life; and they that have done evil, unto the resurrection of judgment.' Now though the word 'first resurrection' is not used in this paragraph, clearly the fact is taught inescapably. What else can we call passing 'out of death into life,' but resurrection? Notice that it is contrasted with the resurrection which takes place when the dead bodies of all men are raised. Notice also that it is said that *all* that are in the tombs shall hear the voice of Christ and come forth. Then, as they come forth from the tombs, the separation takes place into the resurrection of life and the resurrection of judgment. The use of these two terms, 'resurrection of life' and 'resurrection of judgment' in connection with the previous statement that *all* hear Christ's voice and come forth for the separation into the resurrection of life and the resurrection of judgment, in no way indicates a separation in time of a thousand years, as the premillennialists claim, for it distinctly says that all, good and bad, hear the voice and come forth" (*The Basis of Millennial Faith,* p. 117).

These considerations make it quite evident that "the first resurrection" referred to in Revelation 20:4–6 is not to be taken literally, and our conclusion must be that this passage does not support the premillennial doctrine of two or more physical resurrections.

The second passage quoted by premillennialists as supporting the doctrine of two resurrections is,

I Corinthians 15:22–26

"For as in Adam all die, so also in Christ shall all be made alive. But each in his own order: Christ the firstfruits; then they that are Christ's, at his coming. Then cometh the end, when he shall deliver up the kingdom to God, even the Father; when he shall have abolished all rule and all authority and power. For he must reign, till he hath put all his enemies under his feet. The last enemy that shall be abolished is death."

It should be noted first of all that there is no definite statement here that the resurrection is divided into two parts, but, even on premillennial principles, only an implied interval between the resurrection of the saints and the consummation of all things. Actually, in this passage Paul has believers only in mind, and does not say anything at all about a resurrection of unbelievers. The point that he is making is that just as all die in Adam, so all who are made alive are made alive in Christ. Christ and Adam each acted in a representative capacity and as the federal head of his people. Whenever Paul uses the term "in Christ," he includes believers only. Never in his writings, or in other New Testament writings for that matter, are unbelievers said to be "in Christ." Hence in this passage he sets forth only two orders of the resurrection, namely, Christ's resurrection, and they that are Christ's at His coming. Christ is the "firstfruits"; believers belong to the harvest. Nothing is said about unbelievers or about the resurrection of unbelievers in the entire chapter.

And since nothing can be proved from silence, there is no basis at all for the notion that this passage sets forth a period of time between the resurrection of the righteous and that of the wicked.

When Paul speaks of the resurrection of Christ, then of those that are His at His coming, and adds, "Then cometh the end," Premillennialists attempt to get from this statement a long interval of time, and to interpret it to mean the end of the resurrection, that is, the resurrection of the wicked, which they say comes at the end of the Millennium. Dr. Geerhardus Vos, who admittedly is one of the most capable exegetes that the Church has produced, says that the Greek word *eita* (then) in itself may mean sequence with or without chronological interval, but that in this instance the construction indicates rather that it is to be understood with reference to "the close of the great eschatological finale, which leads over from this aeon (age) into the coming one." He adds that the "end" here spoken of follows closely the second coming of Christ and that it is "the giving up of the kingship to God, the Father," and that "this 'giving up' is nothing else but the culminating result of the eschatological process of subduing the enemies" (*The Pauline Eschatology*, p. 244).

Let it be noticed that Paul does not say that after the resurrection of those who are Christ's, then comes "the end of the resurrection," but only that then comes "the end." Where this expression, "the end," is used in other places in Scripture it means the end of all things, or the end of the world. There is no reason why it should be given another meaning here. The natural meaning is that the resurrection of the righteous and the grand finale, the very last end, fall together. Verse 52 tells us that the resurrection of the righteous occurs at "the last trump." Hence since this is *the last trump* there can be no other trump for another resurrection a thousand years later.

Dr. Warfield says concerning this passage:

"Because the resurrection of the wicked is not mentioned it does not at all follow that it is excluded; the whole section has nothing to do with the resurrection of the wicked (which is only incidentally included and not openly stated in the semi-parenthetic explanations of verses 21 and 22), but, like the parallel passage in I Thessalonians, confines itself to the Christian dead. Nor is it exegetically possible to read the resurrection of the wicked into the passage as a third event to take place at a different time from that of the good, as if the apostle had said: 'Each shall rise in his own order; Christ the first-fruits—then Christ's dead at His coming—then, the end of the resurrection, namely, the wicked.' The term, 'the end,' is a perfectly definite one with a set and distinct meaning, and from Matthew (e.g., 24:6, cf. 24:14) throughout the New Testament, and in these very epistles (I Cor. 1:8; II Cor. 1:13,14), is the standing designation of the 'end of the ages,' or the 'end of the world.' It is illegitimate to press it into any other groove here. Relief is not however got by varying the third term, so as to make it say that 'then comes the end, accompanied by the resurrection of the wicked,' for this is importing into the passage what there is absolutely nothing in it to suggest. The word *tagma* does not in the least imply succession; but means 'order' only in the sense of that word in such phrases as 'orders of society.' . . . Not only, however, is there no exegetical basis for this exposition in this passage; the whole theory of a resurrection of the wicked at a later time than the resurrection of the just is excluded by this passage. Briefly, this follows from the statement that after the coming of Christ, 'then comes the end' (verse 24). No doubt the mere word 'then' (*eita*) does not assert immediateness, and for aught necessarily said in it, 'the end' might be only the next event mentioned by the Apostle, although the intervening interval should be vast and crowded with important events. But the context here necessarily limits this 'then' to immediate sequence" (*Biblical and Theological Studies*, p. 484).

When we realize that this is the chief passage in the writings of Paul to which Premillennialists appeal, we see how little support is to be found for this system in his epistles.

The third passage that is alleged to teach two resurrections is,

I Thessalonians 4:13-17

"But we would not have you ignorant, brethren, concerning them that fall asleep; that ye sorrow not, even as the rest, who have no hope. For if we believe that Jesus died and rose again, even so them also that are fallen asleep in Jesus will God bring with him. For this we say unto you by the word of the Lord, that we that are alive, that are left unto the coming of the Lord, shall in no wise precede them that are fallen asleep. For the Lord himself shall descend from heaven with a shout, with the voice of the archangel, and with the trump of God: and the dead in Christ shall rise first; then we that are alive, that are left, shall together with them be caught up in the clouds, to meet the Lord in the air: and so shall we ever be with the Lord."

The controversial statement in this passage is in verse 16: "The dead in Christ shall rise first." Here we find that some of the Christians in the church in Thessalonica who had lost loved ones and who evidently looked for the Lord's return in the near future were worried for fear that when He did come to take those who were living their loved ones who had died would be left behind. Hence Paul writes to assure them that their Christian dead shall not be left behind, but that in fact they shall be raised first, and that then the living and the dead shall be caught up together to meet the Lord in the air.

When the Premillennialist reads Paul's words, "And the dead in Christ shall rise first," he immediately adds in his imagination, "And the dead without Christ shall rise last." But that is not what Paul says. The contrast is not between the resurrection of believers and that of unbelievers, but between the resurrection of believers and the transfiguration or catching up of believers who are alive when Christ returns. Whereas the Thessalonians were afraid their loved ones who had died would not share in the glory of the Lord's return, Paul assures them that they will indeed share in it, that in fact by their resurrection they will be the first to share in it, and that then they and the living believers shall be caught up together to meet the Lord in the air. There is in this passage, as with the others, no reference at all to the resurrection of the wicked. Rather Paul says that the resurrection of the righteous has preference, not in regard to the wicked, but to the catching up or rapturing of the living saints, that the righteous dead shall be not one moment behind the living righteous in gaining the presence of the Lord. There is here, as with the other passages, no basis at all for the doctrine of a second resurrection.

One other verse that sometimes is quoted to prove that there are two resurrections is Philippians 3:11, "If by any means I may attain unto the resurrection from the dead." This is changed to read, the resurrection "from among the dead," or, "the out-resurrection from the dead," implying that the righteous are raised up and out of others who are left behind. It is said that Paul here expressed himself as striving to attain unto the first resurrection, in order that he might share in the millennial reign. But in the Greek the phrase used is *ek nekron*, "from the dead"; and it is left to the reader to decide whether the supplement should be "from (among) the dead," or "from (the place of) the dead," or "from (the state of the) dead." In other instances *nekron* is used without the *ek*, and is translated "of the dead."

This technical argument, however, proves nothing. For in I Corinthians 15:12 *ek nekron* and *nekron* are used interchangeably, where admittedly the reference in both cases is to the resurrection of the righteous: "Now if Christ is preached that he hath been raised from the dead, how say some among you that there is no resurrection of the dead?" Here the resurrection of Christ Himself is cited as a resurrection "from the dead"; hence the expression cannot mean that only the wicked remain for a future resurrection. Again, *nekron* (without *ek*) is used of the righteous in I Corinthians 15:42–44: "So also is the resurrection of the dead. It is sown in corruption; it is raised in incorruption; it is sown in dishonor; it is raised in glory; it is sown in weakness; it is raised in power: it is sown a natural body; it is raised a spiritual body." Actually the terms are interchangeable, and the use of the one or the other determines nothing regarding the time of the resurrection. Snowden points out that this same Greek preposition (*ek*), as used in Philippians 3:11, "occurs in other passages where no one would think it means 'from among,' as in John 6:26, 'because ye ate of the loaves'; and Galatians 3:7, 'they that are of faith.' In most cases this preposition is translated simply 'from' and has no such meaning as this unscholarly premillenarian interpretation seeks to place upon it" (*The Coming of the Lord*, p. 176).

We are told in other passages that *all of the dead* shall hear the voice of the Son of God in the same day and hour and that they shall rise in a general resurrection: "Marvel not at this: for the hour cometh, in which *all that are in the tombs* shall hear his voice, and shall come forth; they that have done good, unto the resurrection of life; and they that have done evil, unto the resurrection of judgment" (John 5:28,29). And in Acts 24:15 we read, "There shall be a resurrection [singular] both of the just and unjust."

Four times in the Gospel of John we are told that Christ will raise up believers "at the last day": "And this is the will of him that sent me, that of all that which he hath given me I should lose nothing, but should raise it up *at the last day*" (6:39); "For this is the will of my Father, that every one that beholdeth the Son, and believeth on him, should have eternal life; and I will raise him up *at the last day*" (6:40); "No man can come to me, except the Father that sent me draw him: and I will raise him up *at the last day*" (6:44); and, "He that eateth my flesh and drinketh my blood hath eternal life; and I will raise him up *at the last day*" (6:54). And according to John 12:48, "the last day" is also the time of the judgment of the wicked: "He that rejecteth me, and receiveth not my sayings, hath one that judgeth him: the word that I spake, the same shall judge him *in the last day*."

Since the resurrection of the righteous is "at the last day," it cannot occur a thousand years before the last day. And since after the last day there are no other days on which the wicked might be raised, their resurrection too must occur at this same time. In I Corinthians 15 and I Thessalonians 4 the resurrection of the wicked was not mentioned, not because they do not rise at the same time, but because they do not rise on the same *principle*. The righteous are represented by and are entitled to life in Christ, and their resurrection bodies, like His, are glorious and incorruptible. But no such principle governs the resurrection of the wicked. No one stands representative for them, or assumes their guilt. Instead each stands alone. Our conclusion must be that all of the dead without exception rise at the same time, in what we call a "general resurrection," at the end of the world. There is but one resurrection, but there are two classes of people —the just and the unjust. As they come forth the separation takes place, into the resurrection of the just and the resurrection of the unjust.

And in contrast with the very long period of time assigned by Premillennialists for the events of the end time, 1000 years, as taken from the highly figurative passage in Revelation 20:1–10, the more didactic portions of Scripture and particularly the writings of Paul indicate that the events will transpire in the shortest possible period. The dead are raised, the living saints are transformed in the twinkling of an eye, and together they are caught up to meet the Lord in the air. These events are represented as practically simultaneous. The judgment, too, occurs on this last day. So almost immediately, it seems, or at least within a relatively short time, Christ and His people return to earth where the judgment takes place. The fact that it is called "the last day" is proof that it is the end of this world, or of this age—not the end of time for us as individuals, for as finite human beings we shall always be creatures of time. In the nature of the case the last day cannot be followed by any other days or time or seasons whatever. These events close what is called "this world" or "this age," and are followed by the age to come, which we call eternity.

A further problem that arises regarding the premillennial scheme is, What becomes of the saints who die during the Millennium? And what becomes of the righteous who are on earth at the end of the Millennium? The answers to these questions may be somewhat startling to the reader, for the fact is: This whole subject is a blank in the system. Premillennialists do not profess to have any Scripture on the subject. All that the Scripture has to say about the resurrection of the saints they apply to those who are raised at the Rapture or at the beginning of the Millennium. For the most part the subject is avoided. Those who have attempted to grapple with this problem have been able to offer nothing more than conjectures or human speculations. One of the older writers, Edward Bickersteth, suggests that both righteous Jews and righteous Gentiles will continue into eternity here on earth, a righteous race, generation after generation, and will therefore be continually propagating their kind and adding more souls to the kingdom. His reasoning is:

"The covenant with Noah was 'an everlasting covenant between God and every living creature of all flesh for perpetual generations.' The covenant with Abraham is called by the Psalmist 'the word which he commanded to a thousand generations.' So Moses describes the Lord as 'keeping covenant and mercy for a thousand generations.' This period of a thousand generations, thus repeatedly mentioned would reach far beyond the close of the millennium. The promises made to Isaiah, concerning the kingdom of Christ, and His reigning on the throne of David, are in the strongest expressions of never-ending continuance. The same promise of perpetuity is often given to the people of Israel: 'Thy people shall be all righteous, they shall inherit the land for ever' (Is. 60:21). Corresponding with this is that very full and clear promise, 'They shall dwell in the land, and they and their children and their children's children for ever, and my servant David shall be their prince for ever.' The plain and obvious meaning of such passages would lead us to the conclusion of a continuance, both of Israel and Gentile nations in a state of righteousness on our earth" (Quoted by David Brown, *The Second Advent*, p. 169).

On Premillennial principles this would seem to be a logical conclusion. It agrees with the view of some more recent Dispensationalists who hold that there are to be two groups of the Lord's people, the Jews on earth, and the Church in heaven, permanently separate. It fails, however, to give due consideration to the statements in II Peter 3:7–10 that the world is to end in fire, which statement Premillennialists in general take literally. One writer suggests that fire falls on the rebel hosts around Jerusalem, but that the city itself is preserved. The argument, however, seems far-fetched.

It is a generally understood principle of interpretation that references to perpetuity are to be extended no further than *the known duration of the thing spoken of*. The Jews, for instance, were commanded to keep such institutions as the Sabbath and the passover "throughout their generations by an ordinance for ever." But that meant not through all eternity, but through the duration of their particular polity—that is, through what we now term the Old Testament period. With the coming of Christ and the institution of the New Covenant those things were fulfilled and done away with. On this principle the references to "perpetual generations," "thousand generations," "inheriting the land for ever," and such like carry no weight. Paul says that after the resurrection, "Then cometh the end" (I Cor. 15:24); and Peter refers to "the end of all things" (I Peter 4:7). But it would seem that according to this theory there is never to be an end of anything!

Chapter XI

THE JUDGMENT

The doctrine of the Judgment traditionally held by the Church and set forth in the great historic confessions of faith is that there is to be a day of Judgment immediately following the resurrection, and that all mankind will be included. But if Dispensationalism sets forth three or four resurrections, it is not less fruitful in reaping a rich harvest of judgments. The Scofield Bible, which as we have seen is the textbook for modern Dispensationalism, sets forth seven, which are as follows:

(1) The Judgment of Believers' Sins.
(2) The Judgment of Self in the Believer.
(3) The Judgment of Believers' Works.
(4) The Judgment of the Living Nations.
(5) The Judgment of Israel.
(6) The Judgment of Fallen Angels.
(7) The Great White Throne Judgment.

Not all Dispensationalists, however, have insisted on as many as seven. Dr. Feinberg distinguishes four: (1) that of believers; (2) that of Israel; (3) that of the living nations at the time Christ returns; and (4) that of the Great White Throne (*Premillennialism Or Amillennialism?* pp. 191-194). For each of these he gives five particulars: the subjects; the time; the place; the basis; and the results. Blackstone likewise distinguishes four, omitting the judgment of Israel, and substituting a judgment of angels, which he says follows that of the Great White Throne. This series of judgments, he tells us, requires intervals of time, and so precludes the idea of a general Judgment (*Jesus Is Coming*, pp. 101-106).

Haldeman also distinguishes four judgments: (1) that of the cross, when Christ took our sins upon Himself; (2) that at the judgment seat of Christ, which takes place in the air immediately after the Rapture and is a judgment of Christians only—they being judged not in regard to life and salvation but only on the basis of their faith and good works, and receiving greater or lesser rewards; (3) that of the living nations, at the Revelation, based on their treatment of the Lord's "brethren" in the flesh, the Jews; and (4) that at the Great White Throne, which occurs at the close of the Millennium (*Ten Sermons on the Second Coming*, p. 299).

Dr. James M. Gray sets forth still another series of judgments. He says that the day of Judgment is a long period of time, during which "several distinct acts or scenes" of judgment take place. These are: a judgment of Christian believers, in the air, after the Rapture; a judgment of the Jewish nation, on the earth; a judgment of the Gentile nations, this also on the earth, after the Revelation; a judgment of Gog and Magog at the close of the Millennium, this also on the earth; and a final judgment of all the dead (*Christ and Glory*, pp. 199–212).

This diversity of opinion among representative Premillennialists indicates that they do not have clear Scripture proof for their views.

Our chief interest, however, has to do with the series of judgments outlined in the Scofield Bible. The first of these, termed, *The Judgment of Believers' Sins,* we are informed took place at Calvary, where Christ took our sins upon Himself and condemned them. It is a fact, of course, that our sins were paid for and blotted out by His suffering and death on the cross. But since no individuals appear in that transaction it is difficult to see on what grounds it should be called a judgment. Christ's work on the cross is more accurately referred to as an expiation or an atonement.

The second, *The Judgment of Self in the Believer,* is a prolonged process in the soul of every Christian, beginning at the time of his conversion and continuing throughout his life as his actions and even his inner thoughts are scrutinized in the light of God's Word. Conscience plays an important part here. We merely point out, however, that the working of conscience is not even in the same category with what we mean when we speak of final judgment, and to speak of it as such only leads to confusion.

The third is, *The Judgment of Believers' Works.* This is said to be based on Paul's words in II Corinthians 5:10: "For we must all be made manifest before the judgment seat of Christ; that each one may receive the things done in the body, according to what he hath done, whether it be good or bad." But there is no reason why these words should not be understood as describing a general judgment at the end of the age. Dispensationalists say that this judgment takes place following the Rapture. They also say that Paul's words were addressed to Christians, and that his use of the pronoun *we* indicates that only Christians will be present at this judgment. But that argument is far from conclusive. As Dr. Murray says: "Even if Paul is addressing Christians and telling them that they must all appear before the judgment seat of Christ, that does not mean that they shall be there by themselves. He is alluding to a universal judgment which shall be experienced by all men, Christians included . . . In the context he refers to 'the terror of the Lord.' We can hardly imagine that Paul would associate any terror with our Lord's dealing with the Church 'between the rapture and the revelation' after He had welcomed the church to Himself" (*Millennial Studies,* p. 163). There is no reason why this should not be the same judgment referred to in Revelation 20, where John says that "the dead, the great and the small" stand before the throne, and that they are judged "according to their works" (vs. 12). John says that "every man" is judged, and Paul says that "all" are judged, so that "each one may receive the things done in the body" (II Corinthians 5:10). In each case the judgment is according to their works.

The fourth is, *The Judgment of the Living Nations.* This is one of the most important judgments in the dispensational system, for it determines what nations are to enter the millennial kingdom. The Scripture alleged to teach this judgment is Matthew 25:31–46, where the shepherd separates the sheep from the goats. For this judgment all of the nations of the earth existing at the time of Christ's return, that is, at the time of the Revelation when He returns to earth with His saints, are gathered together before Him as Judge, and they are judged on the basis of the treatment they have accorded His "brethren," that is, the Jews, during the Great Tribulation. The "sheep nations," those that have befriended the Jews, enter the millennial kingdom; and the "goat nations," those that have persecuted the Jews, are destroyed. Scofield says: "This judgment is to be distinguished from the judgment of the great white throne. Here there is no resurrection. No books are opened. Three classes are present: sheep, goats, and brethren. The time is the return of Christ and the scene is on the earth . . . The test in this matter is the treatment accorded by the nations to those whom Christ here calls 'my brethren.' These 'brethren' are the Jewish Remnant who will have preached the Gospel of the kingdom to all nations during the tribulation" (p. 1036).

Dispensationalists identify the location of this judgment as "The valley of Jehosaphat," a valley on the east of Jerusalem separating it from the Mount of Olives. No explanation is given as to how the nations can be assembled within such a limited area, or how they shall be transported there, or whether or not this judgment is made through representatives. They do insist, however, that the decrees of this judgment have nothing to do with individauls but only with nations in their corporate existence. But the fact of the matter is that a nation has no existence apart from the individuals who compose it, and that it is impossible to reward or punish a nation except by rewarding or punishing the individuals that make up that nation. If any nation as such were to have pronounced upon it the words of blessing pronounced in this judgment, "Come ye blessed of my Father, inherit the kingdom prepared for you from the foundation of the world," or the words of condemnation, "Depart from me, ye cursed, into the eternal fire which is prepared for the Devil and his angels" (vss. 34,41), then, since it is the nation in its corporate existence that is judged, all of the individuals of such a nation would inevitably receive the same reward or suffer the same punishment. In reality no nation is composed altogether of good people, or of bad people. When Peter came to the house of Cornelius he said: "Of a truth I perceive that God is no respecter of persons: but *in every nation* he that feareth him, and worketh righteousness, is acceptable to him" (Acts 10:34,35). And when God was about to destroy Sodom Abraham's momentous question was, even regarding wicked Sodon, "Wilt thou consume the righteous with the wicked?" (Gen. 18:23). The

answer is that as regards inheriting the kingdom or being consigned to the eternal fire, which are the sentences pronounced
in this judgment, the individual stands on his merits regardless
of the state of the majority of the nation. In our own nation of
America no doubt only a minority of the people can be described
as truly Christian; yet if Christ were to come today would any-
body insist that the minority should be punished along with the
majority? Or are we to believe that today we as individuals are
to be held responsible for all that our government does? We
certainly hope not.

That the judgment scene in Matthew 25 has to do not with
nations but with individuals should be clear from the fact that
the things the righteous did and the unrighteous failed to do are
things normally done by individuals—the giving of food and
water and clothes and shelter, and particularly their visiting
Him when He was in prison. Furthermore, if the wicked nations
are sent into eternal punishment at the beginning of the Millennium, there would be no such nations left on earth during the
Millennium over which Christ is supposed to rule with a rod of
iron! Nor would there be any wicked nations at the close of the
Millennium, concerning which we are told Satan is to "come forth
to deceive the nations which are in the four corners of the earth,
Gog and Magog, to gather them together to the war: the number
of whom is as the sand of the sea," Rev. 20:8—unless the Millennium is to be looked upon as more of a period for apostasy than
for evangelism!

The correct interpretation of the judgment scene in Matthew 25 hinges on the meaning of the expression, "all the nations"
(vs. 32). A few chapters later this same expression is used in
giving The Great Commission: "Go ye therefore, and make disciples of all the nations, baptizing them in the name of the Father
and of the Son and of the Holy Spirit: teaching them to observe
all things whatsoever I commanded you: and lo, I am with you
always, even unto the end of the world" (28:19,20). Here it
clearly means the individuals of the whole human race, since
only individuals can be taught and baptized. So why should
it have any other meaning in Matthew 25:32? Paul uses the same
expression in Romans 16:26 to mean everyone in general when
he says that the mystery of the Gospel which was not revealed

in earlier ages now "is made known unto all the nations." There is no reason to believe that it has any other meaning in Matthew 25:32.

And how unreasonable it is to suppose that Christ would pronounce nations righteous or blessed merely because they had treated non-Christian or anti-Christian Jews in a kindly manner! God took their nation away from them and drove them out because they rejected His Christ; and as long as they remain in that apostate state there hangs over them the sentence recorded in I Thessalonians 2:16, that "wrath is come upon them to the uttermost." Furthermore, there is no reason to believe that Jesus would use the term "brethren" for those who are unsaved merely because they are Jewish nationals. On ten different occasions in the Gospels He used the terms "my brethren" or "my brother," and these emphasize that for Him the spiritual ties of faith in Himself and obedience to God the Father supersede the ties of race and family, as when He said, "Whosoever shall do the will of my Father who is in heaven, he is my brother, and sister, and mother" (Matt. 12:50). Never once does he use one of these terms to include unbelieving Jews. Rather He denounced unbelieving Jews as "of your father the Devil" (John 8:44). Furthermore, it is worth noting, as Grier points out, that "While the word 'nations' is a neuter noun (in Greek), the pronoun immediately following is masculine. 'Before him shall be gathered all the nations (neuter), and he shall separate them (masculine) one from another, as a shepherd divideth his sheep from the goats.' The use of the masculine pronoun points to individuals rather than nations" (The Momentous Event, p. 50). Rutgers remarks that "It would almost seem superfluous to refute such a wild hypothesis that the nations are judged as nations, the basis of their judgment being their treatment of the Jews. As salvation is personal, individual, so too the judgment will be personal, each one being rewarded or punished according to his deserts" (Premillennialism in America, p. 223). And Brown says that this interpretation is "so preposterous that nothing but the exigencies of a hard pressed theory could ever have suggested it" (The Second Advent, p. 253).

We have given this particular judgment of the dispensational system a disproportionately lengthy treatment because it forms such a vital part of that doctrine. If this is shown to be without foundation there does not remain much reason for holding on to the other separate judgments.

The fifth is *The Judgment of Israel.* Not all Dispensationalists acknowledge that there is to be a separate judgment of Israel. As we pointed out earlier, some have as few as four. But Scofield has seven, and this is one of them. It seems somewhat inconsistent that there should be a judgment of Israel after Christ returns, for according to this theory the Jews, gathered in Palestine before His return, are to be converted *en masse* at the mere sight of their Messiah. Also Paul makes the statement that "All Israel shall be saved" (Rom. 11:26), generally understood by Dispensationalists as referring to those on earth at the time of His return. Some writers connect this with the Great Tribulation, the continuing seven year period between the Rapture and the Revelation, these visitations of suffering on Israel being a form of judgment so that a remnant calls on the name of the Lord and he comes to their deliverance. But W. L. Pettingill, one of the collaborators in the production of the Scofield Bible, says:

"This judgment will take place on earth in the wilderness of Judea after the return of Christ in His glory, and will be for the purpose of sifting out the rebels against Jehovah and His rule. These will be kept from entering into the Land of Promise in connection with the setting up of the kingdom of David. Study Ezekiel 20:35 and 34 and Psalm 50 for details" (*God's Prophecies for Plain People,* p. 44).

The sixth is, *The Judgment of Fallen Angels.* This judgment is based on Paul's words in I Corinthians 6:3: "Know ye not that ye shall judge angels?" The Church is to be associated with Christ in this judgment. Dispensationalism has not been able to fix the time and place. However, Murray well says in criticism that, "There does not need to be any doubt as to when this shall take place. Scripture is so plain and definite on that matter that only an inordinate affection for numbers would lead men to regard the judgment of fallen angels as a separate judgment. 'And the angels which kept not their estate, but left their own habitation, he hath reserved in everlasting chains under darkness unto the judgment of the GREAT DAY' (Jude 6). The Great

Day is the day of which Christ, Paul and others have spoken when all humanity shall appear before God's throne of judgment." (*Millennial Studies*, p. 171).

The seventh and last of this series is, *The Great White Throne Judgment*. This is based on Revelation 20:11–15. It occurs at the very end of the Millennium, and is a judgment of the wicked dead only. None of the righteous can appear, for they are all said to have been included in the "first resurrection" and the "Judgment of Believers' Works" which occurred at the Rapture. It would seem, however, that the righteous who died during the Millennium, as well as those on the earth at the end of the Millennium, should be included in this final judgment, otherwise they have no judgment at all. The only way to avoid this conclusion is to assume still another and special resurrection and judgment for them, such are the vagaries to which this theory leads.

But that Revelation 20:11–15 describes not a judgment of the wicked only, but of both the righteous and the wicked is strongly indicated by the fact that the *book of life* is opened and the judgment proceeds from that. The statement that, "*If any was not found* written in the book of life, he was cast into the lake of fire," instead of proving that only the wicked are judged actually indicates the opposite, namely, that the large majority *were* found written there, and were saved, and that it was only an occasional name that was not found. This agrees with our view expressed earlier that eventually the large majority of the human race will be saved, and that heaven is immensely larger than hell. It would in fact seem a mockery of the worst kind to have this precious record of God's redeeming love brought into court only to be used as an instrument for condemning to hell all who are then judged. What a strange use the Dispensationalists make of the "book of life"! Surely we would expect the book of life to be used in a positive way, proclaiming that those whose names are written in it are pronounced just and assigned to their heavenly rewards.

The Dispensational scheme is, therefore, so seriously defective in its doctrine of the Judgment that this alone is sufficient to call in question, if in fact it does not destroy, the whole system. Who can read all this guessing about a continuing series of judgments without realizing how wrong is a system which leads to such results? These distinctions find no basis in Scripture, but are the product of a fertile imagination and a wrong method of interpretation. Christ said: "The hour cometh, in which *all* that are in the tombs shall hear his voice, and shall come forth; they that have done good unto the resurrection of life; and they that have done evil unto the resurrection of judgment" (John 5:28,29). At the same voice *all* come forth to Judgment. None of His hearers could have understood the Lord to have spoken of a series of judgments extending over a period of a thousand years. Paul says: "He hath appointed a day in which he will judge the world in righteousness by the man whom he hath ordained" (Act 17:31). On different occasions Christ spoke of "the judgment," implying that there would be but one (cf: Matt. 5:21,22; 12:41,42). Repeatedly He spoke of "the day of judgment." We are convinced that there is but one general universal Judgment, that it occurs at the end of the world, and that it includes all men, believers and unbelievers, the living and the dead. The two most prominent judgment passages in Scripture are Matthew 25:31–46 and Revelation 20:11–15. These two describe the same event. Matthew places the emphasis on what happens to the living, while Revelation tells what happens to the dead. Matthew makes no mention of a resurrection; and Revelation, describing the event as occurring after the end of the world, makes no mention of any living. The uniform view in Scripture is that the coming of Christ is the occasion for Judgment. On the other hand Dispensationalism divides into several parts and distributes over a period of a thousand years that which the Scriptures represent as one unified, majestic, divine transaction.

Chapter XII

THE KINGDOM

The primary difference between the post- and amillennial view on the one hand and the premillennial view on the other as regards the Kingdom has to do with whether or not the Kingdom is spiritual in nature, now present in the hearts of men, the outward manifestation of which is the Church, or whether it is political and economic, absent from the earth at the present time but to be established in outward form when Christ returns.

There is indeed a considerable difference between these two viewpoints, as is shown by the quite divergent systems of theology that have developed around them. The postmillennial view leads its advocates to feel that they are now engaged in an age-long and world-wide campaign to establish the Kingdom in the hearts of men everywhere, and to take a high view of the Church, regarding it as the divinely established agency through which that conquest is to be made effective. The premillennial view, on the other hand, leads its advocates to believe that the Kingdom is not in the world at the present time, that its establishment and glory and accomplishments belong to a future age that is to be quite different from the present age, and so fosters a comparatively low view of the Church as a temporary or interim agency. Amillennialism agrees in the main with Postmillennialism in its view of the Kingdom, although it does not hold that the world is to be converted to Christianity.

In discussing the Kingdom postponement theory we said that Dispensationalism holds that the Kingdom was offered to the Jews at the first advent, but that when they rejected the offer it was withdrawn and that it now is held in abeyance until the return of Christ, at which time it is to be established by overwhelming power. "No Kingdom without the King," is their motto. One writer says: "Jesus will be a King in as direct and positive a sense as any ruler the world has ever known, but with larger and more autocratic sway" (Dr. G. Campbell Morgan, *God's Methods With Man,* p. 115). And another says: "Our hearts may well rejoice because some day, and probably very soon, Christ will return to this earth and in mighty power will rule the nations with a rod of iron. He will force all nations to bow to Him and obey His Word, and Jerusalem will become the capital of the world" (Article in *The Commentator,* organ of The Kansas City Bible College, Nov. 1953).

That the Kingdom is now in the world and a present reality is taught in the following references: "And being asked by the Pharisees, when the kingdom of God cometh, he answered them and said, The kingdom of God cometh not with observation: neither shall they say, Lo, here! or, There! for lo, the kingdom of God is within you" [present tense] (Luke 17:20,21). "For the kingdom of God is not eating and drinking, but righteousness and peace and joy in the Holy Spirit" (Rom. 14:17)—things which are a present day reality in Christian experience and enjoyed by God's people everywhere. We are to give thanks to God the Father, ". . . who delivered us out of the power of darkness, and translated us [past tense] into the kingdom of the Son of his love" (Col. 1:13). "But seek ye first his kingdom, and his righteousness; and all these things shall be added unto you" (Matt. 6:33). This implies that the Kingdom is obtainable now by the believer, and that as it is obtained these other things also are given to him. That Paul throughout his ministry preached the kingdom as a present reality is made clear from his words to the elders of Ephesus as he reminded them that for three years he had dwelt among them "preaching the kingdom" (Acts 20:25), and from the closing verses of the book of Acts: "And he abode two whole years in his own hired dwelling, and received all that went in unto him, preaching the kingdom of God, and teaching the things concerning the Lord Jesus Christ with all boldness, none forbidding him" (Acts 28:30,31). These verses disprove the idea that the Kingdom is only future.

Entrance into the Kingdom is through regeneration. When we receive the new birth we are born into the Kingdom. Entrance into it is thus not through racial origin, nor Church membership, nor even good works, but of God's choosing. Good works are the fruits and proof, not the cause, of membership. The Kingdom of God in this world is, of course, as yet far from its consummation. It is essentially an eschatological concept, and reaches its goal only in the eternal state. It is begun here, and it is perfected hereafter. The sovereignty of Christ is essentially a moral and spiritual sovereignty. It is the redemptive rule of God in the hearts of men, and wherever men are in a state of salvation there Christ is King. That of which Christians have a foretaste in this life will be brought to perfection in the life to come. In other words, the Messianic or mediatorial reign of Christ in this world has already begun. As the world becomes more and more Christian the Kingdom assumes an ever-increasing influence in the lives of men, until in a truly Christianized world it will be the dominating and controlling factor. It was for the accomplishment of this purpose that "all authority . . . in heaven and on earth" was given to Christ, and He in turn commanded His disciples to go and put this Kingdom into effect by making disciples of all the nations, promising that He would be with them always, even unto the end of the world (Matt. 28:18–20). And Paul says: "He must reign, till he hath put all his enemies under his feet. The last enemy that shall be abolished is death" (I Cor. 15:25,26).

When this present stage of the Kingdom has been completed and Christ's whole work of redemption has been accomplished, He will surrender the Kingdom to the Father, and then the triune God, Father, Son, and Holy Spirit, will reign throughout eternity in the perfected Kingdom—"And when all things have been subjected unto him, then shall the Son also himself be subject unto him that did subject all things unto him, that God may be all in all" (I Cor. 15:28). This, then, does not mean that there are two Kingdoms, one on earth and the other in heaven, but rather that there are two states or two phases of the same Kingdom, and that its basic character is not altered by this transition.

At the time of the first advent the Jews expected the re-establishment of the Davidic kingdom as a world power kingdom of Jewish supremacy. But such was not to be. Old Testament prophecy simply was not clear enough for them to form detailed ideas about the coming of the Messiah and the kind of Kingdom that would be established. Even the disciples shared the notion of a political kingdom and disputed among themselves concerning the chief places. When Jesus announced to them that He must go to Jerusalem and be killed, and the third day be raised up, Peter rebuked Him, saying, "Be it far from thee, Lord; this shall never be unto thee" (Matt. 16:22). But at Pentecost the disciples were delivered from that erroneous notion, and from that day on we hear nothing more from them concerning a worldly kingdom.

But strange as it may seem, after nearly twenty centuries of enlightenment by the Holy Spirit, this same idea of a world power kingdom of Jewish supremacy has been taken up by all types of Premillennialism and made the main plank in their system. Though the modern advocates have eliminated some of the grosser elements, they still look for a political and military kingdom, with Christ sitting on a throne built by human hands in the earthly city of Jerusalem, exercising a rod-of-iron rule, administering justice to the people, and dispensing those blessings which result so largely in world prosperity. But, embellish it as they will, what an anti-climax it would be for the Lord Jesus to be brought down from the indescribably glorious throne in heaven to occupy for a thousand years a cramped earthly throne of human origin!

Premillennialism thus perverts the Biblical doctrine of the return of Christ, and misdirects the blessed hope of Christians to things earthly and temporal. It implements a vain hope of earthly dominance and glory in the hearts of its adherents, and particularly in the hearts of the Jewish people, inspiring in them false hopes that can never be realized. Surely the Jewish people have suffered enough without this further deception. Nowhere in the Bible is such a kingdom promised to God's people on this earth, and any kingdom established and maintained by force is absolutely contrary to the spirituality of the Kingdom as taught by Christ and the apostles. As we have already pointed out, the Old Testament prophecies which, taken literally, nourish or foster the earthly, nationalistic expectations of the Jews are in the New Testament interpreted in a spiritual or universalistic sense.

And is not this whole idea of bringing Christ down from His heavenly throne to rule in an earthly kingdom in Jerusalem only a childish attempt to give Him now what they feel was unjustly denied to Him at the first advent? What purpose could such a return serve? Since none of those who were on earth at the time of His first advent and who were responsible for rejecting and crucifying Him are now here, and since such a demotion from heaven to earth for 1000 years would be no honor at all, is not this whole idea only a lingering desire for that earthly kingdom that for so long fascinated the Jewish people? In other words, Is not this whole system merely a resurgence of Judaism? We have seen that it was this desire for an earthly king more than any other one thing that caused the Jews to reject and crucify the Messiah. Furthermore, the Bible tells us that heaven is God's throne, and that the earth is only His footstool. We may be sure that the earth will never become His throne.

We insist that the idea of an earth-centered divine kingdom is wrong in principle. Now, as at the time of the first advent, that idea is doing untold harm in the Church in that it promotes false doctrine, divides Christians and causes them to dissipate their strength in controversies among themselves when they should be working together to carry out the last great command to the Church, the command to evangelize the world.

When John the Baptist announced that the Kingdom of Heaven was at hand, it really was; and nothing that was done by the Jewish mob or the Roman army could prevent its being set up. The Old Testament prophecies and promises regarding the throne and kingdom of David are being fulfilled in Christ's reign in the Church during the present age. He is now "at the right hand of God" (Rom. 8:34), which is the position of power and influence; and His reign is made effective through the instrumentality of the Holy Spirit who is the efficient agent of the Trinity in the present world order.

In conformity with all this, the Westminster Confession states that the visible Church is "the kingdom of the Lord Jesus Christ" (Chap. XXV, 2); and the Westminster Shorter Catechism, in answer to the question, "How doth Christ execute the office of a king?" says: "Christ executeth the office of a king, in subduing us to himself, in ruling and defending us, and in restraining and conquering all his and our enemies." This kingdom as it now exists in the world, and of which the Church is the outward manifestation, is as yet in its preliminary stage. It will continue to advance through the present Church age, and it will come to fruition in all its glory in the heavenly state after the return of Christ. The Kingdom of Grace is already present. The Kingdom of Glory will be manifested in due time.

Chapter XIII

THE MILLENNIUM

A fair example, we believe, of what the Millennium, based on a literal interpretation of Scripture, means to most Premillennialists is found in Gavin Hamilton's book, *Maranatha* (not to be confused with Floyd E. Hamilton). With the nations judged, Christendom purged, and Satan bound, he says the "Golden Age" will begin, and he gives the following "outstanding features":

"FIRST. There shall be peace on earth. The command to nations shall be issued: 'Beat your swords into plowshares, and your spears into pruning hooks' (Is. 2:4). Disarmament shall be enforced. The nations shall learn war no more.

"SECOND. It will be a time of prosperity. Famines, poverty, lack of good food, shall be things of the past. They belong to man's day. The ground shall yield her increase. Every man shall sit under his vine, and under his fig tree, and no one shall make him afraid. 'The seed shall be prosperous; the vine shall give her fruit, and the ground shall give her increase, and the heavens shall give their dew' (Zech. 8:12). Moreover, God says: 'For brass I will bring gold, and for iron I will bring silver; and for wood, brass; and for stones, iron' (Is. 60:17). All that men need shall be at their disposal in abundance.

"THIRD. Longevity shall be restored. It is true that there shall be isolated cases both of sickness and death, for the King shall punish thus those who wilfully disobey his word. This Isaiah and Zechariah plainly state (Is. 65:20; Zech. 14:17-19). But in the main, long life shall be enjoyed. All redeemed ones that enter the kingdom shall never know sickness, pain or death. They shall be alive at the end of the reign and pass into the eternal state . . .

"FOURTH. Creation shall be delivered from its present bondage. The curse shall be removed. This shall affect the lower creation also. 'The wolf and the lamb shall feed together, and the lion shall eat straw like the ox. The sucking child shall play on the hole of the asp, and the weaned child shall put his hand on the cockatrice' den. They shall not hurt nor destroy in all my holy mountain' (Is. 65:25; 11:8,9). No longer shall the bee sting, the dog bite, the serpent smite; no longer shall man be afraid of any creature. Indeed, the blessing of creation shall extend to the utmost bounds. Both winds and waves shall be under control. Nevermore shall volcanoes belch forth their burning lava. Hurricanes and tornadoes, tidal waves and stormy seas, earthquakes and earth tremors shall be unknown. The weather shall be perfect, with the seasons regulated for production of crops and the physical good of man.

"FIFTH. The kingdom shall be run by the King and His people. It is highly probably that Paul the Apostle shall be the Prime Minister [some may not agree with this], and the twelve apostles of the Lamb the Cabinet. Then shall rank next those who have faithfully and sacrificially and affectionately served their Lord. All the nations shall be under His benign and benevolent sway, and all shall have their orders from Him and through His own" (pp. 131–133).

And Dr. Morgan, with typical eloquence, gives the following description of childhood in the Millennium: "What is the King's ideal for child-life? Play! With what shall they play? With that from which today we carefully and necessarily guard our little ones. 'The weaned child shall put his hand on the basilisk's den'; while a little dimpled fist shall be entwined in the mane of the lion to lead about that royal playmate!" (*God's Methods With Man*, p. 124).

In our discussion of Postmillennialism we indicated what we believe the general features of the Millennium will be. Hence it will not be necessary to repeat those comments here.

Another difficulty that arises in the premillennial system has to do with the large number of the wicked who live during the Millennium. They say that the "sheep and goats" judgment in Matthew 25 is a judgment of the nations that are in existence at the time Christ returns. Assuming this to be so, it then becomes clear that all of the evil nations are destroyed, and presumably only a comparatively small minority, those which constitute the righteous nations, remain to enter the Millennium, for Matthew says: "And these shall go away into eternal punishment: but the righteous into eternal life" (vs. 46). The Jews remain, of course, according to this theory; but they are said to be converted at the mere sight of their Messiah; and the Church, let it be remembered, was raptured out of the world before the Tribulation began. Whence then come those evil nations over which during the Millennium Christ is supposed to rule with a rod of iron? Are we to believe that during the blessed millennial reign of Christ wickedness shall so increase from a comparatively small beginning that it will account for those nations that have to be kept down, and which at the end of the Millennium rise in an overwhelming rebellion? Surely this cannot be! Dispensationalism holds that during each of six preceding dispensations man has been tested regarding some distinctive principle, but that each time he has failed, proving that no human system will work. During this seventh dispensation or kingdom age God is supposed to show what He can do with a world under divine rule. But according to their reasoning it would seem that the Millennium proves to be as great a failure as each of the preceding dispensations is alleged to have been.

There is no adequate explanation for the vast population that is supposed to exist during the Millennium. The wicked nations, which are assumed to be the large majority, the world having grown worse and worse before the coming of Christ, are sent to perdition at the beginning of the Millennium; and the resurrected and translated saints will not have bodies capable of giving birth to children, for Jesus said: "The sons of this world marry, and are given in marriage; but they that are accounted worthy to attain to that world, and the resurrection from the dead, neither marry, nor are given in marriage: for neither can they die any more: for they are equal unto the angels; and are sons of God, being sons of the resurrection" (Luke 20:34-36). Those who enter the millennial kingdom are only the Jews and that minority of nations that are friendly to the Jews during the Great Tribulation. In fact it would seem that during the Millennium the Jews are to constitute a much larger proportion of the world's population than they do now.

THE "ROD-OF-IRON" RULE

A distinctive doctrine of all types of Premillennialism is the claim that during the Millennium peace will be maintained throughout the earth by Christ's "rod-of-iron" rule over nations and individuals. But that the real meaning of these words is quite different from that generally understood is brought out by Floyd E. Hamilton. His explanation is as follows, and since this deals with an important phase of Premillennialism we quote him quite fully:

"One of the fundamental claims of the premillennialists is that the Messiah will rule over the nations, that is, the Gentile nations, from His millennial capital, Jerusalem, with a stern, just rule, with 'a rod of iron,' symbolizing forceful, effective rule over people who are rebellious at heart but who are forced to bow to the Messianic rule against their wills (Cp. Gaebelein, *The Return of the Lord*, p. 108). At the close of the alleged millennium Satan is said to gather them to war against the saints (Rev. 20:8), in number as the sands of the sea. This thought of a stern, just rule over rebellious nations during the millennium, is taken from the English translation of three passages in the Revelation, namely: 'He shall rule them with a rod of iron, as the vessels of the potter are broken to shivers' (2:27); 'And she was delivered of a son, a man child, who is to rule all the nations with a rod of iron; and her child was caught up unto God, and unto his throne' (12:5); 'And out of his mouth proceedeth a sharp sword, that with it he should smite the nations; and he shall rule them with a rod of iron; and he treadeth the winepress of the fierceness of the wrath of God, the Almighty (19:15).

"At first sight the premillennial argument from these passages for a stern, harsh but just reign of the Messiah over the Gentile nations during the millennium, seems peculiarly strong, particularly the Revelation 12:5 passage . . . So important is this 'rod of iron' rule for the premillennial theory that if the evidence for it breaks down, it would seem to destroy almost the very heart of the premillennial theory."

Hamilton points out that the Greek word, *poimaino*, is translated "rule" in the English versions. "The question for discussion, then," he says, "is whether the word 'rule' correctly translates the Greek word 'poimaino' . . . In 7 of the 11 instances of the use of the word poimaino in the New Testament, it is actually translated 'feed.' These instances are Luke 17:7; John 21:16; Acts 20:28; I Cor. 9:7; I Peter 5:2; Jude 12; and Rev. 7:17. In Matthew 2:6 it is translated, 'who shall rule my people Israel,' but the revised version gives 'who shall be shepherd of my people Israel.' That leaves only three 'rod of iron' passages in Revelation to be translated 'rule.'

". . . In the New Testament there are three words from the same root as poimaino. The words are poimnion, 'flock,' poimne, 'flock,' and poimen, 'shepherd.' Apparently these words, with the verb poimaino, are always connected with flocks and shepherds, and the care of flocks. (The word is used once of 'feeding cattle,' so it was apparently used for feeding any animals or caring for them) . . . We must notice that in the 39 instances of the use of these four words from the same root, it always elsewhere means 'flock,' 'shepherd,' or 'caring for the flock' in some way (once in connection with cattle), so the word apparently had a fixed meaning.

"Let us now turn to the words 'rod of iron' to look for further light on the passage in question. The *Concise Bible Dictionary,* published in connection with the Nelson Bible, says the following in regard to the 'rod': 'The rod and staff of Psalm 23:4 probably refer to two instruments still used by Eastern shepherds, the first, a heavy-headed club for driving off wild animals, the second a curved stick for guiding the sheep . . . The shepherd of Palestine carried an oak staff, six feet long, and a weapon, in the form of an oak club, two feet long, (the rod of Ps. 23:4) the thick end of which is studded with nails'. *The Students' Commentary* says (p. 314), 'He is provided with a club and a crook.' Dummelow's *Commentary* says: 'The rod was a sort of oaken club for defense; the staff a longer pole for use in climbing or leaning upon, and the Eastern shepherd still carries both.'

"All this seems to show that the 'rod of iron' used in connection with the shepherd word *poimaino,* refers not to ruling over the nations with the rod of iron, but to acting toward the nations as a shepherd would act toward wild animals attacking the sheep! How would a shepherd act toward the enemies of the sheep? Certainly by using his rod to dash them to pieces if he could do so! Now for the meaning of the word *poimaino,* since it is really equivalent to 'being a shepherd,' we suggest that a meaning which would exactly fit the root meaning of the word and the context in every place where it is used in the New Testament is, 'to act the part of a shepherd.' In this case in these 'rod of iron' passages, it should be translated, 'He shall act the part of a shepherd toward the nations with a rod of iron, as the vessels of the potter are broken to shivers' (Rev. 12:5). That is, the Messiah, to protect His flock, the true people of God, from their enemies, will execute vengeance on the unbelieving nations who have been persecuting God's people. Just as a shepherd would in righteous wrath dash out the brain of the wild beasts who were tearing the lambs to pieces, so the Messiah will vindicate His people with a terrible scene of vengeance upon the enemies of God's people. In other words we have a picture of a terrible judgment visited on the wicked nations who have been troubling Christian saints, the 'little flock' of Jesus Christ.

". . . The shepherd may, perhaps, be said to 'rule over' the flock in a kindly, protecting way, but not with his 'rod,' and he certainly does not dash his flock to pieces as 'a potter's vessel is broken to shivers!' A shepherd's rule over his flock is peaceful and loving, not 'stern' or harsh. Imagine a true shepherd striking his sheep with a rod of iron! Sheep have delicate bones, easily broken with a blow of a club! Is it not obvious, even if we did not know these 'rods' are used only to protect the flock from their enemies, that a shepherd would not use his rod of iron *against* his flock? If the Gentile nations are the object of the shepherd's activity with the rod of iron, then the only possible activity in view of the context, is that he should *strike* them with the 'rod of iron'! . . . Thus we see that the 'rod of iron' passages give no justification for thinking that the Messiah will rule over the unbelieving nations with a rod of iron during some future kingdom period.

"This meaning gives us exactly the same picture as that of II Thessalonians 1:7–10, when Christ comes, 'rendering vengeance to them that know not God, and to them that obey not the gospel of our Lord Jesus; who shall suffer punishment, even eternal destruction from the face of the Lord.

"Thus we see that the 'rod of iron' passages give us no justification for thinking that the Messiah will rule over unbelieving nations with a rod of iron during some future kingdom period. These passages all refer to the same picture of vengeance taken by God against the persecutors of God's elect church. The Revelation 19:15 passage, when translated, 'And out of his mouth proceedeth a sharp sword, that with it he should smite the nations: and he shall act the part of a shepherd (or, he shall act as a shepherd would act) toward them with a rod of iron; and he treadeth the winepress of the fierceness of the wrath of God, the Almighty,' gives us a unified picture of just vengeance against the wicked nations who have followed Satan in war against the saints before the rapture.

"So we see that instead of these passages about the 'rod of iron' offering a strong argument for premillennialism, they really reinforce our arguments that the wicked are all punished at the same time, when Christ comes again, and that no unbeliever will be left alive on the earth after Christ comes again. They will all be broken to pieces as the 'potter's vessel is broken to shivers'" (*The Basis of Millennial Faith*, pp. 84–90).

Hence the "rod-of-iron" passages teach that while Christ protects His people, He really does not rule over, but destroys, their enemies.

RESURRECTION SAINTS AND MEN STILL IN THE FLESH TO MINGLE DURING THE MILLENNIUM?

A curious situation arises when, according to this theory, Christ and the resurrected and translated saints return to this earth at the Revelation to set up the millennial kingdom and to mingle freely with men still in the flesh. Some say that the angels too are included. Dr. John R. Rice, for instance, says that Christ comes "with saints and angels to take over the reins of world government in a literal kingdom" (*The Coming of Christ*, p. 118). Some speak of "the open vision of Christ," or of "continued personal access to Christ," or of Jerusalem as the city "on which, or over which, the glory of the New Jerusalem is to rest, like Jehovah's pillar of fire on the tabernacle in the wilderness, or the more awful glory on the top of Sinai."

This condition, semi-heavenly and semi-earthly, Christ reigning in Jerusalem, with two radically different types of people, the saints in glorified resurrection bodies and ordinary mortals still in the flesh yet mingling freely throughout the world for the long and almost unending period of one thousand years, strikes us as so unreal and absurd that we wonder how anyone can take it seriously. Such a mixed state of mortals and immortals, terrestrial and celestial, surely would be a monstrosity. It would be as incongruous as for the holy angels now to mingle in their work and pleasure and worship with the present population of the world, bringing heavenly splendor into a sinful environment. Exalt the Millennium as you please, it still remains far below heaven. It cannot be other than a great anti-climax for those who have tasted of the heavenly glory but who then are brought back to have a part in it. Such positions of authority and rulership as might be given them in this world would be poor compensation for the glory that they have enjoyed in heaven.

In developing their ideas of what conditions will be like during the Millennium, Premillennialists fail to take into consideration the over-powering majesty of the risen and glorified Christ. They imagine that men will be in personal contact with Him as He reigns from an earthly throne. Such a view is based on the assumption that He will again be as He was in the days of His humiliation. At His first advent He came as a perfectly normal human being. He was then, as now, Deity incarnate, but His divine glory was veiled to human eyes. In order to redeem man it was necessary that He, as man's substitute, should take man's place before the law that had been broken. Hence He was born as a babe in Bethlehem, and grew in a perfectly normal way through boyhood and into manhood. He was "in all points tempted like as we are, yet without sin" (Heb. 4:15). But on one occasion even then His glory was manifested as on the Mount of Transfiguration He talked with Moses and Elijah in the presence of His disciples, and we are told that "he was transfigured before them; and his face did shine as the sun, and his garments became white as the light" (Matt. 17:2). Even after His resurrection, in order to give His disciples indisputable proof of His resurrection and while making preparation for the establishment of His Church, He still appeared to the disciples in a form that they could see and handle. But when the ascended and glorified Christ appeared to Saul on the road to Damascus, Saul was stricken blind by the light and fell to the ground. When the Apostle John saw the ascended and glorified Christ, "his countenance was as the sun, shining in its strength." And, says John, "When I saw him I fell at his feet as one dead" (Rev. 1:16,17). John was the beloved disciple who had leaned on Jesus' breast at the last supper. And if such glory was so overwhelming that the beloved disciple fell at His feet as one dead, how much less shall ordinary sinners be able to stand before Him! Paul describes Him as "the blessed and only Potentate, the King of kings and Lord of lords; who only hath immortality, dwelling in light unapproachable; whom no man hath seen, nor can see" (I Tim. 6:15,16). We are told of the appearance of one of His angels on the resurrection morning, and of his effect on the guard of Roman soldiers—"His appearance was as lightning, and his raiment white as snow: and for fear of him the watchers did quake, and became as dead men" (Matt. 28:3,4). When Christ returns in His own glory and that of the Father, with all the holy angels, certainly no mere man, who by comparison is but as a worm of the dust, shall be able to stand before Him. His period of humiliation is now over, and His divine glory forbids the approach of those who are tainted with sin. No mortal man can come into that presence and not be overwhelmed by it. That vision is reserved for Heaven. This world and the people in it cannot stand such glory.

Furthermore, regarding the millennial state, conditions during that time are to remain essentially unchanged, with those who still are in the flesh eating and drinking, planting and building, marrying and rearing families. Problems of government, education, transportation, communication, health and sanitation, etc., will have to be reckoned with even as they are now. The over-all direction of these things will be much more enlightened and efficient, but particularly as regards the unconverted portion of mankind these will remain real problems. Also let it be remembered that the resurrection saints of all the ages who come back for this kingdom will far outnumber those who still are in the flesh.

The idea of a provisional kingdom in which glorified saints and mortal men mingle finds no support anywhere in Scripture. When the saints are caught up to meet the Lord in the air it is

said, "So shall we ever be with the Lord" (I Thess. 4:17). There
is no hint of coming back to the earth before the time of the
new heavens and the new earth of the eternal state. A return to
the present earth would involve either a re-transformation from
resurrection bodies to natural bodies, in order that they might
again be in harmony with the earthly environment, or reigning
in their "spiritual" bodies (I Cor. 15:44), which would mean no
end of confusion. Our natural bodies cannot enter the heavenly
kingdom, and we may be sure that the resurrection bodies of the
saints would be equally out of place if brought back to live in
this environment. Paul tells us concerning the glorified body:

"Now this I say, brethren, that flesh and blood cannot inherit
the kingdom of God; neither doth corruption inherit incorruption.
Behold, I tell you a mystery: We all shall not sleep, but we
shall all be changed, in a moment, in the twinkling of an eye, at
the last trump: for the trumpet shall sound, and the dead shall be
raised incorruptible, and we shall be changed. For this corruptible must put on incorruption, and this mortal must put on immortality. But when this corruptible shall have put on incorruption, and this mortal shall have put on immortality, then shall
come to pass the saying that is written, Death is swallowed up in
victory" (I Cor. 15:50–54).

Paul's teaching here parallels that of Christ who said:

"The sons of this world marry, and are given in marriage:
but they that are accounted worthy to attain to that world, and
the resurrection from the dead, neither marry nor are given in
marriage: for neither can they die any more: for they are equal
unto the angels; and are sons of God, being sons of the resurrection" (Luke 20:34–36).

Hamilton points out that if Paul's words are understood as
having "reference to an alleged millennial kingdom, then this
passage asserts that all those, Jews and Gentiles, who 'inherit
the kingdom of God' that follows the resurrection of the righteous, will have glorified bodies. There is no room here for the
assertion that the Jews will enter the millennial kingdom with
mortal bodies, for 'flesh and blood cannot inherit the kingdom of
God.' This cannot refer to the Church as distinct from the Jewish
remnant, for according to Premillennialists those Jews decidedly
do 'inherit the kingdom.' Anyone, Jew or Gentile, who inherits

this kingdom in the text, following immediately upon the resurrection of the righteous, will be like the angels in heaven. There is no room for unsaved people in that kingdom, for they will not be present in mortal bodies. Whoever is present will have immortal bodies. There will be no people there whom Satan could deceive at the end of the alleged millennium" (*The Basis of Millennial Faith*, p. 99).

Furthermore, in the parable of the Ten Virgins, that of the Talents, and in the general discourse on the judgment as given in Matthew 25, Jesus associates universal judgment with His second advent, and so excludes the premillennial notion of an earthly kingdom. His second coming is definitely set forth as a coming to judgment which ushers in the eternal state. Christ and the saints have resurrection bodies, which are not "flesh and blood," but are incorruptible, glorious, and immortal. How then can they live and work harmoniously on earth with those who still are in the flesh?

Berkhof says concerning this mingling of mortals and immortals in an earthly kingdom:

"The premillennial theory entangles itself in all kinds of insuperable difficulties with its doctrine of the millennium. It is impossible to understand how a part of the old world and of sinful humanity can exist alongside of a part of the new earth and of a humanity that is glorified. How can perfect saints in glorified bodies live in this sin-laden atmosphere and amid scenes of death and decay? How can the Lord of glory, the glorified Christ, establish His throne on earth as long as it has not yet been renewed? The twenty-first chapter of Revelation informs us that God and the Church of the redeemed will take up their dwelling place on earth after heaven and earth have been renewed; how then can it be maintained that Christ and the saints will dwell there a thousand years before this renewal? How will sinners and saints in the flesh be able to stand in the presence of the glorified Christ, seeing that even Paul and John were completely overwhelmed by the vision of Him, Acts 26:12–14; Rev. 1:17" (*Systematic Theology*, p. 715).

Years ago David Brown wrote: "What a mongrel state of things is this! What an abhorrent mixture of things totally inconsistent with each other!" And again, "This system almost inevitably engenders much confusion. The fundamental principle of the system—contemporaneousness and co-existence of the state of grace and the state of glory—of mortality and immortality—of an upper and a lower—a celestial and a terrestrial department of one and the same kingdom—this principle destroys the real nature of both and the things which it places in juxtaposition" (*The Second Advent*, p. 384).

The Premillennialist seems not to realize how utterly inconsistent is his scheme to bring glorified saints back to this world order. Once the saints have passed through the portals of death they have attained a state too exalted for any earthly millennium. Regardless of how attractively the millennial state may be pictured, those who have been nourished on the first-fruits of the heavenly life can never again find earth life attractive or significant. The heavenly bliss that the saints enjoy is incomparably superior to even the most glowing representation of any earthly kingdom that can be imagined.

Not all Premillennialists hold these views, and there is much difference of opinion among them regarding the outstanding features of the millennial reign. Some have felt the incongruous situation that arises when the holy and the sinful, the mortals and the immortals, are thrown together. Dr. J. Oliver Buswell, for instance, suggests a theory—only a theory, he says—that after Christ returns His seat of government will be not in the city of Jerusalem but in the *clouds*. This view, he says, offers a possible solution to some of the problems that arise in our minds regarding the mingling of the risen saints and those still in the flesh.

"The theory," he says, "is that the central place of the visible government of the kingdom of Christ over the earth during the millennium or the thousand years will be that place in the clouds where He catches up His own to meet Him. This is appropriate in connection with those Scriptures which refer to the nations of the earth as being gathered before His throne. If His throne is in that trysting place in the clouds, then the whole round earth spins beneath the footstool of His feet in His immediate presence and He visibly executes judgment over all nations. This suggestion does not for a moment deny the specific connection with the surface of this earth which is implied in Messianic prophecy. The city of Jerusalem will doubtless be visited in person by our glorious Lord . . . 'his feet shall stand in that day upon the Mount of Olives' (Zech. 14:4) . . . The theory that the clouds are the specific locus of His visible government helps to explain certain problems which arise in our minds in regard to the relationship of the risen saints in glorified bodies, with the people of the earth who are ruled in perfect righteousness, many of whom are ready to rebel at the final apostasy" (*Unfulfilled Prophecies*, p. 81).

We do not see that this helps much toward solving the problem. While it may keep the risen saints and the people of earth separate, the idea that the throne of Christ is stationary in the clouds while the earth spins beneath His feet impresses us as particularly fantastic.

We confess that as regards the whole idea of a millennial kingdom we feel very much as does Dr. Berkhof when he says:

"It is a conundrum to me how they who belong to the Church, for whom the promises given to Israel do not apply, can derive special comfort from the fact that Jesus at His return will establish a temporal Jewish kingdom on earth, how they can find it a specially consoling thought that Jesus, who after His resurrection was already endowed as Mediator with an endless life and as such could not remain in this sinful world, but had to ascend to heaven, will after His return again dwell on earth for a thousand years in a world in which sin and death still hold sway; and how they can find it a cause for special rejoicing that Christ will again have to descend from His heavenly throne for a prolonged stay on earth, which is still under the curse of sin and death and still a scene of wickedness and lawlessness, of sickness and sorrow; and that with His saints will also for a thousand years have to exchange their bliss and glory for an environment that is not at all suited to their glorified conditions" (*The Second Coming of Christ*, p. 93).

Two Permanently Separate Peoples

Still another distinctive feature of the dispensational system is that it holds that Israel and the Church are two separate and distinct peoples, and that they are to remain so not only in this world but throughout all eternity. This means that the kingdom promises made through the prophets were literal promises to a literal Jewish nation which is yet to rule the world as a kind of super-state. Israel is to remain permanently on earth after the Church is taken to heaven. Scofield goes even further and divides the saved into four separate groups. Says he: "Israel has her place, the tribulation saints will have their place, the redeemed during the kingdom age [millennium] will have their place. The soul that goes out to Him in this long period of His kingdom and believes in Him . . . Such men belong to another group of the saved. They have another place. They are a new body (the Church)" (Address, Philadelphia Bible Conference, 1914. Reprinted, *Bibliotheca Sacra*, Jan. 1952).

Chafer asserts that Judaism and Christianity are two permanently separate religions, continuing into eternity as such, each having its own doctrine of salvation and its own doctrine of last things. "They incorporate," he says, "similar features—God, man, righteousness, sin, redemption, salvation, human responsibility, and human destiny; but these similarities do not establish identity since the dissimilarities far outnumber the similarities." "The Bible," he says, "distinguishes between God's consistent and eternal *earthly* purpose, which is the substance of Judaism; and His consistent and eternal *heavenly* purpose, which is the substance of Christianity, and it is as illogical and fanciful to contend that Judaism and Christianity ever merge as it would be to contend that heaven and earth cease to exist as separate spheres" (*Dispensationalism*, p. 41).

Dispensationalism holds that the Rapture of the Church, which leaves unbelieving Israel on the earth, prepares the way for the literal fulfillment of the Old Testament kingdom promises to the Jews as an earthly people. The breaking down of the middle wall of partition between Jew and Gentile was only temporary, only for the duration of the Church age. It will be re-established in the period between the Rapture and the Revelation, so that this period and the Millennium will witness, in Chafer's words, the "restoration of Judaism" (*Dispensationalism*, p. 46).

Furthermore, the seven year period between the Rapture and the Revelation, and particularly the millennial period which follows is, on premillennial principles, to be pre-eminently the day of salvation—we may even say, the day of mass salvation.

For the Jew "will then be the missionary, and to the very nations now called Christian," so that "the enormous majority of earth's inhabitants will be saved" (*Scofield Bible*, (pp. 973, 977). In the Millennium the Mosaic laws, the Levitical sacrifices and the feasts will be re-established, and will serve as "memorials." Salvation will be based, not on faith in the cross of Christ, which is the Gospel of the Church Age, but on obedience to the King. Surely this is a restoration of Judaism with a vengeance! And surely, on this basis, the future does belong to the Jew!

In opposition to this we insist that the doctrine that Israel and the Church form two separate groups is contrary to Scripture, that Christ founded the Church as the true and lawful successor to Old Testament Israel, and that God's purpose with Israel having been finished, Judaism should have disappeared and Israel should have ceased to exist as a religious body. In the Old Testament there was no recognized division between Israel and those who united with Israel from among the Gentiles. Rather, those who joined Israel from among the Gentiles merged into the common body. The separation was between this body and the heathen world. Also in the New Testament the division is between the Church and the unbelieving world, not between the Church and fleshly Israel. The elect are gathered out of Jews and Gentiles, out of all tribes and tongues and races and nations, and they become one people. "There is one body, and one Spirit, even as also ye were called in one hope of your calling; one Lord, one faith, one baptism, one God and Father of all, who is over all, and through all, and in all" (Eph. 4:4,5). There is but one vine, one good olive tree, one body, one holy nation, one bride, and one holy city whose unity is symbolized by the names of the twelve apostles written on its foundations and the names of the twelve tribes on its gates.

Dispensationalism holds that the constitution of the millennial kingdom is outlined in the Sermon on the Mount, and that this and most of the material found in the Gospels is kingdom literature given by Christ at the time He was offering the kingdom to the Jews. This material, therefore, does not begin to serve its real purpose until the millennial kingdom is inaugurated. Less emphasis has been placed on this point in recent years, and many even among the Dispensationalists now reject it.

Chapter XIV

THE GOSPEL OF THE KINGDOM
AND OF THE CROSS

A very important question arises regarding the nature of the gospel that is to be preached by the Jewish remnant during the Tribulation period. Will the 144,000 preach the gospel of the cross, which is the gospel as we know it; or will they preach the gospel of the kingdom, which offers salvation apart from the cross? The 144,000 quite clearly are not Christians, for at the Rapture every believer is removed from the earth. Not a single Christian remains. Scofield says that, "During the church-age the remnant is composed of believing Jews (Rom. 11:4,5) . . . During the great tribulation a remnant of all Israel will turn to Jesus as Messiah, and will become His witnesses after the removal of the church (Rev. 7:3–6)" (p. 1205). Darby indicates that there will be a believing remnant of Jews who go through the Rapture and remain on earth after the Church has been removed, Jews who look for the Messiah as King but who do not accept Christ as Saviour. He says: "That there will be a Jewish remnant at the close, delivered and blessed by the Lord at His coming, blessed on earth, is, beyond all controversy, the doctrine of Scripture" (*Collected Writings*, xi, p. 182).

Scofield draws a strong contrast between what is termed "The Gospel of the Kingdom" and "The Gospel of the Grace of God" (p. 1343). Concerning the Gospel of the Kingdom he says:

"This is the good news that God proposes to set up on the earth, in fulfillment of the Davidic covenant (II Sam. 7:16 and Ref.) a kingdom, political, spiritual, Israelitish, universal, over which God's Son, David's heir, shall be King, and which shall be, for one thousand years, the manifestation of the righteousness of God in human affairs." He says there are "two preachings" of this Gospel, ". . . one past, beginning with the ministry of

John the Baptist, continued by our Lord and His disciples, and ending with the Jewish rejection of the King. The other is yet future (Matt. 24:14), during the great tribulation, and immediately preceding the coming of the King of glory" (p. 1343). He says further: "The kingdom is to be established by power, not persuasion, and is to follow divine judgment upon the Gentile world powers" (p. 977); and that "When Christ appeared to the Jewish people, the next thing, in the order of revelation as it then stood, should have been the setting up of the Davidic kingdom" (p. 998).

Concerning the Gospel of the Grace of God he says: "This is the good news that Jesus Christ, the rejected King, has died on the cross for the sins of the world, that He was raised from the dead for our justification, and that by him all that believe are justified from all things" (p. 1343).

The contrast between these two gospels is brought out by the statement that the Sermon on the Mount, which belongs to the Gospel of the Kingdom, is said to be not the ideal standard for living in this present age, but to be the "constitution" for the kingdom of heaven which was offered to the Jews at the first advent. The Sermon on the Mount is said to be "pure law"; "there is not a ray of grace in it, nor a drop of blood" (p. 1000). This means that the Gospel of the Kingdom does not require nor involve the Cross. The Kingdom as it was offered to the Jews, and as it is to be set up in the Millennium, is a reign of law, not of grace.

Dr. Allis has given an effective reply to this kind of reasoning. Says he:

"We have seen that the most serious objection to the claim of Dispensationalists, that the declaration that 'the kingdom of heaven is at hand' meant that it could be set up 'at any moment,' was the fact that this involved the ignoring of the definite teaching of Jesus that the 'Christ must suffer and enter into his glory.' It made the Cross unnecessary by implying that the glorious kingdom of Messiah could be set up immediately. It left no room for the Cross since Messiah's kingdom was to be without end. It led to the conclusion that had Israel accepted Jesus as Messiah, the Old Testament ritual of sacrifice would have sufficed for sin, that it was only the enormity of the crucifixion which made the Cross necessary. Darby tells us quite definitely: 'Supposing, for a moment that Christ had not been rejected, the kingdom would have been set up on earth. It could not have been so, no doubt, but it shows the difference between the kingdom and the Church' (*Lectures on the Second Advent*, p. 113). The only conclusion which can be drawn from such a statement is this, that the Church required the Cross while the kingdom did not, that the gospel of the kingdom did not include the Cross, while the gospel of the grace of God did include it. . . . This we believe to be the inevitable result of Darby's doctrine of the remnant; and we hold it to be utterly irreconcilable with the teaching of the Bible, that 'the word of the cross is to them that perish foolishness; but unto us who are saved it is the power of God.' No Jew who in this gospel age during which Christ is preached as Saviour rejects the Saviour while waiting for the King can be called 'godly' or 'pious' or 'blessed' of God. Christ has died on the cross. To reject Him as Saviour is for the Jew as well as for the Gentile to spurn the offer of salvation and merit the wrath and curse of God" (*Prophecy and the Church*, pp. 230–232).

Truly there is no other Gospel than that of the Cross. We are reminded of Paul's stern words: "But though we, or an angel from heaven, should preach unto you any gospel other than that which we preached unto you, let him be anathema" (Gal. 1:8).

Scofield says that "The kingdom is to be established by power, not by persuasion," and that during that age "the enormous majority of earth's inhabitants will be saved" (p. 977), this to be made possible because of "the removal of Satan from the scene." Thus the Gospel of the Kingdom is set forth as far more efficacious in the salvation of souls than is the Gospel of the Grace of God. But Dr. Allis asks pointedly: "How will this 'enormous majority of earth dwellers' be able to join with the Church-saints in singing praises to the Lamb that was slain, and hath redeemed us by His precious blood? What meaning will the Cross have for those who have attained to a legal righteousness in the Kingdom age?" (*The Evangelical quarterly*, London. Jan., 1936).

Dispensationalists tell us that the Gospel of the Kingdom, which was preached before the Cross, will be preached again by a Jewish remnant during the Great Tribulation, apparently without change or addition. This Jewish remnant, numbering 144,000, supposedly remains on earth because they are expecting the Kingdom and refuse to accept the Gospel as preached by the Church. A "great multitude which no man could number" is said to be saved by their preaching. But again, Dr. Allis, to whom we are indebted for an especially clear analysis of this subject, reminds us that,

"It is not stated in Revelation 7 that the multitude owe their salvation to the preaching of the 144,000. More important still, it is expressly declared that this multitude that are arrayed in white robes 'have washed their robes and made them white in the blood of the Lamb' (7:14). This can only mean that they have accepted, not the 'gospel of the kingdom' which, as defined by Scofield, makes no mention of the Cross, but 'the gospel of the grace of God' which is 'the good news that Jesus Christ . . . has died on the Cross for the sins of the world.' It will have been the preaching of the Cross, whether by a Jewish remnant or by Church saints, to which they will owe their salvation" (*Prophecy and the Church*, p. 233).

Dispensationalists profess to be strictly orthodox and boast of their loyalty to the Bible, even going to an extreme in interpreting the Bible literally. And yet, as we study their sharp distinction between the Gospel of the Kingdom and the Gospel of the Grace of God, we come back to the question: where in the Gospel of the Kingdom does the Cross and the atoning work of Christ come in? Where is there any place for the fulfillment of the Old Testament prophecies which assert in detail the suffering of the Messiah, e.g., Isaiah 53 and Psalm 22? Or where is there any place for the truth taught in the sacrificial system of the Old Testament by which the penalty due the sinner is transferred to an innocent victim? If the Jews had accepted the kingdom, what necessity would there ever have been for the Cross? When could Christ ever have been put off the throne and crucified? The fact of the matter is that Dispensationalism contains a strong element of Modernism, even to the extent of asserting that in the Kingdom age salvation is possible apart from the work of Christ on the Cross. That man can be saved apart from the suffering of Christ is in fact the very heart of the Modernistic heresy, and there is no doctrine of Scripture that the Modernists would more gladly be rid of than that of blood atonement. To say that during the Tribulation period, or during the Millennium, man can be saved by obedience to the King, that is, by good works, is to repudiate the only system of salvation set forth in the Bible. We do not say that Dispensationalists do this purposefully or even consciously. But we do say that those who make the Church only an unpredicted and unforeseen interlude between a past Jewish kingdom and a future Jewish kingdom in which salvation depends on obedience to the King fall into this error.

Dispensationalists fail to see that man's opportunity to earn salvation by living righteously, that is, by obedience, was limited to his probation under the covenant of works in the Garden of Eden, and that the Mosaic law was not a covenant of works at all but a preliminary form of the covenant of grace. It fails to see that the Church is the fulfillment and fruitage of the Old Testament Kingdom of Israel, and treats it rather as something alien and contrary to the divine plan. In substituting six separate dispensations for the covenant of grace it represents God as repeatedly changing plans, and it represents all of these dispensations except the last as ending in failure because they are thwarted by the will of man.

Chapter XV

THE JEWS AND PALESTINE

The assumption of modern Premillennialism, and particularly of Dispensationalism, that at the Coming of Christ a Jewish kingdom will be re-established in Palestine proceeds on a false principle, which is that God still has a special purpose to be served by the Jewish people as a nation. But the fact of the matter is that there is no further need for such a kingdom. In Old Testament times there was reason for the selection of a particular people, and reason why they should be settled in one particular land. No full revelation had then been given concerning the way of salvation. God's plan of salvation, which was to be worked out through the life and death of a promised Redeemer, required that a particular nation be set aside in which He should appear, and that until His work was accomplished that nation should be kept separate from all of the other nations which were completely given over to heathenism.

The Jewish nation was at that time the exclusive channel through which God chose to reveal Himself to the world, the instrument through which preparation was being made for the coming of the Messiah. Israel thus became the divinely appointed missionary nation to the rest of the world. It was chosen not for its own sake, nor because it was a large or powerful nation, for it was in reality one of the smallest; nor because of any past accomplishments, for the original choice was confined to one individual, Abraham, whose seed was to be developed into this nation. Hence the choice really was made before it had any existence as a nation. This purpose was clearly stated in the words spoken to Moses at Sinai, immediately preceding the giving of the Ten Commandments—"Now therefore, if ye will obey my voice indeed, and keep my covenant, then ye shall be mine own possession from among all peoples: for all the world is mine:

and ye shall be unto me a nation of priests, and a holy nation"
(Ex. 19:5,6).

In Old Testament times revelation was in an elementary
stage. But now the Messiah has come and God's revelation to
mankind has been completed—written in a book and made available to the people of all nations, with nothing more to be added,
and in fact with a curse pronounced upon anyone who attempts
to add to or to take away from that revelation (Rev. 22:18,19).
There is no further need for a separate people or nation to serve
that purpose. But until that purpose was accomplished, the
selection of Israel as a separated nation, and the gift to them of
a particular country, Palestine, was all one unit with the other
distinctive elements of the system—the priesthood, the temple,
the ritual, the sacrificial system, the seventh day sabbath, the
line of inspired prophets, and the special laws that set them
apart from the other peoples of the world. All of this was by
divine appointment, and no element in it could be ignored.

But since the Messiah has come and has performed His work
of atonement, the special role assigned to the Jews has been
fulfilled. Hence there remains no reason whatever for the reviving
or re-establishing of any one or more of the elements of the old
system. All of those elements belonged to the kindergarten stage
of redemption, and on the completion of that redemption at
Calvary all of those things passed away together. What Paul
terms "the middle wall of partition" between Jew and Gentile
has been broken down, and it is never to be built back. Christ
died equally for men of all nationalities and races, and it now
makes no difference whether one be Jew, American, Japanese,
German, Russian, white or colored, he has the same right of
approach to God through Christ, the same forgiveness of sins,
and the same hope of heaven.

We want to say most emphatically that when Christ died on
Calvary the old Mosaic order died, never to be revived. That
was the meaning of the supernatural rending of the curtain
which separated the holy place from the holy of holies in the
temple, symbolizing that the last sacrifice, which was Christ
Himself, had been offered, and that God was leaving His temple,
never to return. By that divine act the old order of ritual and
incense, of the sacrificial blood of bulls and goats, of the temple

and a human priesthood, and of the Jews as a separate people and Palestine as a separate land—all of that as a unit had fulfilled its purpose and was abolished forever.

But while the Jews no longer occupy a place of special favor in the divine plan, this does not mean that God has cast them off. *Nothing has been taken from the Jews as individuals.* Only the external forms have been abolished. The blessings and privileges of salvation which they enjoyed during the Old Testament dispensation have been magnified and heightened and extended to all nations and races alike. After the Jews had forfeited their rights as a chosen nation, or, to put it more accurately, after God had completed His purpose with the Jews as a separate people, they continued to have the privileges of full and free salvation individually. Jews and Gentiles alike from that time on were no longer under law, but under grace. Hence there are two, and only two, great divisions, or dispensations, in God's dealings with men,—that of the Old Covenant, and that of the New Covenant, or as we are more accustomed to refer to them, that of the Old Testament and that of the New Testament. Nor is there to be any other until the end of the world.

We find a very significant statement in this regard in the words of Jesus as recorded in Luke 21:24—"And they shall fall by the edge of the sword, and shall be led captive into all the nations, and Jerusalem shall be trodden down of the Gentiles *until the times of the Gentiles be fulfilled.*" The Old Testament era was the times of the Jews. The New Testament era is the times of the Gentiles. Judaism is a thing of the past. It is a glorious memory, despite its limitations and its failings. But it can never be revived. The assumption that there is to be a national conversion of the Jews at the Second Coming of Christ, after the close of "the times of the Gentiles," and that they are to evangelize the world in a seven year period, is entirely unwarranted. The Church will be in the world until the end of the age, and it is the only agency that God has commissioned to carry the message of salvation.

Speaking of the Jews nationally Jesus said: "The kingdom of God shall be taken away from you and shall be given to a nation bringing forth the fruits thereof" (Matt. 21:43). And after the woes pronounced upon the Scribes and Pharisees, He said: "Behold, your house is left unto you desolate" (Matt. 23:38). Interpreting those words in the light of history, we see that the privilege of being God's representative in the world and of proclaiming the Gospel to the world has been taken away from Israel as a nation and has been given to the Christian Church. Similarly, the Apostle Paul, also speaking of the Jews nationally, said that "wrath is come upon them to the uttermost" (I Thess. 2:16)—which again leaves no room for a revival of Judaism, nor for a Jewish era of any kind. But it does leave room for the conversion of Jews as individuals along with individuals from all other national groups, even for the large majority of individuals within these groups, as the Church progresses in the world.

Judaism as a legitimate religious system was brought to its full end and abolished by the crucifixion of Christ, not merely because the nation acting officially through its Sanhedrin rejected the Messiah, but because God's purpose with it was finished. With the establishment of the Christian Church Judaism should have made a smooth and willing transition into Christianity, and should thereby have disappeared as the flower falls away before the developing fruit. Its continued existence as a bitter rival and enemy of the Christian Church after the time of Christ, and particularly its revival after the judgment of God had fallen on it so heavily in the destruction of Jerusalem and the dispersal of the people in 70 A. D., was sinful. No divine favor could rest upon such a movement, but only divine disfavor—such as it indeed has suffered through the centuries. Bitter persecution of any Jews who accepted Christianity became a characteristic and distinguished mark of this revived Judaism as it followed the traditions of the Pharisees and Sadducees who had opposed Christ so bitterly during the days of His flesh. Jews who became Christians, thus ostracized from their fellow Jews, tended to merge into the Gentile communities in which they found themselves, which was the natural and the providentially appointed thing for them to do. Revived Judaism made it extremely hard to reach individual Jews with the Gospel. In a broader treatment of this whole subject Dr. Albertus Pieters, in a book entitled, *The Seed of Abraham,* has shown very conclusively that the Christian Church is the legitimate heir and successor of Old

Testament Israel, and that the Old Testament prophecies and promises so far as they remain unfulfilled are to be fulfilled not to the Jews as a national group but to the Church which is the New Testament Israel.

Furthermore, this revived Judaism built again the middle wall of partition and so made it possible to perpetuate through the centuries the distinction between Jews and Gentiles. The continuance of this bitterly anti-Christian racial group has brought no good to themselves, and there has been strife and antagonism in practically every nation where they have gone. They have not been a happy people. One need only think of the pogroms in Russia, the ghettos of eastern Europe, the many restrictions and persecutions that they have suffered in Italy, Spain, Poland, and other countries, and in our own day the campaign of extermination waged against them in Germany by Hitler. At the present time we see this problem in a particularly aggravated form in the Near East, where the recently established nation of Israel has ruthlessly displaced an Arab population and seeks to expand further into the surrounding regions, some 900,000 Arabs in refugee camps around the borders of Israel being one of the chief continuing causes for bitterness. There a nation of less than two million Jews is surrounded by a solid block of Arab nations with a population of some 40 million. Israel is not a self-sustaining nation, and her existence to date has been heavily subsidized by American money and equipment—much of it undoubtedly having been given for the purpose of influencing the Jewish vote in this country. There is no indication that the age-old rivalry between Jew and Arab can be settled in the foreseeable future. Indeed, on several occasions it has seemed that World War Three might easily be triggered by a rash or provocative act either by Israel or the Arab states, e.g., an act such as Israel's invasion of Egypt in 1956. The mere fact that these people are Jews does not in itself give them any more moral or legal right to Palestine than to the United States or any other part of the world. This does not mean, of course, that the Arabs are any less anti-Christian or any less inclined toward provocative acts than are the Jews. But the fact of the matter is that the existence of Israel as a nation and its support by the West has done more than all other causes combined to alienate the Arab world with its rich resources of oil and to drive it toward the Russian sphere of influence.

An illustration of the role that the Jewish people might have played in uplifting and leavening all other nations of the world, in accordance with their divine mission and with great credit to themselves, may be seen in the blending of nationalities that went into the formation of our own American nation, as English, Scotch, Irish, Germans, French, Hollanders, Swedes, Norwegians, Italians, Spaniards, and others, came across the Atlantic, forgot their old racisms and languages and peculiarities and, uniting in a common cause, formed this new nation which became quite different from any of the others, a strong, progressive, rich nation, with freedom of religion, freedom of the press, freedom of assembly, and many other virtues—in which, perhaps with pardonable pride, we do not hesitate to say that we prefer to be a part rather than in any other nation of the world. The present writer finds four of the above mentioned nationalities represented in his family tree, and proudly acknowledges each of them. Even if it were possible, not many Americans would be willing to exchange what they believe to be their typical American personality for that typical of any country from which their ancestors came. This illustrates to some extent the valuable contribution that the Jewish people might have rendered to the world at large had they been willing, with the greatest of all assets in their possession, the true religion. But that they refused to do. Rather they have chosen to set themselves apart in the strongest opposition to the true religion, and the results have been tragic, both for themselves and for the world at large.

And now to return to the subject of Old Testament prophecy and promises and their bearing on the present and future state of the Jews. Dispensationalism holds that the promises were given expressly to "the house of Israel and the house of Judah" (cf. Jer. 31:31-34), and that they must therefore be fulfilled to the people of Israel and Judah. Dr. Pieters has replied to this in considerable detail and with the most penetrating analysis of the whole problem that we have seen anywhere. He says:

"This is entirely correct, and it is to the house of Israel that the fulfillment came. The objection arises from a failure to perceive that the Christian Church in its origin was an Israelitish body, fully qualified to claim the promises to Israel. Dr. A. M. Berkhof speaks of 'the Church from among the Gentiles'; but there is no such church. The Christian church once having been established many Gentiles came into it, but that did not make it a 'Church from among the Gentiles,' any more than the naturalization of many Italians in our country makes it a nation from among the Italians.

"To make clear how thoroughly the Christian church in its origin was an Israelitish body, let us go back in thought to what happened when Jesus Christ came into the world. He presented Himself as the promised King, of the seed of David . . . Although the rulers of the people rejected Christ and they were supported therein by a majority of the rank and file, there were some who did accept Him. They were but a little flock, but to them it was said: 'Fear not, little flock, for it is your Father's good pleasure to give you the kingdom' (Luke 12:32). Did those who thus accepted Christ thereby lose their standing and rights as the Seed of Abraham, the covenant people of God? God forbid! On the contrary, 'little flock' as they were, those who accepted the Son of God as King of Israel continued without interruption to be what they were before, 'The House of Israel and the House of Judah,' the legitimate heirs to all that God had promised. That they were few in number makes no difference. If anything, it confirms their title, for St. Paul says: 'Isaiah crieth concerning Israel, If the number of the children of Israel be as the sand of the sea, it is the remnant that shall be saved' (Rom. 9:27). You can not object that these believers in Christ were 'from among the Gentiles.' They were not, they were all Israelite members of the Old Covenant people of God, to whom the promise had been made. Strictly in line with the promise and with the prevailing principle of the covenant history, to them, the believing remnant, the promise of the New Covenant was fulfilled . . . That promise was, 'To the House of Israel and the House of Judah,' and to the designated parties the fulfillment came; to all who were, in the sight of God and according to a just interpretation of history, still worthy of the name: 'Israel and Judah.'

"What of the others? Is it not clear that those who refused to acknowledge the King whom God had sent to them and to enter the New Covenant which He had promised, by that very act lost their standing as the people of God and were cut off from the Seed of Abraham? In what covenant relation could they still stand to God? The Old Covenant was gone—'done away in Christ' (II Cor. 3:14) and in the New Covenant they had no part . . .

"Just as it would have been impossible for any Israelite to refuse God's offer in the Sinaitic Covenant and still retain his standing and rights under the Abrahamic Covenant, so it was equally impossible for those under the Sinaitic Covenant to refuse to accept the New Covenant in Christ and still retain their standing and privileges as the Seed of Abraham. There is always but one group that is recognized by God as being the Seed of Abraham, the community with which He is in covenant, and that group, after the rejection of Jesus by the rulers and the majority of the Old Covenant Israel, was the remnant with whom He set up the New Covenant in His blood. The Lord then deposed the unfaithful rulers of Israel and appointed the apostles as the new head of the covenant people (Matt. 21:43–45; 19:28).

"Do I say these things by my own authority, or does the word of God also say them? Listen: 'Therefore I say unto you, the kingdom of God shall be taken away from you, and it shall be given to a nation bringing forth the fruit thereof' (Matt. 21:43). These words are the words of Jesus, after having spoken the parable of the wicked husbandmen, which the rulers rightly understood to refer to themselves. Now, what did those wicked men have of the kingdom of God that could be taken away from them? Only this, that they were the visible people of God, the Seed of Abraham under the Abrahamic and Sinaitic Covenants. *This* was to be taken away . . .

"Exactly similar is St. Paul's teaching under the figure of the Olive Tree, in the 11th chapter of the Epistle to the Romans. From this tree, he says, certain branches had been cut off. Here the tree represents the Seed of Abraham, the continuing covenanted people of God. From it those who refused to accept Christ and enter the New Covenant had been cut off. They were no longer of the Seed of Abraham in the covenant sense. Certain other branches, however, were not cut off because they accepted the Mediator of the New Covenant and the New Covenant which He came to bring. Did not these now constitute the tree, the Seed of Abraham, the House of Israel and the House of Judah? Later—some years later—other branches were grafted in, but this did not in the least alter the standing of those branches that had never been cut off. With these the Lord established the New Covenant, according to the promise in Jeremiah and constituted the Lord's Supper as its feast. This New Covenant Israel is therefore identical with the Christian Church . . .

"In all this, are we spiritualizing the prophecy, as some allege? Not at all. We are stating an historical fact, clearly contained in the sacred records, that in or about the spring of the year 30 A. D., the mass of those who then called themselves Israelites ceased to be such for prophetic and covenant purposes, having forfeited their citizenship in the commonwealth of Israel by refusing to accept the Messiah, and that after this event all the privileges of the Abrahamic Covenant and all the promises of God belonged to the believing remnant, and to them only; which remnant was therefore and thereafter the true Israel and Judah, the Seed of Abraham, the Christian Church. Thus the promise was fulfilled strictly and definitely to the designated parties.

"That this means the Visible Church is involved in the whole transaction. Before that, the Israelites were all together the visible people of God. To that visible people the New Covenant has been promised, and to that same visible people it must needs be fulfilled. Note that, as already remarked, this New Covenant was established, was promised, with the House of Israel and the House of Judah, and with no one else—distinctly not with any Gentiles. For the first ten or twenty years very few Gentiles came in, and when they began to come in, through the work of Peter, Paul and Barnabas, the New Covenant Israel was well established and a going concern. Their coming in made no difference in the New Covenant, but it did make a difference in the status of those who came in. Before that, they had been 'alienated from the commonwealth of Israel and strangers to the covenants of the promises'—(one promise, three covenants)—but after they had come in they were 'no more strangers and

sojourners, but fellow-citizens with the saints and of the household of God,' being henceforth 'fellow-heirs and fellow-members
of the body, and fellow-partakers of the promise in Christ Jesus
through the Gospel' (Eph. 2:11,19; 3:6)" (*The Seed of Abraham,*
pp. 71–77).

There is a little known prophecy in Leviticus 26:27–33, in
which God speaking through Moses says that, if after being
punished for her sins Israel does not repent, her punishment
will be increased seven times longer. It apparently was with this
warning in mind that Daniel gave the remarkable prophecy of
the "70 weeks," which generally are understood to mean weeks
of years, 7 times 70, or 490 years (9:24–27). Daniel was the
prophet with the exiles in Babylon at the end of the 70 years
exile that had been foretold by Jeremiah (25:11,12; 29:10).
When he understood from the Scriptures that the 70 years were
at an end (Dan. 9:2), he earnestly besought God for the deliverance of his people. However, Israel as a nation did not repent
as a result of the Babylonian captivity. Only a small remnant
had faith enough to return to Jerusalem with Ezra and Nehemiah, and the Jews who were reestablished in Palestine had only
a very precarious existence, successively under Persian, Greek,
and Roman rule, and were under such kings or governors as
Antiochus Epiphanes, Herod, and Pilate, until the coming of
Christ. Daniel's prophecy, we believe, was fulfilled in the later
history of Israel, extending from that time until the coming of
the Messiah, the accomplishment of His work of redemption on
Calvary, and ending in the destruction of the city of Jerusalem—
extending "even unto the full end" (Dan. 9:27) of the role
assigned to Israel in the Divine plan.

It may seem harsh to say that, "God is through with the
Jews." But the fact of the matter is that He is through with them
as a unified national group having anything more to do with the
evangelization of the world. That mission has been taken from
them and given to the Christian Church (Matt. 21:43). For the
past nineteen centuries the Church has been the trustee of the
Gospel, preserving, studying, and purifying its text, and proclaiming its message to the world by means of the printed page
and through the preaching of its ministers and missionaries.

Jewish opposition to the Church began to be felt very early, the apostles themselves being the objects of it. Paul's words regarding his own countrymen show to what an extent it had affected his ministry, for he said that they ". . . both killed the Lord Jesus and the prophets, and drove out us, and please not God, and are contrary to all men; forbidding us to speak to the Gentiles that they might be saved; to fill up their sins always: but the wrath of God is come upon them to the uttermost"— that is, as long as they remain in Judaism (I Thess. 2:15,16). And these apparently are the ones that John had in mind when in the message to the Church in Smyrna we read: "I know thy tribulation, and thy poverty (but thou art rich), and the blasphemy of them that say they are Jews, and they are not, but are a synagogue of Satan," and in the message to the Church in Philadelphia: "Behold, I give of the synagogue of Satan, of them that say they are Jews, and they are not, but do lie" (Rev. 2:9; 3:9).

For individual Jews, yes, the way is open as it has always been. Nothing has been taken from them. No impediment has been placed in their way. Many have become true Christians. These are the "natural branches" who again are "grafted into their own olive tree" (Rom. 11:24). They are the "remnant" of fleshly Israel that is to be saved (Rom. 9:27). And it is these individuals, not Israel in a national capacity, who are to undergo conversion. It was these that Paul had in mind when he wrote: "Now if their fall is the riches of the world, and their loss the riches of the Gentiles; how much more their fulness? . . . For if the casting away of them is the reconciling of the world, what shall the receiving of them be but life from the dead?" (Rom. 11:12,15). There are no other people, we believe, who when they are converted and turn to the Messiah are more appreciative or more zealous for the faith than are the Jews. They seem to have a particularly deep religious nature. It was indeed not without reason that God chose the Hebrew race as the channel through which His revelation should be given to the world.

During Old Testament times the nation of Israel, despite its frequent lapses into apostasy, had a glorious history far surpassing that of any other people. The remarkable line of the prophets and other great men and the moral and spiritual grandeur of their writings, produced under divine inspiration, are immeasurably superior to anything found in any other nation. But that glory is in the past. With the fulfillment and passing away of the Old Covenant, and the institution of the New, the special mission of the Jews in the divine plan was at an end. With the establishment of the New Covenant a new principle was involved and a new method of procedure was established with everything dependent on Christ, of whom it was said that He should be, "A light for revelation to the Gentiles, *And the glory of his people Israel*" (Luke 2:32). Would that the Jews could see that Christ is the glory of His people Israel, that they might turn to Him in whole-hearted trust and obedience!

This does not mean, of course, that the Jews will never go back to Palestine—as indeed some of them have already established the nation of Israel, a little less than 2 million out of an estimated world Jewish population of 12 million now being in that country. But it does mean that as any of them go back they do so entirely on their own, apart from any covenanted purpose to that end and entirely outside of Scripture prophecy. No Scripture blessing is promised for a project of that kind.

The prophecies that Premillennialists point to as indicating a return of the Jews to Palestine are found in the Old Testament and either were given before the return from the Babylonian captivity and so were fulfilled by that event, or, as in the case of Zechariah 8:7,8, were given while that return still was in process, it having occurred over a period of years. It is particularly significant that no New Testament writer mentions a future return—for the very obvious reason that the return of which the prophets spoke was behind them. Had such a return been still future their failure to mention it would have been inexcusable.

It may be that in years to come the Jews will possess a larger part, or even all, of Palestine. We do not know. But if they do they will secure it as other nations secure property, through negotiation, or purchase, or conquest, not by virtue of any as yet unfulfilled prophecies or promises. There are no such prophecies or promises. In the meantime Premillennialism must bear part of the responsibility for the evil and dangerous situation that has arisen in the Middle East, since it has encouraged the Jews to believe that they are the rightful owners of that land and that it is divinely ordained that they are again to possess it, not merely the small portion that they now occupy but all of Palestine and great areas of the surrounding territory from the Euphrates River to the border of Egypt.

Inherent in the dispensational system is the idea that the Jews bear some special relationship to God so that they are in themselves a people favored above all others in the world, that they are to be blessed for their own sake and because they are Jews. Dr. Ladd, a Premillennialist but not a Dispensationalist, says concerning Dispensationalism: "The heart of the system is not seven dispensations, nor a pretribulation rapture of the Church. It is the notion that God has two peoples, Israel and the Church, and two programs—a theocratic program for Israel and a redemptive program for the Church. Israel is a national people with material blessings and an earthly destiny; the Church is a universal people with spiritual blessings and a heavenly destiny" (Article in *Christianity Today*, Oct. 12, 1959). To that we would simply add that with the coming of the Messiah God's purpose with Israel as a nation was accomplished and their mission as a separate people was at an end.

We want to call particular attention to the fact that the priesthood, as well as the sacrificial system, the ritual, the temple, the Jews as a separate people, and the land as a divinely appointed possession of the Jews, has served its purpose and has passed away. In the Epistle to the Hebrews we read that Christ, "through his own blood, entered in *once for all* into the holy place, having obtained eternal redemption," and that He has offered "*one sacrifice for sins for ever*" (9:12; 10:12). The chief function and privilege of a priest is that he has access to God. Under the New Testament dispensation of grace all believers have that privilege,—the rending of the veil between the holy place and the holy of holies at the time of the crucifixion having symbolized that the way of access to God is now open to all. The apostle Peter, writing to the members of the Christian Church who were scattered abroad, said: "But ye are an elect race, *a royal priesthood*, a holy nation, a people of God's own possession" (I Peter 2:9); and in Revelation 1:6 John says that Christ "made us to be a kingdom, to be priests unto his God and father." Hence the New Testament teaches the universal priesthood of believers, in that all believers now have direct access to God. Christ alone is our true Priest. The special order of priests such as functioned in Old Testament times has been abolished forever.

An enlightening article in the Chicago Lutheran Theological Seminary Record, July, 1952, somewhat abbreviated, has this to say about the priesthood:

"The writers of the New Testament had two separate words for *elder* and *priest*. They do not mean the same thing at all, and the New Testament never confuses them. It never says *presbuteros*, elder, when it means *priest*. The New Testament word for priest is *hiereus*. In Greek, from Homer down, this word had a single unambiguous meaning. It meant a man appointed, or consecrated, or otherwise endowed with power to perform certain technical functions of ritual worship, especially to offer acceptable sacrifices, and to make effectual prayers. Likewise in the Septuagint *hiereus* is the regular if not invariable translation of the Old Testament *kohen* and *kahen*, the only Hebrew word for priest. It occurs more than 400 times in the Old Testament in this sense. In the New Testament *hiereus* always means priest, never means elder. There is not anywhere in the New Testament the shadow of an allusion to a Christian priest in the ordinary sense of the word, that is, a man qualified as over against others not qualified for the special functions of offering sacrifice, making priestly intercessions, or performing any other act which only a priest can perform. The Epistle to the Hebrews attributes both priesthood and high-priesthood to Christ and to Him alone. The argument of the Epistle not only indicates that a Christian priesthood was unknown to the writer, but that such a priesthood is unallowable. It is to Jesus only that Christians look as to a priest. He has performed perfectly and permanently the functions of a priest for all believers. His priesthood, being perfect and eternal, renders a continuous human priesthood both needless and anachronistic."

Consequently we reject all merely human and earthly priests, whether in the Roman Catholic Church or in heathen religions, and look upon the continuation of a human priesthood as simply an attempt to usurp divine authority.

Chapter XVI

DATE—SETTING

The business of date-setting seems to have a fatal fascination for premillennial writers and practically all of them engage in it to some extent. There is scarcely a premillennial book that fails to record the conviction of the writer that the time for the return of Christ is near. However, they have profited by the experience of earlier writers at least to this extent, that nowadays they seldom set exact dates but only say that the Lord's coming is near without attempting to say how near. But the setting of an approximate date is the same in principle as exact date-setting and makes it evident that those who do it would fix the exact year and day if they could, or dared.

The early disciples inherited from Judaism the idea of an earthly kingdom which they assumed would soon be set up. They had expected it during the time of Christ's public ministry. After His death some of the early Christians, perhaps a majority of them, still clung to the hope that He would return speedily and set up an earthly kingdom. As Jesus was leading the disciples out to the Mount of Olives shortly before His ascension they asked wistfully, "Lord, dost thou at this time restore the kingdom to Israel?" (Acts 1:6). But He replied, *"It is not for you to know* times or seasons, which the Father hath set within his own authority" (vs. 7). To those who on one occasion during His public ministry "supposed that the kingdom of God was immediately to appear" (Luke 19:11), He gave the Parable of the Pounds, in which a nobleman "went into a far country, to receive for himself a kingdom" (vs. 12)—a project which normally would require a considerable amount of time, and the date of whose return therefore would be very uncertain. He also gave the Parable of the Talents, in which "after a long time" the lord of those servants returned to make a reckoning with them (Matt. 25:19). In the Olivet discourse in response to the question of the disciples, "What shall be the sign of thy coming?" (Matt. 24:3), He said, "But of that day and hour knoweth no one, not even the angels in heaven, neither the Son, but the Father only . . . Watch therefore: for ye know not on what day your Lord cometh . . . Therefore be ye also ready; for in an hour that ye think not the Son of man cometh" (Matt. 24:36,42,44). And again: "But take heed to yourselves, lest happily your hearts be over-charged with surfeiting, and drunkenness, and cares of this life, and that day come on you suddenly as a snare: for so shall it come upon all them that dwell on the face of all the earth" (Luke 21:34,35).

In these verses we are told that the time of the Second Coming is unknown not only to mortal man and immortal angels, but that in His human nature it was unknown even to Christ Himself. Hence let us not be so presumptuous as to know what Christ Himself did not know when He was on earth. Much supernatural knowledge was revealed to Him during His earthly ministry, but the time of His Second Coming was in reality in the far distant future and had no immediate bearing on His work of atonement. Hence He did not seek that knowledge, and it was not revealed to Him. Moreover, we are told that His coming not only will be at a time that is unknown, but that it will be at a time when Christians generally do not expect it. Hence all attempts to set a date for the Second Coming are both futile and unscriptural.

It should be clear that when Christ said, "I come quickly" (Rev. 22:20), He did not mean that He was coming *soon*—as is shown by the long time that has elapsed since. Hence He must have had reference to one of two things: (1) the *manner* of His coming, as sudden, without warning; or, (2) His coming for His loved ones at the time of their death. Either of these is a possible interpretation. But to hold that He encouraged His people to look for His final coming within their lifetime is not permissible, for that would have meant that He was encouraging a false hope.

The Apostle Paul did not set dates for the Lord's return, not even an approximate date. When the expectation of an early return came to a climax in the Thessalonian church and some neglected their daily work because they believed the Lord's return was so near, Paul wrote his second epistle to correct that belief, and his injunction was to go back to work (II Thess. 2:2; 3:10–12). He certainly did not believe in an "any moment" rapture, for in this same epistle he wrote that "the falling away" and "the man of sin" must first come before the end could come (II Thess. 2:3). Those events did not occur during his lifetime; hence he could not at any time have expected the return in the near future. In his later life he knew that his death would occur before certain other events, for he said to the elders from Ephesus: "I know that after my departure grievous wolves shall enter in among you, not sparing the flock" (Acts 20:29); and to his faithful companion Timothy he wrote: "For I am already being offered, and the time of my departure is come," II Tim. 4:6. In his Epistle to the Romans he displayed a truly long range historical perspective when he wrote: ". . . a hardening in part hath befallen Israel, until the fulness of the Gentiles be come in" (11:25).

How appropriate are those words of Jesus and Paul for our day when many pry curiously into the unrevealed and even forbidden things of the future, into "the times and seasons, which the Father hath set within his own authority," and then announce with great positiveness, if not the exact date at least the approximate date, of the Lord's return—which almost always is said to be in the near future!

In spite of these plain warnings many have attempted to lift the veil that God has left over large portions of the future. Premillennialism, particularly in its dispensational form, goes far in its attempt to satisfy the longing desire of man to peer through that veil and, of course, such practice cannot but meet with a degree of popularity. Multitudes, in an air of expectancy, stand in awe and admiration of the seer who claims special skill in the art of "rightly dividing the word of truth," and who with great positiveness and assurance announces his insight into the subject of prophecy. Needless to say, the myriad predictions, whether fixing the exact or approximate date, that have had their issue, have all failed. But that does not deter the present day date setters, except that they are more inclined to venture only approximate dates, such as "in the near future," "near at hand," "during this generation," etc.

It is, however, not a mark of superior wisdom or piety to

try to unravel the secret of the time of Christ's Coming. It is rather a form of presumption, and shows the unscripturalness of those who endeavor to fix such dates. If that date could be established the Dispensationalists would have quite an exact timetable for all of the remaining events—seven years from the Rapture to the Revelation (which evidently could be pinpointed to the day and hour), to be followed by an exact 1000 years of the millennial kingdom, Satan to be bound at the beginning and to be loosed for a little while at the end, this to be followed by the resurrection and judgment of the wicked, and entrance into the eternal state.

But that the first century Premillennialists (Chiliasts, as they were then called), and all others up to the present time who have taught the imminent return of Christ and who saw "signs" which to them were convincing, have been wrong, seems to have practically no deterrent effect on the present day prophets. Surely the passing of sixty or more generations of mistaken Premillennialists should be sufficient to convince them that they have misunderstood the Scriptures somewhere.

The following illustration should make clear the fallacy of the doctrine of the imminent return of Christ. Suppose a passenger is waiting at the station for a certain train. He is told by the agent that his train is imminent. Nineteen trains, far apart in time, pass the station; but his train still has not arrived. Did the agent tell a falsehood? Or has his train really been imminent all that time? We think it is a misuse of words to say that his train was imminent at any of those earlier periods. Nineteen centuries have passed since the First Advent of Christ, and His Second Advent has not occurred yet. Quite clearly He could not have represented His return as imminent, or He would have been giving false information.

Probably no other group ever was so confident or preached more aggressively the imminent return of Christ than did the so-called Plymouth Brethren, among whom Dispensationalism came into prominence some one hundred and thirty years ago. They were very sure that Christ would return within their lifetime. Time proved them wrong by a wide margin. But their successors continue almost as aggressively as they did to point out signs which they say indicate that the end is near. Recently we heard a prominent Dispensationalist speaking over the radio who went so far as to say that the return might occur even before the broadcast was over. But, it didn't. Another prominent Dispensationalist speaking over the radio said that the establishment of the nation of Israel in Palestine, which occurred on May 14, 1948, was the "budding of the fig tree," and that since we are told that the generation living at the time of the budding of the fig tree shall not pass away until all these things be accomplished, the Lord is sure to return within 40 years from that date (cf. Matt. 24:32–34). He went on to say that the return was more likely to occur in the first half of that period than in the second half. Much harm has been done and discredit has been brought upon the precious truth of the Second Coming by such foolishness.

In so far as the first century Christians looked for the Return of Christ in their generation they were merely reading their wishes into their theology. Their vision of God's redemptive purpose was much too limited. Time has now extended nineteen centuries beyond their horizon, and has shown that God was working out a redemptive plan that was far larger and grander than anything that they ever dreamed of. It may yet be shown that He is also working out a far larger and grander redemptive plan than present day Premillennialists realize. Invariably His plans have been larger than ours. Dr. Augustus H. Strong has said:

"We discern a striking parallel between the predictions of Christ's first, and the predictions of His second advent. In both cases the event was more distant and more grand than those imagined to whom the prophecies first came . . . The fact that every age since Christ ascended has had its Chiliasts and Second Adventists should turn our thoughts away from curious and fruitless prying into the time of Christ's return, and set us at immediate and constant endeavor to be ready, at whatever hour He may appear" (*Systematic Theology*, p. 1007).

And Dr. Pieters has the following to say concerning a similar problem of those who attempt to trace the details of Church History through the Book of Revelation, assigning dates, wars, empires, military leaders, etc., to this or that vision:

"All such schemes rest on the assumption that the book of

Church History is well-nigh closed. Almost of necessity every writer who attempts to draw up such a scheme places himself at the very end, in the period of Laodicea . . . A man must rank his own age well on toward the end, otherwise he cannot attempt to make such a division. Yet how do we know that we are near the end? It is easy to point to many things that seem to be 'signs of the times' and to predict an early return of Christ, but believers have done the same thing in every age since the ascension, and usually with quite as good reason as can be assigned today. They were wrong—how can we be sure we are right? If the world stands for another thousand years, or two, or three, will not our divisions into periods look foolish? . . . We can not know, and where we do not know, let us be silent" (*Studies In The Revelation of St. John*, p. 100).

The final refutation of early Premillennialism was given by the great theologian of the West, Augustine (died, 430, A. D.), and so thoroughly did he do his work that it did not again gain a prominent position until a thousand years later, following the Protestant Reformation.

Since we cannot know the time of Christ's coming we are to be always ready and always watchful. If men knew that the time of His coming was far off, they would tend to become careless and indifferent about moral and spiritual values. On the other hand, if they knew that the time was very near they would become frenzied and excited and neglect their assigned work. In either event they would not live normal lives. God prefers that we do not know the time of the end, either the date of our own death or the end of the world, that our service may be natural, spontaneous, and orderly. He seeks from us that which is the true fruit of our natures, not that which is excited and motivated by the expectation of immediate reward or punishment. This life is for every person primarily a time of testing for character and achievement. But that test could not be carried out with accuracy if our actions were actuated by the hope of immediate rewards or the fear of immediate punishments, or if we were lulled into an attitude of indifference because of knowledge that that accounting was far away. Far from being told when "the day of the Lord" is coming, we are specifically told that it will come as a thief in the night, that is, at an unexpected time. The true believer will not be taken unawares, for he will always be ready.

The Old Testament did not give the date for the first coming of Christ, nor any clear intimation as to whether it would be soon or in the far distant future. The event was predicted many centuries in advance, and there was an intense interest on the part of the people as to when He would come and what the nature of His kingdom would be. The people expected and longed for the coming of Messiah through the centuries, as Christian believers have expected and longed for His Second Advent; and doubtless they interpreted many events of Old Testament history as indications that the time was near. But the New Testament simply says concerning His first coming that He came "in the fulness of time" (Gal. 4:4). He came when God's plan was ready. So it will be in regard to His Second Coming. All calculations of dates are both futile and presumptuous.

It is a matter of record that wars, national crises, plagues, disasters, earthquakes, etc., invariably have given fresh interest and zeal toward a new reading of the signs of the times and a new outbreak of date-setting. We would observe, however, that these things are *not* signs of the Second Coming, but events which continue in more or less profusion and in greater or lesser intensity throughout this entire age. There has not been a decade since the time of Christ when they were not in evidence somewhere. At some times they have been more prominent in Europe and America and less so in Asia. At other times the reverse has been true. In any event they have nothing to do with the return of Christ.

It is interesting and instructive to notice that within the comparatively short span of our own generation we have seen the Premillennialists use successively three different sets of signs to prove that the return of Christ is near. At the time of the sudden outbreak of the First World War (in 1914) after a prolonged period of peace and tranquility among the major nations of the world many Premillennialists were sure that those catastrophic events proved the end was near. It is hard for us of the present day, who have lived through two world wars and a prolonged period of tension and strain between Russia and the free world and who have become somewhat calloused to such events, to realize the terrific impact that the First World War made on the minds of people, particularly on those who were prophetically inclined. The sensational reports of thousands being slaughtered on the battlefields, the distress of the civilian populations, the destruction of ships at sea, and for the first time in warfare the use of airplanes, submarines, tanks, and poison gas, made it seem that nothing was secure.

The second distinct set of signs became particularly prominent in the 1920's. The Jews in increasing numbers were going back to Palestine. Many thought that the rise of Benito Mussolini in Italy, with his bombastic proclamations about the future glory of the Italian kingdom and his increasing power through the following years signaled the restoration of the Roman empire, which they believed was foretold in Daniel. The popular view among Premillennialists was that eventually Mussolini would be revealed as the Antichrist. But with the sudden collapse of his fascist state in World War Two and his ignominious demise, we heard no more about Mussolini and his "restored Roman empire." The rapid growth of atheistic Communism through this period also was considered a sign of the evil times that were to precede the end. Though the previous signs had failed so completely and were scarcely mentioned any more, how avidly these new signs were seized upon, and what a mass of books, articles, sermons and conference lectures pointed to these as proof that we were in the last days of the Laodicean age!

Then came World War Two, with its still greater destruction on land, on the sea, and in the air, including the spectacular atomic bomb, and in 1948 the setting up of the independent nation of Israel in Palestine, which was said by some to be "the budding of the fig tree" spoken of in Matthew 24:32. The signs pointed to forty, or even twenty, years ago have now been forgotten for the most part and remain only in the books and articles written at those times, most of which seem to have been withdrawn as quietly as possible. We may be sure that if the world continues another twenty or forty years a still different group of signs, at least different in part, will be put forth as evidence that the end is near. The fact is that each generation of Premillennialists discovers signs which to it are convincing and goes on preaching the same doctrine of the nearness of the end.

A curious anomaly exists in present day American Premillennialism in that the standard doctrine of Dispensationalism (and most Premillennialists are Dispensationalists) is that the coming of Christ may occur literally *at any moment* and that the coming is "signless." But while this is the official doctrine, a prominent feature in dispensational writings is the pointing to certain events or conditions which they say indicate that the end is near. Darby opposed the tendency to point to signs; yet he as well as others interpreted certain historical events of his day as meaning that the Coming of Christ was near, and probably no other group has been so sure that the return would occur within their lifetime as were the early Plymouth Brethren. Scofield wrote that the interval between the 69th and 70th week of Daniel 9:24–27 is "the period during which the two great divine secrets—the outcalling of the church and the mysteries of the kingdom of heaven, run their course"; and he added, "Both seem well-nigh complete" (*What Do The Prophets Say?* p. 143).

Dr. Allis quite appropriately points out that:

"One of the clearest indications that Dispensationalists do not believe that the rapture is really 'without a sign, without a time limit and unrelated to other prophetic events' (Scofield, *What Do The Prophets Say?* p. 97), is the fact that they cannot write a book on prophecy without devoting a considerable amount of space to 'signs' that this event must be very near at hand. These signs may be wars, famines, pestilences, the political situation—they may even include tanks and airplanes. Blackstone lists eight signs. A recent writer gives fifteen (Bauman, *Light From Bible Prophecy;* 1940). The discussion of these signs occupies fifty pages or approximately one-third of the book. Some years ago L. S. Chafer published a little book entitled *Seven Signs of the Times.* In no respect is the inconsistency of Dispensationalists more glaringly apparent than in their persistent efforts to discover *signs* of the nearness of an event which they emphatically declare to be *signless.* Savage in *The Scroll* (p. 201) appeals to such events, but refuses to call them signs. This shows that he recognized the inconsistency of attempting to prove by *signs* the nearness of an event which is held to be *signless*" (*Prophecy and the Church,* p. 174, and footnote).

One of the most recent books on this subject (1956), written by premillennialist George E. Ladd, points out that the dispensational doctrine of the any moment Rapture, that is, that no prophetic events are to take place before the secret coming of Christ to rapture the Church, is in error because according to their own interpretation of Daniel's seventieth week the Jews must be back in Palestine and in position to make a covenant with Antichrist before that can happen. Says he:

"If this is a correct interpretation of the prophetic future, *the Rapture of the Church is not the next event upon the prophetic calendar;* it is rather the return of Israel to her land. The Rapture of the Church is then preceded by a sign, the 'sign of the fig tree,' the sign of Israel. After the fall of Jerusalem in 70 A. D. and the destruction of the Jewish state and after the dissolution of the Roman empire, the Rapture could not take place until Israel was restored to Palestine as a nation and until there arose another emperor or king who would rule over all Europe. In other words, it would have been impossible for Christ to have returned to rapture the Church during the nineteenth century, or even as late as 1900 when the Turk was ruling Palestine and the Jew was scattered over the earth outside the land. It is therefore quite impossible to imagine the machinery being set in motion to dislodge the Turk, to reverse the course of history and open Palestine to the Jew, to reassemble a few hundred thousand Jews in the land, to forge the national entity of the heterogeneous people, to see an Antichrist arise out of the relatively stable European political scene who would dominate the continent and enter into covenant with restored Israel—all within a few months; and precisely this would be demanded by a true any-moment theory which would admit that Christ could have returned in 1900. Such a complex of historical events is conceivable in a generation, but hardly in a few months" (*The Blessed Hope*, p. 154).

In regard to the time of the final coming Dr. Craig has said: "We are told that certain events, such as the preaching of the Gospel among all the nations (Matt. 24:14), the conversion of the Jews (Rom. 11:25-27), the overthrow of 'every rulership and every authority and power' opposed to Christ (I Cor. 15:24), are to take place before the return of our Lord. It seems clear, therefore that while the time of our Lord's return is unknown, yet it still lies some distance in the future. Just how far in the future we have no way of knowing. No doubt, if events move as slowly in the future as in the past, the coming of the Lord lies far in the future. In view of the fact, however, that events move so much more swiftly than formerly, so that what formerly was accomplished in centuries is now accomplished in a few years, it is quite possible that the return of Christ lies in the comparatively near future. Whether it comes in the near or remote future as measured in the scale of human lives, we may be certain that it lies in the near future as measured in the scales of God according to whom a thousand years is as one day. In view of present conditions, however, there seems to be little or nothing in Scripture to warrant the notion that Jesus will return within the lifetime of the present generation" (*Jesus As He Was And Is,* p. 276).

God is in no hurry. His plans span the thousands of years. We find, for instance, that immediately after the fall of man, recorded early in Genesis, God gave a promise of redemption. But He did not provide redemption immediately. Instead, the whole of the Old Testament period intervened, and it was a time of waiting, prophesying, and testifying of that which was to come. How long that period was we cannot say with accuracy, but it was at a very minimum 4,000 years. Think of it! 4,000 years before the coming of the anxiously awaited Messiah! How slow, how awfully slow that must seem to those who want to rush everything through and who ever since the first coming of Christ have had as one of their cardinal tenets His "near" or "imminent" return! If God took more than 4,000 years *just to make preparation* for this great work of redemption, surely now that a redemption of infinite value has been provided—paid for at the cost of the suffering and death of Christ on the cross, who was incarnate Deity—surely He will not cut the harvest short. While we cannot say what the secret purpose of God is, from the human viewpoint He is at least free to continue this process indefinitely. Surely He will make very extensive use of this great privilege that now is His, and will bring into the Kingdom literally billions upon billions of souls redeemed by grace.

Those who are so anxious to see the end come, and who so enthusiastically preach the "imminent" return or "soon coming" of Christ have too small a view of God's purposes. Surely they are glad that He did not come a hundred, or a thousand years ago, as the Premillennialists of those days expected and hoped; for in that event they themselves would have been deprived of the privilege of living. A recent premillennial writer comments on what he terms God's "extraordinary reluctance" to send Christ in His second coming, then later in the same article says, "O, how I thank God that Jesus Christ did not come in my lifetime before I was saved. That longsuffering meant salvation to every Christian reading this message. If God had come before we were saved, we would have been doomed to the fire and anguish of the Great Tribulation."

Christ will return in His own good time. But for us to be overly anxious for His return is to cut off those who are yet to be converted and all those who are to live in the ages to come. His coming may be for us, as it was for the first century Christians, an event of the far distant future.

No discussion of the subject of date-setting would be complete without reference to some of the more outstanding predictions that have been made throughout the centuries. It obviously is impossible to detail the literally hundreds of such predictions that have been made.

Even in the apostolic age the rumor spread that Christ would return before the Apostle John died. Some of the Christians in the church in Thessalonica believed that the coming of the Lord was just at hand, and had to be set right by the Apostle Paul (II Thess. 2:2). Early church history tells of numerous groups that expected the return of the Lord, some of which set dates.

As the year 1000 approached many believed that the thousand years spoken of in Revelation 20 was nearing completion and that Christ would then come back to conduct the judgment of the world. Many pious but poorly informed people became convinced that it was folly to work for the realization of their earthly needs and ideals. Some sold their homes and lands and made final disposition of their earthly goods, and waited for the Lord's return.

In the Middle ages an Italian monk who was inclined to mysticism and ecstasy, Joachim of Floris, calculated that the 1260 days mentioned in Daniel and Revelation were to be understood as years, and that the new order under the reign of Christ would begin in the year 1260. In Bohemia a forerunner of John Huss, Melitz by name, fixed the end of the world as falling between 1365 and 1367. Luther was convinced that the rising power of the Papacy and the approach of the Turks combined to herald the near return of Christ. It was the common opinion of the Reformers that the Pope as the head of the persecuting and oppressive Roman Catholic Church was the Antichrist, the Man of Sin spoken of by Paul. Also in this period an independent group of Christians with headquarters at Munster, Germany, set up their New Zion in anticipation of the momentary return of Christ as their King. The city of Munster became the center of unrestrained fanaticism and the movement had to be forcibly suppressed by the government. "Mother Shipton," in her numerous curious prophecies written early in the sixteenth century, ventured among other things the prediction that "The world to an end will come, In eighteen hundred and eighty-one."

In the seventeenth century the "Fifth Monarchy men" arose in England as opponents of Cromwell and said that the fifth kingdom prophesied by Daniel was just ready to be set up, which would mean the personal rule of Christ on earth. Isaac Newton set the date as 1715. Later in the eighteenth century Immanuel Swedenborg gave forth with his many special revelations. The famous Greek scholar, Bengel, so often quoted by Premillennialists, predicted the Lord's return in 1836. Then came the Irvingites, followers of Edward Irving, a Scottish minister of great eloquence preaching in London, with definite predictions of the return of Christ in 1864. Joanna Southcott was in the limelight for some time with her "visions," and said that Christ would come on October 19, 1884.

The French Revolution and the Napoleonic wars, with the "Tyrant," the "Man of Destiny," bestriding Europe and the Near East like a Colossus, afforded a field day for the prophecy-mongers as they were sure that the Antichrist had come and that the return of Christ was very near.

The Plymouth Brethren arose in Ireland and England about 1830, with John N. Darby as their most prominent leader, and as we have already had occasion to observe, they placed very strong emphasis on the imminent return of Christ, which they were sure would occur within the lifetime of the generation then living.

The most famous example and the greatest excitement occasioned by any millennial prediction occurred in our own country as a result of the preaching of William Miller. Miller was a converted deist and a farmer with but limited education. He began to lecture in New York state in 1831, and took as the foundation text for his theory Daniel 8:14, a verse that has tripped up many another self-appointed prophet, and which reads: "Unto two thousand and three hundred days; then shall the sanctuary be cleansed." On the basis of his calculations he fixed the date of Christ's Second Coming at midnight, October 22, 1843. He lectured widely, and his followers, known as "Millerites," were thrown into great excitement as the date approached. All who did not believe were to be lost. Property was given away, crops were left to spoil in the fields, and as the hour approached people climbed to the hill tops and house tops to await the event by which they would be "caught up to meet the Lord in the air." As midnight approached bon-fires were lighted, and there were scenes of wild confusion. But when the time passed and nothing happened, anticipation turned to disappointment and disgust. Miller acknowledged his error, but concluded that he had miscalculated by a year, and again fixed the date exactly a year later, in 1844. He declared, "There is no possibility of mistake this time," and that "All who reject the light will be lost." Again the day passed without regard to Miller's figures. The results were pathetic. Many of his loyal followers were left destitute, some drifted into other isms of the day or into infidelity. Miller was bitterly disappointed and acknowledged that his calculations had been mistaken. His health gradually failed and he died in 1849. The event had again shown the folly of all such calculations and speculations which attempt to fix the time of the Lord's return. The marvel is that so many believed him. The credulity of his followers was due largely to the positiveness with which he asserted that this was the revelation of the infallible word of God, and further because they believed that God had given their group immediate inspiration to understand and interpret the prophecies of the Bible. But out of this movement there developed the Seventh-day Adventist Church, with Ellen G. White as its prophetess, who claimed to have received visions and special inspiration for her writings. This church is strongly premillennial in doctrine, with a one-sided futurism in its preaching and publications.

Rutgers makes the following comment on the Millerite debacle:

"In Miller and his associates we meet with plain, bald, flat-footed chiliasm; chiliasm with all its fervor, enthusiasm and fanaticism; its pessimism, its biblicism, its legalistic, rabbinistic calculating literalism; its fondness for veiled and obscure portions of prophecy; . . . its preaching of an evangel that subordinates all under one theme, the imminent, fast approaching advent of our Lord, ending this dispensation and introducing a glorious millennial reign of His saints on earth . . . We should, how-ever, not merely concentrate our criticism against the Millerites as is commonly the case because of erroneous dates, but rather seek to point out the underlying principle which accounted for this mistake. And that principle is none other than that on which chiliasm of all ages rests, viz., hard and fast literalism. Modern premillennialists attempt to rid themselves of this unwholesome grievous burden of the Millerites, holding up these mistaken dates, but let them consider that their principle of interpretation by which they distill a restoration of Israel, of the temple, Old Testament sacrifices, etc.—are just as foolish, ridiculous and erroneous, and spring from the same root. All attempts to com-prehend eternal realities, foreshadowed in metaphoric and sym-bolic Old Testament prefigurations must fail miserably, when a carnal, literal rule of interpretation is applied which cramps into narrow confines of space and time incalculable, infinite mys-teries" (*Premillennialism In America*, pp. 91,92,97).

Blackstone, in his book, *Jesus Is Coming*, refers to what he terms "prophetic periods" which are to precede the Rapture and the Revelation, and says: "An honest and prayerful study of them has given us an assured conviction that they are rapidly drawing to a close" (p. 208). He sets forth seven *Signs of Christ's Speedy Coming*, which are as follows: 1. The prevalence of travel and knowledge (Dan. 12:4), 2. Perilous times (II Tim. 3:1), 3. Spiritualism (I Tim. 4:1), 4. Apostasy (II Thess. 2:3; Rev. 3:14–22, the Laodicean age), 5. World-wide evangelism (Matt. 24:14), 6. Rich men (James 5:1,8), and 7. Israel, begin-ning to show signs of national life. When this was written (1878) Palestine still was a part of the Turkish empire. How much surer he would have been that the end was very near if he could have seen what we see, the present day nation of Israel with nearly two million inhabitants!

Scofield, speaking before the Second Annual Philadelphia Bible Conference in 1914, shortly after the outbreak of World War I, said:

"We are certainly near the end. We are in the feet, if not the toes, of the image [Daniel 2] and the last events will be rapidly fulfilled . . . I am impressed that we are right at the threshold of the complete destruction of Gentile world-power . . . Thank God, it [the millennial kingdom] is very near now" (Quoted in *Bibliotheca Sacra,* July-Sept., 1950).

And to a prophetic conference which met in Philadelphia, May 28–30, 1918, while World War I still was in progress, Scofield sent the following message:

"To the Philadelphia Conference on the Return of our Lord, Greetings: I pray that God may guide all your proceedings, especially in the putting forth of a fearless warning that we are in the awful end of the Times of the Gentiles, with no hope for humanity except in the personal return of the Lord of Glory; and also in a statement of the fundamentals of Christian belief, which may form a clear basis for Christian fellowship in a day of apostasy."

Another glaring example of the folly of predicting the time of the Lord's return is found in the preaching of Charles Taze Russell, founder of the sect now known as Jehovah's Witnesses. He boldly proclaimed that Christ would return in 1914. But when that year passed without the return of Christ, and was marked instead by the outbreak of the First World War, he had the nerve to maintain that Christ had indeed returned but that He was then in hiding because of the wickedness of the people and that He eventually would show Himself. Russell's successor, the so-called Judge Rutherford, continued to preach the near return of Christ and the speedy transformation of the living saints, as indeed the group does to the present day.

While the First World War was in progress, in December, 1917, a group of prominent churchmen, including G. Campbell Morgan, F. B. Meyer, and others, met in London and issued a statement on *The Significance of the Hour,* which concluded with such statements as the following:

"1. That the present crisis points toward the close of the

times of the Gentiles, 2. That the revelation of our Lord may be expected at any moment, when He will be manifested as evidently to His disciples as on the evening of His resurrection, and 3. That the completed church will be translated to be 'forever with the Lord.' . . ."

But now, forty years later and after the world has gone through a second and much worse world war, the Lord still has not come, and that document has long since taken its place along with many other such in the limbo of forgotten millennial curiosities and follies.

A few years ago Dr. Chafer spoke of "the mighty truth that Christ is to return and that that return is near," and added: "The return of Christ is so close that He becomes as one who is 'at the door'" (*Bibliotheca Sacra,* July-Sept., 1952).

It almost seems as if these people think they can hasten the Lord's coming by making such pronouncements. We are reminded that Christ Himself said: "Then if any man shall say unto you, Lo, here is the Christ, or, Here; *believe it not*. For there shall arise false Christs, and false prophets, and shall show great signs and wonders; so as to lead astray, if possible, even the elect . . . If therefore they shall say unto you, Behold, he is in the wilderness; go not forth: Behold he is in the inner chambers; *believe it not*" (Matt. 24:23–26).

The rule for the detection of false prophets was given early in the Old Testament. In Deuteronomy 18:21,22 we read: "And if thou say in thy heart, How shall we know the word which Jehovah hath not spoken? when a prophet speaketh in the name of Jehovah, if the thing follow not, nor come to pass, that is the thing which Jehovah hath not spoken: the prophet hath spoken it presumptuously, thou shalt not be afraid of him."

We do not hesitate to say that this warning has proved true as regards all those who have been so presumptuous as to set dates either exact or approximate, for the time of the Lord's return. The pity is that many ministers who are known as true Conservatives and who are firm believers in the verbal inspiration of the Bible have identified themselves with the most extreme type of Dispensationalism, and have not hesitated to set exact or approximate dates, almost invariably holding that Christ's coming is in the near future.

But how different from all this is the attitude of Postmillennialism! It does not disturb the Church and excite the ridicule of the world with vain and foolish calculations and predictions of times and seasons, and it does not profess to know more about the time of the end than did Christ Himself when He was on earth. Briefly, we would say of the Coming of Christ: Don't worry about it, and don't worry other people about it. Our duty is to be ready at all times, and then to go ahead with the work at hand, knowing that if His coming to the world at large is delayed, His coming for us personally will be in the comparatively near future.

Chapter XVII

"THE LAST DAYS";
"THE LATTER DAYS"

In the study of prophecy much confusion has resulted from the failure to recognize that the expressions, "the last days," and "the latter days," relate not exclusively to the closing calendar days of the present age, but to the entire Christian era. As used in the Old Testament the expression "latter days" simply means "in later days," or "in later times," and finds its fulfillment largely in that period—e.g., "And Jacob called unto his sons, and said: Gather yourselves together, that I may tell you that which shall befall you in the latter days" (Gen. 49:1); and Balaam's words to Balak: "Come, and I will advertise thee what this people shall do to thy people in the latter days" (Nu. 24:14). In Isaiah 2:2–4 and Micah 4:1–8 the expression is found in one of the kingdom prophecies which, as we have explained earlier, finds its fulfillment in the later part of the Messianic age: "And it shall come to pass in the latter days, that the mountain of Jehovah's house shall be established on the top of the mountains, and shall be exalted above the hills; and all nations shall flow unto it . . ."

The fact that we are now in "the latter days" does not necessarily mean that we are near the end of the age. As used in the New Testament this and similar expressions include the entire Messianic era. Paul wrote: "But know this, that in the last days grievous times shall come" (II Tim. 3:1); and the context makes it plain that he was speaking of the days then present, for after enumerating the evil things that characterize the grievous times he admonished Timothy, "From these things turn away" (vs. 5). On the day of Pentecost Peter explained the events that were happening as having been prophesied by the prophet Joel, and then proceeded to quote: "And it shall be in the last days, saith God . . ." (Acts 2:16,17). The writer of the Epistle to the

342

Hebrews says, "But now once at the end of the ages hath he been manifested to put away sin by the sacrifice of himself" (Heb. 9:26). James says, "Ye have laid up your treasure in the last days" (5:3). In enumerating the things that happened to the children of Israel during the wilderness journey, Paul said: "Now these things happened unto them by way of example; and they were written for our admonition, upon whom the ends of the ages are come" (I Cor. 10:11). Paul and the people to whom he was writing were those upon whom the ends of the ages had come. Peter says that Christ "was manifested at the end of the times for your sake" (I Peter 1:20); and again, "The end of all things is at hand" (I Peter 4:7).

Hence these expressions often are used with reference to the entire Christian era. We are in "the last days" and have been in them for nearly 2000 years, and for all we know they may last for many more millenniums before the end comes. They began when Jesus was born in Bethlehem, and they continue until the Second Coming. As this expression is used in the New Testament it simply distinguishes the days of the Christian era from those that went before, which were the former days. It tells us nothing at all concerning the time of the Second Advent, whether it is near at hand, or in the distant future. The First Coming of Christ was the dividing line in history. We count time before His Coming as B. C., and since His Coming as A. D. In other words, the incarnation of Christ introduced the final period in the world's history, the last on the divine program.

The consequence of this is well stated by Rev. W. J. Grier: "If this present period is the last, then there remains nothing but the eternal state; there is no place for a millennial age between" (*The Momentous Event*, p. 40). And Dr. Edward J. Young, of Westminster Theological Seminary, says that the expression "in the latter days" literally means "in the uttermost part of the days," and adds that as used in the Old Testament concerning the future worship of the people,

"The phrase tells when this true worship of the Lord will occur. The phrase is eschatological, that is, it has to do with the end of things, the very last part of the days. In the vision of the Old Testament prophets, this was the Messianic age, for the appearance of the Messiah upon the earth was the goal toward which all prophecy pointed . . . The New Testament shows without the shadow of a doubt that the phrase 'the last days' refers to the age which was ushered in by the appearance of Jesus Christ upon the earth" (*Old Testament Prophecy*, p. 68).

In the following paragraph Dr. Craig has pointed out another consequence of the proper use of these terms. Says he:

"It has been hastily assumed by many that what is taught concerning the evils that would exist in the 'latter times' or 'last days' (Comp. I Tim. 4:1; II Tim. 3:1; II Peter 3:33; Jude 18) means that the days immediately preceding the end will be particularly bad. This, however, is to overlook the fact that these phrases as used in the New Testament refer to the whole dispensation of the Spirit, i.e., to the whole period between the first and second advents. (Comp. Acts 2:17). It is illegitimate, therefore, to say that the New Testament teaches that the times will grow worse and worse. Such statements do not necessarily refer to more than the first states of 'the latter times' or 'last days.' For aught that these statements imply, the closing stages of this dispensation may be days in which evil will be completely subjugated. It is only because men have overlooked the technical sense in which these phrases are used in the New Testament that they have supposed that there is any contradiction between the passages in which they are found and such a passage as I Corinthians 15:20–28, where the period in which we are living is spoken of as a period of advancing conquest on the part of Christ" (*Jesus As He Was And Is*, p. 280).

The forms of religion as set forth under the Old Covenant were temporary and typical. But Christianity, the religion of the New Covenant, is permanent. God's great work of preparing the world for the coming of Christ was carried out through long ages of time. Then, in the fullness of time, the Messiah came, and at great cost to Himself accomplished the atonement. What remains now is the harvest period, the gathering of redeemed souls. There is no reason why this period should not be prolonged over a very long period of time during which an incredibly large number of souls should be saved.

When Paul says, "Behold, *now* is the acceptable time; behold, *now* is the day of salvation" (II Cor. 6:2), he means that this present Christian age, and not some future age, is the time when

God's redemptive work comes to fruition. The present Christian era *is* the "end time," and when it terminates there will be no other, but only the eternal age. Dr. Warfield says concerning this verse:

"The period of the preaching of the Gospel is the acceptable time and the day of salvation predicted by the prophets. Paul's meaning is not as it has sometimes been strangely misunderstood, that the day in which we may find acceptance with God is swiftly passing by, but rather that now at length that promised day of salvation has fully come. Now, this time of the preaching of the gospel of reconciliation, is by way of eminence *the day of salvation*. It is not a time in which only a few, here and there, may be saved, while the harvest is delayed. It is the very harvest time itself, in which the field is being reaped. And the field is the world."

He continues: "The implication of a declaration like this is, of course, that God's saving activities have now reached their culmination; there can be nothing beyond this. This implication is present throughout the whole New Testament. It pervades, for instance, the Epistle to the Hebrews, the burden of which is that in this dispensation the climax of God's redemptive work has been attained, and there is nothing to be hoped for after it. In His Son and the salvation provided in His Son God has done His utmost . . . Accordingly these days of the Son and His word are explicitly designated the end of these days (Hebrews 1:2), a phraseology running through the New Testament in various forms of 'the end of the times' (I Peter 1:20), 'the last days' (Acts 2:17; II Tim. 3:1; James 5:3; II Peter 3:3, 'the last time' Jude 18), 'the last hour' (I John 2:18). These 'last days' may themselves terminate in a more pointedly 'last day' (John 6:40; 11:24) or 'last time' (I Peter 1:5)—the very last of the last —but just because they are the last they cannot be succeeded by any day or time or season whatever. They close what is called 'this world' or 'this age' and are followed only by 'the world or age to come,' which is what we commonly call 'eternity.' In the face of this it will be hard to maintain that there yet remains another and different dispensation to be lived through before the end comes" (Article, The Gospel and the Second Coming, in *The Bible Magazine*, April, 1915).

The Vastness of the Universe an Indication of the Magnitude of God's Plan of Redemption

We should like to call attention to another consideration which may help to give some idea of the greatness of God and of the incredibly vast scale on which He works, and which surely has some bearing on the scope of His plan of redemption.

There is evidence from different sources that this is a very old universe and a very old world in which we live. In astronomy the unit of measure is the light year, that is, the distance that light traveling at the rate of 186,000 miles per second travels in one year, or approximately six trillion miles. The 200-inch telescope on Mount Palomar, in California, catches light which it is estimated left certain distant stars about two billion years ago. Such a figure is, of course, only an approximation. Yet there is reason to believe that it is somewhere near reality. In any event it informs us that this universe has been in existence for an incredibly long period of time, and that it is immensely large. And there is no assurance that the Palomar telescope has reached the limits of outer space.

As regards the size of the universe astronomers inform us that the sun is 93,000,000 miles from the earth and that light from the sun traverses that distance in 8 minutes. They go on to say that the nearest fixed star is 4 light years away, that the North Star is 450 light years away, that the Milky Way which is the system in which our sun and earth are located and which resembles a giant disk or cart wheel in shape is so vast that it takes light 100,000 years to travel from one side of it to the other, and that out through space there are literally millions of other such milky ways or star clusters. Undoubtedly there is some proportionate relationship between time and space, between the vast size of the universe and the length of time that it has been in existence. Surely it is unreasonable to acknowledge the vast size of the universe and yet limit its existence to only a few thousand years as some do. Surely those distant stars have been out there a long time or their light would not yet be reaching us. The book of Genesis gives no date for the creation of the universe other than to place it in the remote past. This does not mean that we accept the theory of organic evolution as regards the origin of life. Rather we hold that when the earth had been brought to a sufficiently advanced state of development God by pure supernatural power created life in its various forms and placed it here. There is no necessary conflict between the view that the universe is very large and very old and the Genesis account which states that God created this system and that His providential control has been over it from the beginning.

Also, recent developments in atomic physics have opened up much more accurate methods of estimating the age of the earth than were available a generation ago. Radioactive materials such as uranium and thorium are known to disintegrate at fixed rates regardless of temperature or pressure conditions, with a particular lead isotope as the end product. By knowing this rate and the amount of disintegrated product a rock contains it is possible to estimate the length of time that the process has been going on. Some of the rocks in the earth's crust indicate an age of between two and four billion years. At any rate it is a very old and a very stable world.

Both Astronomy and Geology have much to teach us about the greatness of God. The figures from both as regards the age and size of the universe are so huge that they stagger the imagination. In all probability God's plan for this earth is on a scale that our little minds are utterly incapable of grasping. Clearly God is in no such hurry as we frail human beings so often are.

Surely God has not yet displayed His saving grace to its fullest extent in this world, nor has He shown what He can do with a world truly converted to righteousness. Indeed, what we have seen so far appears to be only a preliminary stage, a temporary triumph of the Devil whose work is to be completely overthrown. God's work spans the ages. Even the millenniums are insignificant to Him who inhabits eternity. Those who seem so certain of the near return of Christ and the end of the present world order, it seems to us, have not given sufficient consideration to the incredibly vast scale on which God works. So marvelous is the universe, so great is the goodness and mercy of God, and so precious are redeemed human souls, that we can only conclude that God may have, and undoubtedly does have, developments in store for the human race which shall be quite startling, developments concerning which we have scarcely dreamed as yet.

Assuming that the world is approximately two billion years old, the two thousand year period that has elapsed since Christ came and accomplished His work of atonement is only the one-millionth part of that time! This means that the length of the Christian era compares with the age of the world as one second compares with eleven and one-half days, or as one minute compares with two years. For God to bring the world to an end now after having spent such a relatively short time working out the fruits of the Christian era would be as if a man were to spend two years building a house and would then live in it only one minute. We know that man has been on the earth at least since 4000 B. C. The time that has elasped since the Coming of Christ has been less than half the length of that period.

Our work ordinarily is in the opposite proportion. If we spend six months building a house or a ship we expect to use it for perhaps a hundred times that long. Its period of usefulness should be many times that of its preparation. Of this we may be sure—God is never in a hurry. If He spent 4000 years bringing man to the point of redemption, surely after the atonement has been purchased at such a great cost to Himself He will have something very great in store for the Christian era, which is the fruitage era. Since God's work in the physical world where we are able to observe it is on such an unbelievably vast scale, surely in His dealings with the human race (man having been created in His image and made the crown and glory of the whole creation) He will continue this process until He has displayed His glory by an incredibly large harvest of souls. Surely His work in the more important spiritual realm will not be cut short either in numbers or in time until He has manifested His glory on an even greater scale than in the physical realm. No limit can be set to that number by man. God alone knows how vast the number is. From the beginning God's program has been on a far grander scale than man has been able to comprehend.

If this reasoning is correct, the human race may yet be in its infancy, with a future course of development in store which may well be utterly beyond the power of our imagination to grasp. In the physical realm we are now only on the threshold of the age of electronics, atomic power, and space travel; and who can predict what limitless fields of expansion and conquest both on the earth and throughout the universe these may open up! Dr. Warfield used to say that we still are in the Primitive Church, and that doctrinally the so-called "church fathers" might better have been called the "church infants." In any event we may be sure that as God's plan for the Church and for the development of His Kingdom at large is revealed to us it will be, like His other works, incredibly greater in time and scope than our little minds can grasp. At the time of man's creation one of the commands given to him was that he should "subdue" the earth (Gen. 1:28–30)—that is, search out the laws of nature, learn to apply them for his own advancement, and so make himself master of all animate and inanimate things which have been placed here for his use. He still is a long way behind on that schedule. But beyond all that, God's work of bringing new souls, infinitely precious souls, into the Kingdom is a continuing work of the utmost importance. How thankful we should be that He did not terminate that work before our time! Let us not be too anxious to wind it up and call a halt to such glorious accomplishment.

Chapter XVIII

A PESSIMISTIC THEORY

One of the results of the dispensational doctrine that the rejection of the Kingdom was followed by the establishment of the Church as an interim agency is that during the present age the Gospel is to be preached only as a "witness" or a "testimony" unto all the nations (Matt. 24:14), without any thought that it shall be successful in making the world Christian. With both the King and the Kingdom absent, the Church is looked upon as an expedient to which Christ resorted for the present age. There is no expectation that permanent betterment or final victory can be brought about through it. The preaching of the Gospel is expected to save only a minority of individuals. It is in fact expected to do little more than complete the body of Christ's elect, and its primary purpose is to bring in those who are to be associated with Him during the millennial reign.

A corollary to this belief is that the world is to grow worse and worse until Christ returns, and that this evil course is to culminate in the reign of the Man of Sin, the Antichrist. "The Kingdom is to be established by power, not by persuasion," says Scofield (p. 977). And G. N. H. Peters says: "The Kingdom shall be established, not as men vainly imagine by the preaching of the gospel, but by the iron rod that shall smite down all opposition and make the enemies of Christ like the broken pieces of a potter's vessel." And again he says: "His supernatural might shall be exerted in behalf of this Kingdom in the most astounding manner" (*The Theocratic Kingdom*, p. 81).

This is indeed a pessimistic outlook. It has ever been the practice of Dispensationalists to speak harshly of the Church. They cite the parables of the Tares, the Drag-net, and particularly the parable of the Leaven, as teaching that evil will be triumphant in the world, that Christendom, or "the professing Church" as they term it, will be completely apostate before

Christ returns, and that in fact that condition will be the sure sign of His coming. John N. Darby, the principal originator of the system, represents the parable of the Leaven as setting forth false doctrine. "It is not faith properly so called," he says, "nor is it life. It is a religion; it is Christendom. A profession of doctrine, in hearts which will bear neither the truth nor God, connects itself always with corruption in the doctrine itself." It is interesting to note that Darby withdrew from the Established Church in Ireland shortly after his ordination because of the conviction that an ordained ministry and church organization was wrong. The Brethren group which he founded refused to recognize any form of church government or any office of the ministry. Darby died in 1882, but his influence continues strong not only in the various branches of Brethrenism but in the dispensational movement which extends to some extent through practically all of the other denominations. This attitude has caused some people to fail to appreciate the value of or even the necessity of church membership, and it has caused some to take an antagonistic attitude toward the Church.

Scofield, too, says that leaven represents "the principle of corruption working subtly"; and that this is "the unvarying symbolical meaning of leaven" (p. 1016). In another connection he says that "The predicted future of the visible Church is apostasy . . . of the true Church glory" (p. 1276).

We must reject, of course, the interpretation which invariably makes leaven represent a principle of evil, and particularly we must reject it in this parable, for here it is expressly said that "The kingdom of heaven is like leaven . . ." We need only remember that the reason the Passover was observed with unleavened bread was not because of any suggestion of corruption attaching to leaven, but solely as a reminder of the unleavened bread which was prepared in haste and eaten the night the Children of Israel were thrust out of Egypt (Ex. 12:39). The Passover was primarily an historical reminder and commemoration of that momentous event. Furthermore, leavened bread was in daily use by the people of Israel, apparently without any suggestion of evil. Surely they would not have been permitted to use leavened bread 51 weeks of the year and commanded to refrain from its use only during Passover week if its symbolical use was always and solely evil. Furthermore, it should be obvious to every reader of the parable that leaven working through the whole lump was intended to illustrate the transforming power of the Gospel as it spread throughout the world.

Premillennialism or Dispensationalism thus looks upon the preaching of the Gospel as a failure so far as the conversion of the world is concerned, and sees no hope for the world during the present dispensation. It regards the Church as essentially bankrupt and doomed to failure as each of the five preceding dispensations supposedly have ended in failure, and asserts that only the Second Coming of Christ can cure the world's ills. In premillennial literature we repeatedly come across such expressions as "this apostate age," "the apostasy deepens," "the Laodicean stage of luke-warmness," etc. Dr. Lewis Sperry Chafer, in an Introduction to Dr. Charles L. Feinberg's book, *Premillennialism or Amillennialism?*, refers to what he terms "the present insane, corrupt condition of the world" (p. vii).

Another corollary of this belief is that the benefits of civilization that have been brought about through the influence of the Church are only illusory, and that all this will be swept away when Christ comes. The writings of such a representative Premillennialist as Dr. Nathaniel West illustrate very clearly the pessimistic nature of the system. He has nothing but ridicule and contempt for our alleged "progress" and "civilization." When he comes to treat this subject he can see nothing but evil in our modern Church and world and writes: "Professedly Christian men shall do the Devil's work teaching this same method of 'progress' . . . 'Great Babylon,' bearing the Christian name, a church on every corner, a preacher on every street, is worse than the Chaldean city whose king was God's rod to 'destroy and make a hissing, and a desolation, of Judah' the Messianic state of the old civilization." "The beast is still unchanged in its heart, anti-Christian still, notwithstanding its Christian order, culture, civilization; a civil structure accepting Christianity externally, the Church accepting the world internally, both parties meeting half-way, the Church and the world making mutual concessions, the Beast Christianized, the Church Beastialized, she the loser, it the gainer, proud intellectual culture, science, and wealth of Christendom, leading thousands away from, and preventing others from coming to, the knowledge of Christ" (*The Thousand Years in Both Testaments*, pp. 439–457).

This being the logic of the system, it is not difficult to see why the outlook as regards the present age should be pessimistic. If we feel that the whole secular order is doomed, and that God has no further interest in it, why, then of course we shall feel little responsibility for it, and no doubt feel that the sooner evil reaches its climax the better. To hold that the preaching of the Gospel under the dispensation of the Holy Spirit can never gain more than a very limited success must inevitably paralyze effort both in the home church and on the mission field. Such an over-emphasis on other-worldliness cannot but mean an under-emphasis and neglect of the here and now. Such views tend to produce slipshod methods both in the home church and on the foreign mission field. It is only by a happy inconsistency that Premillennialists holding these views can take any deep interest in social reform movements, although we are glad to say that many of them do work energetically for social progress and community betterment.

Perhaps the passage most often quoted by Premillennialists to prove that the world is growing worse and worse is II Timothy 3:1–5. There Paul says: "But know this, that in the latter days grievous times shall come. For men shall be lovers of self, lovers of money, boastful, haughty, railers, disobedient to parents, un-thankful, unholy, without natural affection, implacable, slander-ous, without self-control, fierce, no lovers of good, traitors, head-strong, puffed up, lovers of pleasure rather than lovers of God; holding a form of godliness, but having denied the power thereof." But having enumerated these evils, he admonishes Timothy: "From these also turn away." Also in the same chapter he says: "But evil men and imposters shall wax worse and worse, deceiv-ing and being deceived." And again he admonishes Timothy: "But abide thou in the things which thou hast learned and hast been as-sured of" (vss. 13,14). Hence he clearly was describing conditions that were then present and warning against them as present temptations, not predicting a state of affairs that would prevail at the end of the age.

In every generation the alleged apostasy of the Church and the alleged corruption of the world are the standing "signs of the times" with Premillennialists which prove that "the end is near," and that the Coming of Christ is "at hand" or "imminent." The charge of pessimism is usually denied with considerable vehemence, and it seems to be a touchy point; but the representative sermons, teachings, and literature of the system prove it to be true. It would be hard to imagine a theory more pessimistic, more hopeless in principle or, if consistently applied, more calculated to bring about the defeat of the Church's program than this one.

But when we are told that doom hangs over the heads of men and that one crisis is to follow another, let us not be too quick to give up on the world. If we have proper ideas of God's program of redemption we shall see that that program contemplated the entire human race as fallen and all men as equally in need of mercy. We may acknowledge that the present generation in the world deserves punishment for its apostasy and immorality and indifference. But if we are properly impressed with the mercy of God, by which we ourselves have been rescued from sin, we shall not quickly and summarily dismiss the plight of our fellow men as though they are beyond all hope. We shall refuse instead to abandon the world to the Evil One, or to project God's kingdom solely into the future age, and hold rather that our task is to win the entire world for Christ, and that this task can be accomplished if we who profess to be Christians are faithful to the Great Commission that He set before us. We have the example of Abraham who, when he was told that Sodom and Gomorrah would be destroyed, did not merely shrug his shoulders with an air of resignation and let it go at that, but interceded earnestly for the postponement of punishment and presented intelligent reasons to justify the extension of divine mercy. The idea that the world is to be converted only by force, and not by persuasion, is a far cry from the Scriptural principle that the Holy Spirit works in the hearts of men when and where and how He pleases so that they are born again and thereby brought into the spiritual kingdom. Paul says that the Gospel is the power of God unto salvation; that though a stumbling block to the Jews and foolishness to the Gentiles, it has pleased God through what he terms "the foolishness of preaching" to save them that believe (that is, it seems like foolishness to those who do not understand it·). In those words we are taught that there is no other means of salvation than through the preaching of the Gospel. Hence we believe that it is a fundamentally wrong conception of what God intends to accomplish in this age to say that the faithful proclamation of the Gospel is not capable of winning the world for Christ. Premillennialists stress the fact that the Gospel is to be preached as a "testimony" or "witness," and almost completely ignore the fact that we are commanded to "make disciples of all the nations." They forget that God's method of bringing the world to Christ is through the instrumentality of human agents, prepared and led by the Holy Spirit.

Earlier in this study we have called attention to the tremendously great progress that has been accomplished through the work of the Church in raising the moral standards of individuals and of nations and in the improvement of social, economic and cultural standards throughout the world. We have also pointed out that so far as we know the Church may yet be comparatively young, with many more centuries or even millenniums in which to labor before the end comes. In view of the progress that has been made, and in the absence of any clear Scripture teaching that the end of the world is near, we may at least be permitted to believe that the Church, concerning which we are told that "Christ loved the church, and gave himself for it" (Eph. 5:25), will gloriously fulfill her task of making disciples of all the nations and teaching them to observe all that He has commanded.

We have pointed out that the progress of the kingdom as seen from the human viewpoint is not always upward, and that there are periods of advance and periods of decline. Hence, when at times the future looks dark let us keep in mind that in the long run the forces of evil are not going to triumph, and that the Church is not going to be defeated. We have the unqualified promise of Christ Himself, spoken to Peter at the time the establishment of the Church was first announced: "And I also say unto thee, that thou art Peter, and upon this rock I will build my church; and the gates of Hades shall not prevail against it" (Matt. 16:18).

It can be admitted, of course, that the present day Church has many faults, that there is much in it of sin and sham and unbelief. It is badly divided, and in many places it is presenting only a weak testimony when it should be strong. But in the main the faults that attach to it are the faults of individuals. It is made up of fallible individuals. These faults do not mean that the Church as an institution is to be condemned, but rather that more Christian discipline is needed, and that all of us as church members should seek to make our manner of living more consistent with the faith that we profess. The Church is the only divinely established institution for the proclamation of the Gospel. It is the outward manifestation of Christ's Kingdom in this world. We should do all that we can to support it and to safeguard its honor.

Amillennialism, too, is seriously at fault in some of its eschatological views, although it does not share the deep pessimism of Premillennialism as regards the present state of the world. It does deny that the world is to be Christianized before the return of Christ. It holds that there is to be a parallel development of both good and evil, with the relative proportion between the two perhaps remaining much as it now is. It points to the parable of the Tares as teaching that both good and evil continue side by side until the end, and holds that Paul's words, "this present evil world" (Gal. 1:4), are a description of this age through its entire course. It does, however, have a high view of the Church as the one divinely established institution for the advancement of the Kingdom in this world.

Chapter XIX

THE INFLUENCE OF PREMILLENNIALISM IN THE CHURCHES

We have noted the tendency of Dispensationalism to develop an entire system and to multiply events in the eschatological realm. It uses a new prophetic vocabulary which is intricate and puzzling to the uninitiated. It has seven dispensations, eight covenants, two second comings (the Rapture and the Revelation), three or four resurrections, four to seven judgments, an Antichrist, a Tribulation, a millennial Kingdom on earth, a heavenly Kingdom, a three-fold people—church saints, tribulation saints, and believing Jews—and two future and eternally separate realms for the people of God, Israel to be on the earth while the church saints are to be in heaven. It assigns a large portion of both Old Testament and New Testament prophecy (all of the Book of Revelation after chapter 3) to a future fulfillment in the Tribulation and in the millennial Kingdom which it says Christ is to set up on the earth at His coming. That the effects of such an elaborate system on the other doctrines of Scripture is bound to be profound must be obvious to everyone.

Years ago David Brown wrote:

"Some may think it is of small consequence whether this system is true or false; but no one who intelligently surveys its nature and bearing can be of that opinion. Premillennialism is no barren speculation—useless though true, and innocuous though false. It is a method of Scripture interpretation; it impinges upon and effects some of the most commanding points of the Christian faith; and, when suffered to work its unimpeded way, it stops not till it has pervaded with its own genius the entire system of one's theology, and the whole tone of his spiritual character, constructing, I had almost said, a world of its own, so that, holding the same faith, and cherishing the same fundamental hopes as other Christians, he yet sees things through a medium of his own, and finds every thing instinct with the life which this doctrine has generated within him" (*The Second Advent*, p. 6).

Joseph A. Seiss, a Premillennialist, says:

"There is scarcely a doctrine which is not more or less affected by the ground we take upon this question. Our decision will and must affect our views of the resurrection, of the kingdom of God, of death, and life beyond death, of the second coming itself, of the nature and purpose of the present dispensation, particularly of the judgment and what is to come after it, and the whole condition of life of the finally redeemed" (*Millennialism and the Second Advent*, p. 67).

Snowden says that the difference between Pre- and Postmillennialism is not merely, ". . . a difference relating to a single syllable, 'pre' and 'post,' 'before' and 'after' an event concerning which no one knows the time when it may occur . . . A single syllable may be the pivot on which turns a large issue, as the divinity of Christ once trembled on a single Greek letter, and that the smallest in the alphabet. The question relates to the future course of Christianity and fate of the world, and so large a matter cannot be unimportant. It may not be vital to Christian faith and life as many do hold this faith and live this life without holding any definite view on this subject. Yet it is a question of great interest and cannot be without its proper consequences . . . Millenarianism is not a theory which can be confined within narrow limits, but is a principle that sends its roots under and its branches through all other doctrines of the Christian faith and duty. It is a pervasive spirit that insinuates itself everywhere . . . In our judgment millenarianism drives a dislocating plowshare through the Bible from beginning to end. It is therefore of great importance that we subject these contending theories to the most critical investigation and seek to determine where the truth lies" (*The Coming of the Lord*, pp. 9–11).

And Pieters, writing with special reference to the Scofield Bible says:

"Through its influence there have arisen here and there 'tabernacles' and 'undenominational churches," composed of people no longer at home in the established orthodox denominations, because they do not get there the sort of teaching they find in the Scofield Bible. In many other churches, where this development has not yet reached the point of separation, the presence of Sunday-school teachers and others who consider themselves illuminated by the Scofield Bible beyond their pastors, form a troublesome element. Periodicals like the 'Sunday School Times' and the 'Moody Monthly' frequently refer to it, and always with an air of having spoken the final word if they can quote a passage from it to support their views" (Pamphlet, A Candid Examination of the Scofield Bible, p. 4).

Almost always Premillennialism, particularly in its dispensational form, minimizes the creeds of the Church and manifests a tendency toward interdenominationalism or undenominationalism. The primary purpose of creeds, of course, is to systematize and preserve the great mass of positive Bible knowledge that has been gained through the centuries by scholars and Bible students, and to present that knowledge in a form that will be readily understood by the average Christian. The reasons for the attitude manifested by Premillennialism are not far to seek. In the first place, none of the great creeds of the Church state the premillennial doctrine. All of them imply Post- or Amillennialism. And in the second place, Premillennialism does not recognize the Church as the true successor of Old Testament Israel, but rather as an interlude between two phases of the Kingdom and as soon to pass away. Hence it cannot have any particular concern for the doctrinal formulations of the Church, nor can it attach much importance to denominational loyalty. Its intense desire is for a speedy termination of the Church age and a resumption of the Kingdom.

In recent years in particular Premillennialism has become a seriously divisive factor in the evangelical churches. Those who hold these doctrines look upon them as precious "rediscovered truth," and insist on putting them forward as "what the Bible teaches." They insist on talking about them in season and out of season, in setting them forth in magazine articles, and so elevate them that they become in effect "a test of orthodoxy." Those who do not hold them are looked upon as having departed by just that much from the faith. Since these doctrines constitute such a vital part of their thinking, Premillennialists usually feel a stronger fellowship with like believers in another congregation or even in another denomination than they do with fellow members in their own congregation who do not hold these doctrines. History shows the system to have been the cause of much controversy. The Brethren group, in which repeated divisions occurred, is an outstanding example. As a rule Premillennialists are earnest and zealous for their beliefs. But others who cannot accept those doctrines, and who hold them to be serious departures from the historic faith of the Church, cannot but offer opposition. This division within the Church is all the more to be deplored in our day when the battle with Modernism and unbelief rages on all sides. We do not blame the Premillennialists for their zeal; they cannot but speak out for what they believe and feel. Oftentimes their zeal surpasses that of those who hold other views, and in that regard their example might well be followed. But that does not make the consequences any less tragic in the life of the Church.

It is not uncommon for Premillennialists to take a superior attitude and appropriate to themselves such titles as "students of prophecy," "students of the prophetic word," etc., as though those who do not accept their views are not students of prophecy or students of the prophetic word. The system has an aggressive spirit and policy. Probably the most vigorous propagandizing campaign ever launched in this country was that begun by Charles T. Russell, more commonly known as Pastor Russell. That movement has been variously known as Russellism, Millennial Dawnism, Watch Tower, International Bible Students, and more lately as Jehovah's Witnesses. While it has many features that are opposed to the usual premillennial program, it also includes a very definite system of Premillennialism. Its superficial and literalistic method of handling Scripture, its doctrine that the world cannot be Christianized through the preaching of the Gospel, its denunciation of the established churches, its strong emphasis on a 1000 year earthly kingdom, and its indulgence in date-setting, are elements that it has in common with what we have designated as standard Premillennialism. And while it has been strongly opposed by Premillennialists such as Lewis Sperry Chafer, who branded it as a false system along with Spiritualism, Christian Science, and Mormonism, in the thinking of many people its doctrines undoubtedly have done much to prepare the way for Premillennialism. Hence the two cannot be said to be altogether separate, and standard Premillennialism must take a share of responsibility for the origin of that movement.

It must be acknowledged that much of the responsibility for the popularity of Premillennialism lies with the churches themselves, in that most of them place comparatively small emphasis on the study of prophecy. Doctrines such as the second advent, heaven, hell, the resurrection, and the final judgment, usually omitted in liberal and modernistic preaching, have been in part at least pushed to the fore as a result of the premillennial emphasis. A study of the cults will show that in almost every instance they have arisen in an effort to correct some defect in the work or teaching of the established churches. Several of them have had Premillennialism as one of their distinctive doctrines. But that the churches were in some respects at fault does not make any less dangerous or misleading the false systems that have arisen. These systems in turn over-emphasize the doctrine or practice that gave occasion for their rise and make a hobby out of it even to the exclusion of much other vital truth.

To the strong over-emphasis on the study of prophecy that is found in Premillennialism there is wedded a one-sided literalism. Catchy slogans, such as, "Take God at His Word," "Believe what the Bible says," "Don't spiritualize the Bible away," etc., make a strong appeal to the lay-members of the Church. Its literalistic method of interpretation, consistently applied, introduces confusion and conflict into the symbols of Scripture, and leaves each person to interpret them according to his own fancy. It is this method of interpretation that is the vulnerable point of the whole system.

So, acknowledging the prominence of the doctrine of the Second Coming of Christ in Scripture, we nevertheless should not attempt to make it the foundation on which to rear our theological system, as Premillennialism is inclined to do. Logically it should be studied *after*, not *before*, the other basic doctrines. Its purpose, and that of Eschatology in general, is to bring into unity and to crown the unfinished edifice. It is *capstone,* not *foundation.* To reverse this order and make it the starting point is to stand the theological system on its head.

The Second Coming of Christ is, then, a sacred and important truth which is believed by all true Christians. Post-, A-, and Premillennialists differ not in regard to its reality, but in regard to the manner, time, and circumstances of the Lord's coming, the efficacy of the Gospel to win the world, the purpose of the Church in the present dispensation, and in regard to the role to be played by the Jews prior to and following the return of Christ.

We should like to close this chapter with a quotation from Dr. Snowden, a tribute to the Church, which we believe will be more and more appreciated as time goes on. Said he:

"Now the Christian Church is not yet wholly Christian and has spots and stains enough on its robes to satisfy the most envious or venomous critics. But neither was the Church wholly Christian in the beginning when the Spirit was poured out upon it in Pentecostal power. Nevertheless, Christ loved the Church and gave Himself for it, and we should love it too with a jealous love. He loves it still, and only the most jaundiced eye or prejudiced theory can magnify its faults and minimize its virtues. The Church has in it the Spirit of Christ, and today it is better, more Christ-like in spirit and service and self-sacrifice, than it ever was in the past. It is the human channel to which Christ committed His Gospel which is the power of God unto salvation. And on an even greater scale and in greater efficiency it is carrying out the Great Commission as it is making disciples of all the nations . . . Take the Church out of the world, and the light of the world would be lost, and its salt would lose its savor. The Church is more Christian today than it ever was before, and this better Church is making a better world" (*The Coming of the Lord,* p. 267).

Chapter XX

HISTORICAL ASPECTS

From the Apostolic age until the sixteenth century the only type of Premillennialism in existence, then called "Chiliasm," was that which we have characterized as Historic Premillennialism. Those who held it believed that the Church would go through the Tribulation (many who endured the persecutions under the Roman emperors thought they were then in the Tribulation), and that when Christ returned He would immediately set up the millennial kingdom. The early Premillennialists knew nothing about a system of seven dispensations, a secret Rapture seven years before the public appearance of Christ, a seventieth week of Daniel's prophecy to be fulfilled between two future comings of Christ, or a Jewish dominated kingdom. They believed that the events foretold in the Book of Revelation would have their fulfillment in this era before the return of Christ. The expectations of the Jews, both of a territorial restoration and of a revived Judaism, were rejected as fanciful and as contrary to Scripture.

Premillennialists make a great deal of the fact that Premillennialism was found in the early Church, and that it continued in some degree up through the fourth century. But that in itself means practically nothing. The fact of the matter is that numerous errors crept into the early Church almost from the days of the Apostles. That was the age in which Christian Theology existed in its most elementary form. The new Church was traveling an uncharted path, and progress was slow. Centuries were to pass before it had time to recognize and reject erroneous presentations and to state its belief in systematic form. The first real start was made in the Council of Nicaea, 325 A. D., and even then the principal doctrine dealt with was the person of Christ, the Council declaring for His full Deity, as opposed to the Arian heresy which held that He was only the first of created beings and therefore not really Divine.

A brief survey of the errors that came to expression in the early Church should enable us to see more clearly of how little importance was the existence of Premillennialism in that period. Church History records the following heresies:

1. *Docetism.* This error arose before the end of the first century. Its distinguishing feature was the idea that all matter is inherently evil. It held, therefore, that Christ really did not become incarnate, since to have done so would have meant coming in contact with that which was sinful, but that He only seemed to have a human body (from the Greek verb *dokeo,* meaning "to seem").

2. *Gnosticism.* The Gnostics emphasized the intellectual side of Christianity to an exaggerated degree. It was an attempt to re-state Christianity so as to fit it into current philosophy and science.

3. *Montanism.* This originated in Asia Minor, about 156 A. D. Montanus, the leader of the movement, maintained that he was the mouthpiece of the paraclete (comforter, helper, that Christ promised, John 14:16), and that the Second Coming of Christ and the establishment of the New Jerusalem in one of the towns of Phrygia was soon to occur.

4. *Monarchianism.* This error arose in the third century. Its purpose was to prove that Christians do not worship more Gods than one, and to accomplish this it held that the Son and the Holy Spirit either were emanations from God the Father, or that they were different forms in which the Father chose to manifest Himself at different times.

5. *Sabellianism.* This corresponded in general to what we know as Unitarianism. According to this school the terms Father, Son, and Holy Spirit were merely three different modes in which the one God manifested Himself.

6. *Asceticism.* Some believed that the unmarried state was holier than the married state, much as Roman Catholic priests and nuns do today. Those who held this view withdrew from the world, forbade marriage, and lived a secluded life.

7. *Arianism.* This was the most dangerous and widespread error in the early Church. Arius, a presbyter in Alexandria,

Egypt, from whom it takes its name, denied that Christ was the same in substance or equal with the Father in power and glory, and asserted that He was only like, or similar to, the Father, a person between God and man. Arianism denied that the Son had existed from eternity, and held that he was the first creation and that he in turn created the world. This heresy aroused prolonged controversy, was opposed by the great Athanasius, and was condemned by the Council of Nicaea in the year 325.

8. *Apollinarianism.* This teaching denied the true humanity of Jesus. Specifically, it denied that He had a truly human mind, i.e., a reasoning mind that reached conclusions through mental processes as ours does. In effect it asserted that He was God masquerading in human flesh. This error was condemned by the Council of Constantinople in the year 381.

9. *Nestorianism.* Nestorianism so divided the person of Christ as to give Him a dual personality, one Divine and one human, and in effect assumed Him to be two persons in unity. It became very widespread and influential. It was condemned by the Council of Ephesus, in 431, but persisted for centuries in some Eastern groups.

10. *Eutychianism.* This was the opposite of Nestorianism. It so united or blended the two natures as to make a third which was neither Divine nor human. It was condemned by the Council of Chalcedon in 451.

11. *Pelagianism.* Pelagius denied the doctrine of original or inherited sin. He held that mankind was injured by Adam's fall only as it set a bad example. Augustine wrote some of his more important works against this error. It was condemned by the Council of Ephesus in 431.

12. *Apostolic Authority.* The idea of episcopal succession, or the transmission of apostolic authority from importantly placed bishops to their successors, arose quite early and was stressed in the writings of Irenaeus about the year 160. This became the practical doctrine by which authority was transmitted from one pope to another.

Add to these *Premillennialism* and you have a roster of the principal errors in the early Church. Surely those first centuries, in the main the post-apostolic and ante-Nicene era, do not form an ideal period in which to look for purity of doctrine. Rather it was quite fertile in producing false doctrines. It should be noted that all of these errors existed before or during the lifetime of Augustine (died, 430), whom the Premillennialists are in the habit of blaming for having subverted their doctrine. The sweeping claims made by some that the early Church was predominantly premillennial are now known to have been greatly exaggerated. In the writings of only a few of the ante-Nicene church fathers is the subject even mentioned, and when it is mentioned it is in an elementary form having little in common with present day Dispensationalism. It never was strong enough to be written into any of the creeds. In view of the zeal that Premillennialists have for their doctrine we can be quite sure that if they had been in the majority in the early Church they would have written it into the creeds. The two really outstanding theologians of the period, Origen and Augustine, were strongly opposed to Premillennialism. As far as its presence in the early Church is concerned, surely it can be argued with as much reason that it was one of those immature and unscriptural beliefs that flourished before the Church had time to work out the true system of Theology as that its presence at that time is an indication of purity of faith. In any event, so thoroughly did Augustine do his work in refuting it that it practically disappeared for a thousand years as an organized system of thought, and was not seriously put forth again until the time of the Protestant Reformation. At that time it was advocated by numerous independent groups but was solidly opposed by the Reformers themselves. Since that time it has never been strong enough to be written into any of the principal church creeds.

The dispensational interpretation was not even suggested until late in the sixteenth century, and was not taken up by any influential church group until the early nineteenth century. At that time it was essentially a reaction against the rigid formalism and lack of spiritual life in the Church of England. The first activity was manifested in individual study groups in Dublin, Ireland, in 1825. There was then no thought of forming a new denomination. In 1830 a strong movement developed in the town of Plymouth, in southwestern England, from which later came the name "Plymouth Brethren." The most prominent leader in this movement was John N. Darby.

But while the dispensational movement did not gain popular recognition until the rise of the Plymouth Brethren, its real origin is traced to a Jesuit monk, Ribera, who lived in the early Reformation era. The standard Protestant interpretation at that time was that the Pope was the Antichrist, and that the sins of the Roman Catholic Church were set forth in the 17th chapter of the Book of Revelation under the figure of the woman arrayed in purple and scarlet sitting upon the scarlet colored beast. In defense of the Roman Catholic Church the monk Ribera put forth the futurist interpretation of the Book of Revelation.

Dr. H. Grattan Guinness, in his *Approaching End of the Age*, says: "In its present form [the futurist interpretation] it may be said to have originated at the end of the sixteenth century with the Jesuit Ribera, who moved like Alcazar to relieve the Papacy from the terrible stigma cast upon it by the Protestant interpretation, tried to do so by referring these prophecies to the distant future, instead of, like Alcazar, to the distant past" (p. 100).

Eric C. Peters says: "The method was invented by the Jesuit Ribera, in 1585. Strangely, the modern Futurists make no mention of him in their writings, but, be that as it may, to Ribera goes the credit for starting the Futurist fire . . . It was first set adrift by the Roman Catholic Ribera, for the sole purpose of confusing Protestants. The truth of this statement cannot be denied, for copies of Ribera's original book are still in existence" (Booklet, *Antichrist and the Scarlet Woman*, pp. 4,5).

Dr. Allis says: "The futurist interpretation is traced back to the Jesuit Ribera (A. D. 1580) whose aim was to disprove the claim of the Reformers that the Pope was the Antichrist." He adds that, "Its acceptance by the Brethren was not due of course to any objection to the 'Protestant' interpretation as such, but to the fact that their literal interpretation of prophecy and their refusal to admit that predicted events were to precede the rapture made their acceptance of this system of interpretation inevitable" (*Prophecy and the Church*, p. 297).

And Baron Procelli, in a booklet published by the Protestant Truth Society, London, England, says: "Jesuit Ribera was the father of the doctrine of Future Antichrist (i.e., that the Pope is not Antichrist, for Antichrist will not appear till the end of

the age). But how did it become a Protestant dogma? The answer is—Maitland, Todd and Newman. Newman deserted to
Rome and became a Cardinal. These pseudo Protestants trans-
planted Ribera's doctrine into the Protestant Church. It was
quite simple for they were accepted members and influential
leaders of that faith in their day—1825–1845. From Maitland's
time the Futurist pedigree is easy to trace: Maitland, Todd,
Newman, Kelly, Darby, The Plymouth Brethren [who brought
it to the U. S.], Seiss, Dr. Gray, Griffith Thomas and others; and
the many futurists who are still peddling this puerile papist
phantasy."

But while Dispensationalism had its origin abroad, it has
had its greatest success in the United States. Darby made several
visits to the United States and Canada. About 1870 a St. Louis
minister, James H. Brookes, wrote a book, *Maranatha*, or *The
Lord Cometh*, which passed through many editions and was
very influential in spreading dispensational ideas. In 1878 William E. Blackstone, a Methodist minister, published his book,
Jesus is Coming, and, with the exception of the Scofield Bible
this book undoubtedly has done more than any other to popular-
ize the dispensational system. It has been translated into many
languages and its circulation has run into the hundreds of thousands. It deserves to be treated as an authority on the subject
since it carries the unqualified endorsement of many well known
Premillennialists, such as: R. A. Torrey, J. Wilbur Chapman,
A. T. Pierson, James M. Gray, W. J. Erdman, Wm. G. Moorehead,
and others. However, we are inclined to agree with Dr. Snowden
when he says that it is "the most unscholarly book on the subject
we have found," and further that it is "singularly destitute of
historical and critical sense in its interpretation of Scripture,
and no amount of pious language will make up for this lack" (*The
Coming of the Lord,* pp. 30,39).

It should be in order at this point to give some information
about Dr. Scofield. Cyrus Ingerson Scofield was born in Michigan, in 1843. When he was quite young the family moved to
Tennessee, where he grew up. At the outbreak of the Civil War
he enlisted in the Confederate army. He was in a number of
bloody battles. After the war he went to St. Louis where he
began the study of law and entered the legal profession. Later

he became a practicing attorney in Washington, D. C., and was also active in politics. During this time he became a heavy drinker. He was visited on several occasions by another young lawyer who was a Christian and who was the means of his conversion. That was in 1879, and shortly afterward he joined the Congregational Church in St. Louis. He continued the practice of law, but three years later received a call to become the minister of a small Congregational church in Dallas, Texas, and without any intervening theological training was ordained to the ministry. In St. Louis he had become acquainted with James H. Brookes, author of the dispensational book, *Maranatha.* He served the church in Dallas from 1882 to 1895, during which time it had a rapid growth. In 1895 Dwight L. Moody invited him to become pastor of the Congregational church in East Northfield, Massachusetts, which was Moody's own place of worship. This was four years before Moody's death.

THE SCOFIELD BIBLE

As Scofield continued his study of the Bible he was troubled by certain difficult passages. He soon hit upon the idea of making brief notes in the Bible to help him over these. This practice was expanded, and eventually he conceived the idea of a set of explanatory Notes for the entire Bible. His pastorate at East Northfield continued for seven years. In 1902 he gave up this pastorate and returned to the church in Dallas, in order that he might have more time to work on the set of Bible Notes that he was developing. To assist him in this work he sought the assistance of a number of outstanding ministers, and the result was what we know as the *Scofield Reference Bible.* This Bible contained the King James Version with a system of chain references and footnotes of varied character and value, printed in such a way that as a person reads the Bible he is bound also to read the explanatory Notes. For years Scofield had studiously absorbed the doctrines of John N. Darby, and naturally it was this system which found expression in his Notes. He did not accept Darby's doctrine of the Church, but he did accept his eschatology in its totality.

Associated with Scofield in the development of this Bible were the following eight men:

Henry G. Weston, president of Crozer Theological Seminary.
James M. Gray, president of Moody Bible Institute.
William J. Erdman, Niagara Bible Conference, secretary.
Arthur T. Pierson, author, editor, teacher.
W. G. Moorehead, president of Xenia Theological Seminary.
Elmore Harris, president of Toronto Bible Institute.
Arno C. Gaebelein, author, editor of *Our Hope.*
William L. Pettingill, author, editor, teacher.

As we have indicated, the Scofield Bible is, in effect, the standard textbook for all dispensational groups. The fact that approximately 3 million copies of this book have been printed in this country since its publication in 1909 is evidence of its widespread influence. Thousands of Christians make it their principal source of biblical knowledge. Scofield assured himself of a very large reading audience and a very favorable reception to his views, not by presenting his Explanatory Notes in a separate commentary, in which case they probably would have had no more influence than many another book, but by putting them in the Bible in such a way that they would be read as the Bible is read. Imagine the confusion that would result if other schools of thought put out Bibles with notes setting forth postmillennial, amillennial, historic premillennial, Calvinistic, and Arminian systems, not to mention the endless interpretations that would result if the various denominations so presented their views. The best policy, we believe, is that of the British and Foreign Bible Society which, for more than a hundred years as it has printed and distributed the Scriptures, has had as its slogan the words, "Without Note or Comment." This same policy was adopted by the American Bible Society, and it has been approved by the general public and by the rank and file of the Christian Church.

The false sense of authority engendered by printing a set of explanatory notes in the Bible, and the manner in which it has led many astray is well illustrated in the admission of the late Dr. Harry Rimmer, himself a well known Bible scholar and evangelist. "For twenty years," he said, "I also believed and taught that the Roman Empire would be restored in the last days of the age in which we live . . . I must confess that in so doing I depended largely upon the ideas and interpretation which I had imbibed from great and godly teachers, in whom I had unlimited confidence. I did not realize that I was teaching interpretation of the text in place of the Word itself, and had never made an exhaustive study of the Scriptures involved in this idea . . . I went over these prophecies again and was finally led to see that my only authority for maintaining that the Roman Empire would be rebuilt was a footnote in my favorite edition of a study Bible. So for twenty years I had taught as a prophecy of God's Word a human conclusion based upon an ambiguous paragraph" (*The Coming League and the Roman Dream*, pp. 42,44).

The words just quoted reveal the ease with which even ministers can be led astray with assumptions which have no Scriptural foundation, but are merely set forth as standard doctrine by some particular group. We are convinced that much of that which passes for Bible study in the dispensational system ultimately rests on nothing more substantial than a footnote somewhere in the Scofield Bible.

Particularly objectionable, too, is the air of finality with which the Scofield opinions are given, as if they were the assured results of modern biblical knowledge. Opposing views are almost completely ignored, and in fact so far as any mention of them is concerned one would scarcely know that there are any other views. This has been characterized by some who differ with Dispensationalism as, "excellent psychology, employed to teach bad theology." Such procedure shows a glaring lack of scholarship. True scholars do not hesitate to state the position of an opponent, and then expose the errors, if there are any. Such procedure as that followed in the Scofield Bible reveals a conscious weakness in the system, a reluctance to join the battle and face the logical conclusions. It has often been said that a person really does not know either side of a question until he knows both sides. Another item that should also be mentioned is Scofield's use of Usher's Chronology,* through which he assumes responsibility for numerous fixed dates in Old Testament history. Many of these are at best only approximate, and their inclusion in a work such as this gives an appearance of accurate knowledge which in many instances is not available.

Dr. Albertus Pieters, after a discussion of the distinctive dispensational views set forth in this Bible says: "It is easily under-

* *The New Scofield Reference Bible* updates this chronology.

stood that such views as this must seriously influence, first, the interpretation of the Old Testament prophecies, and then the exegesis of numerous passages in the New Testament. And so, indeed, they do. It is not uncommon for those who are introduced to the Scofield Bible to testify in great enthusiasm that it has made the Bible a new book for them. It must be so, if they yield themselves to its influence and accept it as authoritative. Their Bible is then no longer the Bible of the early church, or of the Reformed, or of the fathers of the Reformed faith. It has been transformed into a Jewish book, in the sense that the traditional interpretation of the Synagogue, not of the Church, must be regarded as correct" (*A Candid Examination of the Scofield Bible*, p. 25).

We cite two further quotations from Dr. Pieters. Concerning the wide-spread influence of the Scofield Bible he says: "It may fairly be called one of the most influential—perhaps it is the most influential single book—thrust into the religious life of America during the twentieth century" (p. 5). And after saying that because of the widespread use of the Scofield Bible every minister should make himself familiar with its contents, he adds: "For good as the intentions of the author were, and good as the faith and zeal of his followers are, this book must be pronounced from the standpoint of the Reformed theology, and with a view to the peace and prosperity of our churches, one of the most dangerous books on the market. Its circulation is no aid to sound Bible study and true scriptural knowledge, but rather the contrary. Its use should be quietly and tactfully, but persistently and vigilantly opposed; and our congregations should be diligently instructed in a better interpretation of the Word of God" (p. 27).

The virtue of the Scofield Bible is that it sets forth an evangelical theology. The primary doctrines of the Christian faith, such as the full inspiration and authority of the Scriptures, the Trinity, the Deity of Christ, the atonement, justification by faith, the resurrection of the body, final judgment, heaven and hell, are set forth clearly and without any compromise with Modernism. Its vice, as we have indicated, is that along with these notes there are others setting forth a quite erroneous system of eschatology, as well as errors relating to various other subjects of lesser importance. It is to be noted that in the main the chief opposition to the dispensational system which it sets forth has come from Reformed Theology sources, which with few exceptions have been opposed to Premillennialism in any form.

A revised edition, known as *The New Scofield Reference Bible*, was published in 1967. Some notes have been deleted, and others have been added. But the dispensational system remains unchanged. The members of the revision committee were:

E. Schuyler English, chairman, and editor of Oxford Press's "Pilgrim Edition" of the Bible.

Frank E. Gaebelein, headmaster of Stony Brook School.

William Culbertson, president of Moody Bible Institute.

Charles L. Feinberg, author, director of Talbot Theological Seminary.

Allen A. MacRae, president of Faith Theological Seminary.

Alva J. McClain, president of Grace Theological Seminary.

Clarence E. Mason, Jr., dean of Philadelphia Bible Institute.

Wilbur M. Smith, author, professor in Fuller Theological Seminary.

John F. Walvoord, president of Dallas Theological Seminary.

Concluding Remarks

It is amazing how many of the strongest writers against Premillennialism formerly held that system. David Brown, whose book, *The Second Advent*, was long considered the standard postmillennial work, was formerly a Premillennialist. James H. Snowden, author of *The Coming of the Lord*, came to Postmillennialism from Premillennialism—as a result of reading Brown's book, as he tells us on page 28. Among Amillennialists who formerly held the premillennial faith are: Floyd E. Hamilton, author of *The Basis of Millennial Faith;* Philip Mauro, author of *The Seventy Weeks and the Great Tribulation,* and *The Hope of Israel;* Wm. J. Grier, author of *The Momentous Event;* and Robert Strong, author of a splendid series of magazine articles on the subject. Among premillennial writers who have repudiated dispensational views are: Alexander Reese, author of *The Approaching Advent of Christ,* the strongest condemnation of Dispensationalism to date—Reese wrote: "Premillennialism never had a greater millstone around its neck than the mass of vagaries that the new scheme propounds to us" (p. 295); Henry W. Frost, author of *The Second Coming of Christ;* Nathaniel West, author of *The Thousand Years in Both Testatments;* and W. J. Erdman, a collaborator in the production of the *Scofield Bible.* The famous evangelist, R. A. Torrey, held the dispensational view for a time but later rejected it. The noted Greek scholar, Dean Alford, so often quoted by Premillennialists, is said to have turned from Premillennialism; at any rate late in his life he wrote: "I very much question whether the thorough study of the Scriptures will not make me more and more distrustful of human systematizing, the less willing to hazard a strong assertion on any position on the subject." And Dr. G. Campbell Morgan in 1943, two years before his death, repudiated the dispensational position set forth in his earlier ministry and in substance endorsed the amillennial position. He wrote: "I am quite convinced that all the promises made to Israel have found, are finding, and will find their perfect fulfillment in the Church. It is true that in the past, in my other expositions, I gave definite place to Israel in the purpose of God. I have now come to the conviction that it is the new spiritual Israel that is intended" (Letter to Rev. H. F. Wright, Baptist pastor, Brunswick, Victoria, Australia. The present writer has a photostat copy of that letter. This change in Dr. Morgan's thinking is also reported by Archibald Hughes in his book, *A New Heaven And A New Earth,* pp. 123, 210).

Those who have been the most vigorous defenders of Dispensationalism are its originator, John N. Darby, his successor in England, William Kelly, and in this country, Scofield, Blackstone, Gray, Brookes, Arno C. Gaebelein, Chafer, and more recently, Feinberg and Walvoord.

The fact of the matter is that the Church has never yet debated these eschatological questions out to a final conclusion nor stated her position clearly and positively concerning them as she has done in regard to the other doctrines of the Christian system. Fortunately, however, there is a stern consistency in our thought processes that drives them on to their logical conclusions and separates truth from error. The human mind cannot rest until the inconsistencies are cleared up. Since there is such a radical difference between the millennial systems, particularly between the extremes of Postmillennialism on the one hand

and Dispensationalism on the other, it is a matter of great importance that the true solution should be found. We have set forth the case for Postmillennialism, which we believe is the system taught in Scripture. We believe that Amillennialism is a comparatively mild departure from that system, acknowledging the spiritual nature of the Kingdom that is being set up in this world during the interadventual period, but failing to do justice to the glorious future that God has in store for this Kingdom, specifically that it does not give sufficient weight to what Campbell refers to as "all these bright promises of world-wide salvation which sparkle like stars in the firmament of Holy Writ" (*Israel and the New Covenant*, p. 284).

On the other hand we believe that the principle of literal interpretation which characterizes all types of Premillennialism leads to serious error in that it fails to recognize the truly spiritual nature of the Kingdom in this world as manifested in the Church and sets forth instead an earthly, political kingdom; that it promotes a superficial method of Bible interpretation; and that it is seriously handicapped by its pessimistic view of the future. In its radical form it divides the plan of salvation into mutually exclusive and even conflicting dispensations, sets law over against grace and the Church over against the Kingdom, speaks disparagingly of the Church, and teaches a restoration of Judaism during the time of the millennial kingdom. While Historic Premillennialism is a much less erroneous system than is Dispensationalism, it is only wishful thinking which assumes that the two can be logically separated and kept in watertight compartments. The two systems are basically the same and must stand or fall together. We believe that we have shown that the Scriptures not only fail to teach the premillennial system, but that they definitely exclude it as a possible interpretation.

Chapter XXI

THE OLD AND THE NEW COVENANT, AND THE STATE OF ISRAEL

The establishment of the State of Israel in 1948 was a unique event in that it brought together some of the members (about one-eighth) of a race that has been scattered through the nations for nearly two thousand years. Many believe that in this they are seeing the fulfillment of promises made through the ancient prophets. But there is much difference of opinion concerning this event. The question is, Is this movement of God, or only of men?

A deep tragedy has befallen the Jewish people in that having given Jesus to the world they find themselves in opposition to Him and to the spiritual movement which He established, even though that movement has become the faith of the most civilized and enlightened portion of the human race and today gives peace and hope and satisfying answers to millions of hearts. Yet for centuries the Jews have been trying to erase His name from their memory.

A most remarkable phenomenon in the science of Bible study is that only a very few of those who call themselves evangelical Christians take any notice of the fact that the Old Covenant, which we have in the first part of our Bibles and which we call the Old Testament, was made *exclusively* with the nation of Israel, and that it has now been replaced by the New Covenant, which we call the New Testament, and which was made *exclusively* with the Church. "I am Jehovah thy God, who brought thee out of the land of Egypt, out of the house of bondage," said the Lord God as the Old Covenant was established with the nation of Israel at Mount Sinai (Ex. 20:2). Hence it pointedly was not made with the Egyptians, or the Philistines, or the Edomites or the Assyrians; and they as Gentile proselytes could come into the nation of Israel and into the covenant relationship only through certain prescribed rituals.

The New Testament, which alone is the authoritative document for the Christian Church, should be called the New Covenant. "Testament," as in "last will and testament," means dying counsel. But the New Testament is not the dying counsel of Jesus. Rather it is the fulfillment of the promise found in Jeremiah 31:31-33:

> "Behold, the days come, saith Jehovah, that I will make a new covenant with the house of Israel, and with the house of Judah: not according to the covenant that I made with their fathers in the day that I took them by the hand to bring them out of the land of Egypt; which my covenant they brake, although I was a husband unto them, saith Jehovah. But this is the covenant that I will make with the house of Israel after these days, saith Jehovah: I will put my law in their inward parts, and in their heart will I write it; and I will be their God, and they shall be my people."

The writer of the Epistle to the Hebrews cites this promise (8:1-12). He declares that the New Covenant makes the first Covenant old, and that it is vanishing away (8:13), and that Christ is "the mediator of a new Covenant" (9:15). As the Old Covenant was dedicated with blood, so also is the New Covenant. And since "apart from the shedding of blood there is no remission" (of sin) (9:22), so Christ "now once at the end of the ages hath been manifested to put away sin by the sacrifice of himself" (9:26).

The contrast between the Old and the New Covenant is brought out in that the rituals and sacrifices commanded under the Old Covenant had no efficacy in themselves, but were efficacious only in that they pointed forward to the Messiah who in His own person would be their fulfillment and who would offer Himself as a sacrifice to God to satisfy divine justice and to expiate the sins of His people. Likewise, the prophets, priests and kings of the Old Covenant were but types of the true Prophet,

Priest and King, the Messiah, who would come and perform His work of atonement in the fullness of time. Thus the writer of the Epistle to the Hebrews shows that the Old Covenant has served its purpose and has passed away, and that it has been replaced by the New Covenant.

It is true of course that in the Old Covenant great promises were made to Israel concerning the people, the nation, and the land of Palestine. But those promises were *always* conditioned on obedience, either expressly stated or clearly implied. Time and again the people were warned in so many words that *apostasy would cancel the promise of future blessing,* that *promised blessing could be forfeited.*

For instance, the land of Palestine was given to Abraham and to his seed "for an eternal possession" (Gen. 17:8). But the same thing is said of the perpetual duration of the priesthood of Aaron (Ex. 40:15); the passover (Ex. 12:14); the sabbath (Ex. 31:17); and David's throne (II Sam. 7:13,16,24). But in the light of the New Testament all of those things have passed away. We use the same terminology when a title deed grants to the buyer the use of a piece of land "for ever," or "in perpetuity," not meaning that the buyer will hold it for ever, but that it becomes his for as long as he chooses to hold it, or until present conditions change. Moreover, since the people of Israel were exiled from the land of Palestine for nearly two thousand years, how could it be regarded as a fulfillment of the promise to Abraham if they are now given possession of it for one thousand years, as some expect?

At the very beginning of Israel's national history Moses, in the 28th chapter of Deuteronomy, set before the people a promise of blessing if they were obedient, and a threat of punishment, even to the destruction of the nation, if they were disobedient. See especially verses 13-26,45,46. Jeremiah declared clearly the conditional nature of God's promise to Israel: "And at what instant I shall speak concerning a nation, and concerning a kingdom, to build and to plant it; if they do that which is evil in my sight, that they obey not my voice, then I will repent of the good, wherewith I said I would bless them" (18:9,10). Samuel warned the disobedient Eli: "Therefore Jehovah, the God of Israel, saith, I said indeed that thy house, and the house of thy father, should walk before me for ever: but now Jehovah saith, Be it far from me; for them that honor me I will honor, and they that despise me shall be lightly esteemed" (I Sam. 2:30). Thus the promised blessing was forfeited, and the house of Eli was cut off, never to be re-established.

Immediately after the children of Israel came out of Egypt God gave them this apparently unconditional promise: "The Egyptians whom ye have seen today, ye shall see them again no more for ever" (Ex. 14:13). But in Deuteronomy 28:68, when taking leave of the people, Moses specifically warned them of the consequences of disobedience: "And Jehovah will bring thee into Egypt again with ships, by the way whereof I said unto thee, Thou shalt see it no more again: and there ye shall sell yourselves unto your enemies for bondsmen and bondswomen, and no man shall buy you."

Another classic example of an apparently unconditional promise was that given through the prophet Jonah: "Yet forty days and Nineveh shall be overthrown" (3:4). But when the people of Nineveh repented the city was spared. Although Jonah wanted to see the city destroyed, and was greatly disappointed when it was not, he did not feel that God had violated His promise, for we read: "But it displeased Jonah exceedingly, and he was angry. And he prayed unto Jehovah, and said, I pray thee, O Jehovah, was not this my saying, when I was yet in my country? Therefore I hasted to flee unto Tarshish; for I knew that thou art a gracious God, and merciful, slow to anger, and abundant in loving kindness, and repentest thee of the evil" (4:1–2).

Numerous other such warnings might be cited. But these are sufficient to show that *no promise will be fulfilled to a disobedient and rebellious people*. It was not necessary, and it would not have been good literary form, for the sacred writer to have repeated the threat of punishment or disinheritance every time a promise was given. But it was repeated often enough that the observant reader would know that God would be under no obligation to fulfill any promise to a disobedient Israel. On this basis we have no hesitation in saying that all of the promises that were made to Israel in the Old Testament either have been fulfilled, or they have been forfeited through disobedience.

As regards the nation of Israel, the fact is that when Christ came and was rejected, He deposed the leaders of apostate Judaism, the Pharisees and elders, and appointed a new set of officials, the Apostles, through whom He would establish His Church. To the rulers of Judaism He said, "The kingdom of God shall be taken away from you, and shall be given to a nation [the Church] bringing forth the fruits thereof" (Matt. 21:43). And because of their sin in rejecting and crucifying the Saviour, they were brought into a position in which, as Paul solemnly says, "Wrath is come upon them to the uttermost" (I Thess. 2:16). In accordance with this the entire Old Testament system of Judaism has been abrogated and brought to an end. And in its place the New Covenant has become the authoritative and official instrument for God's dealings with His people, His Church.

It should be remembered that the Church as established by Christ was wholly Jewish and is proved by that very fact to be the continuation and successor of the Old Testament Church. It was not until some time later that it was officially opened to the Gentiles, when Peter was sent to preach to the Roman centurion Cornelius (Acts, chapter 10) and Gentiles began to come into the Church; and it was not until several decades later that the Church became predominantly Gentile. The Gentile branches were grafted into the good olive tree that they might enjoy its fatness and fullness of blessing (Rom. 11:17). As Gentiles came into the church and acknowledged the God of Israel as their God, they became New Testament Israelites, just as the ancient proselytes became Old Testament Israelites. Thus Christian believers originally were and continue to be New Testament Israelites, and the New Covenant relates exclusively to them.

This is in accordance with Paul's teaching elsewhere, for he says, "They that are of faith, the same are sons of Abraham" (Gal. 3:7); and again, "There can be neither Jew nor Greek, there can be neither bond nor free, there can be no male and female; for ye are all one man in Christ Jesus. And if ye are Christ's, then are ye Abraham's seed, heirs according to promise" (Gal. 3:28,29). He says that Christ has broken down "the middle wall of partition" between Jews and Gentiles, that He "might reconcile them both in one body unto God through the cross" (Eph. 2:14–16). Again he refers to New Testament believers as "the Israel of God" (Gal. 6:16). Paul here says that in matters of faith the spiritual relationship takes precedence over the physical, and that all true believers are sons of Abraham. And conversely we may say that those who are not true believers are not sons of Abraham in any sense worthy of the name regardless of what their ancestry may be. Paul uses strong words to assert his teaching on this subject. How could you declare more positively than he does here that the old distinction between Jew and Gentile has been wiped out? In the Church there are no promises or privileges given to any one group or nationality which do not apply equally to all others.

The small minority of Jews who originally constituted the New Testament Church are but another example of the "remnant" doctrine found in various parts of the Bible. Beginning with the family of Abraham, only Isaac was the heir, while Ishmael and the six sons of Keturah were cast off. And of Isaac's sons, not Esau, but only Jacob received the promises. Repeatedly after apostasy in Israel only a small proportion returned to the Lord. Isaiah wrote: "For though thy people, Israel, be as the sand of the sea, only a remnant of them shall return" (from the captivity in Babylon) (10:22). Micah spoke of "the remnant of Israel" (2:12), as also did Zechariah of "the remnant of this people" returning to dwell in Jerusalem (8:6–8). In accordance with this Paul cited "the remnant" of the Jews as constituting the New Testament Church (Rom. 9:27). These alone were the Lord's people, and the others were cast off, never to be reinstated except when they as individuals turn and look to Christ as Saviour.

We should point out further that those who today popularly are called "Jews" are in reality not Jews at all. Legitimate Judaism as it existed in the Old Testament era was of divine origin and had a very definite content of religious and civil laws, priesthood, ritual, sacrifices, temple, sabbath, etc. But with the destruction of Jerusalem and the dispersion of the people in A. D. 70, that system was effectively destroyed. It has since not been practiced anywhere in the world.

Any Jew who acknowledges the authority of the Old Testament finds himself faced with this dilemma: Either he must accept Christ as He is revealed in the New Testament, or there is no way for him to approach God except through a reinstitution of the Old Testament ritual and sacrifices. But present day Jewry is in no mood to reinstitute the ritual and sacrifices. Because of their rejection of Christ, the Jews have been forced to move farther and farther away from the Old Testament, and many have lost faith in any promised Messiah, in any future life, and even in God Himself. Having established the State of Israel, the Jews have found that traditional Judaism is not in harmony with the ideas of twentieth century life, nor is it compatible with the functioning of a modern State. And having come into possession of the city of Jerusalem, the question as to whether or not the temple should be rebuilt has suddenly become a moot question, for present day Judaism has no use for a temple, and in fact would not know what to do with it if it had one.

The present situation is that Judaism has developed for itself a book of rabbinical writings which is a collection of religious and civil laws with commentary, known as the *Talmud*. This was produced after the time of Christ and was completed about the year A. D. 500. It is not of divine origin, but is a man made system of religion which was developed by the rabbis. It has become the primary object of study in the schools and synagogues and has almost completely displaced the Old Testament. Hence present day Judaism is not only different from the religion of the Old Testament; it even belongs to a different class of religions. For the religion of the Old Testament, like that of the New, presented salvation as the free, unmerited grace of God, whereas present day Judaism is in its very essence a system of salvation by works of human merit. Although the Jews of today may think better of Jesus than did those of former times, some even acknowledging him as a great teacher, this is of very little practical importance since they still think of salvation in terms of human merit and human achievement. Hence the system should not be called Judaism, but *Talmudism;* and those who practice that system should not be called Jews, but *Talmudists*.

As these things bear upon the re-establishment of the State of Israel, we must say that this project, carried out almost exclusively by unbelieving Jews, is not of God in the sense that it was foretold by His prophets or that His blessing is upon it. Rather it is a humanistic project, which in all probability is headed for increasingly serious trouble. Although the Jewish people have a consuming zeal for the land of Palestine, their real need is not

Palestine, but Christ. And never will they find real peace, individually or as a nation, until they turn in faith to Him.

THE FATAL ERROR IN PREMILLENNIALISM

Premillennialism holds that Christ in His First Advent came to establish a Kingdom, that He so offered Himself to His people the Jews, but that when they rejected Him and crucified Him he postponed the Kingdom and established the Church as a temporary alternative and substitute, and that this was not foreseen by the Old Testament prophets nor mentioned in the Old Testament. It holds further that at the end of the Church Age Christ will return with overwhelming power, that He will then establish the Kingdom, and that he will reign in Jerusalem for 1,000 years.

On the other hand Post- and Amillennialism hold that in His First Advent Christ came, not to establish an earthly kingdom, but to suffer and die and so to make atonement for the sins of His people. They also hold that He did establish a spiritual Kingdom which is not of this world, but of which the Church is the outward manifestation. And as proof that this kingdom is a present reality they cite the words of Christ when He said, "My kingdom is not of this world," (John 18:36); "The kingdom of God is within you" (Luke 20:21); also the words of Paul to the Colossians when He wrote that God the Father has " . . . delivered us out of the power of darkness, and translated us [past tense] into the kingdom of the Son of his love" (1:13). And John, in the book of Revelation, says, ". . . and he made us [again, past tense] to be a kingdom, to be priests unto his God and Father" (1:16). Hence the Kingdom is here. And its citizens are the born again members of the Church.

But suppose that Christ did come to establish an earthly Kingdom as Premillennialists say. And suppose that the Jews had accepted Him as King. He then would have been reigning in Jerusalem in power and glory. *How then could he possibly have been taken from the throne and crucified?* And what then becomes of the all-important doctrine of the Atonement?

The redemptive work of Christ is the central theme of Old Testament prophecy. From Genesis to Revelation the Bible teaches that salvation was to be provided by a substitute who would take the sinner's place and suffer and die in his stead. All of the animal sacrifices, and especially the passover lamb slain for the passover meal, pointed to that redemptive work. Isaiah 53 tells of Christ's sacrificial death some 700 years before it occurred. John the Baptist introduced Him as "the Lamb of God that taketh away the sin of the world" (John 1:29). In the Garden of Gethsemane Christ prayed most earnestly three times that *if possible* that cup might pass away from Him. *But there was no other way.* In Matthew 20:28 Christ tells us precisely why He came to earth: ". . . the Son of man came not to be ministered unto, but to minister, and to give his life a ransom for many." There He expressly repudiates the idea that He came to reign in any kind of a worldly, political, military kingdom, but to pay the penalty for the sin that rested on His people. Perish the thought that Christ, who was and who continues to be Deity, could have failed in any aspect of His mission!

Some have suggested that salvation might have been provided in some other way, perhaps through animal sacrifices. But that is impossible. There was no saving grace in animal sacrifices. The Old Testament sacrifices were but shadows and symbols of a reality that was to come later.

In the third chapter of Genesis we are told that our forefather Adam, in his capacity as the federal head and representative of all of his descendants, disobeyed God and brought the penalty of death upon the entire human race. That meant not only the separation of the soul from the body as in physical death, but also the separation of the soul from God. For God had decreed that the soul that sinned should die. That penalty rested on the human race just as it rested on the fallen angels who had sinned and who were lost forever. God could not simply pardon man's sin without an adequate penalty. Nor could He do as we sometimes do in a case of bankruptcy, reduce the penalty and accept, as it were, 10 cents on the dollar. God's honor was at stake. The moral law was a transcript of His character. Justice demands that sin must be punished, just as definitely as it demands that righteousness must be rewarded. God would be unjust if He failed to do either. The only way God can forgive sin is by taking that penalty upon Himself.

It may help to make this point somewhat clearer if we compare the creation of man with that of angels. When the angels were created each angel was placed on test as an individual. Those who stood their test were confirmed in their holiness and are now the holy angels in Heaven. Those who rebelled against God were cast out of Heaven and are now the fallen angels or demons, the Devil apparently being the highest one of that order who fell. There is no salvation for angels: "For verily not to angels doth he give help, but he giveth help to the seed of Abraham" (Heb. 2:16). But when God created man He proceeded in a different way. It is as if He said, "This time, if sin is to enter, let it enter through one person, so that salvation also can be provided through one person."

Since man therefore had fallen through a representative, he could be redeemed through a representative. Hence Christ, as Deity incarnate, came to earth specifically for that purpose. He took upon Himself that exact penalty of suffering and death that had rested on His people and so made atonement for their sins. And because He was a person of infinite worth and dignity, His suffering and death were of infinite value, sufficient to redeem as many of the human race as He might call to Himself. Hence the salvation that He brought to His people was not by works of any kind on their part, nor by any combination of works and grace, but by pure grace because of what He had done.

Christ will be King truly enough, and He will reign over His redeemed people. But before He could reign it was necessary that He redeem them from their sin. That exclusively was the great purpose of His First Advent. And in the Divine plan of redemption it is the work of the Holy Spirit to apply that redemption to all those who had been given to the Son by the Father (John 6:37), so that they shall be remade in His heavenly image and His celestial likeness, worthy of such a King!

But now to return to the original question: If Christ had established an earthly kingdom, as Premillennialists say He wanted to do, and if He had been reigning in power and glory in Jerusalem, how could He possibly have been taken from the throne and crucified? How could He possibly have fulfilled the Old Testament prophecies concerning a suffering Messiah?

Surely this is the fatal error in the Premillennial system, for it leaves the very important doctrine of the Atonement hanging in mid air. It destroys the basis on which that doctrine rests. If the Jews had accepted Christ there would have been no need to have postponed the Kingdom, nor would there have been any need to have established the Church. But the Scriptures tell us that He did establish a spiritual Kingdom, and that He also established the Church as the organization in this world through which His people, as they are brought one by one from the kingdom of darkness into the Kingdom of light, may find fellowship and so strengthen and encourage one another as they cooperate in obeying His command to take the message of salvation to the nations. We need only add that when the Church Age is finished Christ will return, not to establish an earthly kingdom but the heavenly Kingdom in all its fullness, and that that Kingdom will continue throughout all eternity.

Chapter XXII

THE MILLENNIUM*
OF REVELATION 20

One of the most helpful things ever written concerning the millennium in Revelation 20 was a 1904 article by Dr. Benjamin B. Warfield, *The Millennium and the Apocalypse,* presently found in a collection of his writings, *Biblical Doctrines.* Much work has been done on the millennial problem since that time, but the Church at large still remains tragically divided concerning this subject.

However, we believe that a recent article by a young Warfield scholar, Martin G. Selbrede, of Thousand Oaks, California, in which he gives an analysis of Revelation 19:11–20:10, taken in connection with the Warfield article, does much to complete that study. We believe that he has worked out the solution of the millennial problem. And that, if true, will eventually be seen as a tremendous accomplishment.

Our purpose here is to reproduce that article in abbreviated and paraphrased form. Mr. Selbrede shows that this section of Scripture embraces the entire Christian era as well as the intermediate state, and that it must be taken as a unit. Dr. Warfield, with all of his brilliant theological insight, was not able to reach a solution that was fully satisfactory even to himself, but referred to what he termed a "black spot" regarding the word "nations" in Revelation 20:3, and said that it must be left for further study. He acknowledged that the word "nations" is the term generally used to describe the anti-Christian hosts of the world. But he found that its use in Revelation 19:15, where Christ is said to smite the nations with the sword that proceeds out of His mouth, and that He is to rule them with a rod of iron, conflicted with his own postmillennial interpretation that the nations are to be progressively Christianized, and that they are to accept willingly and lovingly the benevolent rule of their Master.

* Chapter added in revised edition, 1984.

But Mr. Selbrede points out that in this instance John uses the word in a somewhat different sense in that by that term he means that the wicked from among the nations are to be killed by Christ's ministry of death to the wicked as He subdues the earth, and that they are thereby sealed off from their master Satan so that he becomes progressively more helpless until finally he is left without any helpers to carry on his work. This means that in time, and before the end of history, we shall see a fully Christianized world.

Dr. Warfield's explanation of Revelation 20:1-6 is that it relates not to any earthly kingdom, but to the intermediate state. But where did he make his mistake? The following article by Mr. Selbrede, which is included here with his permission, gives his analysis of this problem.

REVELATION 19:11-20:10
A POSTMILLENNIAL ANALYSIS

Martin G. Selbrede
Paraphrased by Loraine Boettner

Dr. Warfield read the sword in the mouth, in Revelation 19:11-21, as being the gospel, with the vision, on this hypothesis, referring to the complete victory of the gospel throughout the world. He therefore atomized or explained away the imagery of war and death by declaring it to be but the drapery of the symbolism. There is, therefore, no war and death in the physical sense at all. Warfield reached this conclusion by taking the sword out of the mouth to be the key to the passage. It may well be the key, but he misinterpreted it. But he was correct about this: the battle scene described extends between the two advents, and embraces the entire Church Age. This protensive aspect of the vision is almost completely missed by Premillennialists who take this to be a single great battle, perhaps only a day long, that relates to the alleged Great Tribulation.

What Premillennialists have correctly noted, however, is that this is a real *blood and guts battle.* But their theory requires that this battle be visible to the naked eye. As Premillennialists see it, the battle is a prelude to the establishment of Christ's millennial reign on earth. Thus, Christ allegedly returns with His army to destroy the nations gathered against Him and the "tribulation saints" so called.

In other words, Premillennialists teach that the Lord is to use an entirely different instrumentality for destroying these nations and people, than He used in all of the preceding millennia. And this change in the game plan is defended on the basis of the alleged discontinuity between dispensations in terms of the premillennial reading of Revelation 20. Amillennialists differ from this by teaching that this battle is between Christ and the last generation, thereby preceding the eternal state rather than a subsequent earthly dispensation. The battle, though, is still declared to be a short one.

Premillennialists teach that Christ is not now slaying the wicked, certainly not in the sense that Revelation 19 teaches, and that this activity of Christ is yet future, reserved for the tribulation generation. Therefore they hold that Revelation 19:11–21 has no bearing on the present or the past, instead construing it as an essentially eschatological vision limited to the end time.

The premillennial view minimizes the present government of Christ as it relates to the death of the wicked. But the Scriptures declare that the government is on His shoulders, and that He exercises many offices, not the least of which is making His enemies lick the dust, which means death. This ministry is being executed during His present mediatorial reign and is therefore a ministry that ends at the end of that reign, when He gives over the kingdom to the Father. I Corinthians 15:24–26 strongly affirms that the reign of Christ continues, death ministry and all, until Death itself is destroyed: "Then cometh the end, when he shall deliver up the kingdom to God, even the Father; when he shall have abolished all rule and all authority and power. For he must reign, till he hath put all his enemies under his feet. And the last enemy that shall be abolished is death."

REVELATION 19:11–21
Verse-by-verse Exposition

11–13. And I saw heaven opened, and behold a white horse! He who sat upon it is called Faithful and True, and in righteousness he judges and makes war. His eyes are like a flame of fire, and upon

his head are many diadems; and he has a name inscribed which no one knows but himself. He is clad in a robe dipped in blood, and the name by which he is called is The Word of God.

John brings before us a glorious picture of the Lord Jesus Christ. He sees heaven opened, and he is given a "behind the scenes" view of precisely what Christ is doing in His present inter-adventual reign from His seat at the right hand of God the Father, to which He ascended after His resurrection from the dead. What John saw would not have been visible had heaven remained closed. *We* do not see Jesus, for He sits at the right hand of the Father, where no human eye can pierce. But John is allowed this vision to see precisely what it is that Christ is doing. Let us not be surprised if we find that He deals very severely with sin.

In this vision John sees a white horse upon which Christ is seated. Premillennialists see the Second Coming of Christ in these verses. But such an interpretation violates the statement of the angel in Acts 1:11, to the effect that Christ will return "in the same way" that the disciples "saw him go" into heaven. John himself was among those who saw Christ ascend. Hence there can be but one conclusion: this passage makes no reference whatsoever to the Second Coming of Christ. Christ did not ascend on a white horse; He will not return on one. Since this vision shows Jesus sitting upon a white horse, the Second Coming simply is not in view here.

Verse 13 tells us that Christ is arrayed in a garment dipped in blood. This is the blood of His enemies, which is shed as His conquest of the world proceeds.

14. And the armies of heaven, arrayed in fine linen, white and pure, followed him on white horses.

The symbol of the horses is significant, primarily because they *are* symbolic: in heaven equestrian locomotion is superfluous. The symbol is representative of the mission the armies are on, specifically, a mission of war. The vision indicates that Christ's enemies are destroyed solely by the sword out of the Rider's mouth, and therefore the armies with Him do not actually engage in literal destruction, in keeping with the Scripture that "vengeance is mine, saith the Lord."

15. From his mouth issues a sharp sword with which to smite the nations, and he will rule them with a rod of iron; he will tread the wine press of the fury of the wrath of God the Almighty.

It is Christ's distinctive ministry, as the One who holds the keys to Death and Hades (Rev. 1:18), to wield the sharp two-edged sword. The sword is symbolic of death and destruction, and His mission is represented as one of war. Note that the nations are still here, and that they continue yet for a time as nations. Christ's inter-adventual reign progressively fulfills the promise that "the transgressors shall be altogether destroyed, And the posterity of the wicked shall be cut off" (Ps. 37:38). In other words, "All the wicked he will destroy" (Ps. 145:20).

This is consistent with the fact that the world is a condemned world, and that Christ has been given two ministries to execute during His Kingship: to save the world, and to fulfill the terms of the world's condemnation. The process by which He takes a totally condemned world and makes it into a saved world has been progressing now for twenty centuries. It is a miracle of the first order, so great that man's imaginations fail in the face of it. How astonishing that the condemned world is passing away (I John 2:17), being replaced by the rock cut out without hands which grows until it fills the whole earth (Dan. 2:35). For He "came to save the world" (John 12:47); and "God was in Christ reconciling the world unto himself" (II Cor. 5:19). But just as surely as He came to save the world, He also is faithful in bringing righteous wrath upon the condemned portion of it, to utterly destroy every principality and power opposed to God Almighty. Christ executes this office continually, through the Church Age, although the only direct revelation we have of it is here in Revelation 19, where heaven is opened for John actually to see the Lord Jesus at work.

16. On his robe and on his thigh he has a name inscribed, King of kings and Lord of lords.

The certain teaching of this verse is that Christ is now reigning with the totality of divine power given to Him by the Father: "All authority has been given to me in heaven and on earth" (Matt. 28:18). Since He is thus endowed with such limitless sovereignty, who dares claim that His power is not sufficient to convert a condemned world into a saved world?

17, 18. And I saw an angel standing in the sun, and with a loud voice He called to all the birds that fly in midheaven, "Come, gather for the greater supper of God, to eat the flesh of kings, and the flesh of captains, the flesh of mighty men, the flesh of horses and their riders, and the flesh of all men, both free and slave, both small and great."

It is because the world is "condemned already" (John 3:18) that God has called the carrion-eaters to partake of their due. These verses speak of a total devastation of *all* men, both free and slave, both small and great, which can only speak of the passing away of the condemned world, the wicked proliferating into the welcoming arms of Death and Hades. Here the fate of every unbeliever is made manifest, that Christ will see to it that they pay the wages of sin: they shall all die.

19. And I saw the beast and the kings of the earth with their armies gathered to make war against him who sits upon the horse and against his army.

The battle scenes vary throughout history, from the subtleties of blasphemies and heresies to the literal torture and murder of the saints. The battles occur on earth itself, and are but the death-throes of a condemned world. Christ is behind the scenes and, except for the extraordinary case of John, cannot be seen except by the eye of faith. The kings and leaders of iniquity do not see their real Enemy, but their consciences and instincts tell them that there is an enemy of some kind. Very few of them are atheists. But note the present-day defiance of the wicked toward God as they boldly blaspheme His name and go their own defiant, sinful way.

The important point to be grasped in this verse is that the armies are deliberately gathered against an enemy. They are fitted with all the implements of war. The natural meaning is that they will wage literal war. Therefore, the armies against which they will wage war, with human instruments, must also be an army composed of men. The wicked armies (the world forces of evil) have deliberately gathered themselves against an enemy, which they assume to be in some ways like themselves, and which they fully intend to conquer. Such a representation (such an attitude on the part of sinners) would be ridiculous if the Second Coming of Christ with angels in power and glory were in view here for the following reasons: (1) Complete preparation for battle is implied by the wicked hosts' gathering methodically against their enemy. (2) The actual return of Christ in glory would put any human army to flight because of the utter terror of His glory. When the Second Coming of Christ occurs, no human armies will stand against Him. If the beloved disciple John fell as one dead in the presence of the glorified Christ, how much more would His appearance strike sinners with mortal terror! Would not those armies rather cry to the mountains to fall on them, to hide them from the wrath of the Lamb, given this premillennial hypothesis? (3) The superhuman courage of the beast's armies, which enables them to stand up and do battle with their enemy, does not square with what we know of the Lord's glory and terrifying power. The premillennial theory, and indeed any theory that relegates these verses in Revelation 19 to the Second Coming, asks us to believe that men will not so much as flinch at the terrifying return of the Lord of glory; that they will rather fight the more bravely against impossible odds. Surely this scenario smacks of a fairy tale that glorifies man over the presence of Him who dwells in eternal light, He that no man can even approach. Would that more Christians understood that those theories seriously underrate the terrifying glory of the Lord Jesus.

20. And the beast was captured, and with it the false prophet who in its presence had worked the signs by which he deceived those who had received the mark of the beast and those who worshipped its image. These were thrown into the lake of fire that burns with brimstone.

Of all the verses, this is the most compelling, for it represents the fulfillment of Paul's prophecy in II Corinthians 10:3-5: "For though we live in the world, we are not carrying on a worldly war, for the weapons of our warfare are not worldly but have divine power to destroy strongholds."

We destroy false teachings and every proud hindrance to the

knowledge of God. In our day the prophecy is in process of fulfillment as Christ destroys ungodly governments and false religions in His own good time.

21. And the rest were slain by the sword of him who sits upon the horse, the sword that issues from his mouth: and all the birds were gorged with their flesh.

All of Christ's enemies must die. This is the special ministry that God has purposed toward the wicked: it is a ministry of death. Isaiah says of the Messiah that "he shall smite the earth with the rod of his mouth, and with the breath of his lips shall he slay the wicked" (11:4). We see many wicked men dying of supposedly "natural" causes or illnesses. But John sees the shrouds of heaven thrown open to see the real cause, the real avenger of God's wrath.

Since all the wicked must die, there must come a time in history when the wicked have all passed into death, and all that will remain is a world populated by elect believers. Christ's victory over His foes will be total and complete, and the Devil will have nothing at the end of history. This then is the full issue of the mighty salvation wrought on the Cross, that the whole world might be saved through Him whom the Father sent.

And Isaiah said, "Of the increase of his government and of peace there shall be no end" (9:7). This can never be fulfilled unless Messiah fully exercises His government as it relates to the death of the wicked. Since "there is no peace saith the Lord, to the wicked," the wicked *must* perish.

This, then, is the meaning of Revelation 19:11–21. It shows us what Christ is doing throughout this inter-adventual period, that He is now reigning from His throne at the right hand of the Father, the position of power and influence.

How can it be maintained that a final apostasy will occur at the end of history? Since all the wicked are slain by the sword that proceeds out of Christ's mouth ("consumed by the breath of His mouth," II Thess. 2:8b), none will be left alive at the end of the age. Christ returns to destroy them with the *second* death ("destroyed by the brightness of His coming," II Thess. 2:8c) at the general resurrection unto final judgment. God's justice requires this twofold punishment of the reprobate, as Paul sketches for us in the case of the man of sin, the Roman emperor: he, like all the reprobate, must be destroyed by the sword of Christ's mouth, whose breath is a consuming fire, in *this* age, to be subsequently resurrected for final justice and the second death at the Consummation (cf. Dan. 12:2).

As long as Christ reigns, peace will increase. His government is in the business of putting the wicked *out* of business. They will lick the dust. And to lick the dust means to be killed.

SUMMARY OF REVELATION 19:11–21

1. Christ is the Rider upon the white horse.
2. Christ is now reigning from His throne at the right hand of God the Father.
3. The sword symbolizes war, death and destruction.
4. Christ has two distinct ministries to perform: a ministry of saving the world for the righteous; and a ministry of death to the wicked, which ministry is to continue until all the wicked have been cut off.
5. The battle is now in progress upon this present earth, and it continues throughout the Church Age.
6. Christ's victory over all of His enemies will be total and complete.
7. The beast, which symbolizes corrupt government, and the false prophet, who symbolizes false religions, are to be captured and thrown into the lake of fire, which means total destruction.
8. The followers of the beast, and the supporters of false religions will all be slain by the sword of Him who sits upon the horse.
9. There will come a time in history when there will be a fully redeemed world.
10. There is no place here for an end-time apostasy.
11. Any theory which assigns this portion of Scripture to the Second Coming of Christ is in error.

REVELATION CHAPTER 20: A BRIEF OVERVIEW

Dr. Warfield made every effort to impress upon his readers that when apocalyptic symbolism is the object of our exploration, interpretation is more a matter of sympathetic imagination than the use of the fine scales of linguistic science. In other words, it is crucial for the interpreter to gain insight into the seer's method. It is clear from his textbook on New Testament Textual Criticism that Dr. Warfield possessed this remarkable talent, a gift that enabled him to enter into the thought processes of the inspired authors. It is hard to understand why modern expositors have taken a step backward to tread old exegetical ground when they should have continued in his pioneering footsteps. But so often even with conservatives who have written on eschatology, the tendency has been, not to answer his arguments, but merely to ignore them.

The opening verses of Revelation 20 introduce a new symbol, the 1000 years. It soon becomes evident, however, that the 1000 year symbol relates, not to time on earth, but to the intermediate state, that state of the soul as it exists between the death of the body and its resurrection. There the blessed dead are reigning and ruling with Christ, a co-regency in the heavenlies. Hence this symbol definitely does *not* relate to any millennial kingdom on earth. Nor is there any place for a defection of the church on earth, although most Pre-, Post-, and Amillennialists have held that there will be such a defection.

Furthermore, the reign of Christ and His saints does not belong to some far-off realm away out in space, but to the reign that He now is conducting as He is seated at the right hand of God the Father, to which place He ascended after He had completed His work of atonement (Mark 16:19). It relates to that reign spoken of in I Corinthians 15:24-26, where we are told that "he must reign, till he hath put all his enemies under his feet. And the last enemy that shall be abolished is death." That is *what* He is doing, and *this earth* is *where* He is doing it, *now*.

As we have said, Warfield believed that the 1000 years related to the intermediate state and to the blessedness of those Christians who have died and now are with Christ. He noted that John used a *time* symbol to represent the intermediate state, and that it is therefore appropriate that anything that happens *outside* the intermediate state must necessarily be represented by another time symbol, as happening *before* or *after* the 1000 years.

Satan is represented as completely restricted in one area, bound with a great chain, so that he has no access to the saints in the intermediate state. But as Warfield correctly notes, "outside of their charmed circle" Satan's hideous work continues—as indeed we see it is continuing in this world. And John uses another time symbol, "a little time" (v. 3), in contrast with the 1000 years of the intermediate state, this relating to another sphere, the earth. And although we have here two time symbols of varying length, these are not to be thought of as consecutive in terms of worldly chronology, but rather in regard to different spheres. This "little time" during which Satan is loosed relates to the Church Age on earth, and is in reality a recapitulation of Revelation 19:11-21, in which Christ is subduing His enemies. The key point is that the destruction of both wicked men and Satan himself is taught to occur in time and history, thus offering the only complete fulfillment of I Corinthians 15:24-26. If every enemy is to be destroyed while Christ still sits at the Father's right hand, this must include Satan himself, the pre-eminent enemy of the Son. Therefore Jesus will remain there until Satan and Death, the last enemies, are destroyed, and *then* He will return in glory to His redeemed world.

REVELATION 20:1-10
Verse-by-verse Exposition

1. Then I saw an angel coming down from heaven, holding in his hand the key of the bottomless pit and a great chain.

Here we are told that the angel coming down from heaven is holding two distinct objects in his hand: the key to the bottomless pit, and a great chain. These two symbols represent two different instruments.

2, 3(a). And he seized the dragon, that ancient serpent, who is the Devil and Satan, and bound him for a thousand years, and threw him into the pit, and shut it and sealed it over him, that he should deceive the nations no more, till the thousand years were ended.

The angel first seizes Satan and binds him for a thousand years. The binding is accomplished with the great chain. The intermediate state is in view here, and it follows that Satan is bound so that he has no power whatsoever over the *saints* who have died and who are in glory. He cannot assault the saints, although they can and do assault him, since they are engaged with Christ in His intermediatory reign as regards the earth, and He is actively destroying the works of the Devil.

However, after being bound, Satan is also thrown into the bottomless pit, and the door of the pit is shut and sealed over him. This is the purpose of the *key,* that he should be sealed in, locked up. The reason given is that he should deceive the nations no more. This refers to Satan's relationship with the *wicked* after their death, for his army is being slowly decimated by the death of its earthly hosts. Christ's army does not suffer any setback upon the death of its soldiers, for they live and reign with Him in heaven. But Satan's armies are totally sealed off from their leader when they enter the grave. For as we will be told in verse 5, "The rest of the dead lived not until the thousand years should be finished." Satan can no longer use them to do his work on the earth. Thus the Devil is cast into the abyss in the sense that as the non-elect or unregenerate die, they are progressively taken from him. He grows weaker and weaker as Christ's ministry of death to the wicked proceeds, until finally he is left completely helpless. Paraphrasing Warfield, "What happens, does not happen to Satan, but to the reprobate: they are sealed in death where Satan has no power to deceive them or to arm them for the battle against Christ.

3. (b) After that he must be loosed for a little while.

Warfield indicated that the two time symbols, the effulgent 1000 years, and the diminutive "little season," are contrasted in such a way by John as to make it clear that time here on earth is the little season. But since two time symbols are used, they are not overlapped, but are set against each other in chronological sequence, as before and after. But that indicates only a change in symbol, not an actual progression of events. This verse merely says that the sphere of Satan's assaults is restricted to the little season (Rev. 6:11 is a parallel passage), that is, the time on earth—the little time in the life of each individual as that individual is on earth. He has no power regarding the saints gathered in paradise.

Warfield says that resistance to this interpretation is natural enough, since we are reticent to enter into the seer's method; indeed it is difficult for us to enter into the "temporo-spatial machinery" to set forth these things. It should be pointed out that precisely the same technique is used in Revelation 11 respecting the two symbols of three and one-half years and three and one-half days. The periods are not consecutive, but symbolic of the probationary period man lives on earth, en masse and individually.

4 (a). And I saw thrones, and seated upon them were those to whom judgment was committed.

John is here describing the intermediate state, a co-regency of Christ and the saints. In Revelation 3:21 Christ had said, "He that overcometh, I will give to him to sit down with me in my throne, as I also overcame, and sat down with my Father in his throne."

And in I Corinthians 6:3 Paul writes to the Christians at Corinth, "Know ye not that ye shall judge angels?" The fulfillment of this verse is reserved for the intermediate state. The saints co-reign with Christ, and when He lays down the kingdom to the Father, the mediatorial reign ceases for Him and for the saints. Whereas the singular throne of Christ is in view in Revelation 3:21, the promise that believers would sit with Christ in His judgment seat is fulfilled by a *multitude* of thrones in Revelation 20:4. Thus Revelation 3:21, I Corinthians 6:3, and Revelation 20:4 are parallel passages. But they refer to the intermediate state, not to an earthly reign of Christ in Jerusalem.

4 (b). And I saw the souls of those who had been beheaded for their testimony to Jesus and for the word of God, and who had not worshipped the beast or its image, and had not received its mark on their foreheads or their hands.

There has been much difference of opinion concerning the word souls (psuchai) employed by John. The natural use is that of disembodied spirit. But Premillennialists, desiring to establish a basis for a reign of the saints with Christ in Jerusalem, have insisted that this be understood to mean bodily resurrection.

It is the conviction of the present writer that the natural meaning is the correct one, that these are disembodied souls in the intermediate state. Those who die the second death have already died physically once, since the second death is subsequent to the final judgment, for which purpose the wicked were resurrected. Some have argued quite persuasively that the first death is spiritual death, going back to the fall in Adam. But that cannot be, because the second death then would have to be physical death; and that simply does not accord with John's order of events.

There is the first death, which is physical, the phase of existence in which many millions of evil-doers are presently abiding. There is the first resurrection, the phase of existence in which the elect live and reign with Christ in heaven. And there is the second death, the phase of existence reserved for the wicked dead after the final judgment, which is hell.

4 (c). They lived and reigned with Christ a thousand years.

This is the blessedness of those who have gone to be with the Lord. Though dead, they live and reign with Christ in the intermediate state, from heavenly thrones in accordance with Revelation 3:21: "He that overcometh, I will give to sit down with me in my throne, as I also overcame, and sat down with my Father in his throne." The purpose of this declaration is to impress on God's servants the glory that awaits those who die in the Lord. Thus John says, "Though dead, they live. Though buried in the ground, they reign."

Finally, it should be pointed out that while living and reigning in the intermediate state, the elect are warring against Satan and his hosts as well, "judging angels," and exercising authority as co-reigning heirs with Christ.

5. The rest of the dead did not live until the thousand years were ended. This is the first resurrection.

This parenthetical observation is a restatement of verse 3. The reason that the "nations," the wicked hosts who formerly lived on earth, are no longer deceived by Satan is that they are *dead*. But the saints who read this prophecy may ask, If the elect live and reign with Christ after death, will not the wicked also be active? Are there more terrible battles to be waged in heaven after we die? So John adds: Fear not, beloved of God: only the saints will be alive and reign after death. The fate of the wicked is altogether different! Whether or not the wicked retain consciousness as they await the resurrection, we cannot be sure, although the parable of the rich man and Lazarus would seem to indicate that they do; and indeed the fallen angels remain fully alert as they await the judgment.

Thus Satan is definitely sealed away from the wicked dead, or more accurately, they are sealed away from him. He can no longer deceive them into serving his nefarious purpose on earth. Satan's army is progressively being decimated. But when the saints die, Christ's army gets even stronger, for they sit on thrones and reign with Him.

This then was the only oversight on Warfield's part, that he did not recognize the distinction John made between the chain and the sealed pit. Two distinct instrumentalities are at work here, the one with reference to the elect dead, the other being applied to the wicked dead, who are depicted as the nations that Satan can no longer deceive. And John explicitly declares that the estate of the saints in heaven is the first resurrection. That is an estate of blessing beyond anything that we can imagine in this life.

6. Blessed and holy is he who shares in the first resurrection! Over such the second death has no power, but they shall be priests of God and of Christ, and they shall reign with him a thousand years.

The saints completely share in the first resurrection. The second death has no power over them, but it does have power over the reprobate and will soon exercise that power in its fullness. The second death is clearly the lake of fire.

It may be asked, What of the Christians who are alive at the Second Coming? At that point, death is swallowed up in victory. The saints who have been in paradise are given their resurrection bodies, and the corruptible bodies of the living saints are changed "in the twinkling of an eye" into glorified bodies.

7, 8. And when the thousand years are ended, Satan will be loosed from his prison, and will come out to deceive the nations

which are at the four corners of the earth, that is, Gog and Magog, to gather them for battle: their number is like the sand of the sea.

Let us keep it clearly in mind that in these time symbols there is no chronological succession whatever, but only a difference in spheres that is set forth. The two spheres operate concurrently. Satan's little season has reference to time on earth, that is, to the Church Age, in which he is now active. It is the time of trial and tribulation in which the militant Church is in battle with the wicked one and his hosts. The shift is in the symbols only, not in the things symbolized. The intermediate state, in which the saints are, and the little season on earth, where Satan is active, are concurrent realities, that is, they transpire simultaneously as seen from our vantage point.

The little season in which Satan is loosed is recapitulation of the battle described in Revelation 19:11-21. It is Satan who rallies the nations, Gog and Magog, to fight against Christ and His people here in this world.

9, 10. And they marched up over the broad earth and surrounded the camp of the saints and the beloved city: but fire came down from heaven and consumed them. And the devil who had deceived them was thrown into the lake of fire and brimstone where the beast and the false prophet were, and they will be tormented day and night for ever and ever.

As the Church Age comes to an end, Satan and his hosts are brought to naught. The destruction of the enemies of God is initiated and executed from heaven. All the wicked must die; none will remain when Christ returns to His redeemed world. Far from being an end-time event, the fire from heaven is smiting the earth daily, consuming the wicked. In the throne vision that Daniel saw, "A fiery stream issued and came forth from before him" (7:10). Ever since the fall of man in Eden the enemies of God have been persecuting the righteous, scheming to cause their downfall. And ever since that time God has been slaying the wicked. This unrelenting process of punishment initiated and executed by God Himself, described here as fire from heaven, has been slaying the wicked, and it continues until all the wicked have been destroyed.

The Devil himself is destroyed, but not by the instrumentality of fire from heaven, but because he is thrown into the lake of fire. This clears the way for Christ, who at this point is still reigning from the right hand of the Father, to destroy the last enemy, death, since all the preceding enemies (Satan included) have been made the footstool of His feet. The beast and false prophet, symbols of corrupt world government and false religions, are depicted as having been already judged and destroyed.

In the concluding section, verses 11-15, John presents the final judgment, complete with the Final Judge. The throne is white, symbolic perhaps of purity and righteousness. He who sits upon it is ready to judge, and thus the end of the world occurs. And these verses set forth the final judgment in all its glory and terror. The parallel passage is Matthew 25:31-46, there from the standpoint of the living, here from that of the dead.

Thus is embraced, in two short chapters, the past, present and future of the world, and the world beyond, from several varied perspectives. Revelation 19 and 20 form a unit, although not necessarily in a chronological order. As Warfield noted, John's primary concern was to bless and encourage the saints in their work here on earth, and to prepare them for the severe trials and persecutions that lay ahead. We are assured that history is running on God's perfect schedule, and that the final outcome rests entirely in His hands. The marvelous work of redemption, initiated by God Himself, is brought to final fruition with a magnificently saved world.

A further point of interest is the rather widespread assumption that because of the binding of the Devil spoken of in Revelation 20:1-3, he can no longer prevent the gospel's being sent to all the nations of the world, as allegedly he did during the time of Old Testament Israel. The atonement made by Christ on Calvary is assumed to have taken that power from him. And the Scripture commonly assumed to teach this is Matthew 12:29: "How can one enter into the house of the strong man and spoil his goods, except he first bind the strong man? and then he will spoil his house." And this is all the more remarkable since Calvinists are among its strongest supporters.

But this introduces an element of Arminianism into the saving process, since it has been the distinguishing mark of Arminianism that it finds its determining factor in the will of man rather than in the will of the Creator. But certainly that is an inconsistent position for Reformed theologians. For, in technical language, it affirms that Satanology determines soteriology.

The error in this view is that the Devil does not have, nor has he ever had, any power to influence human affairs except as God gives him permission. Since his own fall he has been merely a fallen angel, and like the other fallen angels or demons, "kept in everlasting bonds under darkness unto the judgment of the last day" (Jude 6). Neither under the Old Covenant nor under the New has the Devil ever had any power whatever to prevent God from extending salvation throughout the world whenever or wherever He pleases.

SUMMARY OF REVELATION 20:1-10

1. The angel coming down from heaven had two instruments with which to bind Satan: a key and a great chain.

2. John uses two symbols: "a thousand years," and "a little time."

3. The time symbols have to do not with successive events, but with events in different spheres.

4. When time symbols of varying lengths are used to describe events in different spheres, it is but natural that they should be spoken of as *before* or *after,* when really they are concurrent.

5. Since John saw the souls of those who had been beheaded and who now live and reign with Christ, it is the intermediate state that is in view.

6. The great chain is used to bind Satan so that he cannot attack the saints who are in the intermediate state.

7. The key is used to imprison Satan so that he can no longer deceive the "nations."

8. The "nations," in contrast with the saints in glory, are the hosts of the wicked who have died.

9. The key, used to imprison Satan, assures that he no longer has access to his former servants who did his bidding on earth.

10. As Satan's helpers on earth are taken from him in death, he grows progressively weaker until finally he is left completely helpless.

11. Satan's being loosed for "a little time," relates to his activity on earth during the Church Age, and runs concurrent with the 1000-year reign of the saints in glory.

12. The "little time" during which Satan is loosed is a recapitulation of the battle described in Revelation 19:11-21.

13. The fire that comes down from heaven to destroy the wicked is God's continual providential battle against them.

14. The Devil, and also the beast and the false prophet who are symbols of corrupt government and false religion, are cast into the lake of fire.

15. There is no apostasy at the end of the age.

16. The final judgment and the end of the world occur at the same time.

WILL THERE BE A FINAL APOSTASY?

In regard to this new interpretation of Revelation 19:11–20:10, the following comments should be in order, while the present writer has long been a Postmillennialist, there has always been one element in this system that has seemed to be completely out of harmony with the others, and that is the doctrine that shortly before the end of the Church Age there will be a great apostasy in which practically all of the progress that has been made during the preceding centuries will be lost. As this has usually been presented, the Devil is to be loosed for "a little time" whereupon he gathers his allies and they go up over the face of the earth and surround "the camp of the saints," and "the beloved city," and all but annihilate the true believers. The true believers are saved from that fate only when fire from heaven suddenly comes down and destroys the attackers.

But must there really be an end-time apostasy? Practically all Pre-, Post-, and A-millennialists have so believed. And indeed Revelation 20, verses 3 and 7–10 do seem to teach that. But such an outcome seems like a great anti-climax to the glorious Church Age as that has been set forth in the postmillennial system. Indeed in many places the Scriptures indicate that the Church Age is to end in victory for Christ and His Church. The prophet Isaiah wrote concerning the coming Messiah that "of the increase of his government and of peace there shall be no end"

(9:7). John says that "God sent not his Son into the world to judge the world; but that the world should be saved through him" (3:17). In Mark 16:19 we are told that after Christ's ascension He sat down at the right hand of God—which is the position of power and rulership. Paul says that "he must reign, till he hath put all his enemies under his feet" (I Cor. 15:25); and again, that "Christ loved the church, and gave himself up for it" (Eph. 5:25). Certainly the Church is His most precious possession, purchased by Him at an enormous cost. Hence an end-time apostasy in which the Church is allowed to fall victim to its enemies even for a very short time, seems definitely out of harmony with the rest of the system.

But as we have seen in the preceding article, Mr. Selbrede has suggested an interpretation that seems to solve that problem. He has shown that Revelation 19:11–21 is *not* a prophecy of Christ's Second Coming, as has been so generally assumed, but that it is a description of His providential coming to earth on a mission of death to His enemies, and that this mission continues throughout the Church Age. The sword that proceeds out of His mouth symbolizes war, death, and destruction. The passage is in reality a picture of a great battle, a real *blood and guts battle,* as he has described it, although it is not visible to the naked eye. In harmony with this Paul says that "our wrestling is not against flesh and blood, but against the principalities, against the powers, against the world-rulers of this darkness, against the spiritual hosts of wickedness in the heavenly places" (Eph. 6:12). And in this work Christ exercises the "all power" that was given to Him before He sent forth the apostles to make disciples of all the nations (Matt. 28:19). The battle results in total victory for Christ and His Church as He changes a fallen world into a redeemed world.

This cannot be a description of the Second Coming of Christ, for when that occurs His enemies will be utterly terrified at His brightness and majesty and will have no incentive whatever to stand up and fight. Instead they will call for the mountains to fall on them and cover them from the wrath of the Lamb (Rev. 6:16). There will be no battle at the time of the Second Coming. Ever since the fall in Adam unregenerate man has been simply terrified at any appearance of the supernatural. But here Christ and His army contend mightily against an opposing army and win an overwhelming victory. The shrouds of heaven are withdrawn so that John can see what is really happening in the heavenlies, and there is portrayed before him a tremendous battle in which Christ and

His army are engaged with the Devil and his armies. All the imagery of war, the sword, blood, the horses, the dead corpses and carcasses on the battlefield, and the invitation to the vultures of the air to come and feast on the flesh of kings and captains and horses and men, are all designed to teach this very thing. These are symbols of normal although some-what rare procedures on this earth, not of the end-time coming of Christ and of the resurrection of the saints.

Now let us turn to Revelation 20:1–10. Here we are told that the Devil is bound with a great chain and imprisoned for "a thousand years," and that after the thousand years he must be loosed for "a little time." Verses 4 through 6 tell of the blessed state of the saints who have died and who are now reigning and ruling with Christ in glory—indeed many have already reigned and ruled with Him much longer than a literal one thousand years. They are those who have been "beheaded" for their testimony of Jesus and for the Word of God. They therefore cannot be living people in a millennial kingdom on this earth. We have here two symbols, the "thousand years," and the "little time." When these are contrasted or used in opposition to each other, it is but natural that they should be spoken of as "before" and "after." But in reality they refer not to successive earthly time periods, but to different spheres—to time in the intermediate state, and to time on earth. And as such they are *concurrent*.

The Devil is bound for a thousand years in the sense that he cannot attack or molest the saints who are in the intermediate state as he did attack them when they were on earth. Instead, they have perfect peace. And the little time for which he is loosed relates to his activity in this world, during the Church Age, and is a *recapitulation* of Revelation 19:11–21, in which he is battling against Christ and the saints.

The "little time" is, for the individual, but a short period and is soon over, compared with the "thousand years" spent by the saints who are in the intermediate state. But during that time Christ as the Redeemer of His people is, as we have seen, engaged in a tremendous battle with the forces of evil as in His providential control of all things He slays the wicked and wins the world for Himself and His people. The result is a truly Christianized world before His work of redemption is finished. How long it may continue in that redeemed state before His final coming we are not told. But it is at least possible that it may continue for some considerable time.

Up until the present time no one of the millennial systems, neither

Pre-, nor Post-, nor A-millennialism, has been able to present through its ablest scholars convincing proof against the other two. And that for the very good reason that each has had within itself elements of error, even quite serious error. But here is an explanation that is different, one that brings in some new ideas. In the main it substantiates the basic principles of the postmillennial system. But in clarifying that system it does away with the idea of a final apostasy, it gives a really new interpretation to Revelation 19:11–21, and it solves the problem about the loosing of Satan for "a little time."

Against Premillennialism this explanation holds that it is in serious error in that it teaches that the Church will become apostate, that true believers will be raptured away more than a thousand years before the end of the world, that seven years of great tribulation will follow the rapture, during which time Anti-Christ will rule on earth; then Christ and all of His saints will return and will then establish a literal 1000 year earthly kingdom in Jerusalem. It also holds that after that kingdom has been completed, the Devil will be loosed for a little time, whereupon he goes out over the earth, gathers his allies, and shuts up the saints in Jerusalem, until suddenly fire from heaven comes down and destroys the attackers. But how can anyone accept such an inglorious end to a millennial reign of Christ? This system also calls for three or four resurrections and four or five judgments, for which we find no sufficient evidence in Scripture. So dependent is Premillennialism on the first 10 verses in Revelation 20, which it takes literally and then relies primarily on Old Testament kingdom prophecies for proof, that had it not been for this misinterpretation, the system as such probably never would have arisen.

And against Amillennialism, which is a much less elaborate system, this explanation holds that it too is in serious error in that it teaches that Christ will not win a final victory before the end of the world, that the world will continue until the end in much the same condition that it is now in, and that there will be a final great tribulation.

Again we must say that if this is the true explanation of the millennial problem, as we believe that it is, it is an event of great importance. This does not mean that the problem will soon fade away. The history of theological doctrines shows that such changes come very slowly. But if this problem can be eliminated, it will remove a main cause of rivalry and division that has plagued the Church since the first centuries of the Christian era.

POSTMILLENNIALISM

The Great Commission. Matt. 28:18-20: "And Jesus came to them and spake unto them, saying, All authority hath been given unto me in heaven and on earth. 19 Go ye therefore, and make disciples of all the nations, baptizing them in the name of the Father and of the Son and of the Holy Spirit: 20 teaching them to observe all things whatsoever I have commanded you: and lo, I am with you always, even unto the end of the world."

Here we are told that **all authority, in heaven and on earth,** has been given to the risen and ascended and reigning Christ. On the basis of that authority He has commanded His disciples to go and make disciples of all the nations. And He has promised that He will be with them always, even unto the end of the world. His declared purpose is the **Christianizing** of the world during this present Church Age. Hence we ask, What will He be able to do in a 1000 year millennium, seated on a throne in Jerusalem, that He cannot do now? He already has **all authority, all power,** in heaven and on earth. He can never have any more power or any more authority than He has now. He has commanded His followers to go **now,** and **make disciples of all the nations,** and that those people are to be baptized in the name of the Father and of the Son and of the Holy Spirit. But only true believers are to be baptized. Hence this clearly means that the people of those nations are to become true Christians. It cannot mean a merely superficial announcement of the Gospel to those nations, as some say, but a truly effective Christianizing of the world. Hence we ask again: What will Christ be able to do, seated on a throne in Jerusalem during a 1000 year millennium, that He cannot do now? Or What conceivable need is there for such a millennium?

The Triumphant March of the Church. Matt. 16:18: "And I say unto thee, that thou art Peter, and upon this rock I will build my church: and the gates of hell shall not prevail against it."

This verse, following immediately after Peter's magnificent confession of Jesus as the Christ, gives us special confidence for believing in the future progress of the Church. It has usually been understood to mean that the Church which Christ established will be able to defend itself against all its foes, that even the worst that the enemies of the Gospel will be able to bring against it will not be able to destroy it. We believe, however, that the real meaning is quite different. "Gates" are not **offensive,** but **defensive** weapons. They are stationary. They do not make the attack. In that day the gates were strongly fortified instruments designed for the defense of the city, designed to withstand the strongest on- slaughts of the attackers. As such they did not move. Hence the real meaning of this verse is, not that the Church will be able to defend itself against all attacks, but that it will make the attack, that it will advance throughout the world, and that nothing, literally nothing, will be able to resist its onward march. Not even the fortress of hell itself will be able to resist it. All will fall before it. Before the end comes the Church will make a clean sweep of everything. Even the strongest fortresses of the enemy will be laid waste before it. Surely that is Postmillennialism with a vengeance! !

BIBLIOGRAPHY

Postmillennial:

Brown, David, The Second Advent, 1849. Reprinted, 1953, under the title, Christ's Second Coming.

Campbell, Roderick, Israel and the New Covenant, 1954, 326 pages.

Hodge, Charles, Systematic Theology, 1871, vol. iii. Pages 771-868.

Hulse, Erroll, The Restoration of Israel, 1968. 167 pages.

Kik, J. Marcellus, An Eschatology of Victory, 1974. 268 pages. (Highly recommended).

Selbrede, Martin G., Revelation 19:11–20:10, A Postmillennial Analysis. Article. 1983.

Shedd, W. G. T., Dogmatic Theology, 1888. Vol. ii. Pages 591-754.

Snowden, James H., The Coming of the Lord, 1919. 279 pages.

Strong, Augustus H., Systematic Theology, 1907. Pages 981-1056.

Warfield, B. B., Article, The Millennium and the Apocalypse, 1904, reprinted in Biblical Doctrines, 1929. Also various other articles.

Amillennial:

Berkhof, Louis, Systematic Theology, 1941. Pages 661-738.

    The Second Coming of Christ, 1953. 102 pages.

Canfield, Joseph M. The Incredible Scofield and His Book, 1984. 289 pages.

Carver, Everett I., When Jesus Comes Again, 1979. 327 pages. (Highly recommended).

Graebner, Theodore, War in the Light of Prophecy, 1941. 140 pages.

Grier, Wm. J., The Momentous Event, 1945, 98 pages.

Hamilton, Floyd E., The Basis of Millennial Faith, 1942. 144 pages.

Hendriksen, William, More than Conquerors, 1939. 256 pages.

Hodges, Jesse Wilson, Christ's Kingdom and Coming, 1957. 233 pages.

Hughes, Archibald, A New Heaven and A New Earth, 1958. 233 pages.

Kuyper, A., Chiliasm, or The Doctrine of Premillennialism, 1934. 36 pages.

Masselink, William, Why Thousand Years? 1930. 222 pages.

Mauro, Philip, The Seventy Weeks and the Great Tribulation, 1944. 273 pages.

    The Gospel of the Kingdom, 1928.

Murray, George L., Millennial Studies, 1948. 200 pages.

Pieters, Albertus, The Seed of Abraham, 1950. 161 pages.

    Studies in the Revelation of St. John, 1937. 342 pages.

    A Candid Examination of the Scofield Bible, 1938. 27 pages (pamphlet).

Rutgers, William H., Premillenialism in America, 1930. 290 pages.
Wyngaarden, Martin J., The Future of the Kingdom, 1934. 193 pages.
Vos, Geerhardus, The Pauline Eschatology, 1930. 316 pages.

Anti-Chiliast:

Allis, Oswald T., Prophecy and the Church, 1945. 284 pages.

Historic Premillennial:

Alford, The Greek Testament, 1874.

Frost, Henry W., The Second Coming of Christ, 1934.

Guinness, H. Grattan, The Approaching End of the Age, 1880.

Kellogg, S. H., The Jews, or Prediction and Fulfillment, 1883.

Ladd, George E., Crucial Questions about the Kingdom of God, 183 pages. 1952; The Blessed Hope, 1956. 167 pages.

Reese, Alexander, The Approaching Advent of Christ, 1917.

West Nathaniel, The Thousand Years in Both Testaments, 1880. 493 pages.

Dispensational:

Blackstone, Wm. E., Jesus Is Coming, 1878; revised 1908. 245 pages.

Brookes, James M., Maranatha, 1876; 10th ed., 1889, 544 pages.

Chafer, L. S., Systematic Theology, 1948. Dispensationalism, art., 1936, reprinted 1951. 108 pages.

Darby, John N., Synopsis of the Books of the Bible, 5 vols.

Feinberg, Charles L., Premillennialism or Amillennialism? 1936; enlarged, 1954. 350 pages.

Gaebelein, Arno C., The Harmony of the Prophetic Word, 1907; The Return of the Lord, 1925.

Gray, James M., Prophecy and the Lord's Return, 1917. 118 pages.

Haldeman, I. M., The Coming of Christ, Both Premillennial and Imminent, 1906; The Signs of the Times, 1913.

Ironside, H. A., Lectures on the Revelation, 1930, 366 pages; The Lamp of Prophecy, 1940.

Morgan, G. Campbell, God's Methods with Man, 1898. 188 pages.

Pentecost, J. Dwight, Things to Come, 1958. 583 pages.

Peters, G. H. N., The Theocratic Kingdom, 3 vols., 1884.

Scofield Reference Bible, 1909, revised 1917.

Scofield, C. I., Rightly Dividing the Word of Truth, 64 pages.

Seiss, Joseph A., Millennialism and the Second Advent.

Silver, Jesse F., The Lord's Return, 1914. 297 pages.

Walvoord, John F., The Rapture Question, 1957.

INDEX OF AUTHORS

413

INDEX OF SUBJECTS

415